Left Radicalism in India

Left radicalism in India was rooted in the nationalist movement and was set in motion in the 1920s with the formation of the Communist Party. The communist movement manifested itself differently in each phase of India's political history and communism continues to remain a meaningful alternative ideological discourse in India.

This book examines left politics in India, focusing on its rise, consolidation and relative decline in the present century. Left radicalism in India is a distinct ideological phenomenon which is articulated in two complementary ways: while the parliamentary left remains social democratic in character, its bête noire, the left-wing extremists, continue to uphold the classical Marxist, Leninist and Maoist notion of violent revolution. Concentrating on the nature and also the activities of these two versions of left radicalism, this book is a thorough study of the phenomenon. The author analyses the states of Kerala, West Bengal and Tripura and presents a variety of case studies of communist movements. He argues that the political power of the left parties depends on the degree to which they have built organizational strength, political hegemony and a broad social base through legal and extra-parliamentary struggles.

An in-depth study of socio-economic circumstances that remain critical in conceptualizing radical extremism, *Left Radicalism in India* will be of interest to those studying Indian Politics, South Asian History, Development Studies and Global Politics.

Bidyut Chakrabarty is Professor in Political Science, University of Delhi, India. His publications include *Corporate Social Responsibility* (Routledge 2011), *Maoism in India* (Routledge 2010), *Social and Political Thought of Mahatma Gandhi* (Routledge 2006) and *Indian Society and Politics* (Routledge 2008).

Routledge contemporary South Asia series

1 **Pakistan**
Social and cultural transformations in a Muslim nation
Mohammad A. Qadeer

2 **Labor, Democratization and Development in India and Pakistan**
Christopher Candland

3 **China–India Relations**
Contemporary dynamics
Amardeep Athwal

4 **Madrasas in South Asia**
Teaching terror?
Jamal Malik

5 **Labor, Globalization and the State**
Workers, women and migrants confront neoliberalism
Edited by Debdas Banerjee and Michael Goldfield

6 **Indian Literature and Popular Cinema**
Recasting classics
Edited by Heidi R.M. Pauwels

7 **Islamist Militancy in Bangladesh**
A complex web
Ali Riaz

8 **Regionalism in South Asia**
Negotiating cooperation, institutional structures
Kishore C. Dash

9 **Federalism, Nationalism and Development**
India and the Punjab economy
Pritam Singh

10 **Human Development and Social Power**
Perspectives from South Asia
Ananya Mukherjee Reed

11 **The South Asian Diaspora**
Transnational networks and changing identities
Edited by Rajesh Rai and Peter Reeves

12 **Pakistan–Japan Relations**
Continuity and change in economic relations and security interests
Ahmad Rashid Malik

13 **Himalayan Frontiers of India**
Historical, geo-political and strategic perspectives
K. Warikoo

14 **India's Open-Economy Policy**
Globalism, rivalry, continuity
Jalal Alamgir

15 **The Separatist Conflict in Sri Lanka**
Terrorism, ethnicity, political economy
Asoka Bandarage

16 **India's Energy Security**
Edited by Ligia Noronha and Anant Sudarshan

17 **Globalization and the Middle Classes in India**
The social and cultural impact of neoliberal reforms
Ruchira Ganguly-Scrase and Timothy J. Scrase

18 **Water Policy Processes in India**
Discourses of power and resistance
Vandana Asthana

19 **Minority Governments in India**
The puzzle of elusive majorities
Csaba Nikolenyi

20 **The Maoist Insurgency in Nepal**
Revolution in the twenty-first century
Edited by Mahendra Lawoti and Anup K. Pahari

21 **Global Capital and Peripheral Labour**
The history and political economy of plantation workers in India
K. Ravi Raman

22 **Maoism in India**
Reincarnation of ultra-left wing extremism in the 21st century
Bidyut Chakrabarty and Rajat Kujur

23 **Economic and Human Development in Contemporary India**
Cronyism and fragility
Debdas Banerjee

24 **Culture and the Environment in the Himalaya**
Arjun Guneratne

25 **The Rise of Ethnic Politics in Nepal**
Democracy in the margins
Susan I. Hangen

26 **The Multiplex in India**
A cultural economy of urban leisure
Adrian Athique and Douglas Hill

27 **Tsunami Recovery in Sri Lanka**
Ethnic and regional dimensions
Dennis B. McGilvray and Michele R. Gamburd

28 **Development, Democracy and the State**
Critiquing the Kerala model of development
K. Ravi Raman

29 **Mohajir Militancy in Pakistan**
Violence and transformation in the Karachi conflict
Nichola Khan

30 **Nationbuilding, Gender and War Crimes in South Asia**
Bina D'Costa

31 **The State in India after Liberalization**
Interdisciplinary perspectives
Edited by Akhil Gupta and K. Sivaramakrishnan

32 **National Identities in Pakistan**
The 1971 war in contemporary Pakistani fiction
Cara Cilano

33 **Political Islam and Governance in Bangladesh**
Edited by Ali Riaz and C. Christine Fair

34 **Bengali Cinema**
'An Other Nation'
Sharmistha Gooptu

35 **NGOs in India**
The challenges of women's empowerment and accountability
Patrick Kilby

36 **The Labour Movement in the Global South**
Trade unions in Sri Lanka
S. Janaka Biyanwila

37 **Building Bangalore**
Architecture and urban transformation in India's Silicon Valley
John C. Stallmeyer

38 **Conflict and Peacebuilding in Sri Lanka**
Caught in the peace trap?
Edited by Jonathan Goodhand, Jonathan Spencer and Benedict Korf

39 **Microcredit and Women's Empowerment**
A case study of Bangladesh
Amunui Faraizi, Jim McAllister and Taskinur Rahman

40 **South Asia in the New World Order**
The role of regional cooperation
Shahid Javed Burki

41 **Explaining Pakistan's Foreign Policy**
Escaping India
Aparna Pande

42 **Development-induced Displacement, Rehabilitation and Resettlement in India**
Current issues and challenges
Edited by Sakarama Somayaji and Smrithi Talwar

43 **The Politics of Belonging in India**
Becoming adivasi
Edited by Daniel J. Rycroft and Sangeeta Dasgupta

44 **Re-Orientalism and South Asian Identity Politics**
The oriental other within
Edited by Lisa Lau and Ana Cristina Mendes

45 **Islamic Revival in Nepal**
Religion and a new nation
Megan Adamson Sijapati

46 **Education and Inequality in India**
A classroom view
Manabi Majumdar and Jos Mooij

47 **The Culturalization of Caste in India**
Identity and inequality in a multicultural age
Balmurli Natrajan

48 **Corporate Social Responsibility in India**
Bidyut Chakrabarty

49 **Pakistan's Stability Paradox**
Domestic, regional and international dimensions
Edited by Ashutosh Misra and Michael E. Clarke

50 **Transforming Urban Water Supplies in India**
The role of reform and partnerships in globalization
Govind Gopakumar

51 **South Asian Security**
21st century discourses
Sagarika Dutt and Alok Bansal

52 **Non-discrimination and Equality in India**
Contesting boundaries of social justice
Vidhu Verma

53 **Being Middle-class in India**
A way of life
Henrike Donner

54 **Kashmir's Right to Secede**
A critical examination of contemporary theories of secession
Matthew J. Webb

55 **Bollywood Travels**
Culture, diaspora and border crossings in popular Hindi cinema
Rajinder Dudrah

56 **Nation, Territory, and Globalization in Pakistan**
Traversing the margins
Chad Haines

57 **The Politics of Ethnicity in Pakistan**
The Baloch, Sindhi and Mohajir ethnic movements
Farhan Hanif Siddiqi

58 **Nationalism and Ethnic Conflict**
Identities and mobilization after 1990
Edited by Mahendra Lawoti and Susan Hangen

59 **Islam and Higher Education**
Concepts, challenges and opportunities
Marodsilton Muborakshoeva

60 **Religious Freedom in India**
Sovereignty and (anti) conversion
Goldie Osuri

61 **Everyday Ethnicity in Sri Lanka**
Up-country Tamil identity politics
Daniel Bass

62 **Ritual and Recovery in Post-Conflict Sri Lanka**
Eloquent bodies
Jane Derges

63 **Bollywood and Globalisation**
The global power of popular Hindi cinema
Edited by David J. Schaefer and Kavita Karan

64 **Regional Economic Integration in South Asia**
Trapped in conflict?
Amita Batra

65 **Architecture and Nationalism in Sri Lanka**
The trouser under the cloth
Anoma Pieris

66 **Civil Society and Democratization in India**
Institutions, ideologies and interests
Sarbeswar Sahoo

67 **Contemporary Pakistani Fiction in English**
Idea, nation, state
Cara N. Cilano

68 **Transitional Justice in South Asia**
A study of Afghanistan and Nepal
Tazreena Sajjad

69 **Displacement and Resettlement in India**
The human cost of development
Hari Mohan Mathur

70 **Water, Democracy and Neoliberalism in India**
The power to reform
Vicky Walters

71 **Capitalist Development in India's Informal Economy**
Elisabetta Basile

72 **Nation, Constitutionalism and Buddhism in Sri Lanka**
Roshan de Silva Wijeyeratne

73 **Counterinsurgency, Democracy, and the Politics of Identity in India**
From warfare to welfare?
Mona Bhan

74 **Enterprise Culture in Neoliberal India**
Studies in youth, class, work and media
Edited by Nandini Gooptu

75 **The Politics of Economic Restructuring in India**
Economic governance and state spatial rescaling
Loraine Kennedy

76 **The Other in South Asian Religion, Literature and Film**
Perspectives on Otherism and Otherness
Edited by Diana Dimitrova

77 **Being Bengali**
At home and in the world
Edited by Mridula Nath Chakraborty

78 **The Political Economy of Ethnic Conflict in Sri Lanka**
Nikolaos Biziouras

79 **Indian Arranged Marriages**
A social psychological perspective
Tulika Jaiswal

80 **Writing the City in British Asian Diasporas**
Edited by Seán McLoughlin, William Gould, Ananya Jahanara Kabir and Emma Tomalin

81 **Post-9/11 Espionage Fiction in the US and Pakistan**
Spies and 'terrorists'
Cara Cilano

82 **Left Radicalism in India**
Bidyut Chakrabarty

83 **"Nation-State" and Minority Rights in India**
Comparative perspectives on Muslim and Sikh identities
Tanweer Fazal

Left Radicalism in India

Bidyut Chakrabarty

LONDON AND NEW YORK

First published 2015
by Routledge
2 Park Square, Milton Park, Abingdon, Oxon OX14 4RN

and by Routledge
711 Third Avenue, New York, NY 10017

First issued in paperback 2017

Routledge is an imprint of the Taylor & Francis Group, an informa business

© 2015 Bidyut Chakrabarty

The right of Bidyut Chakrabarty to be identified as author of this work has been asserted by him in accordance with sections 77 and 78 of the Copyright, Designs and Patents Act 1988.

All rights reserved. No part of this book may be reprinted or reproduced or utilized in any form or by any electronic, mechanical, or other means, now known or hereafter invented, including photocopying and recording, or in any information storage or retrieval system, without permission in writing from the publishers.

Trademark notice: Product or corporate names may be trademarks or registered trademarks, and are used only for identification and explanation without intent to infringe.

British Library Cataloguing in Publication Data
A catalogue record for this book is available from the British Library

Library of Congress Cataloging in Publication Data
Chakrabarty, Bidyut, 1958–
Left radicalism in India / Bidyut Chakrabarty.
   pages cm. – (Routledge studies in South Asian politics ; 82)
   Includes bibliographical references and index.
   1. Communism–India–History. 2. Communist parties–India–History.
3. India–Politics and government–21st century. I. Title.
   HX393.5.C34 2014
   324.254'075–dc23   2013049588

ISBN 13: 978-1-138-49154-0 (pbk)
ISBN 13: 978-0-415-81032-6 (hbk)

Typeset in Times New Roman
by Wearset Ltd, Boldon, Tyne and Wear

Dedicated to my teachers, students and fellow travellers who sustain my zeal to remain academically active

Contents

List of illustrations	xiii
Preface	xv
List of abbreviations	xvii
Introduction	1

PART I
Setting the scene: consolidation of left radicalism in India 23

1 Socio-economic contexts of left radicalism in India 25
2 Constituents of left radicalism in India 48

PART II
Parliamentary left in India: articulating social democracy as a universal theoretical design 81

3 Parliamentary left in Tripura: social democracy in a new mould 85

4 Parliamentary left in West Bengal: the rise and fall of a hegemonic regime 100

5 Parliamentary left in Kerala: redesigning parliamentary democracy amidst ideological elasticity 133

PART III
Left-wing extremism in India: an indigenous endeavour at ideological innovation(?) 161

IN COLLABORATION WITH RAJAT KUJUR

6 Historical roots and gradual consolidation of the Maoist left radicalism 163

7 Left-wing radicalism in practice in Orissa: a field-based analysis 187

Conclusion 215

Select bibliography 227
Index 239

Illustrations

Figure

6.1	Left-wing extremist affected areas in India	164

Tables

2.1	Outcome of the encounters between CPI (ML) Party Unity and CPI (ML) Liberation, 1994–7	70
3.1	Duration of the government	88
3.2	Performance of the contending parties in assembly elections, 1983–2008	89
3.3	The results of the 2013 state assembly election	89
3.4	Left Front's share of seats and popular votes, 2013 assembly election	91
3.5	Share of seats and popular votes of the Congress and its allies, 2013 assembly election	91
3.6a	Share of seats and popular votes, Left Front in 2013 assembly election	92
3.6b	Share of seats and popular votes of the Congress and its allies in 2013 assembly election	92
3.7a	Results of the 2009 Lok Sabha poll (Tripura West)	93
3.7b	Results of the 2014 Lok Sabha poll (Tripura West)	93
3.7c	Results of the 2009 Lok Sabha poll (Tripura East)	93
3.7d	Results of the 2014 Lok Sabha poll (Tripura East)	93
3.8	Percentage vote by community in 2009 and 2014 Lok Sabha poll	94
3.9	Health status of the people of Tripura	96
3.10	Literacy in districts of Tripura, 2011	96
4.1	Seats and share of votes	106
4.2	The 2006 West Bengal assembly results	107
4.3	Percentage share of the Left Front votes in the *Panchayats* and *Zila Parishads*	109
4.4	The number of candidates who won unopposed	110

xiv *Illustrations*

4.5	Share of parliamentary seats and share of popular votes, 2004 and 2009	113
4.6	Comparing the 2011 and 2006 West Bengal assembly results	116
4.7	District-wise West Bengal assembly election results 2011	117
4.8	Results of the *Panchayat Samiti* election, 2008	119
4.9	Results of the *Panchayat Samiti* election, 2013	119
4.10	Increase and decrease of CPI (M) members in the districts of West Bengal, 2008–11	124
4.11	Decrease in members from among the workers in CPI (M) in selected districts in West Bengal, 2008–11	124
4.12	Decrease of agricultural labourer members in CPI (M) in selected districts in West Bengal, 2008–11	125
4.13	Decrease of women members in CPI (M) in selected districts in West Bengal, 2008–11	125
5.1	Elections in Kerala, 1982–2011	147
5.2	The results of the 2006 Kerala state assembly election	151
5.3	Results of the 2009 Lok Sabha election	152
5.4	Comparative assessment of the poll outcome of local elections, 2005 and 2010	153
5.5	Comparative assessment of seats won by the UDF and LDF in 2010 local elections	153
5.6	The outcome of 2011 state assembly election	154
7.1	Mineral resources of Orissa	204

Preface

The book took a while to get to its final shape for a variety of reasons, including the difficulty in comprehending left radicalism in the rapidly changing socio-economic context of India especially following the acceptance of the 1991 New Economic Policy. In my considered opinion, India joining the neo-liberal bandwagon is a defining moment of her history, politics and economy. Whether one accepts or rejects the New Economic Policy one cannot remain aloof from its impact. This was what the left radicals, despite being critical, had to confront while taking a position on neo-liberal economic reforms. Here, too, they were not unanimous in their views: the division among the parliamentary communists was visible; for the left-wing extremists, the uncritical acceptance of economic reforms by the state was an opportunity for mobilization for their ideological goal. India's political scene is thus full of various kinds of possibilities which mean various kinds of challenges to grapple with while seeking to understand the phenomenon in its entirety.

The project is ambitious and also difficult because of the complex nature of left radicalism in India which is neither purely derivative nor exactly indigenous. This was also an opportunity for me to intervene in the debate on its nature on the basis of the inputs that I have derived from the available literature and field studies. I cannot claim to have written a bias-free account which, to me, is inconceivable since I have my own understanding of the situation in which the battle for human dignity is being constantly waged. Nonetheless, it was a project which brought me in touch with my colleagues and graduate students who also upheld an identical discomfort with the available scholarly works that sought to address a rather non-fashionable field of enquiry. The book would not have attained the sophistication that it has without the intellectual support of Dr B.L. Biju of the department of Political Science, University of Hyderabad, Dr Rajat Kumar Kujur of the department of Political Science, Sambalpur University, and Dr Arindam Kumar Roy of the department of Political Science, University of Burdwan. I am thankful to them. I also appreciate the Routledge editors Dorothea and Jillian and their team members for being so cooperative during the preparation of the manuscript for the book.

An author engaged in academic works is always a lonely person. I am no exception. My children, Barbie and Pablo, never allowed my loneliness to be overpowering by their creative though mischievous interventions at regular intervals. My friends in academia kept in me the zeal for creativity despite odds. This preface shall remain incomplete if I do not acknowledge the contribution of my students in various university campuses in different continents. With their innovative ideas and penetrating questions, they have always inspired me to venture into the unknown, but challenging, domain of human interaction, which helped me grapple with newer tools of analysis from sister disciplines in social sciences. It would not have been possible for me to be appreciative of inter-disciplinary borrowing without their constant engagement with me on issues of identical concern.

This book is about a topical subject which is difficult to capture in a single monograph. I am aware that this book cannot be conclusive and will have raised more questions than have had their answers. If the book provokes debates and deliberations on such an important area of enquiry, I shall have achieved my intellectual goal.

Bidyut Chakrabarty
Delhi, 2014

Abbreviations

AICCCR	All-India Committee of Communist Revolutionaries
AITMC	All-India Trinamul Congress
BCLA	Bengal Criminal Law Amendment Ordinance
BJP	Bharatiya Janata Party
CPI	Communist Party of India
CPI (M)	Communist Party of India (Marxist)
CPI (Maoist)	Communist Party of India (Maoist)
CPI (ML)	Communist Party of India (Marxist-Leninist)
CSP	Congress Socialist Party
INC	Indian National Congress
IOR	India Office Records, London
IPF	Indian People's Front
JSC	Jungle Surakhya Committee (Forest Protection Committee)
KKC	Krantikari Kisan Committee (Revolutionary Farmers' Committee)
KMPP	Kishan Mazdoor Praja Party
KPCC	Kerala Pradesh Congress Committee
KSP	Kerala Socialist Party
LCC	Left Consolidation Committee
MCC	Maoist Communist Centre
MP	Member of Parliament
NCP	National Congress Party
NDA	National Democratic Alliance
NSS	Nair Service Society
OSCC	Orissa State Coordination Committee
PCC	Party Central Committee
PDS	Public distribution system
PGA	People's Guerrilla Army
POC	Provincial Organizing Committee
PPC	People's Plan Campaign
PSP	Praja Socialist Party
PWG	Peoples' War Group
RGMVP	Rajiv Gandhi Mahila Vikas Pariyojana (Raviv Gandhi Developmental Plans for Women)

RSP	Revolutionary Socialist Party
SEZ	Special Economic Zone
SHG	Self-help group
SNDP	Sree Narayana Dharma Paripalana Yogam
SRP	Socialist Revolutionary Party
TTAADC	Tripura Tribal Areas Autonomous District Council
TTNC	Travancore Tamil Nadu Congress
TUJS	Tripura Upajati Juva Samity
UDF	United Democratic Front
UNDP	United Nations Development Program
UPA	United Progressive Alliance
WPP	Workers and Peasants Party

Introduction

I

Indian nationalism was multi-dimensional. While Mahatma Gandhi reigned supreme in India's struggle for freedom, there were competing ideological strands that also motivated masses to fight for their rights in adverse circumstances. Despite its typical western roots, left radicalism remained perhaps the most powerful ideology in mobilizing Indian masses during the freedom struggle and its aftermath. By seeking to articulate the voice of the underprivileged, not only did the left radicals catapult the workers and peasants onto the centre stage of the Indian nationalist movement, they also addressed serious ideological weaknesses that the Gandhi-led Congress leadership had by making the workers and peasants integral to India's freedom struggle. In that sense, left radicalism was a significant ideological strand that fulfilled a specific political role in the anti-British struggle for independence. What was striking was the growing importance of left radicalism especially among the socio-economically underprivileged in a context when the Gandhian *ahimsa* (non-violence) became more or less an uncontested instrument for political mobilization. This perhaps confirms that, despite its alien ideological roots, left radicalism struck organic roots in India because of its persuasive appeal to that section of the struggling masses that remained disconnected with what the nationalist Congress stood for. As is evident in history, besides being a powerful ideological voice during the freedom struggle, left radicalism sustained and also expanded its ideological reach by adopting specific socio-economic programmes for the poor who had to toil hard in factories and agriculture for mere survival. Despite being aware of the issues, the nationalist Congress appears to have been restrained in its response to the struggle of the subalterns presumably because of its class background. With the growing importance of peasants and workers as constituencies in the nationalist movement, it was difficult for the Congress to ignore them completely in the light of its declared objective of expanding its organizational base beyond its conventional sphere of influence. But its class bias against the peripherals, which Gandhi also did not strongly challenge presumably because of the probable adverse repercussion on the organization, held the Congress leadership back from extending uncritical support to the genuine demands that the peasants and workers regularly made. So it was a deliberate ideological choice for the Congress not to pursue the causes of the peasants and workers to the extent it was expected especially in the context of the freedom struggle which unleashed massive popular energy against the foreign ruler and vested interests. It is true that the Congress addressed this weakness later though not fully because of its class prejudices against the underprivileged which created an environment in which left radicalism struck roots and gradually expanded its acceptability among those who fought individually and in specific areas, but never became part of the organized assault on the vested interests protective of feudal land relations and industrial capital. So, left radicalism was a unique voice of protest which the Congress was reluctant to articulate given the constraints that the Congress leadership failed to overcome, primarily due to its clear tilt towards vested social and economic interests. The distinct ideological stance notwithstanding, left radicalism was a powerful articulation of a voice that was not adequately represented in the initial stages of India's freedom struggle. In other words, politically vibrant and ideologically innovative, left radicalism created and nurtured its constituency by constantly being sensitive to the genuine socio-economic demands of the toiling masses which, for specific ideological constraints, never became critical to the Congress leadership though some of the top left radicals in India were politically baptized by the Congress. What was paradoxical was the failure of the Congress to meaningfully address the real socio-economic grievances of the downtrodden despite having understood their criticality in political mobilization against the alien rule. Left radicalism was a contextual response in circumstances where there were hardly any organized political forces to take care of those who so far remained peripheral in the struggle against colonialism. It was thus not merely an ideologically meaningful construct for political mobilization, but also a persuasive plan of action for the victims of the skewed development that the well-entrenched vested interests pursued in collaboration with their colonial masters.

II

Left radicalism in India was rooted in India's nationalist movement. Embedded in mass discontent over genuine social economic grievances which the dominant Gandhi-led Congress leadership failed to address, the left radicals struck an emotional chord with the victims of colonialism. Despite its visible success in political mobilization, nationalism never became an all-inclusive political ideology, given its focus on political freedom from British rule. Nonetheless, it created an environment in which other competing ideologies emerged which not only expanded the sphere of the political, but also contributed to movements involving the disempowered sections of the masses. For the newly emerged left radical leadership, mere political independence, though critical, was not adequate to bring about human emancipation in its real connotation. Hence leftism was defined to mean 'anti-imperialism' and 'socialism'. For the Congress-minded left radicals, '[a] genuine anti-imperialist is one who believes in undiluted independence (not Mahatma Gandhi's substance of independence) as the political objective and in uncompromising national struggle as the means for attaining it'.[1] With the attainment of 'independence', leftism meant 'Socialism and the task before the people will then be the reconstruction of national life on a Socialist basis'.[2] It was obviously a difficult task because the leftists needed to fight on two fronts; on the one hand, they had to fight 'the foreign Imperialism and its Indian allies, and on the other, our milk-water-nationalists, the Rightists who are prepared for a deal with Imperialism … and will stoop to any degree of ruthlessness in the persecution of the Leftists'.[3] As is evident, leftism in the nationalist perspective was certainly about political freedom from imperialism which would create an environment in which the struggle for genuine socio-economic transformation could successfully be waged. Here socialism is a metaphor referring to the absence of exploitation of human beings by human beings. Leftism thus became an alternative ideological tool in India's freedom struggle which evolved partly due to the failure of the Gandhi-led right-wing Congress leadership to effectively address the genuine socio-economic grievances of the disempowered, especially the peasants and workers.

Disillusioned with the conservative Congress leadership, left radicals strongly felt that radical socio-economic transformation needed a completely different ideological commitment which the Congress had miserably lacked. They were attracted to Marxism and other socialist ideas because they offered not only a well-articulated programme of socio-economic changes, but also powerful theoretical tools to understand and analyse the nature of capitalism that engendered colonialism. With their effective intervention, Indian nationalism no longer remained a mere political struggle, but became a multifaceted battle for liberation not only from political bondage, but also from social and economic atrocities which were intrinsic to India's social fabric.

Left radicalism was an ideologically inspiring endeavour which immediately attracted the youth who were politically baptized by revolutionary terrorism that had organic roots, especially in Bengal, Punjab and Maharashtra. An Intelligence Bureau report of 1927 made clear that a substantial section of revolutionary terrorists had come to the view that, unless peasants and workers were involved in the anti-British struggle, the nationalist movement would never be strong enough to achieve India's independence. Evidence of growing discontent, the report continued,

> was to be found in the proceedings of the Political Sufferers' Conference at Gauhati [in Assam] and was voiced by Bhupendranath Dutta [brother of Vivekananda] in his presidential address. The speech was openly communistic and it [was] said to have created a profound impression on the minds of the youths to whom it was addressed. Dutta advocated for an organization of the peasants and workers and the formation of people's party.[4]

In his personal recollections, Tridib Chaudhuri, a member of the revolutionary outfit, Anushilan Samity, who later became a leader of the Revolutionary Socialist Party (RSP), corroborated this. According to him, by the early 1920s, the

Anushilan Party in particular adopted definite policies and programmes along socialist lines in order to reach beyond 'the world of the middle class dominated *bhadralok* politics'.[5] Side by side with indigenous movement designed to include hitherto neglected political actors, there were also attempts by the Communist International through its emissaries, such as M.N. Roy, Abani Mukherjee and Gopen Chakrabarty, to spread socialist ideas. Although the Third International succeeded in attracting a sizeable section of the revolutionary terrorists, there was opposition too. Jadugopal Mukherjee, himself a revolutionary terrorist, recollected in his memoirs that the majority of the Anushilan members never liked the idea of launching a nationalist movement under the direction of a foreign country.[6]

Whatever the principal reason for this ideological change in Bengal, the above evidence indicates the awareness among the revolutionary terrorists, who increasingly dominated the Congress, particularly in Bengal, after the days of C.R. Das, of the importance of building an organization involving the peasantry and workers. In a programme of action, published in 1931 by the Chittagong revolutionaries, the aim was clearly stated by underlining that:

> The Congress platform is to be availed of. Then follow orders for the capture of trade unions, the formation of ryot associations, secret entry into social and philanthropic organization and the formation of unity to offer armed resistance to troops and police. Revolutionary students should join university training corps for observation of military methods. A women's committee should be coopted for the duty of revolutioning the women folk and selecting from them active members for direct service.[7]

Though declaring that the Congress was dominated by selfish commercial interests and the creed of *ahimsa* [non-violence] was futile as a means of achieving independence, this document appreciated Gandhism because 'it count[ed] on mass action. It had paved the way for the proletarian revolution by trying to harness it, however realistically or crudely to its own political programme. The revolutionaries must give the angel his due.'[8] The awareness of linking the peasant and working-class movements with the wider anti-British struggle was also manifested in the Congress decision to incorporate the demands of the peasants and workers in its policies and programmes in the 1929 Rangpur session of the Bengal Congress. The Congress failure to adopt a concrete agrarian programme[9] and the fact that the majority of east Bengal peasantry were Muslims and the visible social prejudices of the Hindu landed gentry towards the Muslims enabled the non-Congress and communal organization to flourish at its expense. Among the workers, the Congress had built a support base, but its national democratic line of maintaining an amicable understanding between the workers and the native industrialists prevented any consolidation of its position.

This was thus an era of possibilities in which competitive ideologies were articulated to address new socio-economic and political issues involving the politically disempowered sections. The contemporary document shows that in addition to the Congress that sought to expand its base among the peasants and workers, the revolutionary terrorists were reported to have changed their strategy because they realized that 'a handful of terrorists, however determined they might be, could never win swaraj for India unless they had the support of mass of populace'.[10] The involvement with the mass movement led a group of revolutionary terrorists to realize, as Gopal Halder, himself a member of a revolutionary outfit, called Jugantor, noted, 'how strong a movement involving the people could be if it was properly organized'.[11] With this new realization, they searched simultaneously for new ideologies. One of the sources which shaped their thinking was certainly the influence of the Moscow-returned Bengali revolutionary terrorist. Nalini Gupta and Abani Mukherjee who sought recruits from among their old acquaintances to their new ideology aimed at a mass revolution following the Russian model. By convincing the former revolutionary terrorists of the importance of building organizations among the students, peasants and workers, the left radicals contributed to a shift in their ideological orientation. The ideological shift which started in the early 1920s was manifested in the formation of new organizations involving workers and peasants. The Labour-Swaraj Party was an example. Founded in 1925, this party became in 1926 the Workers and Peasants Party (WPP) which united members of both the revolutionary groups, Anushilan and Jugantor,[12] who were persuaded to believe that terrorism was politically suicidal.

The WPP became a rallying point for the workers and its emergence was hailed. For R.P. Dutt who was instrumental in popularizing Marxism in India, it was complementary to India's freedom in the real sense of the term. As he mentioned,

> [t]he new factor which developed for the first time in the middle years of the nineteen-twenties and gave a decisive impetus to the new wave of struggle, though not yet its leadership, was the emergence of the industrial working class as an independent forces, conducting its own struggle with unexampled energy and heroism.... With its advance, the new ideology of the working class or Socialism began to develop for the first time as a political factor in India and the influence of its ideas began to penetrate the youth and left section of Indian Nationalism, bringing new life and energy and wider horizons.[13]

It was the dawn of a new era in which the disempowered sections became integral to the political processes and with the formation of the WPP their role was formalized. In that respect, the WPP was a unique chapter in India's working-class struggle which, so far, did not figure prominently in the nationalist agenda presumably because of the hegemonic middle-class leadership and the restricted social expanse of the nationalist movement. With the party's arrival on the political scene, the workers got a forum to raise and also support their genuine socio-economic demands. Immediately after the WPP made its formal appearance, a charter of demand was prepared and placed to improve the conditions of the factory workers across industries which are as follows:

(1) Eight hour day (two weeks holiday with pay per year); (2) abolition of child labour; (3) abolition of the system of fine; (4) minimum living wage; (5) state support for unemployed, old age pensions, maternity benefit and sickness benefits; (6) improvement of laws regarding workmen's compensation and that of employers; (7) installation of modern safety appliances in factories and mines and (8) abolition of the system of *sirdars*.[14]

These demands drew the attention of the jute workers. An official recorded that 'Reds are prominent and active ... in most of the jute workers' union'.[15] The WPP had a decisive a role in the 1928–9 strike of jute workers. Although its militant section, the Bengal Jute Workers' Association, led the strike, the WPP always provided organizational support. The strike was not a success because the workers returned on the conditions proposed by the jute mill owners. Nevertheless, the strike and the WPP's role in it demonstrated a new phase of working-class history signifying a new dimension in working-class militancy. In his study, Dipesh Chakrabarty has shown how the communist influence became decisive in the jute workers' defiance of authority during the 1930s.[16]

The WPP also strove to mobilize the peasantry. As early as 1928, the party put forward the following demands aimed at ameliorating the peasants' conditions:

(1) Elimination of all mid agencies between the peasants and the state; (2) direct representation of the peasant on the state apparatus, through peasant *Panchayats*; (3) immediate provisions for land from big estates; (4) substantial reduction in rent; (5) review of the debt and interest obligations through peasant courts, and (6) state credit to the peasants.[17]

In comparison with its organizational strength among the jute workers, the WPP was less significant among the peasantry. Despite its marginal role, it had contributed to the formation of Kishan Sabha (a peasant organization) which gradually became strong among the peasants in parts of Bengal and other states in eastern India.

This brief scan of the evolution of left radicalism in India confirms that the situation at the grassroots was restive and those involved in factory production and also agriculture bore the brunt of development which the colonial power pursued to strengthen its foundation. Discontent simmered for obvious reasons. With the formation of the WPP and Kishan Sabha, the workers and peasants found organizational platforms through which to ventilate their grievances and also possibly to seek redress. In fact, these outfits expanded the horizon of the freedom struggle by making classes other than the middle class, which so far remained the mainstay, integral to the political battle that the nationalist Congress had launched in alliance with several other organizations. Political freedom from colonialism was necessary, but not adequate to bring about radical socio-economic transformation in circumstances where vested interests are well entrenched and powerful enough to scuttle efforts towards changing the class balances in society. This was the concern which M.N. Roy, one of the earliest left radicals in India with faith in Marxism, expressed when he mentioned that '[o]ur object is to create discontent everywhere against the present system of exploitation and to intensify it wherever it exists. Thus will the ideal of Swaraj be brought within the understanding of the workers and peasants of India.'[18] In two ways, Roy attempted to galvanize the exploited masses into revolutionary actions: on the one hand, he always appreciated the importance of the party in creating and sustaining the revolutionary zeal among the discontented masses; he thus appreciated the role of the WPP and Kishan Sabha which, in his opinion, set in motion certain activities towards that effect; on the other hand, as a true Marxist, he also paid equal emphasis to the level of consciousness that not only contributed, but also sustained the revolutionary potentials of the victims of the exploitation. He thus argued that '[o]ur task is to develop in the minds of the masses this consciousness of their own power, to awaken their interest and develop their indomitable will to conquer freedom [and they] will do the rest'.[19]

In this growth and consolidation of left radicalism in India, the role of the WPP and its sympathizers was most critical and cannot thus be denied. It was difficult to sustain an organization that drew on Marxism-Leninism in circumstances where, besides the brutal colonial state apparatus, there were competing ideologies of nationalism and divisive communalism which gained remarkably in the period of organizational weakness and decline. Nonetheless, the WPP, by evolving a new political alternative drawing on class contradictions, put forward a new format of mass struggle challenging 'the deliberate occlusion of social interests of the exploited in mainstream politics'.[20] Opposed to 'the class oligarchy of the nationalist leadership', they put forward a new ideological format challenging not only 'the opportunistic and reformist' elements in 'the struggle for human emancipation', but also 'the alliance defending vested interests'.[21] It was therefore a breakthrough in India's battle for political freedom which created circumstances for the left radicals not only to mobilize the disempowered, but also to articulate new idioms of politics privileging class-contradiction over class-reconciliation.

III

As is evident, left radicalism was not just externally induced because it had indigenous roots. The usual argument attributing the emergence of the communist movement championing left radicalism to the initiatives of the Comintern and Soviet Union thus speaks the half-truth because it 'tends to gloss over the role of the peasants and labour movements in ... the development of the socialistic organizations'.[22] With clear organic roots in the contemporary agrarian and industrial milieu, the WPP was perhaps the first organized endeavour to create a movement involving both the peasantry and factory workers. There is no doubt that in the dissemination of left radicalism in India, the WPP had played a critical role which was complemented by several other political outfits with the same ideological mission. One of the most striking developments in this regard was the consolidation of an ideological left group within the Congress which sought to reorient the nationalist movement by drawing on the classical socialistic texts, including that of Marxism. While reminiscing about the growth of the left in the Congress, Subhas Chandra Bose, one of the firebrands within the group, mentioned that in the formation of the Swaraj Party, the left had a critical role though at the beginning it had 'drawn elements from the Right and the Left. During the life time of [C.R. Das], the Left elements had the upper hand because he himself belonged to the Left', added Bose.[23] The first concrete step in which the left was recognized as integral to the Congress was taken in the 1927 Madras Congress. The youth brigade within the Congress comprising Jawaharlal Nehru, Subhas Chandra Bose and Shuaib Quereshi, carried a resolution in favour of complete independence which, though defeated, set in motion processes for its adoption in the 1929 Lahore Congress. Along with this resolution, the Madras Congress also took a significant step in appointing these three left-oriented Congressmen to the highest decision-making authority in the Congress, the Congress Working Committee. So, the Madras Congress, according to Bose, 'may be regarded as standing for a definite orientation towards the Left'.[24] The Bose–Nehru duo represented the left in the Congress because both of them seem to have been inspired by the libertarian aspect of communism. For Bose, communism was preferred because it represented an ideological commitment to equality whereas Nehru was attracted because it was 'not hypocritical and nor imperialistic ... nor insisting on a doctrinal adherence ... besides the tremendous changes in Russia'.[25] Despite being inspired by communism as an ideology, Nehru was however very critical of the communists who 'often irritated [him] by their dictatorial ways, their aggressive and rather vulgar methods, their habit of denouncing everybody who did not agree with them'.[26] Nonetheless, his support for the left radical stance in the Congress consolidated a new ideologically charged group of youth within the nationalist movement. In this sense, the 1927 Madras Congress was a watershed in left radicalism in India because not only did it formally recognize the left wing in the Congress hierarchy, but it also created an environment in which the left radicals became an integral part of the nationalist movement. It was evident in a Congress meeting in 1928 in Calcutta when the left wing sought an amendment to the resolution that Gandhi moved in support of the dominion status for India by insisting that 'the Congress would be content with nothing short of independence, which implied severance of the British connection'.[27] The amendment was defeated by 973 to 1,350 votes not because of its merit, but because of the moral blackmail that the Mahatma resorted to by threatening that 'if his resolution was defeated he would retire from the Congress'. So many endorsed the resolution 'not out of conviction, but because they did not want to be a party to forcing the Mahatma out of the Congress'.[28] It is true that the left wing failed to accomplish its mission in the face of Gandhi's frontal opposition. Nonetheless, the voting showed, as Bose zealously stated, that 'the Left Wing was strong and influential'.[29]

The consolidation of the WPP and the increasing importance of the left wing within the Congress, despite the towering presence of Gandhi, reflected a new era in India's nationalist movement in which left radicalism gained prominence. It was the beginning of a new type of politics which sought to capture the restive marginalized section of the society by raising socio-economic issues that so far had remained peripheral in the nationalist purview. The growing importance of the left in the Congress and also its popularity among the youth were a source of concern to the British authority, as was evident in a secret government circular of 21 February 1929 which characterized the 1928 Calcutta meeting of the All-India Congress Committee as 'a clear triumph for extremism'.[30] Indicating how alarmed the authority was, the circular further added that:

> if the experience of the Calcutta Congress is any guide, the decision of future policy appears to lie almost entirely with the young men, notably Pandit Jawaharlal Nehru and Babu Subhas Chandra Bose. There is a tendency for the political and communist revolutionaries to join hands, and Pandit Jawaharlal, an extreme nationalist, who is at the same time genuinely attracted by some of the Communist doctrines, stands at the meeting point.... The situation contains serious potentialities of danger.... If the extremist leaders press on with their programme, it appears to the Government of India that they should not have a free hand to develop their organization, and increase their following with a view to striking at the moment most favourable to themselves.[31]

Both Bose and Nehru were ardent admirers of Marxism and the Soviet Union which represented a great hope to mankind. In fact, in his assessment of the Soviet Union, Nehru was always appreciative of the achievement that the Leninist Soviet Union had accomplished following the 1917 socialist revolution. In his words: 'I have no doubt that the Soviet Revolution had advanced human society by a great leap and had lit a bright flame which could not be smothered, and that it had laid the foundation for that new civilization towards which the world could advance.'[32] For obvious reasons, Nehru's proclivity towards socialism did not augur well with the right wingers who felt that 'vodka has gone to his head'.[33] Despite being appreciative of Marxist ideas of radical socio-economic transformation, he was also swayed by Gandhi who, he felt, 'knew India better than [anybody else], he was a man who could command such tremendous devotion and loyalty that he must have something in him that corresponded to the needs and aspirations of the masses'.[34] It was 'an interesting position', argued Bose who, along with Nehru, opposed the Gandhi-led right-wing Congress leadership, because '[Nehru's] ideas and views are of a radical nature and he calls himself a full-blooded socialist – but in practice he is a loyal follower of the Mahatma. It would probably be correct to say', he further added, 'that while his brain is with the Left Wingers, his heart is with Mahatma Gandhi.'[35] By the 1929 Lahore Congress, it was clear that Nehru had shifted his loyalty to Gandhi when he did not allow Subhas Chandra Bose, Srinivas Iyengar and other prominent left-wingers to become members of the All-India Congress Committee because 'the Mahatma ... wanted a committee of one mind and he wanted his list to be passed

10 *Introduction*

in its entirety'.[36] So the 1929 Lahore Congress was 'a great victory' for Gandhi in two ways: on the one hand, Nehru was 'won over by him' and this undoubtedly strengthened Gandhi's position in Congress High Command and, on the other hand, his success caused irreparable damage to the left radical forces in a context when '[t]he Mahatma could henceforward proceed with his own plans without fear of opposition within the [committee], and whenever any opposition was raised he could always coerce the public by threatening to retire from the Congress or to fast unto death'.[37]

IV

The gradual decline of the left-wingers in the Congress notwithstanding, parallel efforts were made to consolidate the left radicals to create an alternative leadership to lead the nationalist campaign differently. The idea was broached in an informal meeting among a young group of socialists who were serving prison sentences in the Nasik (Bombay) central jail. It was decided to form a block of opposition within the Congress to prevent 'its drift towards neo-constitutionalism' and also to 'broaden the basis of the movement by organizing the masses on an economic and class-conscious basis'.[38] A new political outfit, christened the Congress Socialist Party (CSP), was born in 1934 which found its largest support in the United Provinces and Bombay, especially among those who were disillusioned with the Gandhi-led right-wing Congress leadership. Despite being unhappy with the Congress, the socialists agreed to operate from within the Congress since it was the only organization that ignited the mass inspiration for political freedom from British rule. As the existing nationalist battle was bourgeois-nationalistic in character, it would be suicidal, they also felt, to dissociate from the struggle that the Congress launched under Gandhi's stewardship. For practical purposes, the socialists decided to join the Congress to pursue their ideological mission of 'reorienting the masses towards the goal of socialism'.[39] It was thus publicly announced at the first All-India Socialists' Conference at the Anjuman-i-Islamia Hall in Patna on 17 May 1934 that the primary object of the conference was to mobilize the masses to prevent 'an outright drift to constitutionalism and to put a more dynamic programme before the country'.[40] Along with the pursuing of the nationalist goal, the socialists were asked 'to fervently and persistently agitate within the Congress for the adoption of an economic programme with a view to socialize the nationalist struggle'.[41] Soon after the Patna conference, the socialists met again in Bombay in October 1934 to prepare the constitution and reinforce the claim that, besides winning political independence, the party also aimed at achieving 'the establishment of a socialist society in India'[42] through the implementation of a fifteen-point charter of demands[43] which are as follows:

1 transfer of all power to the producing masses;
2 development of economic life of the country to be planned and controlled by the state;

3 socialization of key industries (steel, cotton, jute, railways, shipping, plantations and mines), insurance and public utilities with a view to the progressive socialization of the instruments of production, distribution and exchange;
4 state monopoly of foreign trade;
5 organization of cooperatives for production, distribution and credit in the unorganized sector of the economic life;
6 elimination of princes and landlords and all other classes of exploiters without compensation;
7 redistribution of land to the peasants;
8 state to encourage and control cooperative and collective farming;
9 liquidation of debts owned by peasants and workers;
10 recognition of the right to work or maintenance by the state;
11 'to everyone according to his needs' is to be the basis of distribution of economic goods;
12 adult franchise which shall be on the functional basis;
13 state shall neither support nor discriminate between religions nor recognize any distinction on caste or community;
14 state shall not discriminate between the sexes;
15 repudiation of the so-called public debt of India.

A perusal of the above charter shows that the CSP sought to evolve a third ideological perspective by combining the features of Fabian socialism and Marxism-Leninism. It was an Indian version of left radicalism that took into account the distinctive Indian socio-economic circumstances while chalking-out its list of programmes. As well as being ideologically distinctive, the CSP was unique in that its plan of action was supported both by advocates of armed struggle (Jayaprakash Narayan) and by those insisting on the typical Gandhian non-violence (Narendra Deva). Supporting decentralized socialism, the CSP favoured cooperatives and trade unions as effective devices for meaningful participation by the people in governance. Unlike the Gandhians who considered community as critical to unity, with their commitment to the Marxist theoretical framework, the CSP found in class solidarity an effective means to combat communal schism and bitterness. Nonetheless, the party continued to remain an appendage to the Congress in order to strengthen and mould its policies towards achieving its primary ideological mission of attaining socialism in India. For the CSP members, the Congress gradually became a solid anti-imperialist platform for its sustained activities among the masses which made it the strongest mass organization. So the task before the CSP was to complement the political campaign that the Congress had undertaken. It was thus not surprising when Jayaprakash Narayan, one of the firebrand CSP members, stated that '[t]he Congress alone is the country's salvation. And let us remember that the Congress means the whole and not part of it. A limb torn from the body does not have its proportionate strength and ability. It merely dies.'[44]

The CSP was a fresh ideological intervention during the nationalist struggle in India. By seeking to evolve as a conscience-keeper for the anti-British nationalist campaign, the CSP fulfilled two significant ideological goals: on the one hand, with their pronounced socialist inclinations, the CSP members reconsolidated the left radicals within the Congress despite the Gandhian onslaught; on the other, the arrival of the CSP on the political scene kindled hopes among the masses who seemed to have lost hope in the Gandhi-led right-wing Congress leadership. Nonetheless, the party never became powerful as a movement presumably because none of the top-ranking Congress leaders was associated with it. While explaining the failure of the CSP to rise 'as an alternative leadership in place of the Gandhian leadership which had monopolized the political field since 1920', Subhas Chandra Bose thus argued that '[t]he Congress Socialist Party had the historic opportunity to throw up an effective alternative leadership in the Congress ... if Pandit Jawaharlal Nehru, who gave his moral support to that party, had openly joined it and accepted its leadership'.[45] There is no doubt that the CSP failed to generate mass support and create independent constituencies of support among the peasantry or workers except in certain areas of Bombay and the United Provinces. The party remained an appendage to the Congress and it was therefore not possible to strike an emotional chord with the toiling masses in the factories or paddy fields. Bose thus laments by saying that:

> the Congress Socialist Party contains within itself the promise of a great future [and] ... it has been able to draw towards itself the radical elements in Indian National Congress ... [it] has unfortunately fallen a victim to the same confusion of ideas which has seized the present day Congress leaders.[46]

In such hopeless circumstances, 'masses will', he further added, 'ultimately turn to some other party for their salvation'.[47]

Disillusioned with the Gandhi-led nationalist leadership, a section within the Congress made another serious endeavour in 1939 to unite the left radicals by forming the Left Consolidation Committee (LCC) which included all leftist groups involved in the nationalist struggle. This new organization was nothing but a pressure group within the Congress. It sought to provide a general platform for the left; it was also an attempt to win over the majority within the Congress to its viewpoints and it proposed to mobilize for the resumption of the nationalist struggle under the Congress banner.[48] The Committee however collapsed soon because of the serious differences of opinion among the constituents over the observance of All-India protest day, on 9 July 1939, against the All-India Congress Committee resolution banning civil disobedience without prior permission of the provincial Congress committee, which was actually an attempt to clip the wings of Subhas Chandra Bose, who was one of the architects of the LCC, in Bengal. The Communist Party of India (CPI) and the socialist leader, Jayaprakash Narayan, accorded first priority to Congress unity; it was, they thought, in jeopardy as a result of such a call.[49] And they thus decided to stay away from the LCC. M.N. Roy felt that in the light of the national movement, the decision to challenge the Congress was 'a great blunder'.[50] Having seceded from the LCC, he was alleged to have pressed Nehru to persuade the CSP to dissociate from it which, according to Bose, 'amounted to a betrayal of the Leftist cause'.[51] By July 1939, one month after its formation, all the major constituents had left the LCC with the exception of the Kishan Sabha and a few Anushilan Marxists from Bengal.

V

The above narrative shows that left radicalism was both indigenous and externally driven: while the WPP was rooted in the resentment of the disempowered which the established nationalist leadership failed to address, the Congress left-wingers consolidated their position because of the weaknesses of the nationalist ideology to address genuine socio-economic grievances. In addition to these two major trends, the Communist Party of India was also a major component of left radicalism that gradually thrived in India not only during her colonial-imperial phase, but also in the aftermath. Unlike the nationalist parties, the Communist Party did not seem to have indigenous roots since it was founded in India at the initiative of the Comintern. It is true that a large number of revolutionary terrorists were drawn to the Marxist ideas of human emancipation which acted favourably when the idea of the party was broached by the Communist Party of Great Britain. With the formal inauguration of the party, a succession of British communists including Shapurja Saklatvala, the Dutt brothers (Clemens P. Dutt and Rajni P. Dutt), Philip Spratt and Ben Bradley came to India to actively engage with communist activities in India. Two of the British emissaries (Philip Spratt and Ben Bradley) were arrested in the 1929 Meerut conspiracy case in which leading communists were incarcerated for their involvement in instigating movements against the state. It was also the beginning of a new phase in India's nationalist struggle when the communists joined the anti-imperial struggle under the direction of the Comintern.

Set in motion in the 1920s with the formation of the Communist Party of India, the communist movement had manifested differently in different phases of India's political history. It played the role of a catalyst rather than being a decisive political force during the nationalist movement for freedom from British rule. Despite their critical role in mobilizing peasants and workers in their fight against vested socio-economic interests, the Indian communist had a rare distinction of being 'collaborators' with British rule during the Second World War so long as it remained a mere imperial war according to the former Soviet Union. Hence the Communist Party activists justified their indifference towards the Gandhi-led 1942 open rebellion which alienated them from the mainstream nationalist politics. They became suspects to the nationalists even when they revised their political stance once the Second World War was interpreted differently, following the participation of the former Soviet Union in the war. The imperial war suddenly became the people's war once the Soviet Union got involved in the aftermath of Hitler's attack on Moscow. For the Soviet Union, this was a defensive attack and was thus justified. But for the Indian communists, their initial withdrawal from the 1942 Quit

India movement had cost them dearly. The party was criticized severely for being supportive of the imperial power when the nationalists were thrashed brutally for their campaign against the state. Because of its failure to understand the nationalist mindset, the CPI failed to strike an emotional chord with the people at large. There was hardly a leader who could 'harness the radical forces arising from the socioeconomic and political environment'.[52] The Communist Party never became a significant political force in India's struggle for freedom because it was, argued Nehru,

> completely divorced from, and [was] ignorant of, the national traditions that [filled] the minds of the people.... The Communist Party [could] not take advantage of [the mass resentment] because it [had] cut itself off from the springs of national sentiment and [spoke] in a language which [found] no echo in the hearts of the people.[53]

Its ideological appeal to students and factory workers notwithstanding, the CPI failed to emerge as an effective alternative to the Congress as it was unable to strike organic roots in India. Explanations for its decline vary: for the nationalists, its foreign roots were primarily responsible; for others, its uncritical faith in a set of dogmas accounted for its failure to reach out to the masses. It has been cogently argued by the experts that:

> Communism in India failed because it was founded on dogma [that] has had many facets that the proletariat is infallible, that the international leadership is infallible, that the Party can do no wrong, that Parliaments are the instruments of the exploiting classes, and that the inevitable sweep of history will bring the Party to power ... [and] whenever reality contradicted dogma, Communists have often turned their back on the reality.[54]

As is shown, the failure of the Communist Party to emerge as an acceptable alternative during the freedom struggle was attributed to (a) its alien roots and (b) its obsession with the doctrinal and also derivative ideas of political mobilization which failed to evoke any natural response from among the masses. Despite its well-publicized emancipatory nature, the Communist Party could never become a part of the mass psyche largely because of these limitations from which it never could recover, especially during the nationalist phase. Nonetheless, the sustained political activities by the communist cadres among the peasants and workers helped the party create constituencies in parts of West Bengal and Telangana region of the erstwhile princely state of Hyderabad. The results were visible soon; the Communist Party led mass uprisings in these areas against the state which set in motion a different kind of political mobilization involving the so-called wretched of the earth. The Communist Party was thus banned in independent India, presumably because of the decision to launch an armed struggle first in West Bengal, championing the cause of the peasantry, and later in Telangana opposing the feudal ruler of Hyderabad. The ban was withdrawn in

1950 and the Communist Party agreed to participate in parliamentary politics.[55] However, this is only one part of the story because the communist movement also morphed into armed struggle, as was the case with the Naxalite movement in the late 1960s and later Maoist insurrection in the twenty-first century. In other words, the communist movement had different shapes in independent India ranging from parliamentary left to violent armed struggle of the Maoists in recent years. History thus shows not a single path of evolution across all regions presumably because of the contextual differences in which left radicalism of the communist variety was articulated. Its nature had gradually become more Indian and 'less communist'[56] which meant that the Communist Party that gained salience in independent India took into account India's contextual peculiarities while determining its ideological priorities regardless of the classical doctrinal Marxist approach to political mobilization. To understand this, one has to look at the strategies of the regional units and the varying social milieu and political atmosphere in different regions which play a critical role in redefining the communist model of human emancipation with reference to the contexts. For instance, the strategy of the Communist Party was not uniform in Travancore and Cochin compared to Malabar in Kerala, which was part of British India: while in the former, the Communist Party preferred to follow the parliamentary path, in Malabar, in order to fulfil its revolutionary goal, the party resorted to violent means. In fact, this was the familiar pattern of the communist mobilization in India after 1957 when the Communist Party agreed to adopt parliamentary means for human salvation. Despite the acceptance of democratic election, which led to the formation of the first communist government in Kerala in 1957, a section within the party was never reconciled to this position because it amounted to a clear dilution of the fundamental principles of Marxism-Leninism.[57] The group supporting violent revolution was easily bypassed because it was a minority. In its fifth Party Congress, held in Amritsar in 1958, it was thus announced that:

> [t]he CPI strives to achieve full democracy and socialism by peaceful means. It considers that by developing a powerful mass movement, by winning a majority in the Parliament and by backing it with mass sanctions, the working class and its allies can overcome the resistance of forces of reaction and ensure that Parliament becomes an instrument of people's will for effecting fundamental changes in economic, social and state structure.[58]

As is evident, the majority in the Communist Party believed that radical socio-economic transformation in India was possible through ballot and accordingly the party participated in electoral politics in India. The radical section thought otherwise. True to their commitment to the violent revolutionary path of mass struggle, the left radicals who were opposed to parliamentary means were never persuaded. For them, radical change remained 'an elusive goal' so long as the communists evaded 'the violent revolutionary path'.[59] This was not merely a convenient way of looking at Marxism-Leninism, but also a serious distortion, it was further argued, of basic Marxist-Leninist belief undermining its dynamism. They were critical of the Kerala experience by saying that it heightened parliamentary illusions because

> reformism grew in the party as a result of the Kerala victory [which] they found it particularly dangerous as it could lead to erroneous conceptions that the state could be changed by its electoral capture, and socialism could be built without smashing the received machinery of the bourgeois state.[60]

Given the manifestation of communism in two diametrically opposite ways, the Indian experiment is perhaps the most creative articulation of an ideological discourse that drew on moral values which are based on respect and struggle for the freedom of the individual – values that are integral to Marxism.

VI

The aim of this exercise is to focus on the two versions of left radicalism in India that evolved with context-specific distinctive characteristics. While the parliamentary left, by regularly participating in elections, represents one version of communism, those critical of parliamentary forms of governance seem to have reinvented Marxism in a non-industrial context by defending the violent revolutionary path as perhaps the only way to radically alter the prevalent class relations. What is therefore striking is the fact that in India both versions of left radicalism are relevant and ideologically meaningful in mobilizing those supportive for their respective causes. It is true that, by eschewing violence immediately after independence, the Indian communists were drawn to parliamentary politics to pursue their ideology-driven goals. There is no doubt that the communist rule in Kerala, West Bengal and Tripura brought about significant changes in governance by adopting, for instance, radical land reforms which were not pursued seriously in the past for obvious class constraints. The principal argument that this book makes thus relates to the growing importance of the left parties in India's liberal democratic governance. It is now evident that there has been a clear ideological shift from a revolutionary to a reformist orientation and the parliamentary left parties, instead of emphasizing 'class antagonism' as a means for the establishment of an egalitarian society, seem to have been favourably inclined towards significant socio-economic transformation through electoral politics. The parliamentary left appears to have flourished in circumstances in which the state is utilized for facilitating 'development with redistribution'.[61] Drawn on a social alliance of apparently contradictory class forces, the reformist left parties sustain their viability as a democratically elected government within an economy which is not favourably disposed towards the left ideological goal.

At the national level, the role of the communist parties was never so significant except for their symbolic presence in the Indian Parliament presumably because they hardly had noticeable numerical strength in the national legislature, except during the period of the V.P. Singh-led National Front government, between 1989 and 1991, and later during the first United Progressive Alliance (UPA) government (2004–9) when the left parties, including the Communist Party of India (Marxist), agreed to support the Congress-led coalition against the so-called communal forces, led by the Bharatiya Janata Party (BJP) and its allies. Despite their meaningful roles in crafting a different kind of administration in the constituent provinces, the left parties failed to expand their influence beyond their traditional strongholds of Kerala, West Bengal and Tripura. Given their historical involvement in mobilizing workers and peasantry for political causes, the left parties continue to remain critical in reconceptualizing their role in the changed environment. So, the trajectory of the parliamentary left is indicative of an alternative political discourse that also thrived in a typical liberal democratic framework.

The story of left radicalism is equally interesting for two specific reasons. First, by espousing the communist goal of establishing an exploitation-free society through violent means, the left extremists seem to have articulated a powerful ideological discourse for the socio-economically downtrodden sections. This is a clear re-evaluation of how salient is the left extremist ideology at the grassroots. Second, the increasing popularity of Maoism and the growing existence of the so-called 'red corridor' in contemporary India further confirms the importance of left extremism in mobilizing the disempowered even under adverse circumstances. Indicative of the growing discontent of the masses, Maoism, perhaps the most virulent form of the communist movement, seems to have emerged as the most successful ideological discourse (at the popular and also intellectual levels) in contemporary India, which has set in motion very meaningful processes of political mobilization for the hitherto peripheral sections of Indian society.

Based on an in-depth study of socio-economic circumstances that remain critical in conceptualizing radical extremism drawing on Marxism-Leninism and also its Maoist articulation, this book seeks to provide a synthetic account of the rise and consolidation of left radicalism in India, This is a contextual study of the phenomenon by reference to its articulation by the parliamentary left and also the outlawed left-extremist groups. By focusing on two different (and also mutually antagonistic) versions of left radicalism, the aim of the book is to analytically account for its changing texture.

Since it is a contextual study of left radicalism in India, the book begins, in Part I, with a detailed exposition of the context in which the contemporary versions of left radicalism are articulated and put into practice. Chapter 1 provides an analytical account of the changing nature of India's socio-economic environment since India became politically free in 1947. By accepting liberal democracy of the Westminster variety, independent India continued with more or less the identical political system which gradually underwent changes to accommodate the contextual needs of the polity. Enamoured by the success of state-led development in the erstwhile Soviet Union, the first generation nationalist leadership uncritically accepted state-sponsored planning for uniform development in India. With the failure of the planned development to accomplish the goal, the idea lost its credibility, especially following the onset of globalization. After having set the socio-economic context, the book unfolds with an elaborate discussion of the parliamentary left and also its militant version that pursues a violent revolutionary means to capture power. 'Who constitute the parliamentary left in India?' is the question for which answers are sought in Chapter 2. In India, the task is less complicated because, due to ideological compatibility, the constituents of the left have formed a compact, known as the Left Front in West Bengal and Tripura and the Left Democratic Front in Kerala. By dwelling on each of the constituents, this chapter seeks to situate them in a historical perspective. It is true that in the formation and also continuity of the parliamentary left, the role of the dominant partner, the Communist Party of India (Marxist) is most critical though the partners remain integral to the collectivity showing perhaps the significance of an ideological bond in a coalition.

Part II dwells on the parliamentary left in India, with reference to its rise and consolidation since the formation of the Communist Party of India in the 1920s. Chapter 3 focuses on the increasing importance of the parliamentary left in Kerala and Tripura: while Kerala has the distinction of having the first elected communist government in India, study of the latter shows the growth and consolidation of the parliamentary left in an insurgency-prone north-eastern state of India. The parliamentary left in West Bengal has created history by holding the state for thirty-four uninterrupted years. Chapter 4 provides an analytical narrative of this unique experiment of left radicalism that sustained its acceptability among the voters largely because of pro-people welfare policies that the Left Front government pursued during its rule and also a well-entrenched organization that held its social base by decimating, coercively on occasions, the opposition in the state. Chapter 5 focuses on the experiment of parliamentary left in Kerala since 1957 when the first communist government was formed through election.

Part III focuses on the left-wing extremism which has had its varied manifestations in different phases of India's recent political history. The most important left-wing extremist movement was the one that the Naxalite had organized in 1967 for a Maoist revolution in India by mobilizing the wretched of the earth. Chapter 6 thus concentrates on the historical evolution of Maoism in India with reference to the socio-economic context in which mass poverty shaped an ideological assault on the state that was charged with pursuing discriminatory policies towards the disempowered. Drawing on field data from Orissa, an Indian province in the east in which Maoism is a strong politico-ideological force, Chapter 7 is an in-depth contextual study of the phenomenon that has gradually gained salience in contemporary politics since it has ignited hopes among those who always remain peripheral in the present socio-economic dispensation. Maoism is, as the book argues, a product of the prevalent socio-economic circumstances in which those on the lower rungs continue to suffer because of the class bias of the ruling authority. Maoists have capitalized on this to build and sustain an organized movement against the state. The growing importance of Maoist left-wing extremism confirms that Maoism is not merely a powerful statement on India's growth trajectory, but also an equally powerful critique of the state-led development paradigm that the nationalist leadership has preferred to bring about uniform socio-economic development in independent India.

In view of its unique texture, the Indian variety of left radicalism does not fit in to the available theoretical framework. One has to be sensitive to the rapidly changing socio-economic milieu to comprehend the phenomenon in its entirety. This is a book that seeks to grasp and also conceptualize the changing nature of the communist ideology with reference to its articulation in governance and also ideologically charged political movements for radical socio-economic metamorphosis. By drawing on the left experiments in Kerala, West Bengal and Tripura, the book will provide an analytical account of how it was possible for the left parties to remain in power in pockets in circumstances which were not exactly conducive. While the parliamentary left is well entrenched, its failure to emerge as a meaningful ideological alternative is also visible with the growing importance of the extra-parliamentary left in India. With the Maoist intervention, various new issues – environment, forest rights, displacement due to the creation of special economic zones (SEZs), food entitlement, alternative health programmes – have become critical in political mobilization. Given the growing importance of Maoism in the so-called 'red corridor' stretching between Pashupati in Nepal to Tirupati in Andhra Pradesh, the argument that Maoism is not just a mere ripple appears to have gained credibility.

Notes

1 Subhas Chandra Bose, *The Indian Struggle, 1920–42*, Asia Publishing House, London, 1964, p. 409.
2 Bose, *The Indian Struggle*, p. 409.
3 Bose, *The Indian Struggle*, p. 409.
4 IOR L/PO/3, extract from a daily report of the Director of the Intelligence Bureau, Home Department, Government of India, New Delhi, 10 February 1927.
5 Foreword by Tridib Chaudhuri in B. Bhattacharyya, *Origins of the Revolutionary Socialist Party: from national revolutionary politics to non-conformist communism*, Publicity Concern, Calcutta, 1982, p. 5.
6 Jadugopal Mukherjee, *Biplabi Jibaner Smriti* [Memoirs], Academic Publishers, Calcutta, 1982, p. 398.
7 'Our Aims', published in *The Statesman*, Calcutta, 23 December 1931.
8 'Our Aims'.
9 I have elaborated this argument in my 'Bengal Congress and the peasantry, 1928–38', *South Asia Research*, vol. 5, no. 1, May 1985, pp. 18–38.
10 *India and Communism*, Home, Government of India, Calcutta, 1935, p. 234.
11 Gopal Halder, foreword in Jadugopal Mukherjee, *Biplabi Jibaner Smriti*, Academic Publishers, Calcutta, 1982, p. 10.
12 *Communism in India*, Home, Government of India, Calcutta, 1927, p. 139.
13 R.P. Dutt, *India Today*, Manisha, Calcutta, 1979 (reprint), p. 357.
14 G. Adhikari, *Documents on the History of the Communist Party of India*, vol. 3 (c), Progressive Publications, New Delhi, 1982, p. 275.
15 West Bengal State Archives, Calcutta, home-Poll, 148/1927, 'Report on jute mill situation', District Magistrate, 24 Pargana to Chief Secretary, Government of Bengal, 7 August 1927.

20 *Introduction*

16 Dipesh Chakrabarty, 'On deifying and defying authority: managers and workers in the jute mills of Bengal, 1890–1940, *Past and Present* 100, August 1983, pp. 144–5.
17 Adhikari, *Documents on the History of the Communist Party of India*, vol. 3 (c), p. 278.
18 M.N. Roy, *India in transition*, Nachiketa Publications Limited, Bombay, 1971 (reprint), p. 284.
19 Roy, *India in transition*, p. 284.
20 Suchetana Chattopadhyay, *An Early Communist: Muzaffar Ahmad in Calcutta, 1913–1929*, Tulika Books, New Delhi, 2012, p. 232.
21 Muzaffar Ahmad, 'Gorai golod' (lapse at the beginning), *Ganabani*, 4 October 1928 – reproduced in Muzaffar Ahmad, *Prabandha Sankalon* (A collection of essays), National Book Agency, Calcutta, 1970, p. 155.
22 Subho Basu, *Does Class Matter? Colonial capital and workers' resistance in Bengal (1890–1937)*, Oxford University Press, New Delhi, 2004, p. 199.
23 Bose, *The Indian Struggle*, p. 117.
24 Bose, *The Indian Struggle*, p. 146.
25 Jawaharlal Nehru, *An Autobiography: with musings on recent events in India*, John Lane, London, 1941, p. 163.
26 Nehru, *Autobiography*, p. 163.
27 Bose, *The Indian Struggle*, p. 157.
28 Bose, *The Indian Struggle*, p. 157.
29 Bose, *The Indian Struggle*, p. 158.
30 IOR L/PO/3–4, daily report of the Director of the Intelligence Bureau, Home Department, Government of India, 21 February 1929.
31 IOR L/PO/3–4, daily report of the Director of the Intelligence Bureau, Home Department, Government of India, 21 February 1929.
32 Jawaharlal Nehru, *The Discovery of India*, Oxford University Press, Delhi, 1989, p. 29.
33 Patricia Kendell, *India and the British*, Charles Scribner's Sons, London, 1931, p. 426.
34 Nehru, *Autobiography*, p. 255.
35 Bose, *The Indian Struggle*, p. 29.
36 Bose, *The Indian Struggle*, p. 175.
37 Bose, *The Indian Struggle*, p. 175.
38 Yusuf Meherally (ed.), *Jayaprakash Narayan, Towards Struggle*, Padma Publications, Bombay, 1946, p. 9.
39 Yusuf Meherally (ed.), *Acharya Narendra Deva, Socialism and the National Revolution*, Padma Publications, Bombay, 1946, pp. 4–5.
40 Meherally, *Acharya Narendra Deva*, p. xii.
41 Meherally, *Acharya Narendra Deva*, pp. 28–9.
42 *Times of India*, 21 October 1934.
43 Meherally, *Jayaprakash Narayan*, pp. 101–2.
44 Meherally, *Jayaprakash Narayan*, pp. 139–40.
45 Bose, *The Indian Struggle*, p. 325.
46 Bose, *The Indian Struggle*, p. 385.
47 Bose, *The Indian Struggle*, p. 385.
48 Subhas Chandra Bose, *All Power to the People*, All-India Forward Bloc, Calcutta, 1940, p. 27.
49 Meherally, *Jayaprakash Narayan*, pp. 137–8.
50 M.N. Roy to Amarendranath Chatterjee, 1 December 1939, Nehru Memorial Museum and Library, New Delhi, M.N. Roy Papers.
51 Bose, *The Indian Struggle*, p. 404.
52 Satyabrata Rai Chowdhuri, *Leftist Movements in India, 1917–1947*, Minerva, Calcutta, 1977, p. 242.

53 Nehru, *The Discovery of India*, pp. 516–17.
54 Gene D. Overstreet and Marshall Windmiller, *Communism in India*, University of California Press, Berkeley, 1959, p. 537.
55 Valerian Rodrigues has elaborated the phases of the communist movement in his 'The Communist Parties in India', in Peter Ronald deSouza and E. Sridharan (eds), *India's Political Parties*, Sage, New Delhi, 2006, pp. 199–252.
56 Overstreet and Windmiller, *Communism in India*, p. 539.
57 B.T. Ranadive, 'The devil strikes back?' *New Age*, April 1956.
58 Ajoy Ghosh, 'On the party constitution', *New Age*, February 1958.
59 A group of firebrand members of the party from West Bengal raised their objection to the acceptance of 'the parliamentary path' and 'peaceful means' of revolutionary transformation. Several pamphlets were circulated at the 1958 Amritsar Congress of the party in which party activists supporting the violent revolutionary path for meaningful socio-economic and political change raised their voice while issue was allowed to be debated.
60 Sudipta Kaviraj, 'The split in the communist movement in India', PhD dissertation, Jawaharlal Nehru University, New Delhi, 1979, p. 436.
61 Bose, *The Indian Struggle*, p. 383.

Part I
Setting the scene
Consolidation of left radicalism in India

An ideology ceases to be an ideology if it does not develop organic roots. Hence it is conceptually inaccurate to conceptualize ideology as a universal category precisely because of its context-driven nature. It is the historical context which adds meaning to an ideology, representing ideas, norms and values of a specific age of history reflective of a definite mindset. This means that opinions, statements, propositions and systems of ideas are not taken at their face value, but 'are interpreted', argues Karl Mannheim, 'in the light of the life situation of the one who experiences them ... [signifying] that the specific character and life-situation of the subject influence his opinions, perceptions and interpretations'.[1] Two features thus stand out: on the one hand, ideology is situation-specific, seeking to evolve a bunch of ideas which are meaningful and motivating; because it is also transcendental in terms of its reach, ideology upholds, on the other hand, a universal spirit which makes sense in an identical socio-economic and political context. Ideology is both ideating and inspirational since it sets in motion significant processes which are also reflective of an urge for transforming the prevalent system of thinking.

Left radicalism in India is highly context driven. Drawing on the passion for substantial socio-economic changes to the prevalent class imbalances, not only did the left radicals craft an alternative discourse of change, they also raised newer issues involving the marginalized by directing successful protest movements in different phases of India's recent political history. During the struggle for freedom, they mobilized masses for socio-political aims which did not always please the nationalist leadership presumably because of their specific class prejudices. Nonetheless, their sustained endeavour at the grassroots was politically innovative since they drew on an ideology which sought to combine political freedom with substantial socio-economic changes at the grassroots to accomplish human emancipation in the real sense of the term. Despite not being successful in altering the prevalent class relations in contemporary India, left radicalism remains an important ideological force that is both meaningful and provocative in the sense of raising issues which usually escape the notice of the well-established liberal political outfits for obvious class bias. Hence this part is most fundamental in laying out the socio-economic and political context in which the Indian variety of left radicalism emerged and continues to remain pertinent in the political processes.

Note

1 Karl Mannheim, *Ideology and Utopia: an introduction to the sociology of knowledge*, Routledge & Kegan Paul, London, 1979 (reprint), p. 50.

1 Socio-economic contexts of left radicalism in India

The aim of the chapter is to provide an account of the socio-economic circumstances that remain critical in conceptualizing left and radical politics drawing on Marxism-Leninism and its Maoist articulation in contemporary India. This is also a study of a specific kind of social-democratic model that India's parliamentary left sought to articulate by adopting pro-people schemes through well-established legislative procedures within the constraints of parliamentary democracy. This is not a unique theoretical design because it had its manifestations elsewhere in the globe as well. What is unique, however, is the application of the model in three differently textured socio-economic circumstances of Kerala, West Bengal and Tripura that enabled the parliamentary left to strike organic roots. This is not the entire story because there exists side-by-side an ultra-left-wing extremism as a powerful mobilizing ideology, in the form of Maoism, even in the left-ruled state of West Bengal. Presumably because of the failure of the state in fulfilling the aspirations of the people at the grassroots, Maoism seems to have gained an easy acceptance among the victims of 'state-led-development' who remain socio-economically peripheral in post-independent India in which the benefits of planned economy are appropriated by a specific segment of society. This also explains the alienation of the Gorkhas in Darjeeling in West Bengal or the tribals in Tripura from the prevalent left governments. One is thus better equipped to understand the complexities of the situation by reference to a rigorous contextual analysis of the probable factors responsible for the growth, consolidation and relative decline of the left in India. Just like the parliamentary left, there are indications of the decline of Maoism as an ideology-driven political movement. A contextual study of Maoism in Orissa and Chhattisgarh reveals that the Maoist ideological alternative does not seem to remain as inspiring as before, presumably because of the Maoist failure to ameliorate the conditions of the poor on the one hand and, on the other hand, the success of the state in meaningfully implementing developmental packages for people in the affected areas, besides, of course, the coercive role of the government-sponsored military and paramilitary forces in liquidating the left wing elements wherever they constitute a formidable opponent. In view of its historical role in shaping India's polity, left radicalism continues to remain a critical ideological component in conceptualizing its nature. Despite having drawn its ideological linage from the derivative Marxist-Leninist-Maoist model of analysis, the Indian version of left radicalism also remains indigenous in its spirit and articulation. The parliamentary left and its militant counterpart have sustained their ideological appeal largely due to the fact that they are rooted in the Indian soil. In other words, despite being inspired by a derivative ideology, left radicalism continues to remain a significant political force in contemporary India since it is meaningful to the majority of the disempowered sections across the country.

There is no doubt that context is always critical in shaping a specific ideological response. This is true of the Indian variety of left radicalism which, despite being anchored in the Marxist-Leninist tradition, has hardly a uniform character across the country because of the diverse socio-economic characteristics. For instance, there is hardly a difference in perception between the parliamentary left and other leading bourgeois political parties on the neo-liberal path for economic reforms, as the discussion below shows: by agreeing to follow a neo-liberal path of development, both the left and its right-wing bête noire do not appear to be ideologically different at all.

Neo-liberal economic reforms in India

With the onset of macroeconomic reforms in the 1990s, the state-led developmental plans seem to have lost their significance in a situation where the non-state actors have grown in importance in redefining the state agenda.[1] India has adopted reforms in perhaps a very guarded manner. One probably cannot simply wish away the theoretical justification of state intervention in a transitional economy. Reasons are plenty. Socialist principles may not have been forgotten, but the importance of the state in the social sector cannot be minimized unless a meaningful alternative is mooted. This is reflected in the obvious distortions in India's economy.

It is true that economic liberalization is a significant influence and yet, the importance of the prevalent politico-institutional context cannot be underestimated while conceptualizing the impact of economic reform in India. In a significant way, the institutional legacy of a well-entrenched state affected the post-reform possibilities in India.

What thus proliferate across India are 'state-guided routes to liberalization rather than market fundamentalism'.[2] This has resulted in an obvious tension in the economy which is neither appreciative of market hegemony nor fully supportive of the erstwhile state-led development paradigm. In fact, here lie roots of severe social discontent fuelling ideological political movements, including a militant Maoist movement, challenging the state for its failure to protect the marginalized. The situation has thus become far more complicated because there is evidence to confirm that the state has miserably failed to address the genuine socio-economic grievances of the majority of the people, especially in rural India, leading to the consolidation of people-centric political movements redrawing the contour of Indian politics that cannot be formatted in the available theoretical discourses.

The political economy of India as a nation state

India's post-colonial political economy is neither purely capitalist nor feudal but a peculiar admixture of the two. Hence the path of development that India adopted can never be conceptualized in a straightforward manner like India's evolution as a nation in the aftermath of decolonization in 1947. The Preamble to the Constitution of India laid the foundation of the socialist pattern of society in which the state remained the most critical player. Accordingly, the Directive Principles of State Policy (Part IV of the Constitution) emphasize that the goal of the Indian polity is not unbridled laissez-faire but a welfare state where the state has a positive duty to ensure for its citizens social and economic justice with dignity of the individual consistent with the unity and integrity of the nation. By making these principles fundamental in the governance and law-making of the country and making it the duty of the state to apply these principles, the founding fathers made it the responsibility of future governments to find a middle way between individual liberty and the public good, between preserving the property and privilege of the few and bestowing benefits on the many in order to liberate the powers of men and women equally for contributions to the common good.[3] This led, as a commentator rightly points out, to 'paradoxical socialism' in India that approximated to what the Fabian socialists championed as socialism. Fabian socialism, it was further argued, was

> an intellectual tool [that] facilitated, when required, a distancing of oneself from the revolutionary left while still maintaining a claim to socialism; and, possibly more importantly, justifying a socialism brought about by an elite who were great believers in science.[4]

Independence in 1947 provided the founding fathers with a chance to translate their ideological vision into concrete development programmes in which the role of state was hailed as a prime mover. The new institutional matrix that the state-led development programmes provided, consisted of 'a regulatory regime' comprising (a) public sector expansion, (b) discretionary controls over markets and private economic activities and (c) stringent foreign exchange and import controls. The first two had their roots in the ideology of socialism while the last had its roots in economic nationalism. Taken together, they articulated 'activism of the newly established nation state'[5] to guide the economic system 'in a desired direction by means of intentionally planned and rationally coordinated state policies'.[6]

In this model of state-directed development, the most significant instrument was the Planning Commission that came into being in January 1950 despite serious opposition of the Gandhians within the Congress Working Committee. However, the cabinet resolution that finally led to the creation of the commission underlined three major principles as special terms of reference in the preparation of the plans which largely defused opposition. These principles were: (a) that citizens, men and women equally, have the right to an adequate means of livelihood; (b) that the ownership and control of the material resources of the country

28 *Setting the scene*

are so distributed as best to serve the common good; (c) that the operation of the economic system does not result in the concentration of wealth and means of production to the common detriment.[7] Underlining the ideological commitment of the nation, the 1948 Industrial Policy Resolution therefore begins by stating that:

> [t]he nation has now set itself to establish a social order where justice and equality of opportunity shall be secured to all the people. For this purpose, careful planning and integrated efforts over the whole field of national activity are necessary; and the Government of India propose to establish a National Planning Commission to formulate programmes of development and to secure its execution. (para 1)

Accordingly, the resolution insisted that the state should play a progressive active role in the development of critical industries, such as (a) industries manufacturing arms and ammunition, production and control of atomic energy and the ownership and management of railway transport; (b) basic industries such as iron, coal and steel, aircraft manufacture, ship building, mineral oils. This resolution was reiterated in the 1955 Avadi session of the Congress by underlining that in view of the declared objective of being a socialist pattern of society, the state shall play a vital role in planning and development. The next landmark event confirming the intention of an activist state was the Industrial Policy Resolution of 1956 that was adopted after Parliament had accepted in December 1954 a socialist pattern of society as the objective of social and economic policy and the Second Five Year Plan (also known as Mahalanobis Plan) articulated this ideological goal in formal terms. P.C. Mahalanobis, the architect of the plan, argued for state-controlled economic development for accelerating the tempo of growth under 'the autarkic industrialization strategy'.[8] Hence he insisted that the basic and heavy industries should remain in the public sector for two reasons: (a) the private sector might not be able to raise adequate resources for these very capital-intensive industries and even if it managed it would command a monopolistic control that was deemed detrimental to social welfare; and (b) by controlling the allocation of output of basic and heavy industries according to social priorities, it was certain that the government would be able to channel private sector growth to fulfil its ideological goal. In seeking to achieve the objective of a socialist pattern of society, the Nehru-led government envisaged an expanded role for the public sector and the importance of planning in all-round development of the country.

Planning for development: a panacea or failure(?)

As an operational tool, planning seems formidable to structure the role of the state in accordance with its ideological underpinning. Therefore not only is planning as an instrument tuned to economic regeneration, it is inextricably tied to the regime's political preferences as well. This is however not to conceptualize the relationship between planning and the ideological slant of the regime in a deterministic way, but to underline the complex interdependence which entails, at the same time, an interplay of various pulls and pressures in a rapidly changing social fabric. Planning is thus 'an exercise of instrumental rationality ... institutionalized ... outside the normal processes of representative politics [and executed] through a developmental administration'.[9] Notwithstanding the critical significance of planning, the developmental project in India, argues Aseema Sinha, 'was and continues to be constrained by the pattern of mediation between the centre and regions'.[10] Furthermore, centralized planning also led to the expansion for regionalism in India presumably because of haphazard and unequal development of constituent provinces. Regional differences and politico-economic conflicts arising out of a centrally engineered scheme remain critical in post-independent India's political economy, besides the exogenous influences in the wake of globalization.

Historically, the Congress was persuaded by the arguments supporting planning for development. Contrary to Gandhi's explicit opposition to 'planned development', the Congress Party showed ample interest in socialistic means, including planning and heavy industrialization, as 'essential to make revolutionary changes in the present economic and social structure of society and to remove gross inequalities' since 1929. Within two years, the 1931 Karachi Congress adopted a resolution insisting on state ownership of 'key industries and services, mineral resources, railways, waterways, shipping and other means of public transport'.[11] However in 1934, the Congress Working Committee passed a resolution at Banaras stressing that 'large and organized industries are in no need of the services of Congress organizations or of any Congress effort on their behalf'. Critical of the above, Jawaharlal Nehru rallied support to reformulate the resolution with a view to soliciting Congress backing for industrialization and planning which, he believed, was the only available means to attain substantial economic development in India. A compromise formula was reached in Bombay at the Congress Working Committee meeting in September 1934. Accordingly, top priority was accorded to small-scale cottage industries. Encouraged by partial support of the party, as neither the Congress fund nor its organizational support was available, Nehru in his 1936 Faizpur presidential address argued strongly in favour of heavy industrialization and coordination of human resources through planning.

Planning seems to have provided the Congress stalwarts with a platform to articulate different ideological positions. Drawing on their respective ideological leanings, Nehru hailed industrialism while Gandhi opposed it since he felt that instead of contributing to the general welfare, machine civilization would not only expose Indians to a worse kind of exploitation but also lead to a general degradation of human life. Although Nehru and Gandhi were poles apart on occasions, the former, unlike his militant colleague Subhas Bose, never pursued his differences with the latter to the extent of causing a split within the Congress. Despite the adverse ideological implication of aligning with Gandhi, Nehru as a pragmatist participated wholeheartedly in the Gandhi-led freedom struggle for

30 *Setting the scene*

he knew that the attainment of independence was prior to ideology. So, the controversy involving Gandhi and Nehru vis-à-vis planning and industrialization was just a signpost indicating the tension which was most likely in view of the Congress effort to create an anti-British platform incorporating even contradictory ideologies. By making a case for planning and industrialization there is no doubt that Nehru ushered in a new era in the Indian independence struggle.[12]

This detailed description of the evolution of planning illustrates Nehru's uncritical faith in planning though he acknowledged that it was to be guided by what he characterized as 'integrated planning'. Hence he observed,

> [The] Planning Commission has performed an essential task; without which it could not have progressed.... We are a federal structure and it has served to bring the various states together and have integrated planning. If it had not been there, the central government could not have done its job because immediately difficulties would have arisen that the central government was encroaching on the rights of the States.[13]

It was almost natural that planning was to become an important instrument for development once Nehru took over as India's Prime Minister. Planning was envisaged as 'a pre-condition' and was based on the assumption that 'spontaneous development cannot be expected'.[14] Economic planning in South Asia is, as Myrdal further argues, 'not [therefore] the result of development, but is employed to foster development.... The underdeveloped countries in this region are thus compelled to undertake what in the light of Western history appears as a short-cut.'[15] Despite the euphoria over planning, it left a large number of people below the poverty line. Even those sympathetic to the strategy of planned development believed that 'If Indian society values growth with equity, as plan documents repeatedly emphasize, India has still a long way to go in adapting institutions and aspirations in that direction'.[16] While explaining the failure of planning to accomplish the Nehruvian goal of 'balanced and equitable growth', Sukhamoy Chakravarty, who was otherwise a supporter of the state-led development programme, attributed the failure to the lack of coordination among those involved in the framing of planning and also 'the information failure'. In his words,

> plans did not work because the desired coordination among the different actors was faulty, either because 'messages' were faulty, or because they were transmitted with delay, or went contrary to the specific interests of the actors involved and were therefore evaded.[17]

Besides the inherent weaknesses of the planning processes, India's development strategy did not yield the desired results presumably because of the failure to evolve 'a broad political consensus on priorities'.[18] It is true that planning failed to evolve a mechanism for equitable distribution of economic resources and was also detrimental to capitalist development in India. Planning was merely an ideological tool of the state to intrude, rather mechanically, into the economic processes which may not always follow what is planned in advance. As Meghnad Desai argues, 'the Green Revolution, and the context of owner-cultivation in which it made its impact, brought capitalism irreversibly to the country side'. This is a significant structural change in the Indian economy which 'came independently of planning'. What it showed was the gradual but steady decline of planning as an instrument of rapid economic development in India where capitalism had a skewed growth due to a variety of historical reasons. Desai thus concludes that 'planning has lost the driving seat it once had [because] ... the driving force will come from the capitalist social relations in the Indian economy'.[19] Instead of altogether rejecting planning, what it suggests is the changing role of the Planning Commission based on appreciating the capitalist path of development. In the words of Desai,

> Planning [requires to be] interactive and predictive in an econometric way. It will be strategic rather than pervasive. It will start with a given growth rate. The growth rate that will emerge from the interactive predictive quinquennial exercise will set a feasible bound. It will require further iterative and counterfactual work with the available models to explore whether a higher growth path is achievable, and if so, what constraints need to be removed.[20]

This is the quintessence of the argument which Desai puts forward to reorient the instruments for economic development, including planning for a well-defined scheme drawn on the basic principles of capitalist growth, as explained by classical Marxism. Hence 'planning designed for an insulated national economy ... is not appropriate'.[21] Instead, it has to take into account the new material conditions involving the growing importance of the global economy, especially the non-state actors like the International Monetary Fund, the World Bank and other transnational donor agencies. One cannot simply ignore this changed milieu, and hence the national economies need to come to terms with them as best as they could. So, the most meaningful step for steady economic growth is 'a rapid integration of the Indian economy into capitalism'.[22] The formula works in a spectacular way in the case of China, Taiwan and Korea where capitalism is not discriminatory but pro-people as well. Socialism in India failed in its basic objective. Those at the bottom continued to suffer. The mixed-economy strategy which sought also to pursue state-led capitalist development thus largely failed because the Indian economy 'had grown too slowly to qualify as a capitalist economy ... [and] by its failure to reduce inequalities had forfeited any claims to being socialist'.[23] Such an argument led Desai to believe that 'India's problem is not so much capitalism but that it is stuck with a backward version of capitalism'.[24] So economic growth is, as Desai argues, rooted in a complete overhauling of the economy, supported by a strong political will endorsing, for instance, various anti-poverty programmes and cutting the subsidies to the rich. Under these changed circumstances, it is possible for the state to play a dynamic role in pursuing an economic agenda in favour of those at the bottom who have always suffered in the name of much euphoric socialistic planning. While explaining the failure of the state-led development paradigm in India, Atul Kohli thus argues that:

> the Achilles heel of Indian political economy is not so much its statist model of development as much as the mismatch between the statist model and the limited capacity of the state to guide social and economic change.... [By] trying to reconcile political preferences of both the left and right in the context of a fragmented state, [the Indian policy-makers] failed both at radical redistribution and at ruthless capitalism-led economic growth.[25]

The euphoria over the role of the public sector for a balanced economic growth was short-lived. Except for financial enterprises in banking and insurance and petroleum-producing enterprises, none of the public sector units became viable.[26] This created a paradoxical situation. While socialist rhetoric was useful for building and sustaining a stable political base for the ruling authority, the pro-poor policies were hardly seriously pursed. As a result, not only were the business houses alienated, the poor also felt cheated. This perhaps explains why 'the state-led economic growth or political efforts at redistributions and poverty alleviation' did not succeed to the same extent as was possible in Korea where the state pushed capitalist growth (rather ruthlessly) or in China which followed state-directed radical poverty alleviation.[27]

With the consolidation of globalization, it is true that there is no alternative to economic reforms. It is also true that, without a proper political backing, economic reforms are just mere devices without much substance. In India, the same political leadership that had been the guardian of the old order emerged as the champion of the new. Is this 'a genuine change or [mere] electoral window dressing?', Desai asks.[28] Given the present dispensation of power in India, the future of economic reform does not appear to be as bright as in South East Asian countries or China. One of the primary conditions for a sustained reform package is a government which is ideologically compatible with an adequate numerical strength in the legislature. As of now, the political system does not appear to be stable due to too frequent elections and is thus not equipped to pursue economic reforms in a sustained manner. 'An unreformed political system is', Desai laments, 'an obstacle to fundamental and irreversible economic reform.'[29] There is no magical way. What is required is a change of attitude because 'it is quite clear that India must liberalize' for sustained economic growth. Indian resistance to liberalization, as Desai argues, comes from the elite interests and not from the poor. At the forefront are the organized sector industrialists who benefited from the policy of protection and are now scared of competition. The state has a crucial role to play in the changed circumstances. What must be junked is 'state ownership [of non-profit and non-viable otherwise] as it has proven to be wasteful and growth-retarding'. Still, 'reform is a contentious issue [and] India, [as of now], is not an enthusiastic reformer'.[30] Yet, there is no doubt that reform is a sure contributor to economic growth, as the examples from South East Asia demonstrate. For India, clinging to liberalization is 'a resumption of history [because] India as a trading and manufacturing nation [was] able to compete on a world scale [in] cotton textile in the days before independence'.[31]

The changing economic horizon

The introduction of macroeconomic reforms in 1991 was a serious challenge to the state-led development plans and programmes. Given the clear failure of the Nehruvian socialistic pattern of society that was espoused so zealously by the political leadership immediately after India's decolonization in 1947, the 1991 New Economic Policy did not appear to have raised many eyebrows. Nonetheless, the principles governing the socialistic pattern of society cannot be said to have completely disappeared; instead, the Indian state seems to have adopted a context-specific strategy in which state intervention is appreciated so long as a meaningful alternative is unavailable. Furthermore, one cannot simply gloss over larger political-philosophical issues involved here. The argument that the march of the market economy has been resisted by Indian elites' infatuation for socialistic principles does not appear persuasive in the light of the visible mass opposition to economic liberalization. As Pranab Bardhan argues,

> our collective passion for group equity, for group rather than individual rights and the deep suspicion of competition in which the larger economic interests are given an opportunity to gobble up the small, work against the forces of market and allocational efficiency.[32]

This passion was particularly strengthened by Gandhi who gave 'sensitive and eloquent expression to this anti-market, anti-big capital, small-is-beautiful populism' while mobilizing masses against the British for freedom.[33] Economic reforms have created conditions in which those persuaded by the Gandhian moral critique of market expansion and competition are even drawn to the left-radical forces for building active grassroots movements all over the country for the protection of the environment, of women's rights and of the traditional livelihood of the indigenous people. In such circumstances, development or market seems to be synonymous with 'dispossession of the little people and with despoliation of the environment'. Major strands in the political culture thus, as Bardhan rightly concludes, 'provide a none-too-hospitable climate for market reforms'.[34]

Economic liberalization in India ushered in reforms 'by stealth'[35] as it was more or less accepted as a *fait accompli* to avoid the massive balance of payment crisis in 1991. Apart from domestic compulsion, internationally two major events undermined 'the basic premises of the earlier social consensus regarding the development strategy'.[36] The first was the collapse of the former Soviet Union and its East European satellite states that moved towards a market-oriented economic system eschewing altogether the model of planned economic development. Second, the spectacular success of the socialist market economy of China with the opening of the economy since 1978 and its concomitant favourable economic fall-out cast serious doubts on India's development strategy based on economic nationalism.

Nonetheless, the importance of the prevalent politico-institutional context cannot be undermined while conceptualizing the impact of economic reform in India. In a significant way, the institutional legacy of a well-entrenched state affected the post-reform possibilities in India. As a commentator argues,

> India's bureaucratized regime – the license-quota-permit raj – has had major, unintended consequences on post-transition patterns: all [state] governments and central regimes continue to rely on state-led strategies of reform; there is no 'Washington Consensus' or 'neo-liberal' route to reforms in India.[37]

There is no doubt that economic reforms brought about radical changes in India's political economy. Yet, the old regulatory regime of the bygone era remained critical in the path and processes of liberalization in a very decisive way. What thus proliferates across India are 'state-guided routes to liberalization rather than market fundamentalism'.[38] This is reflected in the obvious distortions in India's economy. On the basis of an empirical study in Andhra Pradesh and other supporting data, the author thus argues that 'two economies – one affluent and the other predominantly agricultural economy – are emerging ... and this division can be seen across the social and regional landscape of India'.[39] The technology-based export-oriented city-centred economy is flourishing in the new economic environment while the agricultural economy remains backward and those associated with this 'have little expectation of a better future [and] remain preoccupied with the daily struggle to secure a livelihood'.[40] The contribution of agriculture to national income has, in recent years, fallen dramatically but more than 600 million Indians still depend on farming. This is a matter of concern, for obvious reasons. In fact, the growing divergence between the share of agriculture in GDP and in the workforce alerts 'to the urgent imperative of raising farm productivity in India [which] languishes far below potential'.[41]

While agriculture remains 'a bargain sector', industrialization is hailed as the panacea for Indian economic ills since the economy is growing fast even when agriculture stagnates. Seeking to articulate the typical Indian response to liberalization, the 1991 Industrial Policy Resolution thus suggested several steps to 'unshackle the Indian industrial economy from the cobwebs of unnecessary bureaucratic control' though within the overall control of the state.[42] Four specific steps were recommended: first, the government decided to abolish industrial licensing policy except for a short list of industries related to security and strategic concerns, social reasons, hazardous chemicals and overriding environmental reasons. Second, the government also endorsed direct foreign investment of up to 51 per cent foreign equity in high-priority industries. To avoid bottlenecks, an amendment to the 1973 Foreign Exchange Regulation Act was suggested. Third, it was also decided to withdraw protection of 'the sick public sector units' and there would be 'a greater thrust on performance improvement' to ensure accountability of those involved in these state-sponsored enterprises. Finally, the 1991 policy sought to remove the threshold limits of assets in respect of those companies functioning under the Monopolies Restrictive Trade Practices Act. By seeking to amend this act, the 1991 policy suggested elimination of 'the requirement of prior approval of the Union Government for establishment of new undertakings, expansion of undertakings, merger, amalgamation and take over and appointments of Directors under certain circumstances'. The Indian response to economic liberalization is most creative, if judged contextually. The Nehruvian socialist pattern of society cannot be so easily dispensed with for historical reasons while globalization may not be an appropriate strategy for economic development in a poor country like India because in its present form, argues Joseph Stiglitz, it seems like 'a pact with the devil'. A few people may have become wealthier, but for most people, closer integration into the global economy 'has brought greater volatility and insecurity, and more inequality'.[43] Economic liberalization is thus a double-edged device which while improving the lives of some Indian has also left millions more untouched. Hence it has been rightly pointed out that the essence of economic liberalization in India can be captured by a Buddhist proverb suggesting that 'the key to the gate of heaven is also the key that could open the gate to hell'. Indeed, the danger and opportunity are so intricately intermingled in economic reforms that 'the journey to the promised land of [economic prosperity] could easily turn into a hellish nightmare of poverty and widening inequality for the majority'.[44]

Economic reforms and special economic zones (SEZs)

The introduction of market-driven economic reforms in 1991 in India was perhaps due to the fiscal crisis that Indian was only able to overcome with financial support from the World Bank and International Monetary Fund. This support was not of significant benefit to the marginalized sections of the population. Instead, the creation of SEZs for industrial purposes out of prime agricultural land in various parts of India renders land-dependent populations jobless and homeless. The SEZs are those specially earmarked territories which are duty-free and tax-free enclaves that are considered 'privileged territories' for trade operations and tariffs. This is a policy decision supportive of private investment for rapid economic development in which the state becomes a facilitator. True to its newly acquired neo-liberal role, the state seems to have unleashed 'a policy of terror' to forcibly acquire land for these private operators. This has led to massive protests in Chhattisgarh, Jharkhand and other parts of the country where left-wing extremism is a strong ideological force because it has resulted in the displacement and dispossession of the indigenous population. A party document underlines the adverse human consequence of SEZ, stating,

> today the reactionary ruling classes of the country are bent upon transforming vast tracts of fertile agricultural land into neo-colonial enclaves if it

means enacting blood-baths all over the country. Thousands of *crores* of rupees have already flown from big business and imperialists Multinational Corporations into the coffers of the ruling class in India. It is clear that the battle-lines are drawn for an uncompromising war between the haves and have-nots between those who want to turn our mother land into a heaven for the international capital, the Indian big business and the handful filthy rich on the one hand and the vast majority of the destitute, poverty-stricken masses, particularly the peasantry, on the other. There is no middle ground: either one is with the vast masses or with the filthy rich. Two hundred and thirty seven SEZs have already been approved and of acres of fertile agricultural land are being forcibly acquired by the various state and central governments. In Orissa, Jharkhand, Chhattisgarh, Andhra Pradesh, Maharashtra, Haryana and several other states, of the people are rendered homeless due to anti-people projects. The CPI (Maoist) calls upon the oppressed masses, particularly the peasantry, to transform every SEZ into a battle zone, to kick out the real outsiders – the rapacious MNCs [multinational corporations], comprador big business houses, their (boot lickers) and the land mafia – who are snatching away their lands and all means of livelihood and colonizing the country.[45]

As a result, the state that zealously pursued the path of reforms seems to have lost its credibility to those involved in the everyday struggle for survival. The period since the late 1980s has thus seen growing resistance to such policies by the dispossessed groups in different parts of the country. The 'red corridor' is also the mineral corridor, given the rich reserve of minerals in this large tract of tribe-inhabited areas and the Maoists aim to resist 'the handover mineral wealth of India to multinationals and foreign capitalists'[46] transforms the area into a war zone. This is a different kind of war being waged in parts of India where people 'are fighting in their own territory to save their land, forest, water, minerals from being grabbed and they are convinced that they have an alternate vision, not just for themselves, the Adivasis, but for Indian people as a whole'.[47] In such volatile circumstances, the installation of the SEZs seems to have provoked new discussions and also resistance movements even in areas which are free from Maoist radical politics. This is therefore not just coincidental, as will be shown in Chapter 4, that localities rose in rebellion against the ruling parliamentary left in West Bengal when the incumbent Left Front forcibly took over land from the farmers in Nandigram and Singur. Maoists were reported to have participated in the movement against forcible land acquisition which was basically a spontaneous mass outburst in opposition to the policy of dispossession. Even though not ideologically compatible, several bourgeois political groups joined the resistance movement against land acquisition, suggesting perhaps the building of a powerful critique by raising pertinent questions regarding the applicability of neo-liberal economic reforms in India where the proportion of people living below the poverty line is staggeringly high. So, SEZs are not merely an articulation of a specific form of economic development, they are also an ideological tool to pursue an alternative path of development in which the stakeholders are informed but not at all consulted while seeking to integrate India with global capitalism through neo-liberal economic reforms.

The changing texture of Indian politics

Along with the dramatic changes in India's political economy following the acceptance of neo-liberal economic reforms, a significant transformation is also visible in India's political texture. Indian politics is now regionalized and coalition governments have become an important ingredient of political articulation. Reflective of the socio-political and cultural diversity of the country, the regional parties that provide the numerical legislative strength hold the balance of power in a political situation where none of the so-called national parties have the magic number of parliamentarians to justify their independent claim. So, despite their distinct identities, the national parties hardly remain as decisive as they were in the environment of coalition politics where they cannot afford to ignore the regional parties entirely. This is suggestive of unique socio-political processes whereby regional issues gain immense importance in governance both at the central and provincial levels. On occasions, this results in tight-rope walking for both the regional and national parties where the support of the regional parties is absolutely crucial for the survival of the coalition. Under such circumstances, political blackmail by the coalition partners cannot be ruled out to squeeze advantage when the coalition is most vulnerable. The collapse of the 1996–8 United Front government is illustrative here because the withdrawal of the Congress support led to its loss of majority in Parliament. This is not the situation, however, if the leading partner holds a majority in the legislature and thus can survive even if the partners withdraw support. For instance, the Left Front governments owed their stability largely to the adequate strength of CPI (M) in the state assemblies. Here, the political existence of the partners is better protected within the coalition and hence, the differences are usually sorted out through meaningful dialogues and discussions. These two different varieties of coalitions articulate two different theoretical positions: on the one hand, the ideological congruity among the partners provides greater possibilities for the coalition to coagulate better for a stable formation; its lack, on the other hand, simply weakens the coalition unless the partners appreciate the importance of coming together in opposition to a common political foe or to fulfil a common political agenda, prepared by those constituting the coalition. The success of the BJP-led National Democratic Alliance (NDA) in completing its term of five years is illustrative here. Glued by the common minimum programme avoiding contentious issues, the NDA survived by drawing on a clear understanding between the numerically strong BJP and other smaller regional parties. Articulating a new wave in Indian politics, the NDA is perhaps the most successful experiment in India's recent political history of a coalition of apparently ideologically incompatible but politically congruent partners due largely to acceptable common minimum programmes. The formation of another coalition government, led by the Congress, is a continuance of the trend that began in 1999. While NDA was a majority coalition in the sense that its constituents had a majority in Parliament, the first United Progressive Alliance government, of which the Congress is a leading partner, owes its survival in a no-confidence motion to the outside support provided by the CPI (M) and Samajwadi Party with a tally of ninety-seven seats in total. Like its predecessor, the present UPA that came into being in 2009 consolidated its support base, at least at the outset, by evolving common minimum programmes which its partners agreed to respect. Apart from programmatic compatibility among its constituents, the compulsion of pushing the BJP and its allies away from power has cemented the bond despite serious ideological differences among them.

Coalition in India is a region-dictated political phenomenon. The rise of the regional parties as a combined force bidding for power at the centre is possibly due to the following factors: first, the decline of the Congress as an institutionalized party representing various and also conflicting socio-economic interests. It lost its hegemony due to, inter alia, the departure of the nationalist generation, the demise of internal democracy and the emergence of personalized mass appeal of the top leadership. No longer did the Congress remain a party capable of accommodating conflicting social interests and fulfilling the individual ambitions of those involved in its expansion at the provincial and local levels. The vacuum created by the progressive self-destruction of the Congress Party has been filled in different ways in different parts of the country, though invariably by the parties drawing on the support of the other backward classes and other lower castes. This has further deepened regionalism underlining the growing importance of region-specific issues in national politics. Indicative of a new political trend, regionalism has also ushered in a certain democratization involving the hitherto neglected sections of socio-political groups. Second, with successive elections, new social groups and strata are being introduced to the political processes. Since the entrenched groups in the dominant party tended to impede their entry to the political processes these new entrants found it easier to make their debut through non-Congress parties or occasionally even founded new parties. So, the emergence of new parties outside the BJP and Congress fold to articulate hitherto neglected socio-political interests seems to be a major factor that has contributed to the consolidation of coalition with a seemingly different ideological perspective.

What are the consequences of shifting power to the regions? Given the well-entrenched processes of centralization under the Congress governments in the past, the growing decentring of power is certainly a corrective step to restore the vitality of democratic institutions and the federal character of the Indian constitution. Regional issues can be sorted out amicably through conscious democratic processes, rather than through imposition from the centre. The fragmentation of power seems to have given an opportunity for relocating India's democracy in a perspective in which region-specific issues are equally important. Furthermore, the presence of the regional and state-based political parties accords a wider basis to governmental policies by providing inputs from those areas and regions

Socio-economic contexts 39

to which they belong. In view of the indisputable role of these smaller parties, coalition governments are also an institutional device for participation by hitherto marginalized sections in the policy-making processes. As India's party system is still volatile, it is difficult to say whether the two mainstream parties – Congress and BJP – will continue to remain the nucleus of a stable coalition government. A great deal depends on the strategies of mobilization adopted by these parties in the context of the growing politicization of peripheral sections of society and also the linkages between the global and domestic political economies that one cannot simply gloss over in today's globalizing world. Unlike the European states which are more or less uniform ethno-linguistically and thus culturally, the Indian version of coalition is a significant contribution to democracy by locating the experiment in an essentially multi-cultural society. Coalition is this complementary to democratic processes, articulated not only in the ritualistic participation of the people in election, but also in their day-to-day involvement in governmental activities. In this fundamental sense, coalitions are unavoidable and cannot be wished away as a mere ripple.

The regionalization of Indian federalism

The 2006 West Bengal poll outcome seems to have contributed to a process of genuine federalization of the Indian polity that began with the decimation of Congress rule in various states in the 1967 state assembly election. The growing importance of the regional parties, including the CPI (M) which, despite its national existence, at least ideologically is still confined to three Indian states, led to the decline of the pan-Indian parties, namely the BJP and Congress. The scene was completely different during the heyday of the 'Congress system' when the Congress Party controlled all the state governments and also the union. What was symptomatic in 1967 seems to have evolved into a well-entrenched pattern now with the clear political ascendance of the regional parties. The leading member of either of the major coalitions at the pan-Indian level can afford to ignore them only at their political peril. Following the rise of the regional parties as formidable partners in governance, the constituent states in federal India are growing stronger gradually and steadily. Not only are they now capable of articulating their demands effectively, they have, on occasions, become decisive in policy-making. Politically, it seems to be a sign of 'adulthood' of Indian states which may create the US confederal type polity with strong units and a centre as a mere monitoring instrument. The adulthood of states is not at all a romantic conceptualization of the growing importance of Indian states, but is premised on a particular variety of political consciousness, drawing on the inherent diverse socio-cultural realities of India as a nation. There are instances which may be cited to substantiate that adulthood disrupts national integrity and hence is despicable. But a thorough study of the so-called 'disruptive movements' championing regional autonomy may reveal that the outcome would have probably been otherwise had they been dealt with differently at the outset. To put it bluntly, the carefully crafted tendency to essentialize multi-cultural Indian identity boomeranged and the sooner it is understood by those who preside over India's political destiny the better it isfor the country.

Silent revolution in rural India[48]

The Indian countryside is undergoing slow but noticeable changes. While neo-liberal economic reforms have divided public opinion into watertight compartments the growing politicization of women largely due to recent democratic churning at the grassroots has made them integral to socio-political processes in rural India; they appear to be the instigators of change and not merely mute recipients of what is given by the state as a favour. An extensive interaction with several self-help groups (SHGs) in eastern Uttar Pradesh is more than a mere indication of the silent revolution at the grassroots involving women. It is amazing to see how popular the SHGs in rural empowerment are. Initiated by the Rajiv Gandhi Mahila Vikas Pariyojana (RGMVP), these women-driven SHGs have become a harbinger of change in recent years. Introduced in 2002, this programme seems to have awoken rural women not only about their duties towards the community, but about their entitlements that they have been denied because of obvious social constraints. Unlike so many of the organizations that are reportedly committed to gender empowerment, RGMVP has succeeded in putting across the message of inclusion to the socially peripheral sections of eastern Uttar Pradesh. In order to translate into reality the aim that 'the poor have a strong desire and innate ability to overcome poverty', the RGMVP has undertaken several specific programmes to inculcate community feelings and also to promote financial independence, healthcare, livelihood enhancement, education and healthy environment by involving the stakeholders in forty districts in Uttar Pradesh. With 47,000 SHGs across the state, the Pariyojana seems to have taken off as a realistic plan of action which is likely to radically alter the socio-economic balance in villages.

Prepared by well-trained and committed members of the programme, the RGMVP model draws on the idea that women are a central change agent and this is made possible through financial empowerment. Instead of pursuing the plan in a piecemeal manner which was prevalent with previous schemes for gender empowerment, this programme seeks to promote confidence and connectivity among the poor to meaningfully articulate its mission. Rather than making ideological statements, the Pariyojana is translated into action by creating several institutions linked with various kinds of activities which are integral to women's empowerment in the area in which it operates. The activities are conducted by a three-tier organizational set-up: SHGs at the bottom which form village- and block-level federations comprising primarily the office holders at the constituent SHGs. Once they are in place, they form four different committees relating to (a) liaison with the banks for credit, (b) making people aware of the importance of education and basic health and (c) creating an awareness among the rural people of being connected with each other to effectively combat poverty and also other sources of atrocities against women.

Socio-economic contexts   41

The stories that came out of my interaction with these proactive women in Seshpur Samodha village in Raebareilly reveal how effective the Pariyojana programme is in mitigating poverty and also in empowering village women. Out of 982 families, the other backward classes constitute a majority, followed by those belonging to the general castes and scheduled castes; the social engineering is so effective that the Muslims with 3 per cent of the total demography remain connected with the programme. In most of the villages where the SGHs are formed, what is noticeable is the zeal with which the village women participate in activities relating to the villages. Given women's proactive role, the banks have become sensitized to women's power and this is reflected when bank authorities no longer refuse to open a bank account on the flimsy grounds of the applicant's gender. It is thus not surprising that, in the Bank of India branch in this village, the number of bank accounts surpasses the number of families, showing the faith of the villagers in bank transactions and also the transformation of the attitude of bank officials in accepting the village folk as reliable customers. The proactive role of the village women was also visible recently in regard to the midday meal in a village school in Seshpur. With repeated complaints from the students about the quality of food in the primary school, the members of the SGHs resorted to available democratic means to convey their displeasure and also to request that this problem be immediately addressed by regular monitoring of the quality of food. This went unheeded. Left with no choice, they then met the authorities responsible for providing rice and other ingredients; after several rounds of discussion, the district authority was persuaded to supply the ingredients directly, bypassing the authority of the village Pradhan. which caused consternation at the outset; but with the threat of a sustained agitation involving SHGs in other villages, the village *Panchayat* agreed to the new system of supply in which the Pradhan lost his control over the supply chain. There is another incident involving the distribution of subsidized fertilizer: the local suppliers used to hoard the supply of subsidized fertilizer; the same pattern was evident here: with the *gherao* of the shop by the SHGs, the shop-owner was forced to distribute fertilizer in accordance with government rules. These widely publicized incidents have created an environment in which women are not only treated fairly, but also with respect, regardless of caste. It is thus not surprising that a majority of governmental developmental plans and programmes, like Mahatma Gandhi National Rural Employment Guarantee Act, National Rural Health Mission, Indira Abas Yojana, and Sarv Siksha Aviyan,[49] do not lose their focus largely because of the presence of the vigilant SGHs, supported by equally proactive Vinay Kumari, Rekha, Manorama or Kamla, the faceless women who have become a critical part of the development processes as stakeholders.

With the increasing involvement of the SHGs in village reconstruction, what is most striking is the growing awareness of village women about the methods of family planning, not only the use of various kinds of contraceptive methods, but also pre- and post-natal care of mothers. It is not surprising thus that in the villages in which SGHs are most effective family planning remains most effective. These activities apart, the SHGs, by standing by the poorest of the poor in the village, whenever needed, have become an integral part of rural being, which is not a mean achievement in the midst of rivalries over caste, class and clan. In the event of crises – whether flood or fire – the villagers are not left to themselves, as came out very clearly during the brief interaction that I had with the village women. There was a heart-breaking story about a villager who lost everything in an accidental fire. The SHGs immediately plunged into action by *annadan* (offering food), besides helping him to rebuild his house out of the corpus fund that they had accumulated in the bank from the deposit of Rs 1,000 per family per month. On the basis of their own financial strength, supported by supplementary credit from the bank, the SHGs have set in motion an empowering design of self-dependence which was unthinkable in the past because of the hegemonic and debilitating presence of the money-lenders as saviours in financial stress.

The SGHs are an empowering device whereby village women have acquired a self-esteem that was elusive until quite recently because of social constraints due to age-old patriarchal practices, supported by equally authoritarian devices denying gender equality. The village women in those villages where SHGs are most active are now fairly treated and can claim an equal status with their male counterparts not only in the villages, but also elsewhere in their interaction with the authorities while claiming their entitlement in a spirit of equality and fairness. That they have gained recognition at par with the rest of the society is how Nirmala Devi summarized while identifying the achievement of the SHGs in eastern Uttar Pradesh. This is the crux of the silent revolution involving half of India's demography.[50]

A transformative context

In a departure from the conventional pattern, this long chapter is more than a mere elaboration of the context for four important reasons. First, this book is a contextual study of a phenomenon that was articulated in two diametrically opposite ways: by clinging to the social-democratic ways, the parliamentary left finds the prevalent democratic institutions of governance useful to create conditions for the fulfilment of the Marxist-Leninist goal of establishing a classless society. Democracy, even the liberal variety, seems to be an effective ideological instrument in the transitional phase and hence it cannot be dispensed with. Contrarily, for the other version – ultra-left-wing extremism – radical social change in the sense of dramatically altering existent class relations is inconceivable under parliamentary democracy because it is simply a smokescreen to justify the age-old system of class exploitation with a different label. Once the system of governance is appropriated by those with vested socio-economic interests, which is usually the case, the institutions, despite being sensitive to the needs of the underprivileged, always reflect class prejudices when attempts to change the prevalent class relations are made. There are innumerable instances of the involvement of the landed gentry in the Maoist movement to protect their class interests. As is shown by field data, the landlords belonging to Kurmi castes in Bihar supported left-wing extremism 'not due to any ideological commitment to the poor peasants, but to re-establish their dominance in the region'.[51]

Second, in order the capture the complex evolution of left radicalism in India within a time span of more than half a century, this chapter also focuses on the social, economic and political metamorphosis of a country that has a visible colonial legacy not only in the institutions of power, but also in the ideological surroundings supportive of liberal democracy of the Westminster type. Change is visible though governance is articulated largely in liberal democratic terms whereby dissenting voices are accommodated so long as they do not disrupt the prevalent social, economic and political order. And, also the state's response to dissent is far more calibrated than ever, presumably because of the change of circumstances when protest movements, if articulated in a liberal-democratic format, are considered as important sources of refreshing socio-economic and political inputs from the grassroots which are also useful to reinvent strategies for long-term gain.

Third, by attempting a contextual explanation of the growth of several constituencies of power outside the arena of the state, this chapter draws on the wider social, economic and political milieu to grasp its importance in shaping and also defending a movement that challenges the conventional conceptualization of transformation of grassroots socio-political discontent into effective ideological onslaughts. This is largely the outcome of a deepening of democracy over the years in which 'the bulk of ... the population acquires binding, protected, relatively equal claims on a government's agents, activities and resources'.[52] As is shown above, the importance of *vox populi* is not merely felt during the elections; the involvement of various strata of people in the regular political processes through innumerable (formal and informal) instruments of empowerment at the grassroots ensures that the voice of the people continues to remain critical beyond elections.

Finally, with India being integrated to global capital following the acceptance of neo-liberal economic reforms in 1991, new contradictions have emerged that need new responses. The scene has become far more complicated with the arrival of new players in the economic arena with no emotional obligation to the indigenous population at all. With the state supporting the private operators and their local representatives for specific political gains, these investors find no shackles to the fulfilment of their partisan goal of making profit at any cost, except perhaps the organized mass confrontations, including those at the Maoist behest in India's tribal lands. The mass protests provoked by well-planned efforts by global capital to radically alter the prevalent socio-economic and political texture of the polity are also symptomatic of the processes of the deepening of democracy in areas which have traditionally remained outside the organized world of parliamentary and extra-parliamentary politics. Thus it is not strange to see the growing importance of gender, ethnicity or region as critical constituencies in contemporary politics. Debates, discussions, deliberations and tolerance, the constituents of the culture of democracy, which I define as the 'hardwire of democracy', seems to have brought about revolutionary changes not only in social constituencies of protest movements, but also in our conceptualization which has set in motion new debates involving new political actors seeking to articulate their role differently by imbibing the spirit of the era.

Concluding observations

Based on the assumption that texts and contexts are dialectically interlinked, this chapter confirms the argument by drawing on the socio-economic circumstances that shape the Indian variety of left radicalism. What is most interesting to observe is the fact that both versions of left radicalism seem to be critical in contemporary India for contextual reasons: by changing ideological priorities, the parliamentary left survives and even thrives on occasions in a social-democratic environment proving perhaps the viability of non-liberal ideological preferences in India; similarly, the Maoists, clinging to the violent revolutionary path, reigned supreme in what is euphemistically designated 'the red corridor', by emotionally involving the people in a movement for genuine socio-economic changes for the poor and disempowered. In other words, India is perhaps a unique case illustrating the prevalence of two types of left radicalism with definite organic roots in contemporary India. Seeking to achieve human emancipation, the parliamentary left and its militant counterpart do not seem to substantially differ in ideological terms because of their faith in the role of a centralized political authority for genuine socio-economic changes, though their views hardly coalesce in regard to the methods that they resort to for the fulfilment of an identical ideological goal: while for the parliamentary left, the ballot is more powerful than violence and revolutionary changes can be possible within a liberal democratic form of governance, the left extremists are simply not persuaded by the claim that bourgeois democratic means are adequate for meaningful socio-economic changes for the underprivileged sections. This is a fundamental difference which puts these two varieties of left radicalism in watertight compartments. Nonetheless, given their salience in contemporary Indian politics, they can neither be dismissed nor bypassed if one seeks to make an objective assessment of India's democratic experience since she became politically free from British rule in 1947.

As is evident, in the articulation of left and radical politics in India, the context remains most critical. What is striking is the prevalence of different types of political outfits with different ideological perspectives. There exist liberal, right-wing and also radical political parties seeking to pursue specific ideological lines of thinking which is what makes India an interesting case study. This has set in motion interesting processes of inter-party communication which perhaps encourage the parties to learn from one another. There are instances when even the political parties with clear left leanings join hands with liberal political parties. It was thus not ideologically incongruent for the CPI to support the Congress in order to thwart the fundamentalists. Similarly, the CPI (M) did not find it strange when it extended outside support to the Congress-led UPA in its first tenure. One may attribute this process of coming together to political opportunism or a smart art of political survival and in that sense, it is also politically expedient. Nonetheless, this is also reflective of circumstances in which ideology is sought to be redefined to accommodate political desires regardless of ideology. The context and the nature of politics are thus dialectically linked and in that respect, one simply cannot gloss over the importance of socio-economic and political environment in the shaping of the left and radical politics in contemporary India.

A perusal of India's recent political history confirms that there have been radical socio-economic transformations in India especially following intensive processes of deepening of democracy. Especially since the late 1980s, changes are visible in the popular response to the issues of governance. Instead of being mere recipients, citizens have become instigators of change in an era of heightened mass awareness. Political parties have reinvented themselves to remain viable in the changed environment. It is therefore not surprising to find that the left radicals, like their liberal counterparts, focus more on local issues rather than idolizing those ideological issues (of a general nature) which are not contextually relevant. In the Indian context, democratization is translated into greater involvement of people not as 'individuals', which is a staple of liberal discourse, but as communities or groups. Individuals are in the public sphere not as atomized individuals but as members of 'primordial' communities, drawn on religious, caste or *jati* identity. The processes of steady democratization have contributed to the articulation of a political voice, hitherto unheard, which is reflective of radical changes in the texture of the political. The expanding circle of democratic participation since independence has thus transformed 'the character of politics as previously subordinate groups have gained a voice'.[53] By helping to articulate the political voice of the marginalized, democracy in India has led to a loosening of social strictures and empowered the peripherals to be confident of their ability to improve their socio-economic conditions. This is a significant political process that has led to what Christophe Jaffrelot describes as 'a silent revolution' through a meaningful transfer of power from the upper caste elites to various subaltern groups within the democratic framework of public governance.[54] Here too, the context underlining the process of social churning at the grassroots provides cues to understanding the popular proclivity towards left-radical ideological belief which becomes transformational by being accommodative of the genuine socio-economic needs of those who, so far, have remained peripheral in India's state-directed development strategies.

Notes

1 For details, see Ashutosh Varshney, 'India's democratic challenge', *Foreign Affairs*, vol. 86, no. 2, March/April 2007, pp. 93–106.
2 Aseema Sinha, 'The changing political economy of federalism in India: a historical institutional approach', *India Review*, vol 3, no. 1, January, 2004, p. 55.
3 Articles 38 and 39 of the Constitution of India spell out the sentiments. Article 46 underlines the concern for the weaker sections, including scheduled castes and scheduled tribes.
4 Benjamin Zachariah, *Developing India: an intellectual and social history*, Oxford University Press, New Delhi, 2005, p. 235. Zachariah, while making this argument, draws on Stephen Howe's *Anti-colonialism in British Politics: the left and the end of empire, 1918–1954* (Clarendon Press, Oxford, 1993). According to Howe, many of the strands of anti-colonial policies in Britain originated in romantic identification with downtrodden peoples rather than in critiques of imperialism and capitalism.

5 Suresh D. Tendulkar and T.A. Bhavani, *Understanding Reforms: post 1991 India*, Oxford University Press, Delhi, 2007, pp. 18–19.
6 Gunnar Myrdal, *Asian Drama: an inquiry into the poverty of nations*, vol. 2, Pantheon, New York, 1968, pp. 709–10.
7 Francine R. Frankel, *India's Political Economy, 1947–2004*, Oxford University Press, 2005, p. 85.
8 Tendulkar and Bhavani, *Understanding reforms*, p. 24.
9 Partha Chatterjee, 'Development planning and the Indian state', in Partha Chatterjee (ed.), *State and Politics in India*, Oxford University Press, Delhi, 1997, pp. 271, 279.
10 Aseema Sinha, *The Regional Roots of Developmental Politics in India: a divided leviathan*, Indiana University Press, Bloomington and Indianapolis, 2005, p. 277.
11 *Hindustan Standard*, 27 September 1934.
12 I have dwelt on this aspect of the freedom struggle in my 'Jawaharlal Nehru and planning, 1938–41: India at the crossroads', *Modern Asian Studies*, vol. 26, no. 2, 1992, pp. 275–87.
13 Jawaharlal Nehru on planning (a press release), *Hindustan Times*, 17 August 1963.
14 Myrdal, *Asian Drama*, p. 739.
15 Myrdal, *Asian Drama*, p. 739.
16 Sukhamoy Chakravarty, *Development Planning: the Indian experience*, Clarendon Press, Oxford, 1987, p. 89.
17 Chakravarty, *Development Planning*, pp. 39–40.
18 According to Sukhamoy Chakravarty, India's development prospects

> cannot be ensured merely by technocratically inclined civil servants. While technocrats can obviously suggest more efficient means for pre-designed goals, the problem of goal-setting is inherently a socio-historical process. Societies which have grown fast during the recent period have done so not because the sum total of problem solving effort has been vastly greater in any measurable sense, but because they could succeed in evolving a broad consensus on priorities.
>
> Chakravarty, *Development Planning*, p. 89

19 Meghnad Desai, Development and Nationhood: essays in the political economy of South Asia, Oxford University Press, New Delhi, 2005, p. 121.
20 Desai, *Development and Nationhood*, p. 139.
21 Desai, *Development and Nationhood*, p. 137.
22 Desai, *Development and Nationhood*, p. 157.
23 Jagdish N. Bhagwati, 'Indian economic policy and performance: a framework for a progressive society', in his *Essays in Development Economics*, MIT Press, Cambridge, MA, 1985 quoted in Ramchandra Guha, *India after Gandhi: the history of the world's largest democracy*, Picador, London, p. 469.
24 Desai, *Development and Nationhood*, p. 158.
25 Atul Kohli, *State-directed Development: global power and industrialization in the global periphery*, Cambridge University Press, Cambridge, 2005, p. 258.
26 Pranab Bardhan provides a graphic illustration of the performance of the public sector in the first three decades of India's independence in his *The Political Economy of Development*, Oxford University Press, New Delhi, 2008 (reprint), pp. 63–4.
27 Kohli, *State-Directed Development*, p. 279.
28 Desai, *Development and Nationhood*, p. 161.
29 Desai, *Development and Nationhood*, p. 175.
30 Desai, *Development and Nationhood*, p. 189.
31 Desai, *Development and Nationhood*, p. 196.
32 Bardhan, *The Political Economy of Development*, p. 136.
33 Bardhan, *The Political Economy of Development*, p. 136.
34 Bardhan, *The Political Economy of Development*, p. 137.
35 Rob Jenkins, *Democratic Politics and Economic Reform in India*, Cambridge Univer-

sity Press, Cambridge, 1999, pp. 172–207. Since economic reforms were not strategy-based but crisis-driven, India hardly had a choice and was thus more or less forced to accept the conditionalities imposed by the donor agencies.
36 Tendulkar and Bhavani, *Understanding Reforms*, p. 85.
37 Sinha, 'The changing political economy', p. 51.
38 Sinha, 'The changing political economy', p. 55.
39 Frankel, *India's Political Economy*, p. 625.
40 Frankel, *India's Political Economy*, p. 625.
41 Mihir Shah, 'Governance reform key to NREGA (National Rural Employment Guarantee Act) success', *The Hindu*, 14 March 2008.
42 *Hindustan Times*, 21 April 1992.
43 Joseph Stiglitz, *Making Globalization Work: the next steps to global justice*, Allen Lane, London, 2006, p. 292. This argument was forcefully made by Margit Bussmann in her 'When globalization discontent turns violent: foreign economic liberalization and internal war', *International Studies Quarterly*, vol. 51, no. 1, March 2007, pp. 79–97.
44 Amit Bhaduri and Deepak Nayyar, *The Intelligent Person's Guide to Liberalization*, Penguin, New Delhi, 1996, p. 159.
45 Statement of the Communist Party of India (Maoist), Central Committee, 16 March 2007 (obtained from a Maoist activist in Orissa).
46 Gautam Navlakha, *Days and Nights in the Heartland of Rebellion*, Penguin, New Delhi, 2012, p. 78.
47 Navlakha, *Days and Nights in the Heartland of Rebellion*, p. 202.
48 Based on my personal study of a self-help group in the district of Raebareilly and Amethi in Uttar Pradesh in October–November 2012 and March 2013. I am thankful to my colleagues, Sampth and Surender who contributed immensely to the entire study.
49 These are all major government of India flagship programmes, aimed at providing employment, housing, healthcare and education to the marginalized sections of rural India.
50 Personal interaction with Nirmala Devi, an active member of the self-help group in Seshpur in Raebareilly.
51 Georege J. Kunnath, 'Smouldering Dalit fires in Bihar, India', *Dialectical Anthropology*, vol. 33, 2009, p. 321.
52 Charles Tilly, 'Processes and mechanisms of democratization', *Sociological Theory*, vol. 18, March 2000, p. 8.
53 Katharine Adeney and Andrew Wyatt, 'Democracy in South Asia: getting beyond the structure–agency dichotomy', *Political Studies*, vol. 52, no. 1, 2004, p. 1.
54 Christophe Jaffrelot, *India's Silent Revolution: the rise of the low castes in north Indian politics*, Permanent Black, New Delhi, 2003.

2 Constituents of left radicalism in India

Left radicalism in India is both derivative and indigenous. Inspired by Marxism, Leninism and Maoism, left radicals in India built an alternative ideological tradition which complemented the mass struggle for democracy and human dignity. Interestingly, the tradition was not exactly imitative of the efforts elsewhere, presumably because it had distinct contextual flavours. Despite being derivative, left radicalism was thus indigenous too. As political forces championing radicalism, the left radicals thus seem to have redefined the derivative ideological perspectives creatively to understand the reality in which they had clear organic roots. It has thus been argued that, in striking contrast to the liberal-nationalist discourse, left radicalism in India did not grow organically in the country's own political and spiritual climate. It emerged in India when 'a section of radical nationalists, utterly dissatisfied with the leadership of Gandhi, started groping for a more militant ideology and found in the Marxist-Leninist revolutionary doctrine an answer to Gandhism'.[1] This confirms two important theoretical points: on the one hand, the argument for indigenous roots of left radicalism upholds 'the universalist-humanistic nature' of Marxism, Leninism and Maoism when it comes to political mobilization for genuine human emancipation; that they are not static and can thus be adapted to the specific contexts also highlights, on the other, their universal applicability in battling against exploitation of human beings by human beings. In another significant way, the dialectics between the text and context help develop new conceptual categories in grasping the specific socio-economic milieu in which people rise to revolt. The growing importance of 'new democracy' as a conceptual tool in understanding the socio-political processes at the grassroots in India is illustrative here. By developing an effective multi-class political platform, the parliamentary left not only remains well entrenched in West Bengal, Kerala and Tripura, but also became a powerful political force in national politics in the context of coalition politics when neither of the pan-Indian political parties, the Congress and Bharatiya Janata Party (BJP), was capable of forming a majority in the Parliament without the numerical support of the parliamentarians belonging to the left. In a similar vein, the Maoist endeavour to consolidate the social base by drawing on the indigenous tribal traditions in the areas in which left-wing extremism has flourished reflects the attempts at indigenizing the Marxist, Leninist and Maoist traditions which do not have, for obvious reasons, organic roots in India. For the impoverished, Maoism is a powerful voice to pursue an ideological mission for creating an exploitation-free society, a society which is alien to the artificial barriers between human beings. To a Maoist activist, the complex theoretical nuances of Maoism may not have a bearing; but what is most appealing is its success in initiating a campaign against the age-old and also customized forms of social, economic and political exploitation which go unabated for obvious class prejudices of those holding authority across the length and breadth of the country. Hence Maoism is not alien to the exploited, but an enabling ideological device in the midst of hopelessness.

As is evident, both the parliamentary left in India and Maoists have evolved definite ideological roots by being involved in those people-centric activities which none of the well-established political outfits seem to have paid adequate attention to while setting an agenda, because of obvious class constraints. Where the parliamentary left fails, the Maoists appear to have gained. In that sense, these are ideologically refreshing endeavours in the context of the state-led development that India favoured immediately after independence in 1947 and later in the era of neo-liberal economic reforms following ascendancy of the liberalized-privatized-globalized (LPG) regime in India. The aim of this chapter is to provide a brief biographical sketch of political outfits that constitute the parliamentary left and left-wing extremists respectively. This is an informative exercise since these labels are used rather loosely in day-to-day conversations and also academic literature. Due to space constraints, the chapter concentrates only on those constituents which are relatively well known for their sustained political activities among the people at the grassroots. There are innumerable organizations which neither have joined any of the formally recognized political outfits nor have institutionalized existence in India's political map though they are meaningfully engaged in pro-people activities in both rural and urban India. Their activities are visible, but their existence may not always be noticed, presumably because they are not institutionalized as political outfits. Nonetheless, this chapter, by focusing on the institutionalized constituents of left radicals in India, helps us understand the nature and ideological contours of those seeking to constitute an alternative ideological discourse in India. Divided into two parts, this delves first into the constituents of the parliamentary left and later those of the left-wing extremist variety.

Constituents of the parliamentary left

The parliamentary left is distinct because of its ideological commitment to parliamentary democracy and other attendant social, economic and political values. For those supportive of this path of political change, election is a cornerstone of democracy and also people's meaningful involvement not only in the formation of the government but also in its regular functioning. There are many parties which cling to the parliamentary path; here, we will focus on those that are critical to the formation and sustaining of the parliamentary left in India.

Prominent among them are Communist Party of India, Communist Party of India (Marxist), Revolutionary Socialist Party, Socialist Unity Centre of India and Forward Bloc.

Communist Party of India (CPI)

The Communist Party of India was formed in 1920 at Tashkent in the former USSR by a couple of revolutionary émigrés from India, M.N. Roy and Abani Mukerjee. Why did the Communist Party of India begin its journey aboard? To answer this question we have to recapitulate the history of leftism in India. Leftism in India 'emerged out of the matrix of the Indian national movement'.[2] The left-wing faction within the Indian National Congress (later grouped under the banner of Congress Socialist Party (CSP)), that was very keen to bring about radical socio-economic changes along with national liberation, found the Gandhian method of non-violence grossly inadequate. On the contrary, the newly acquainted philosophy of revolutionary socialism of Marx and Lenin appeared to them quite promising.

Apprehensive of the increasing radicalization of demands from the CSP, the colonial administration had adopted a series of pre-emptive measures. The national revolutionaries and congress socialists had to bear the brunt. The Alipore bombing incident had provided the colonial administration with a solid pretext for launching an all-out attack against the revolutionaries. In the face of the colonial crackdown, a sizeable section of bright young men with revolutionary zeal fled the country in quest of money and arms for liberating their homeland. Notable among them were Har Dayal, Virendranath Chattopadhyaya, Barkatullah, Abani Mukherjee, Surendranath Kar, Bhupendranath Dutta and many others. Among those expatriates Abani Mukherjee and M.N. Roy took the initiative to lay the foundation stone of a communist party for India. However, in India there was no such support base for a communist party. M.N. Roy took an active interest in cultivating communism on Indian soil. As well as publishing a fortnightly magazine called the *Vanguard of Indian Independence*, he kept close contact with his Indian counterparts. Back home, there was a typical rise of communist consciousness in the form of a proliferation of communist groups and socialist magazines and journals. However, the colonial oppression continued in tandem. Anxious about a sudden rise of radicalism among the revolutionaries and freedom fighters, the British government had slapped a series of draconian conspiracy cases such as the Peshawar Conspiracy Case (1922–3) and the Kanpur Bolshevik Conspiracy Case (1924) against the budding communist organizations in India. However, these pre-emptive strikes could not quench the ember of radicalization of the anti-imperialist movement. In the meanwhile, M.N. Roy and others in the Communist International had spawned several fragmented groups throughout the country. The leftists across the country had realized the importance of bringing the communists under a single umbrella. Accordingly, the indigenized version of CPI came into being in 1925 at Kanpur. In the meanwhile (between 1926 and 1928), to consolidate their position among their traditional constituency, the Workers and the Peasants Party (WPP) was set up first in Bengal and subsequently in Bombay and United Provinces. As a mass organization, WPP started working along with with the Indian National Congress (INC) which led to the growth of a left-wing faction within INC.[3] However, WPP emerged as a separate organization, with a leadership which had been largely drawn from communists and revolutionaries. The birth of the left-wing faction of the INC could be attributed to the relative recession in the activities of INC following Mahatma Gandhi's withdrawal of non-cooperation movement. The militant and class-based workers' and peasant parties began to mushroom in this relatively serene phase, culminating in a series of strikes and demonstrations and the birth of WPP.[4] Perturbed by rising workers' and peasant activities, the empire struck back with the same legal weapons of clampdown with the infamous Meerut Conspiracy Case (1929). The communist leaders who took WPP as a potential legal cover,[5] were also booked under the conspiracy case with the national revolutionaries. The organization of WPP was disbanded. The trial continued for more than three years, giving the sagging organization of communism a real morale boost up in terms of publicity.[6] In the meanwhile, a directive from the Comminist International, especially its strategy vis-à-vis the national bourgeoisie, taken at the Sixth Congress in 1928 had further confused the Indian communists. Unlike, its earlier stand of abstaining from nationalist movements for independence, the decision was taken that communists and the working class would participate in the nationalist movement. It was directed that CPI should directly take the lead in the national movement in India. The Congress further directed to expose bourgeois nationalist organizations including the INC. As a result of this directive, CPI was pitted directly against INC. Historically speaking, this dissociation from INC and the movement it spearheaded proved very costly for CPI as it had been increasingly detached from the mass movement. During this phase, when INC under the leadership of Mahatma Gandhi launched another county-wide mass mobilization, CPI was gradually reduced to a non-performing party until it was declared illegal in 1934.

The period spanning from 1947 to 1951 had witnessed as many as four different stands[7] by the CPI. The differences officially surfaced for the first time during the second congress of the party at Calcutta, revealing a crack in the supposedly monolithic structure of CPI.[8] A brief discussion of these blocks would help one navigate the communist movement in India.

The first stand was more or less moderate. It hailed the independence from imperialistic subjugation and extended full support to the popular government. This position held the post-independent regime as progressive, though not totally free from the influence of imperialism and feudalism.

The second position was a total reversal of its earlier position. Instead of viewing independence as progressive one, this position, inspired by the Soviet and Chinese categorization, viewed Indian independence as a 'sham' and the Indian state as a 'supplicant before imperialism'. This particular section did not confine itself to castigating Indian independence alone. In fact, it went to the extreme extent of proposing armed seizure of state apparatuses all over India accompanied by mass uprising, popularly known as the 'Ranadive line'.[9] The party in its second congress held at Calcutta in 1948 had endorsed the above stand. The resolution of that congress read:

> though the bourgeois leadership parade the story that independence has been won, the fact is that the freedom struggle has been betrayed and the national leadership has struck a treacherous deal behind the back of the starving people, betraying every slogan of the democratic revolution.[10]

The radical stand adopted in the congress can be attributed to the West Bengal unit of CPI. It was due to the stiff opposition from the state unit of the party against the all-Indian party line of mending fences with the progressive elements of INC, that the party took a radical stand in the Calcutta Congress (1948). In fact, the socio-economic condition in West Bengal in the wake of partition was ripe for revolutionary change.[11] The element of truth notwithstanding, the very timing and the tone of the vitriolic observation of the party regarding the nature of independence and its subsequent activities like violent demonstrations and damage to public property in search of an alternative freedom, were proved to be counter-productive for the party. For such a stand, on the one hand, provoked huge government offensive in the form of massive crackdowns on party functionaries; and on the other hand created a negative repercussion about the party among the animated citizens eagerly waiting for independence. Consequently, the party was decimated organizationally. Hence, the stand proved to be counter-productive and defeating for the party. The failure of this strategy necessitated a change of guard in CPI as the moderates like P.C. Joshi, Ajoy Ghosh and S.A. Dange took over the leadership from B.T. Ranadive.

The third stand, unlike the Soviet-directed line and the Ranadive line, wanted to draw an Indian version of communism. Originating in the local unit of the party in Teleangana region of the Nizam-ruled Hyderabad, the position, popularly known as 'Andhra thesis', held that 'feudalism is the principal contradiction in India. It is the social base of imperialism. The so-called independent regime in India is comprador in character, i.e. it is in the service of both imperialism and feudalism.'[12] It further held that the peasantry was the crucial vehicle of Indian revolution, which would be agrarian in nature. However, this strategy of revolution was not an armed uprising, but 'protracted armed struggle, employing guerrilla methods of combat and establishing base areas leading to liberated areas'.[13] Initially following the above thesis, the party managed to set its foothold in the Nizam's state of Hyderabad and even took on Indian army, that was stationed to police the area. However, this stand had only few takers as the dominant faction of the party was preoccupied with the parliamentary form of governance and constitutional mobilization.

The fourth stand, based on the Programme and Policy Statement of 1951, marked a total departure from the dominant views and paved the way for parliamentary communism in India. The Policy Statement stressed the anti-imperialist and the anti-feudal character of the Indian national movement and wanted the

Communist Party to take part in the democratic revolution leading to the realization of people's democracy and rights. The statement carried a specified roadmap to be pursued. Though notionally it did not repudiate the necessity of revolutionary violence, for tactical reason it never spelt out its detail. On the contrary, strategically it reposed its confidence on the Nehru government and called for a 'broad democratic front' on a 'simple democratic programme'.

Dawn of parliamentary communism

The 1950s dawned a new phase of the communist movement in India as the party finally decided to go to the polls and came out with flying colours. The party fared as the third largest party in the election. Full trade union rights, security of employment and living wages for the workers were the demands on which the party fought the election. However, the ideological ambivalence refused to die down even after its turn to parliamentary communism. Even a section of elected representatives were clueless about their supposed roles in the legislature. Some representatives claimed that they would transform the legislature into a veritable battleground, while others preferred 'wrecking them from within'.[14]

Ideological debates

CPI had been wrestling with a fierce polemical debate within itself over a number of issues, which include among others the role of Congress Party, the role of Nehru, the foreign policy of the government of India, future economic planning, and expanding the public sector. While one section of CPI of West Bengal unit, led by Bhawani Sen, Biswanath Mukherjee and Somnath Lahiri, advocated the need for close cooperation with the INC for a broad-based anti-imperialist united front, another section headed by Promode Das Gupta, Jyoti Basu, Hare Krishna Konar and Binoy Choudhry vociferously objected to the other's opinion as a brazen surrender to Congress.[15] The section headed by Bhawani Sen and Somnath Lahiri, among others, championed the path of peaceful transition through parliamentary means. In fact, a series of events in the national and international arena, like Khrushchev's report on Stalin in the 20th congress of the Communist Party of the Soviet Union, uprisings in Poland and Hungary, Rubenstein's thesis on the non-capitalist path of development, and the expansion of the public sector in the second five-year plan had convinced them that the parliamentary mechanism was the only way to bring socialism. The opponents were sceptical about INC–CPI cooperation and asked for independent initiatives by the Communist Party. The debate reached its climax during the Sino-Indian border dispute in 1962 concerning Chinese aggression on Indian territory. The event had not only rattled CPI but also exposed the party to a sort of factional feud. In November 1962, the faction led by Bhawani Sen prevailed over other factions as the CPI, in its National Council Resolution, had lent its support to the Nehru government by condemning Chinese aggression towards

India. However, the majority of the West Bengal unit of CPI opposed the stand taken by the central committee. The dissident stand by the West Bengal faction was promptly interpreted as anti-national and a sizeable section of the front-ranking leaders were arrested by the police under the Defence of India Rules, leading to the dissolution of the state council. A new ad hoc Provincial Organizing Committee (POC) was entrusted to look after the functions of the state committee. The left faction of the party in West Bengal refused to succumb to state repression and started organizing from within and outside jail. They revolted against the national leadership in general and S.A. Dange in particular. The National Council meeting of the party in 1963 had witnessed a serious tiff within the party as the left faction demanded a probe into Dange's activities following the Meerut Conspiracy Trial. The right-wing faction of the party, however, summarily rejected the demand, causing as many as thirty-two members to walk out. Notable among them were Muzaffar Ahmed, Promode Dasgupta, Samar Mukherjee, Joyti Basu and Hare Krishna Konar. On being suspended, those leaders assembled at a convention at Tenali in July 1964 and decided on the formation of a new party. CPI had convened a party congress in October 1964 to formalize the separation. Accordingly, a new Communist Party came into being, subsequently known as Communist Party of India (Marxist) (hereafter CPI (M)). The spilt not only left CPI emaciated organizationally but also led to a collapse in the social bases of the party. Only the organized sector like trade unions and a large number of intellectuals associated with the undivided CPI, popularly known as 'fellow travellers', stayed with the party, while the organizations of poor peasantry and agricultural labourers sided with CPI (M).[16] Hence, the split provides us with a clue to the puzzle identified at the beginning as to why no single left party claims absolute command over the entire state or why left parties constituting the Left Front individually hold up in different pockets of West Bengal. The formal split did not reduce the enmity between the two communist parties. In fact, both the parties had floated their alliance with the like-minded splinter parties. The communist movement in the post-split phase had been marked by bitter ideological conflict and organizational rivalry between the two quarrelsome parties; with occasional coming together, honouring the popular mood of discontent and protest. Depending upon the ground-level reality, these two estranged kins kept changing their strategies as and when they required.

Coming to power

In 1967 CPI formed a first non-Congress government in West Bengal with the help of CPI (M) led United Left Front and a few non-Congress and independent members of the legislative assembly. However, the United Front government did not last long. Within only three months of its coming into existence, it succumbed to fierce infighting within the party. Soon after the United Front government came to power, factional feuds resurfaced following peasant uprising in the Naxalbari region in the Darjeeling district of West Bengal. Led by the local unit

Constituents of left radicalism 55

of CPI (M), the Naxalbari peasant movement[17] took some radical stands like seizing of lands and crops and subjecting landlords to a peasant trial court in complete disrespect to the rule of law and the constitutional edifice of the country. The United Front government tried to control the peasant uprising by political intervention. But when the attempt to negotiate failed, the government resorted to police action. CPI (M) was quick to condemn the police action and a large section of Naxalbari sympathisers deserted the United Front government, leading to its collapse in November 1967. The renegades, who were sensitive towards the Naxalbari movement, had constituted a coordination committee among the communist revolutionaries. Soon it took an all-India dimension and an All-India Committee of Communist Revolutionaries (AICCCR) came into existence. In West Bengal, Charu Mazumdar, who led the West Bengal AICCCR, had not only lent his support to Naxalbari movement but also advocated annihilation of class enemies and an armed struggle in India. The Naxalbari movement was not confined to three contiguous areas i.e. Naxalbari, Kharibari and Fansidewa of Darjeeling district in North Bengal. This movement coincided with similar armed struggles in two backward tribal pockets – Debra and Gopiballavpur of Midnapur district during 1969–70.[18] The increasing radicalization of left politics coincided with a call for a revolutionary party, which materialized in 1969 with the formation of Communist Party of India (Marxist-Leninist) (CPI (ML)). In the meantime, an interim government headed by P.C. Ghosh was formed but could not survive, leading to the imposition of president's rule. A mid-term election was held in 1969. The United Front government once again came into power with CPI (M) clinching a majority of popular votes. But the second United Front government also succumbed due to the protracted rivalry between the two major communist parties in 1970. The signing of the Indo-Soviet treaty of peace and mutual cooperation, nationalization of fourteen big commercial banks and liberation of Bangladesh had further convinced CPI of the positive intention of Congress. Carried away by the progressive gestures of INC, especially after the major break up of INC in 1969,[19] CPI along with Bangla Congress rallied behind the Congress government to forge an anti-CPI (M) coalition in the state. Accordingly, the Congress swept the poll in 1971. Backed up by the unprecedented electoral success and the apparent discord among the left, the Congress in West Bengal unleashed a veritable 'reign of terror' from 1972 to 1977, under the garb of president's rule, to liquidate CPI (M), CPI (ML) and all the radical variants of the left, though CPI continued to enjoy the confidence of Congress. In the post-Emergency dispensation, CPI was reduced to a mere pressure group, much to the advantage of CPI (M). Consolidation of CPI (M) in the Left Front government began in 1977 and further marginalized CPI in West Bengal politics.

The party from its very beginning shook off the dilemma of its Congress counterpart (the left-wing faction of the Indian National Congress) and launched a frontal attack on both imperialist and national bourgeoisie. The party had spoken out against the class character of Indian National Congress in unambiguous terms for its apparent hobnobbing with bourgeoisie and landlords.

However, such distancing from the Indian National Congress was short-lived as both the national and international circumstances compelled CPI to come in alliance with INC. In a complete volte-face, CPI attempted to mend the fence with INC on the pretext that Congress represented the 'national centre of opposition against imperialism' and joined INC. Soon they started mobilizing factory labourers, sharecroppers, students and youths by remaining within the organizational structure of INC. Moreover, the communists managed to get elected to executive posts in several Congress committees. Hence, the history of the left in India is marked by continuous fragmentations and unifications. The party was not content with full-fledged independence. It urged the abolition of landlordism, full democratic rights for the people, complete transfer of power, and trade union rights for workers. However, the party has never been in a position to decide upon the future course of action. Instead of expediting the revolutionary potential of the peasantry, the Indian left (then the undivided CPI) found themselves more comfortable in the cosy ambience of the classic texts of Marx, Engels, Lenin, Stalin or Mao. They relied mostly on the pronouncements of the Comintern, or the Communist Parties of the Soviet Union and China to make sense of the reality on the ground at home. Such a dependency syndrome among the CPI leadership stymied the initiatives of the Indian left to devise an indigenous theory of revolution.[20] The succumbing of the party to Soviet or Chinese positions was not appreciated by all within the party. For example, Satya Bhakta, a journalist and leader of the Kanpur-based Communist Party who convened the Kanpur communist conference, had strongly argued in favour of a national communism as early as 1925. However, he could not succeed in putting across his ideas due to stiff opposition. Satya Bhakta was not alone in being disowned by the leftists. In fact, the same opinion, though in a different garb, expressed by no less a person than V.I. Lenin, had been blissfully ignored by the Indian socialists on the eve of the formation of the Communist Party of India in 1920. The Indian socialists did not appear to have paid attention to India's unique socioeconomic circumstances while seeking to evolve a distinct ideological path for political mobilization. This was conclusively addressed later, though, at the outset, it was an obvious source of organizational weakness that hardly received adequate attention from them.

Communist Party of India (Marxist) CPI (M)

Born out of a split in CPI in 1964, the CPI (M) has charted a new course for Indian communism. With a view to bringing about a proletarian revolution, a highly regimented, disciplined cadre-based political party was launched. Keeping equidistance from both Moscow and Peking, CPI (M) has ushered in a new tactical line of consolidation and expansion, popularly known as 'govern-and-mobilize'.[21] Drawing on its own assessment of the ground-level realities in India, especially its political culture, CPI (M) has experimented with 'controlled peasant militancy' while keeping the parliamentary option open.

Militant left mobilization

Despite commonalities in worldviews, organizational structures and membership pattern with CPI, CPI (M) managed to put its distinctive features on Indian politics. The party was carved out of CPI with a majority of subaltern constituencies who had been the major source of sustenance for CPI in pre- as well as post-independence phases. The party, ever since it came into being in 1964, had to bear the brunt of factional rivalry and state wrath from time to time. The reasons behind it were hidden in the very aspiration of the party. From the very beginning, in a bid to stake its claim as a 'genuine' Communist Party of India with ideological purity, the party started dissociating itself from CPI and engaged in a series of mobilizational politics, including mobilization of rural peasantry against exploiting landlords. Understandably, such initiatives sent a panic wave among the landed gentry in the rural areas, which in effect put enormous pressure on the Congress governments, both in the centre and in the states. For these landlords held the key to the success of Congress in the countryside. They 'by means of manifold linkages forged by distribution of patronage'[22] had maintained an equilibrium in the countryside and provided a constant support base for the Congress. Hence, Congress was very sceptical about the party since its inception, which got further intensified by its pejorative characterization of Congress. Moreover, from the contextual point of view, the 1960s provided a fertile ground for radical politics against the Congress government in West Bengal. The continuous stream of refugees who had emigrated to the state since Partition had thrown the state out of gear. Inadequate rehabilitation measures, abject poverty and an alarming rate of unemployment, in addition to the discriminatory attitude of the central government towards the cash-strapped state, gave rise to simmering discontent against the Congress rule. The CPI (M) leadership, unlike CPI, seized the opportunity to mobilize the people along with other non-Congress left parties.[23]

Though for tactical reasons CPI (M) joined hands with CPI from time to time, it kept its ideological standpoint pretty clear and separate from the beginning. In 1967, CPI (M) came to power with a host of other local parties. The year 1967 marked a watershed in the history of post-independent India. From the beginning CPI (M) started mobilizing peasants, workers, and tribals against the bourgeois state. The distance between CPI (M) and CPI began to widen on several issues like determining the nature of the Indian state and of the national bourgeoisie, and the relationship with nationalist bourgeois political parties like Indian National Congress, which turned into open hostility on the question of extra-constitutional movements especially the movement spearheaded by the local CPI (M) leadership in the Naxalbari area in North Bengal. CPI, after renouncing the (in)famous Ranadive line and the consequent change of guard,[24] was too keen to distance itself from the radical left movement at Naxalbari, so much so that when, as a part of first United Front government, CPI (M) extended its moral support to the comrades combating feudalism at Naxalbari, CPI was rather lukewarm to the movement and arguably offered tacit support to police action.

58 Setting the scene

But as the peasant militancy turned violent and escalated beyond control, CPI (M) leadership started pacifying the agitating peasantry by administrative and political measures.

Birth of CPI (ML)

Immediately after the 1964 split, the left had another jolt when the militant section of the CPI (M) broke away to form the CPI (Marxist-Leninist). Consequently, dissidents upholding the Naxalbari path formed a new revolutionary party known as CPI (ML). The Congress government at the centre took the opportunity to play the Naxalbari insurrection as the handiwork of CPI (M) and made ground for future state intervention. In fact, the collapse of the second United Front government in 1969 can also be attributed to mutual squabbling between CPI (M) and CPI. CPI's increasing proximity to Congress was the bone of contention. CPI was under the impression that Congress would bring a genuine democratic front. Several progressive gestures by INC like a socialistic pattern of society, bank nationalization and introducing subsidies had further fortified CPI's conviction. Accordingly, along with Bangla Congress, it rallied behind the Congress government to forge an anti-CPI (M) coalition in the state. Consequently, Congress swept the poll in 1971. Inspired by the exceptional electoral success and the apparent dissonance among the left, the Congress in West Bengal under the leadership of Siddhartha Sankar Ray formed the government. Ray was most ruthless during the five-year period (1972–7) when the Congress ruled the state in containing those belonging to CPI (M), CPI (ML) and other ideologically radical groups. CPI (M) was virtually immobilized during this phase. The Emergency had unfolded a couple of alternatives to CPI (M). On the one hand, there was an option of keeping the agitation going; under this option the risk of state oppression could not be entirely ruled out. On the other, there was an option of going into strategic hibernation, and waiting for the opportune moment to strike back. The party leadership, however, adopted a middle course. Once the Emergency was lifted in 1977, CPI (M), along with several splinter groups went to the polls under the loosely formulated coalition popularly known as Left Front and emerged as the single largest communist party in India in the election.[25] Even in power, CPI (M) could not forget those dark days of state repression and gagging of public opinion. Hence the party adopted a tactical line of 'govern and mobilize' and strengthened the mobilization of poorer sections of society in almost all walks of life, which the party had launched at the time of its birth.

Mobilizational politics

Inheriting a solid support base among the peasants and marginalized people, CPI (M), unlike CPI that had been busy primarily with the organized sector, started mobilizing poor peasantry in the countryside from its very inception. Creating a strong support base among the poor and middle-class section as a credible deterrent against state excesses and a potential step towards establishing proletarian counter-hegemony, CPI (M) began to penetrate the villages as early as 1967. This strategy was endorsed by none other than Hare Krishna Konar, who had been largely credited with CPI (M)'s 'substantial penetration of the West Bengal countryside'.[26] In an interview Konar claimed:

> we have found the way in West Bengal to build a militant peasant movement; we know how this is to be done, and we also know that this is the only way the Indian revolution can win. Our task now is to further strengthen the movement in Bengal and to carry it forward to the other states, especially Orissa, Bihar and Uttar Pradesh.[27]

Considering the ground-level reality, soon the CPI (M) leadership in West Bengal devised a revolutionary tactic using parliamentary means. Hence, they shrewdly applied both legal and extra-legal measures to obtain their goal. For there was no 'inherent incompatibility between the communists participating in government on one hand and their task of political-ideological mobilization of the masses along class lines on the other'.[28] The peasant mobilization under the Left Front government had two intermeshing stages: one at the governmental level, being implemented by several government departments; and the second at the party level, being led by the peasant front of CPI (M), which tried to politically socialize the peasantry so that they could grab their legitimate rights, dislodging the recalcitrant rural rich. This mobilizational politics went quite smoothly as there was no perceived threat from the intervening centre as it was in 1960s. However, there was a marked difference in mobilizations between the 1960s and the 1970s. The militant posture of the peasant rebellion of the early 1960s had been replaced by a more pragmatic and moderate programme as the party realized that whipping up political frenzy and peasant militancy would be counter-productive in the long run, especially when the party was in power. In fact, the persistence of peasant militancy would further isolate CPI (M)-led West Bengal from the rest of the country and invite unwanted 'coercive wrath of bourgeoisie'.[29] Such realization coincided with a change of guard in the peasant faction of the party. The emotive rumbling of Hare Krishna Konar during the United Front government in the 1960s was more or less tempered in the 1970s under the leadership of Binoy Krishna Choudhry. With a view to stabilizing left rule in West Bengal, the CPI (M)-led Left Front government adopted the two-pronged strategy, as stated earlier, administrative and political. From the administrative point of view, a series of short-term polices were adopted which included among others the procurement and distribution of food grains, food for relief work and land reform. The political mobilization of the Left Front government was done by the Kisan Sabha. The primary objective of the political mobilization, unlike the model of confrontation of the 1960s based on seizure of surplus land, was polarization of the classes. For CPI (M), polarization, which means a division 'into two sharply contrasting groups', can salvage the poor sections from the clutches of exploiting sections. Hence, from the late 1970s peasant mobilization had been confined to the prevention of eviction of peasants from land and ensuring their legitimate share of the harvest. In a carefully phased incremental scale of mass movement, CPI (M), along with its peasant wing, had chalked out detailed phases of a mobilizational plan, starting from small gatherings of peasants in districts to large assemblies in different districts, demonstrations, and finally struggle. In this new garb, peasant mobilization was 'conducted without any overt peasant militancy, and entirely within the framework of legality'.[30]

However, CPI (M)'s mobilization was not confined to the rural peasantry alone; it systematically penetrated the middle-class and lower middle-class section with its weapon of reaching out to the people. Taking over a disturbing legacy of all-pervading doom in society and polity in West Bengal, CPI (M) decided to undo the typical decadent culture by engaging the middle class. But soon, the CPI (M) leadership and the CPI (M)-led Left Front government realized that penetrating the middle-class constituency was even more difficult than they had realized earlier. Like the rural peasantry, the middle-class constituency was anything but homogenous. CPI (M) encountered as many as three middle classes: weak middle class, 'middle' middle class and the affluent middle class. The well-to-do middle class was an enigma, nicely described by Bhabani Sengupta as a 'bundle of paradoxes', impregnable to any new idea, let alone change.[31] Hence, the initial inhibition notwithstanding, CPI (M) leadership engaged willy-nilly in mobilizing the weaker section of the middle classes – the 'middle' middle class and the weaker middle class – by doling out benefits and instilling much-needed confidence among them. As a part of this mobilizational technique the Left Front government targeted the educated unemployed middle class by offering them an unemployment benefit scheme of Rs50 monthly for a period of three years if the claimant's family income was below Rs500 a month. Initially though there was inhibition among the middle class regarding the scheme until there was assurance on the part of the government. Dr Asok Mitra, the then Finance Minister, had reiterated the conviction of the CPI (M)-led government towards the people in the following words:

> the Government of West Bengal is of the view that the millions of young men and women who are currently unemployed are without jobs not because of any fault of their own but because of the deficiencies of social and economic structure which have inhibited growth. As long as that structure is not demolished, the state owes the young men and women an apology, and it is its Constitutional obligation to organize some form of unemployment assistance for them. If the centre does not arrange for such assistance, the state governments cannot simply sit back.[32]

Such assurance on the part of the government no doubt instilled a lot of confidence among the people regarding the party and the government. The mobilizational techniques of CPI (M) involved primarily two parts – the first part sought to dislodge all the decadent relics from the society; and secondly it intended to replace it with some progressive initiatives in all spheres of society.

In order to make a dent in the middle-class constituency CPI (M) also targeted several occupational categories of middle class. Notable among them were school teachers, college and university teachers, and government employees. Teaching, though adored as a noble and highly dignified profession in Bengali society, was not backed up by a dignified salary structure. Consequently, except for only a few committed individuals, most talented people preferred other professions to school teaching. The scenario did not change much after independence. Schooling in West Bengal suffered from both acute lack of funds and dilapidated infrastructure. CPI (M) realized the centrality of this sector in the future development of the country and tried to penetrate the sector by floating a teachers' wing, subsequently known as All Bengal Teachers' Association to look after the issues pertaining to school education and to moot their professional demands. Similarly, CPI (M) also made inroads into the arena of higher education by organizing college and university teachers under the banner of West Bengal College and University Teacher's Association. It was due to the intervention of CPI (M) that several thousand teachers in private colleges started receiving regular salaries as per University Grants Commission norms. Moreover, CPI (M) was instrumental in streamlining the governance of private colleges in West Bengal. This mobilizational strategy ensured the CPI (M)-led Left Front government a constant support base of thousands of trusted and loyal sympathizers.

Similarly, the CPI (M) leadership found that a loyal, ideologically committed and strong army of government employees could become a vehicle for the implementation of socialist plans and a credible deterrent against bureaucratic vagaries. Accordingly, they started wooing government employees. A series of welfare initiatives, until now unheard of, were introduced, which included the announcement of an ex-gratia allowance to low-paid government employees, popularly known as a bonus, other retirement benefits and so on. In a statement justifying the CPI (M)-led government's strategy of establishing a long-standing rapport with their employees, Dr Asok Mitra said:

> A Left regime dose not treat its employees as hired wage-labourer, but as comrades in the struggle for social transformation. The trade union rights of the employees, snatched away during the gruesome years from 1970 to 1977 have been given back to them in full. Many of the administrative inequities – legacies of the past – have been got rid of. A pay commission is looking into the problems of salary structure and conditions of work; an interim set of recommendations has already been given effect to. For the first time anywhere in the country, an ex-gratia payment, a surrogate of the bonus, has been introduced. Trust begets trust; the state government employees are responding magnificently to these gestures; administrative lethargy is bound to decline in consequence.[33]

Implied in the statement was the rationale of CPI (M)'s mobilizational politics. So profound and incisive had been the intervention of CPI (M) in West Bengal

62 Setting the scene

that the society eventually turned out to be a party-society.[34] Largely due to these mobilizational politics, the left especially CPI (M) had won consecutive elections since 1977 until 2011.

Revolutionary Socialist Party (RSP)

The Revolutionary Socialist Party was formed in March 1940 when a group of revolutionaries[35] of the CSP,[36] under the leadership of Jogesh Chandra Chatterjee, decided to quit the party in protest against its opposition to Subhas Chandra Bose. However, the root of the party can be traced back to prominent revolutionary groups Anushilan Samiti[37] and Hindustan Socialist Republican Army. RSP as a non-conformist Marxist-Leninist party evolved by 'way of ideological and political transformation in the middle and late 1930s from the *Anushilan Samiti* as a national revolutionary party and grew up as an independent Marxist-Leninist toiling people's party'.[38] However, the evolution was neither straightforward nor smooth. During the inter-war period profound changes had transpired both in national and international contexts, which had compelled Anushilan Samiti to change the course of its movement. Anushilan Samiti seemed to have been caught in a dilemma about its future course of action, between, on the one hand, the wave of Gandhian mass movement at home that stirred the imagination with visions of freedom; and on the other hand, the various currents and cross-currents of the communist movement. In addition, government repression continued unabated, leading to serious rethinking on the style of working of the party. The promulgation of the Bengal Criminal Law Amendment Ordinance (BCLA) had added further teeth to the governmental repression. Between 1923 and 1927, most of the front-ranking revolutionary leaders were arrested and overt revolutionary activity came to its nadir. State repression notwithstanding, revolutionaries activities continued apace, albeit in a new covert form.

The Indian revolutionaries started secretly regrouping under the banner of United Party of Indian Revolutionaries. But the plan of unification of the revolutionaries failed to take off due to Congress politics in 1930. After the armed uprising at Chittagong in April 1930, most of the lower- and middle-rung leaders were sent to jail. A series of conspiracy cases were lodged against the revolutionaries: the Inter-provincial Conspiracy Case (1933–5), the Hili Station Railway Mail Raid Case (1933), and the Titagarh Conspiracy Case (1935–6). Even those who could not be framed were booked under BCLA Act. Hence, the revolutionary activities remained suspended till 1938. On their release in 1938, the revolutionaries, including Anushilanites, started thinking of taking on the British by launching a new revolutionary party of the toiling masses. But the Anushilanites had no resources to sustain a party. At that time the CSP was the only viable alternative to the Anushilanites. The leaders, including Jogesh Chandra Chatterjee, Keshav Prasad Sharma, and Tridib Kr. Choudhry, in a meeting with Jay Prakash Narayan in 1938, decided to join the CSP. But the expectations proved to be unfounded as the CSP eventually succumbed to Gandhian ideology and its programme. The difference between CSP and Anushilan Samiti had surfaced for the first time at the Tripuri Congress in 1939, where CSP remained a mute spectator on the Pant resolution (which insisted that Bose should form his working committee only on the advice of Mahatma Gandhi – an attempt to establish Gandhi as the undisputed leader of the Congress). The cleavage between the right and the left factions of INC was exposed very nakedly at this congress though the seeds of contention between them were there in 1938. As Subhas Chandra Bose wrote, 'since 1938 the issues on which we Leftists have found ourselves at loggerheads with Gandhites and on which no compromise has been possible are the resumption of the national struggle for Independence and correct war policy of the Indian people'.[39] His primary objective was to raise the demand for 'ultimate formula' (complete freedom from British rule). The CSP leadership did not toe the line of ultimate formula advocated by Subhas Chandra Bose. Not only that, the CSP leadership also tacitly accepted G.B. Pant's resolution which defied the ultimate formula of Subhas Chandra Bose and reposed its total faith in Gandhian leadership. Considering such incidents as humiliating, Subhas Chandra Bose had resigned from Congress and floated a new party Forward Bloc. The Anushilanites, though they sided with Bose on different issues, refused to merge with Forward Bloc as Bose's wartime political slogan 'All power to the Indian people' smacked of anti-imperialist national democratic revolution. Left with no alternative, ultimately Anushilanites formed a party in 1940, known as RSP.

The party took an avowed stand of waging relentless war against British imperialism. It had been critical of both the CSP and the communists for their misconceived venture of bringing about communism in India. The party believed that neither the CSP nor the CPI could reach the goal of the Communist International as both parties were close to Gandhism and the Soviet Communist Party respectively. The party believed in the principles of Marxism-Leninism. However, it was very much against the Soviet reification of communist internationalism and Stalinist aberration. For the RSP, true internationalism lies in developing class struggles in favour of workers in each country. Hence, the Soviet dictated model of the Communist International must be tested on the empirical grounds of reality. The party also found absolutely no contradiction between the Communist International and the nationalist struggle for independence. Hence, the party extended unambiguous support to Subhas Chandra Bose and took an active part in the Quit India Movement in 1942. By 1947, like many other communist parties working in Indian context, RSP also categorized the Indian state as the repository of capitalism and called for a socialist revolution.

Ideological position

On ideological questions the party was rather uncompromising about the establishment of socialism, which could not be possible by religiously following the dictates from the Soviet Union or Beijing, or by the revisionist programmes of CPI, or by sectarian ultra-leftist prescription for all-out war against the state, as popularized by the Ranadive line. The party was against the programme of National Democracy or People's Democracy as it would eventually blunt the edge of class struggle. The party had also no illusions about the communist rhetoric of Nehru and Krishna Menon. It repudiated the popular distinction of the bourgeoisie as progressive and reactionary. The party was of the opinion that the nature of the government could be judged by its attitude towards the working class. Paying mere lip services to the workers or a few radical postures would not make a government progressive.

Perhaps it was the compulsion of parliamentary communism, as it had unfolded in West Bengal, that, ideological incompatibility and mutual squabbling notwithstanding, led the left-minded parties to converge into alliance to fight bourgeoisie–imperialist combinations. This tendency was not peculiar to the RSP alone; in fact, the electoral compulsion of parliamentary politics had forced all the left-minded parties to forge alliances among themselves at one point of time or other. RSP realized the political reality of India and created an alliance in the first general election itself with the CSP and Forward Bloc on ideological issues like the Communist International, and anti-Stalinism. But those issues appeared to be too remote and fuzzy to the animated citizens of India and RSP or its alliance partners failed to win a single seat. Soon a realization set in among the leadership of the party that contesting election required emphasis on immediate issues affecting the masses. Accordingly, after 1952, RSP started building rapport with like-minded communists, that had been waging endless war against feudalism to establish the rights of the exploited and impoverished section of the masses. This started to produce results as RSP gradually made its mark by securing inspiring results in the successive elections. The party actively participated in both the United Front governments, with two veteran leaders Nani Bhattacharya and Jatin Chakraborty serving as ministers. Nani Bhattacharaya as minister in charge of health earned huge admiration. It was under his adept guidance that the healthcare sector witnessed marked improvements, including the taking over of the management of National Medical College by the government, and the introduction of evening clinics. But the relationship between RSP and left parties did not last long as they were drifting apart from early 1970. The followers of RSP and CPI (M) went to the extent of targeting each other. But RSP did not join the rival eight-party combination led by CPI either. In 1971 the party had decided to go it alone and published a list of forty candidates. CPI (M) tried to cajole RSP to join the anti-Congress Front as any discord in the anti-Congress coalition would benefit Congress. But the electoral alliance between CPI (M) and RSP could not materialize as each imposed several conditions on the other. In 1972, however, once again they came together in the CPI (M)-led alliance. In the meantime, the proclamation of Emergency in 1975 had forced the party to suspend its activities. In 1977, the party joined the CPI (M)-led coalition and remained as an alliance partner for more than three decades.

Socialist Unity Centre of India (Communist) SUCI (C)

Socialist Unity Centre of India (Communist) SUCI (C), known as Socialist Unity Centre of India (SUCI), came into being when a faction of the leadership broke away from the RSP in 1948. Sibdas Ghosh laid the foundation-stone of the party in 1948. However, unlike RSP, SUCI had reposed its faith in the leadership of the Soviet Communist Party in general and Stalin in particular as the supreme leader of the world communist movement. Though, like any other Marxist party, SUCI was organized on the principle of democratic centralism and parliamentary communism, it focused mainly on mass movements and extra-parliamentary struggles. The party however was against the mimicking of either the Soviet or the Chinese model. On the contrary, the party believes that mass mobilization of workers, peasants, students and the middle class is the key to the success of Indian communism. One of the champions of ideological sanctity, SUCI, from its inception, was busy in protecting the quintessential nature of the Communist Party. It had been very critical of other communist parties for their gross aberrations in practising communism. In election, the party which is confined to West Bengal has a marginal presence.

Forward Bloc

Forward Bloc is another leading constituent party of the Left Front. As a result of a fissure in the Congress on the question of complete freedom, Subhas Chandra Bose founded a new political party in 1940, popularly known as Forward Bloc.[40] Convinced that the conservative character of the Congress Party meant that change was not possible, Subhas Chandra Bose charted a new course for the freedom struggle in India. Representing the left-wing faction of the INC, Bose had persistently opposed the right-wing version of gradual accomplishment of freedom. In fact, he had been advocating an ultimate formula of complete freedom. The rift between the left and the right faction of the INC was wide open for the first time at the Tripuri Congress in 1939, when Bose's call for complete freedom was openly turned down by the Pant resolution. In fact, a tactically Gandhian principle prevailed over Bose's ultimate formula. In protest, Bose had resigned from the INC and formed a new party, subsequently known as Forward Bloc. It was originally intended to act as a nucleus 'for bringing about left-consolidation'.[41] It declared itself as a party only at the second All-India Conference held at Nagpur.

The party declared its objective in the following words: 'to rally all the radical and anti-imperialist progressive elements in the country on the basis of a minimum programme, representing the greatest common measure of agreement among the radicals of all shades of opinion'.[42] Soon the party started organizing huge rallies in different parts of the country. Notable among them was a rally at Ramgarh in 1940, which coincided with the annual session of the Congress. The party from the beginning, unlike Congress, had adopted uncompromising stands against British imperialism. Consequently, it became a meeting-ground of radical congressmen. During the Second World War, when Subhas Chandra Bose escaped the country and formed the Indian National Army, Forward Bloc adopted a policy of all-out struggle against the British raj. Consequently, the party came under the scanner of the empire and most of the leaders were thrown into jail. But the end of war did not bring much of a break for the party. In fact, the organization of the party was in shambles as most of the party leaders were behind bars. It was the Congress which reaped a rich harvest from the heroic deeds of Subhas Chandra Bose. A sizeable section of the leadership of the party joined the Congress and contested the election of 1946.

The party did not support the partition plan of Congress as it was an annulment of Bose's ideal. Moreover, the party had developed a strenuous relationship with the communists for the latter's critique of Subhas Chandra Bose. Gradually the party evolved as an ultra-nationalist left party.

In December 1948, the party experienced a split between pro-Marxists and non-Marxists. Claiming the communist leaning of Subhas Chandra Bose, the pro-Marxist leaders of the All-India Forward Bloc wanted to build a united front with the communists. But the anti-Marxist faction, popularly known as Subhasist Forward Bloc, rejected the claim of the pro-Marxists. This faction showed the conciliatory approach of Subhas Bose, by which he intended to synthesise between nationalism and communism.

Summarizing the discussion

As is evident, the parliamentary left in India represented a well-knit ideological group with more or less identical ideological goals. Drawing on the classical Marxism and Leninism, Indian leftists also charted an independent course of action when in power which approximates, to a large extent, to Bernsteinian revisionism. The other significant point relates to the changing ideological priorities of the Left Front partners in response to the prevalent socio-economic circumstances. Once in power, the main concern of the left was not to pursue class struggle to its logical conclusion within the classical Marxist-Leninist perspective, but to find a middle path to accomplish its ideological mission. This was evident in the functioning of the constituents of the left: in the pre-liberalization phase, the parliamentary left was opposed to foreign and private capital; but their attitude towards them underwent a sea-change in the post-1991 period that ushered in economic liberalization in India. There were, of course, differences among the constituents on this issue though they were muted for the sake of left solidarity in the context of stiff political competition in which the left parties were naturally handicapped, given their failure to expand their social bases beyond their strongholds in West Bengal, Kerala and Tripura.

Constituents of left-wing extremism

Left-wing extremism in India has evolved out of very complex processes of ideological churning. Interestingly, most of the parties belonging to the parliamentary left began their journey with an uncritical faith in the Marxist-Leninist method of seizure of political power through violent revolution. The CPI waged a violent war against the state for the underprivileged in the 1940s, first in the south-western part of Bengal and later in the Telangana region of the former

Constituents of left radicalism 67

state of Hyderabad. Once the ban on its activity was withdrawn in independent India, the CPI willingly took part in the first national election in 1952. The same is true of the erstwhile Naxalites who launched a violent struggle for political change in the 1970s. With the gradual decline of their movement, some of the radical Naxalites belonging to the CPI (ML) joined parliamentary politics and took part in elections. However, this part concentrates on those constituents of left-wing extremism which, by drawing on the classical Marxist-Leninist-Maoist path, believes that only through violent revolutions can the prevalent unjust class balances be altered. The left-wing extremists are, in contemporary parlance, known as the Maoists who remain critical to the consolidation of the left-wing revolutionary zeal in an area which is euphemistically characterized as the 'red corridor' in India. By elaborating the distinct characteristics of the constituents, this section will be of use in understanding the unique nature of the Indian variety of left-wing extremism.

Communist Party of India (Marxist-Leninist) Liberation

Historically speaking, the origin of CPI (ML) Liberation dates back to 1974. However, the post-Emergency phase of 1977, when most leaders of the communist movement were released from jail, was the time when the activity of Liberation was first noticed. The Party Central Committee (PCC), in a move to unite the splinter groups owing their origin to CPI (ML), called a meeting from 30 January to 2 February 1981. However the meeting could not derive the expected results.

> From this point onwards whereas the PCC group goes on to become irrelevant and splits up into various factions, the M–L movement begins to polarize between the Marxist-Leninist line of CPI (ML) (Liberation) and the anarchist line of CPI (ML) (People's War).[43]

During 1982, the Indian People's Front (IPF) was launched in New Delhi at a national conference. In due course of time, IPF became the party's open political platform actively intervening in national politics. At the end of the year the Third Party Congress took place at Giridih, Bihar, where the issue of participation in election was clinched. This shift in the outlook of CPI (ML) Liberation proved to be vital in designing its later course of activity within the Naxal movement. As one scholar observes, 'Even though the Liberation group considers itself the true inheritor of the CPI (ML) legacy, its political line has changed dramatically from that of the original CPI (ML).'[44] With this strategic shift in functioning, the CPI (ML) (Liberation) recorded its first electoral victory under the banner of IPF in 1989 and Ara (one Lok Sabha constituency in Central Bihar) sent the first Naxalite member to Parliament.[45] In a special conference convened in July 1990, the party decided to resume open functioning. This decision was formalized at its fifth congress in December 1992. In 1994, the IPF was disbanded. The Election Commission recognized the CPI (ML) in 1995, and since then the party has contested successive elections at national and state levels.

68 *Setting the scene*

The CPI (ML) Liberation, though functioning over ground within the parliamentary democracy set-up, has not completely disbanded the path of armed rebellion.

> The Party does not rule out the possibility that under a set of exceptional national and international circumstances, the balance of social and political forces may even permit a relatively peaceful transfer of central power to revolutionary forces. But in a country where democratic institutions are based on essentially fragile and narrow foundations and where even small victories and partial reforms can only be achieved and maintained on the strength of mass militancy, the party of the proletariat must prepare itself for winning the ultimate decisive victory in an armed revolution. A people's democratic front and a people's army, therefore, remain the two most fundamental weapons of revolution in the arsenal of the Party.[46]

This again points out the dilemmas within the ultra left movement, which is very often reflected in the unpredictable character of the Naxal movement.

The People's War Group (PWG)

PWG is the most important among all the splinter groups representing the Naxal movement because today the dominant line within Naxal politics is the PWG line of thought. Though it is popularly known as PWG or PW, its official nomenclature is Communist Party of India – Marxist-Leninist (People's War). If Naxalism today is considered as the greatest internal security problem, and if today Naxals claim to be running parallel government in different parts of the country, credit for this mostly goes to PWG. 'The CPI (ML) (People's War) was formed on the Lenin's birth anniversary on April 22, 1980.'[47] Kondapalli Seetharamaiah, one of the most influential Naxalite leaders from Andhra Pradesh and a member of the erstwhile Central Organizing Committee of the CPI (ML), is the founding father of PWG; ironically, however, he was later expelled from the group. While elaborating the ideological programme of the party, it was proclaimed that,

> the Programme of our Party has declared that India is a vast 'semi-colonial and semi-feudal country', with about 80 per cent of our population residing in our villages. It is ruled by the big-bourgeois big landlord classes, subservient to imperialism. The contradiction between the alliance of imperialism, feudalism and comprador-bureaucrat-capitalism on the one hand and the broad masses of the people on the other is the principal contradiction in our country. Only a successful People's Democratic Revolution i.e. New Democratic Revolution and the establishment of People's Democratic Dictatorship of the workers, peasants, the middle classes and national bourgeoisie under the leadership of the working class can lead to the liberation of our people from all exploitation and the dictatorship of the reactionary ruling classes and pave the way for building Socialism and Communism in

our country, the ultimate aim of our Party. People's War based on Armed Agrarian Revolution is the only path for achieving people's democracy i.e. new democracy, in our country.[48]

Rejecting the parliamentary democratic system and branding individual annihilation as individual terrorism, PWG declares that people's war is the only path to bring about a people's government in the country. It is clear that there was a set of organizational, strategic and tactical conflicts going on within the CPI (ML) which paved the way for the split and creation of a more radical party. Broadly speaking, the party programmes of CPI (ML) Liberation were mostly focused on the cause of peasants, while the group led by K. Seetharamaiah wanted the party to be a platform for peasants, workers, tribal and other weaker sections of society. It was the prime agenda of Liberation to build up a political front focusing on peasant struggles, whereas PWG was more interested in the formation of mass organizations instead of any democratic front. One of the renowned guerrilla leaders of the erstwhile PWG summarizes the essence of conflict between CPI (ML) Liberation and CPI (ML) People's War by stating:

> In the *Liberation* group, which at one time was one of the strong groups defending Charu Majumdar's revolutionary line, after the martyrdom of Comrade Johar, with the leadership falling into the hands of Vinod Mishra, they began betraying the Indian revolution. As part of a conspiratorial plan, a once revolutionary party was gradually changed into a revisionist party, like the CPI and CPM. The armed resistance struggles against the state's attacks, taking place under the then leadership of *Liberation*, was ended. The armed struggle to crush the feudal private armies was made a secondary task. In this way, they diverted the entire group away from the basic path outlined by the unified CPI (ML), and particularly of its founder, Com. CM – that of protracted people's war – into becoming agents of the ruling classes, by surrendering them to the parliamentary path. They converted the Comrade Johar-led *Liberation*, from being a revolutionary movement, into a legalist, reformist and parliamentary movement; and changed the underground organization into an open opportunist and revisionist organization.[49]

The two official statements of PWG quoted above clearly suggest that the birth of PWG was the result of a split within the CPI (ML) Liberation, and was mostly designed due to the dynamics of conflict among many of its cadres. For a considerable period after its birth the PWG's activities were limited to Andhra Pradesh only, whereas CPI (ML) Liberation continued to hold its turf in Bihar. It was during this period that another organization came into existence on 1 January 1982. It was named the Communist Party of India (ML) Party Unity, which came into existence with a merger between CPI (ML) Unity Organizations and the Central Organizing Committee of CPI (ML). Hereafter, left-wing extremism in India witnessed some of the worst ever conflicts, which again forced many of the organizations to take a position and adopt new tactics. Bihar

70 *Setting the scene*

has always remained a strong battleground for Naxal operations and ironically Bihar witnessed most of the clashes between CPI (ML) Party Unity and CPI (ML) Liberation in the past, as the Table 2.1 illustrates.

While these conflicts were taking their toll on the cadres of both sides, another development was taking place simultaneously. In August 1998, Party Unity merged with CPI (ML) People's War Group and the group came to be known as People's War. 'The merger of the two parties is the culmination of the unity process which began in March '93 and continued for over five years during which differences on several political, ideological and organizational questions were resolved through thread-bare discussion.'[50] The statement continues,

> The emergence of the united Party – the Communist Party of India (Marxist-Leninist) [People's War] – does not mark the completion of the process of unification of the genuine communist revolutionary forces in India. The newly Unified Party will continue its efforts in right earnest to achieve this unification. We also call upon the other genuine revolutionary elements in the various M-L parties in India who are being led astray by both right and left opportunist leadership, to fight against these deviations and rally under the banner of the United Party. The United Party pledges itself to avenge the death of thousands of martyrs who fell in the course of the ongoing democratic revolution in India which will be futile until their cherished goals are accomplished. This is the era of Revolutions.[51]

By this merger PWG became another force to reckon with in Bihar and in other areas where PU had a presence. Further developments suggest that with this merger the armed rebellion path of the Naxal movement became stronger, while Liberation, with its parliamentary practices, was losing its turf to PWG. The same Liberation which once controlled the whole of Central Bihar was losing its territory and supporters to PWG and Maoist Communist Centre (MCC). Not only in Bihar, but everywhere Liberation was being systematically reduced from the map of Naxalite politics. By participating in electoral methods and by not being able to make an impressive mark the Liberation movement became weak and the PWG's armed operation started gaining momentum.

Table 2.1 Outcome of the encounters between CPI (ML) Party Unity (PU) and CPI (ML) Liberation (Lib.), 1994–7

Year	Number of clashes	Number of deaths
1994	5	8 (PU 5, Lib. 3)
1995	16	13 (PU 8, Lib. 5)
1996	36	24 (PU 5, Lib. 19)
1997	21	16 (PU 3, Lib. 3)

Source: *Times of India*, 7 December 1997.

So while Liberation, with its changed modus operandi, was being reduced to any other small political party, PWG in the same period managed to register its presence outside Andhra Pradesh and gradually made strongholds in different areas of Bihar, Orissa, Madhya Pradesh, Jharkhand, Chattisgarh and Maharashtra. Of course, due to this conflict between PU and Liberation, both the groups suffered in terms of loss of considerable number of their cadres, but as we saw this conflict also resulted in the merger of PU and PWG and ultimately resulted in the violent consolidation of the movement.

The formation of People's War also resulted in tactical changes in several aspects of the Naxal movement in general. 'In our agenda for a new democratic revolution, there are two aspects – the agrarian revolution and fight for nationality.'[52] This statement shows the amount of organizational change witnessed by the Naxal movement in all those years. In 1967, it started in the name of agrarian revolution, which gradually took the stance of replacement of the parliamentary form of government, but the question of nationality was never there. This reflects the pattern of conflict between PW and Liberation. By not questioning nationality PW wanted to make it clear that it wanted a broad revolutionary pattern and 'land to tillers' could be a programme but not the sole agenda of the revolution.[53]

Between 15 and 30 November 1995 the PW conducted an All-India Special Conference in some unknown locality of Dandakaranya. There it adopted two important party documents. The 'Party Programme' as adopted at the conference reads,

> India is a semi-feudal, semi-colonial society; here the New Democratic Revolution (NDR) has to be completed victoriously paving way to the Socialist Revolution and to advance towards the ultimate goal of Communism. The Indian people are weighed down by three big mountains: feudalism, imperialism and comprador bureaucratic capital; these are the targets to be overthrown in the present stage of NDR. The four major contradictions in the present-day Indian society are: the contradiction between feudalism and the broad masses; the contradiction between imperialism and the Indian people; the contradiction between capital and labour and the contradiction within the ruling classes. While the first two are fundamental contradictions to be resolved through the NDR, the contradiction between feudalism and the broad masses is the principal contradiction at the present stage. India is a multi-national country – a prison-house of nationalities and all the nationalities have the right to self-determination including secession. When NDR is victoriously completed, India will become a voluntary and genuine federation of all national people's republics.[54]

The second document, which was adopted in the conference, was the document on strategy and tactics. It reads:

> The political strategy to be pursued in the present stage of NDR in India is one of forming a broad united front of all the anti-feudal, anti-imperialist

forces – the working class, the peasantry, the petty bourgeoisie and the national bourgeoisie – under the leadership of the working class to overthrow the common enemies – feudalism, imperialism and comprador bureaucratic capital. The military strategy or the path of Indian Revolution is the path of protracted people's war i.e., liberating the countryside first through area wise seizure of power establishing guerilla zones and base areas and then encircling the cities and finally capturing power throughout the country. The unevenness in the economic, social and political development of Indian society calls for different tactics i.e., forms of struggle and organization, to be pursued in different regions of the country, while the political tactic line throughout the country remains the same. In urban areas the political and mass work should be carried out observing utmost precaution and the organizational work should proceed keeping in view the long-range perspective. Caste is a peculiar problem in India; and appropriate forms of organization and struggle should be evolved vigorously to fight out untouchability, caste discrimination and to finally root out the caste system. The tactics of boycott of elections have to be pursued for a long time in the prevailing conditions in India; and participating in parliamentary and assembly elections under any pretext only weakens the class struggle.[55]

These two documents containing different organizational aspects of PW make a clear-cut demarcation on the issues pertaining to organizational conflict between the Liberation and PW. The People's War, on the basis of its assessment of the people's level of preparedness for an armed struggle, discarded total annihilation of 'class enemies' as the only form of struggle and stressed floating mass organizations. It established several front organizations. During the 1980s, the Radical Students' Union and Rayatu Kuli Sangham had emerged as organizations with an impressive mass following and most of the PWG's present base and political cadres had developed through that practice. However, during the 1990s, the growth of militarization became the characteristic feature of the PWG. The formation of People's Guerrilla Army (PGA), special guerrilla squads, a permanent action team and a special action team were the distinctive features of PWG activities for quite some time before it merged with MCC to form the CPI (Maoist).[56]

Maoist Communist Centre (MCC)

The next important group within the broad spectrum of the Naxal movement is the Maoist Communist Centre (MCC). Among a number of organizations it stands apart as conventionally speaking it never was part of the CPI (ML), which many claim as the mother of all Naxal organizations. 'The MCC, while supporting the Naxalbari struggle, did not join the CPI (ML) because of some tactical differences and on the question of Party formation.'[57] The MCC was formed on 20 October 1969, at the same time as the CPI (ML) was formed; however during those days it was known as Dakshin Desh. It was in 1975 that the group renamed itself as Maoist Communist Centre. In 2003, the MCC merged with the Revolutionary Communist Centre of India-Maoists to form the Maoist Communist Centre-India (MCC-I).

Right from its inception, the MCC stood for taking up arms as the main form of struggle and waging protracted people's war as the central task of the party. This position of the MCC has been repeatedly expressed and emphasized by the Maoists while decoding their strategy. As the *Red Star*, the MCC weekly, firmly declares,

> This armed revolutionary war is the war of the armed people themselves; it is 'Protracted People's War' as shown by Mao Tse Tung. The concrete economic and political condition of India leads to the very conclusion that the path shown by the great leader and teacher, Mao Tse Tung, the path of the Chinese Revolution, that is, and to establish a powerful people's army and people's militia and to establish dependable, strong and self-sufficient base areas in the countryside, to constantly consolidate and expand the people's army and the base areas, gradually to encircle the urban areas from the countryside by liberating the countryside, finally to capture the cities and to establish the state system and political authority of the people themselves by decisively destroying the state power of the reactionaries – this very path of the protracted People's War is the only path of liberation of the people of India, the path of victory of the new democratic revolution.[58]

The Communist Party of India (Maoist)

The Naxal movement in India entered into yet another phase of organizational transformation with the merger of two of the principal armed organizations, PW and MCC-I, which resulted in the formation of the Communist Party of India (Maoist).

> The formation of the unified Communist Party of India (Maoist) is a new milestone in the history of the revolutionary communist movement of India. A unified Maoist party based on Marxism-Leninism-Maoism is a long delayed and highly cherished need of the revolutionary minded and oppressed people of the country, including all our ranks, and also all the Maoist forces of South Asia and internationally. Now, this long-aspired desire and dream has been transformed into a reality.[59]

This statement given by the first secretary of CPI (Maoist) Ganapathy, assumes a great deal of importance as it reflects the organizational politics that were going on all these years between these two organizations representing the Naxal movement.

The exalted aim of the CPI (Maoist), as announced on the occasion of its formation, is to establish a compact revolutionary zone stretching from Nepal to Bihar to Andhra Pradesh and beyond. While continuing their goal of people's democracy the ultimate aim of the CPI (Maoist) is to seize power through protracted armed struggle. According to the press statement issued on the event of announcing the merger,

> The immediate aim and programme of the Maoist party is to carry on and complete the already ongoing and advancing New Democratic Revolution in India as a part of the world proletarian revolution by overthrowing the semi-colonial, semi-feudal system under the neo-colonial form of indirect rule, exploitation and control.[60]

This revolution will remain directed against imperialism, feudalism and comprador bureaucratic capitalism. This revolution will be carried out and completed through armed agrarian revolutionary war, i.e. protracted people's war with the armed seizure of power remaining as its central and principal task, encircling the cities from the countryside and thereby finally capturing them. Hence the countryside as well as the PPW (Protracted People's War) will remain as the 'center of gravity' of the party's work, while urban work will be complementary to it. According to the same press release, the CPI (Maoists) 'will still seek to unite all genuine Maoist groups that remain outside this unified party'.[61]

It is important to examine the significance of the merger particularly when earlier attempts were not successful. In fact, the merger is largely seen as a result of the gradual convergence of views of these two groups on areas such as the role of the party, approaches to revolution and adoption of strategies and tactics. In the formative years, Charu Mazumdar and Kanai Chatterjee represented two irreconcilably different lines and approaches to 'revolution'. At the time of the formation of the CPI (ML) in 1969, the Dakshin Desh, an earlier form of the MCC, remained opposed to the process due to sharp differences with the CPI (ML) over issues such as the formation of a communist party, the existence of revolutionary mass struggle and the preparedness of the people to participate in it. The press statement released by the erstwhile general secretaries of PW and MCC-I highlighted the essence of the merger.

> In the past history there were many splits within the M-L movement. But splits are only one side of the coin; the brighter side was that there were continuous efforts to unify the revolutionaries. The CPI (ML) (PU), though it had its origins in Bengal, it spread and strengthened by unifying several revolutionary groups. The CPI (ML) (PW), though it originated in Andhra Pradesh and Tamil Nadu, unified with revolutionaries in almost all the states where it was working. The MCC too, had originated in Bengal, unified many revolutionaries groups in it in many States and became the MCCI.[62]

This statement underlines the continuous process of organizational politics within the broad spectrum of the Naxalite movement which, on occasions resulted in the organizational conflict.

Looking back, the need for a joint unified platform was felt by the leadership of both the parties as early as 1981.

> The PW and MCC began unity talks from their very first meeting in 1981. However, the reason for the delay in the process was the lack of continuity of leadership. The arrest of Comrade Kondapally Seetaramaiah (KS), the leader of the PW, and later the internal crisis of the PW and split in the Central Committee (CC) delayed the unity process for several years. In the early eighties, the MCC lost its two top leaders Comrades Amulya Sen (AS) and Kanai Chatterjee (KC), which had some negative impact, resulting in further delay in the unity process.[63]

However, this is not to suggest that the formation of CPI (Maoist) is the final stage of the Naxal movement. As one official Maoist document puts it,

> Revolutions never proceed in a straight line. The history of all successful revolutions shows this. The path is zig zag, there are ups and downs, there is victory and defeat repeated a number of times ... before final victory. Of course, there is no final victory until the stage of communism is reached.[64]

This analysis makes one forceful plea that has affected Naxal movement essentially is a political problem and it needs to be examined from the perspective of organizational politics.

The merger of the CPI (ML) PW and MCC-I that resulted in the birth of CPI (Maoist), also successfully brought the dominant faction of CPI (ML) Janashakti to its fold. Amidst speculations of merger, both the Janashakti and CPI (Maoist) presented a united front in 2005. A death toll of 892 persons that year was largely believed to be a result of the merger. The Naxal movement, however, continued to conquer new territories in 2006–7. Other than the escalation in violence, the later part of 2006 also witnessed significant changes in the operational ways of the Naxal movement.

The honeymoon between the CPI (Maoist) and Janashakti could not last longer than a year and in 2006 it became apparent that both were clearly going different ways to occupy operational areas. During the open session of the CPI (Maoist) held in December 2006, Janashakti was asked to make clear its stand on political aims and programmes; Janashakti, however, chose not to attend the session. Consequently, the CPI (Maoist) withdrew the partner status from Janashakti and decided to provide need-based support only in the case of police actions. The conflict between the CPI (Maoist) and Janashakti became public only recently, when the Orissa Janashakti group led by Anna Reddy killed three forest officials on 31 January 2007. The CPI (Maoist) state leadership immediately distanced itself from the killings. Subsequent police enquiry confirmed the involvement of the Janashakti group in the gruesome act.

Of course, things are at a formative stage today; the setting is ready for a possible realignment of the Maoist forces. In Karnataka, which is largely viewed as the new Naxal target, the CPI (Maoist) recently suffered a major set-back as a number of cadres in the state, who disagreed with the Maoist agenda of intensifying the revolution in rural areas first and then spreading it to urban centres, have floated a new party named the Maoist Coordination Committee. It should be noted that the political cracks in Karnataka have now started to extend to other states.

On the basis of the above discussion, three points stand out: first, the history of the Naxal movement is the history of a continuous process of organizational conflicts, splits and mergers. Second, the Naxal movement essentially represents simultaneous but not so peaceful coexistence of many streams, and, looking from this angle the movement does have a presence in all parts of the country. Third, the growth of the Naxal movement is closely linked with the ongoing process of organizational conflict. The ultimate political objective behind all this organizational exercise, according to the statements of various senior Naxalite leaders, is to build a leftist alternative and to mobilize people on issues such as increased 'imperialist intervention' and 'pro-imperialist policies' pursued by the Union government in support of 'revolutionary war' based on Chinese leader Mao's theory of organized peasant insurrection. Similarly, the history of the Naxal movement right from its first phase in 1967 demonstrates that even if there has been a continuous evolution in terms of their understanding of the Indian situation, focus of the movement, character, fighting capabilities and financial resources, the left wing extremists have remained more or less consistent as far as their core ideology is concerned. Barring the Liberation, they all reject parliamentary system of governance and want to bring about a fundamental change in the nature of the Indian state. For this they have adopted the strategy of protracted armed struggle, which entails building up bases in rural and remote areas and transforming them first into guerrilla zones and then liberated zones, besides following the area-wise seizures and encircling cities and finally seizing political power and achieving nation-wide victory.

Concluding observations

Biographies of the constituents of the parliamentary left and left-wing extremists provide useful inputs in understanding the nature and also processes that are critical in the shaping of particular ideological responses. Several political outfits with more or less identical ideological predilections came together to chart out a different course of action in accordance with what the left radicals draw out of their faith in Marxism, Leninism and Maoism. So it was primarily an ideological faith that brought them together since the available political tools did not appear to be adequate to pursue their goals. In formulating their specific responses the context always remained an important variable. The above detailed description thus enables us to grasp the dialectics between text and context. This is an enriching theoretical formulation which also helps us explain the changing left-radical perception about India's contemporary socio-economic and political reality. During the first phase of the Congress-led United Progressive Alliance government (2004–9), it was not therefore difficult for the Left Front to support the government as a preferred strategy to prevent the communal forces from capturing power. It was a clear contextual compulsion that justified the bonhomie between the left and its ideological rival, the Congress Party and its cohorts. In a similar vein, the coming together of the scattered left extremists groups to form the CPI (Maoist) in 2004 was also context driven since division among them made it easier for the Indian state to effectively counter their endeavour at undermining the institutionalized instruments of power. In fact, their growing strength, reflected in their capacity to combat the state-led coercive forces, including the army, is now officially recognized since they are dubbed the worst security threat to India.

As is evident, neither parliamentary left nor its bête noire, the left-wing extremists, are homogeneous in terms of their respective social bases: while the former has developed bases across classes and social strata the latter is usually confined to the rural areas involving those associated with agriculture or without sustained means for survival. In an atmosphere of mass disillusionment, given the failure of the liberal political forces to bring about meaningful changes in the prevalent class balances, not only did the constituents of the left mobilize masses against the well-entrenched class prejudices, but they also provoked a debate on independent India's system of governance by exposing the obvious ideological limitations of derivative liberalism in a post-colonial context. The meteoric rise and equally dramatic fall of the parliamentary left in India's recent political history also underlines the limits of social democracy as an ideology especially in a parliamentary democracy. With a formidable class coalition involving indignant intelligentsia, white-collar unionized public sector employees, and rural poor in its favour, it was easily possible for the parliamentary left to create and consolidate a stable social base in Kerala, West Bengal and Tripura. Through political practice and cultural movements, 'the Left had created a social imaginaire that altered the commonsensical idioms of politics in [the left-ruled states] in favour of such a class coalition'.[65] So, a favourable class coalition, sustained by complementary efforts at mobilizing support for the left, accounts for the continuity of the parliamentary left in those Indian provinces. The poll reversal that it witnessed in the assembly elections also confirms how fragile the class coalition was in retaining power for the left. This was true of the conglomeration called the parliamentary left which also establishes that, given the ideological compatibility among the constituents, the collective draws on the same social base which consolidates the left, if it is stable and strong, and contributes to its decline, if it is weak and unstable. So, the story of the constituents cannot be told differently since their fate is integrally linked with the collective.

Left-wing extremism is diverse since it has different trajectories in different parts of India. Even the issues that they articulate while mobilizing support for mass struggle are different since they are context driven. In contemporary Orissa, the public wrath against private capital provided the Maoists with an effective means for political mobilization, while in Bihar, the issue of caste always remained an integral part of the left radical campaign in rural areas, given

78 *Setting the scene*

the peculiar caste-conscious socio-economic milieu in which the so-called lower castes/untouchables were usually subjected to inhuman atrocities due to the accident of birth. It is also difficult to homogenize issues in view of India's diverse socio-economic texture. Nonetheless, an attempt was made to evolve a pan-India agenda with the coming together of various constituents endorsing left-wing extremism to form the CPI (Maoist) in 2004. In principle, Maoists have become part of the same ideological outfit though they operate in accordance with the context-specific ideological direction provided by the regional leadership in different areas. In its endeavour to bring about a classless society in a typical Maoist way, the party thus allows its regional wings to function independently, within, of course, its overall supervision and control. So, the constituents remain as integral to the Maoist ideological mission as the collective.

Notes

1 Satyabrata Rai Chowdhuri, *Leftism in India (1917–47)*, Minerva, Calcutta, 1977, p. 33.
2 Chowdhuri, *Leftism in India*, p. 26.
3 Valerian Rodrigues, 'The Communist Parties in India', in Peter Ronald deSouza and E. Sridharan (eds), *India's Political Parties*, Sage Publications, New Delhi, 2006, p. 205.
4 T.J. Nossiter, *Marxist State Governments in India: politics, economics and society*, Pinter Publishers, London and New York, p. 14.
5 M.N. Roy laid emphasis on the need for a WPP through which communists could function legally. For more see Chowdhuri, *Leftism in India*, p. 71.
6 For detail see Nossiter, *Marxist State Governments*, p. 14; Chowdhuri, *Leftism in India*, pp. 45–61.
7 Rodrigues, 'The Communist Parties in India', pp. 209–11.
8 Amitava Ray, 'The Left in West Bengal: electoral and mobilizational strategies (1947–1967)', in Rakhahari Chatterjee (ed.), *Politics in West Bengal: institutions, processes and problems*, The World Press Pvt. Ltd, Calcutta, 1985, p. 65.
9 The Ranadive line was known as a stand undertaken by the then General Secretary of the party, B.T. Ranadive.
10 S. Poplai (ed.), *Select Documents on Asian Affairs, India (1947–50)*, vol. 1, Oxford University Press, 1959, p. 511, as quoted by Sudhir Ray, *Marxist Parties of West Bengal: in opposition and in government (1947–2001)*, Progressive Publishers, Kolkata, 2007, p. 18.
11 Marcus Franda, *Radical Politics in West Bengal*, MIT Press, Cambridge, MA, 1971 as cited by Ray, 'The Left in West Bengal', p. 68.
12 Rodrigues, 'The Communist Parties in India', p. 210.
13 Rodrigues, 'The Communist Parties in India', p. 210.
14 Rodrigues, 'The Communist Parties in India', p. 212.
15 Ray, *Marxist Parties of West Bengal*.
16 Rodrigues, 'The Communist Parties in India', p. 214.
17 Ideologically speaking, the Naxalbari peasant movement was inspired by Charu Majumdar. He called for armed struggle by annihilating class enemies. This radical stand and advocacy for a revolutionary party paved the way for the formation of the CPI (ML) in 1969.
18 Apurba Mukhopadhyay, 'The Left in West Bengal: government and movement (1967–82)', in Chatterjee (ed.), *Politics in West Bengal*, p. 90.
19 The split of the INC in 1969 facilitated Indira Gandhi and her Congress ® to acquire credibility in Indian politics.

20 Apurba Kumar Mukhopadhyay, 'Politics – Left, Lefter, Leftest', in Purusottam Bhattacharya, Tridib Chakraborti and Shibashis Chatterjee (eds), *Anatomy of Fear: essays on India's internal security*, Lancer's Books, New Delhi, 2004, p. 232.
21 Bhabani Sengupta, *CPI (M): promises, prospects, problems*, Young Asia Publications, New Delhi and Stockholm, 1979, p. 14.
22 Sengupta, *CPI (M)*, p. 57.
23 Mukhopadhyay, 'The Left in West Bengal', p. 92.
24 Change of guard in CPI happened when the Ranadive line had backfired. P.C. Joshi had replaced Ranadive.
25 Sengupta, *CPI (M)*, pp. 92–5.
26 Sengupta, *CPI (M)*, p. 54.
27 Hare Krishna Konar, quoted in Sengupta, *CPI (M)*, pp. 53–4.
28 Mukhopadhyay, 'The Left in West Bengal', p. 102.
29 Sengupta, *CPI (M)*, p. 100.
30 Sengupta, *CPI (M)*, p. 113.
31 Sengupta, *CPI (M)*, p. 131
32 Asok Mitra as quoted in Sengupta, *CPI (M)*, p. 157.
33 Mitra as quoted in Sengupta, *CPI (M)*, p. 158.
34 The term was coined by Dwipawan Bhattacharaya in 'Of control and factions: the changing party-society in rural West Bengal', *Economic and Political Weekly*, 28 February 2009. By party society he indicated both the intensive and the extensive intervention of the party in societal affairs.
35 They primarily hailed from a prominent revolutionary group, known as Anushilan Samiti in Bengal in pre-independent India.
36 The CSP was established in 1934 at the end of the civil disobedience movement by a number of young Congress workers. Though it started with a socialist dream of transforming the contour of the national movement to a truly anti-imperialist movement, soon the expectations were belied as the party was said to have succumbed to Gandhism. The party, like its mother organization, was amorphous, containing as many as three contradictory strands within its fold: the Marxist socialism of Jay Prakash Narayan and Acharaya Narendra Deva; the social democratic strand of Minoo Masani and Ashok Mehata; and the Gandhian method of non-violent direct action of Achyut Patwardhan and Ram Monohar Lohia.
37 Anushilan Samiti was founded in Calcutta in 1902 as a 'revolutionary cultural and youth organization' and had taken an anti-imperialist national revolutionary stance.
38 Buddhadeva Bhattacharya, *Origin of the Revolutionary Socialist Party: from national revolutionary to non-conformist Marxism*, Publicity Concern, Calcutta, 1982.
39 Bhattacharaya, *Origin of the Revolutionary Socialist Party*, p. 11.
40 Bidyut Chakrabarty, *Subhas Chandra Bose and middle-class radicalism, 1928–1940*, Oxford University Press, Delhi, 1990, pp. 46–8.
41 Bose, *All Power to the People*, p. 27.
42 *Thirty Years of Naxalbari*, an undated publication of CPI (ML) Liberation.
43 *Selected Speeches of Subhas Chandra Bose*, Publication Division, Government of India, New Delhi, 1962, p. 100.
44 Bela Bhatia, 'Naxalite Movement in Central Bihar', *Economic and Political Weekly*, April 9 2005.
45 'History of Naxalism', *Hindustan Times*. www.Hindustantimes.com
46 A party document of CPI (ML) Liberation titled 'The General Programme'.
47 *30 years of Naxalbari*, undated Maoist literature, Vanguard Publication, p. 30. *Vanguard* was the organ of PWG.
48 'Path of People's War in India – Our Tasks!' a comprehensive PWG party document highlighting its aims, objectives and strategies. The document was adopted by All-India Party Congress, 1992. We obtained this document from one of the principal ideologues of the PWG.

80   Setting the scene

49 Sharvan, the then secretary of the Bihar State Committee of CPI (ML) People's War, in an interview given to *People's March*, vol. 2, no. 3, March 2001.
50 People's War literature titled 'Joint declaration by Communist Party of India (ML) People's War and CPI (ML) (Party Unity)', August 1998.
51 People's War, 'Joint declaration'.
52 Interview with Muppalla Lakshmana Rao alias Ganapathy, the then head of the CPI (ML) People's War. www.rediff.com/news/1998/oct/07gana.htm, accessed on 18 January 2013.
53 The issue of nationality remains very critical in Marxism. Among Indian Marxists it was interpreted as ethnicity, which is a source of serious controversy and acrimony among them. Hence PW refused to take the question of nationality into account to avoid schism among the rank and file of its supporters.
54 This report on the special conference was posted on a website (www. cpimlpwg/repression.html) which claimed to be the unofficial website of PW. The website has since been withdrawn. Despite its claim, during my interaction with many PW rank and file I found that it was no less then their official website.
55 Report of the special conference (see note 50).
56 In response to a government decision to launch coordinated action against the Naxalites by police forces of the various Indian states affected by Naxal violence, the PWG formed the PGA, its military wing, in December 2000 by reorganizing its guerrilla force. The PGA functions under a single operational command, the Central Military Commission. In the Indian states where the PGA has a presence, there is a state military commission and in special guerrilla zones there is a zonal military commission. A regional military commission supervises a group of state military commissions or zonal military commissions. Each regional military commission reports to the Central Military Commission. All armed cadres of the PWG are organized under the PGA. 'People's Guerrilla Army', www.satp.org/satporgtp/countries/india/terroristoutfits/peoples_guerrilla_arms_left_wing_extremists.htm, accessed on 23 January 2010.
57 *30 Years of Naxalbari*, p. 36.
58 *Red Star*, special issue, June 2003, p. 20. *Red Star* is the English language organ of the MCC, as quoted by Aloke Banerjee in a pamphlet titled 'Inside MCC Country'. Also quoted in 'MCC India three decades leading battalions of the poor', an article published by A World to Win (www.awtw.org/back_issues/mcc_india.htm). Though it denies it, many treat *Red Star* as the unofficial organ of the Revolutionary Internationalist Movement.
59 Ganapathy, in an interview given on the occasion of the formation of CPI (Maoist). *People's March*, vol. 5, nos 11–12, November–December 2004.
60 'Maoist-influenced revolutionary organizations in India', at www.massline.info/India/Indian_Groups.htm, accessed on 18 April 2011.
61 'Maoist-influenced revolutionary organizations in India'.
62 Ganapathy, interview.
63 Ganapathy, interview.
64 'State repression', document posted to the unofficial website of PWG, www. cpimlpwg/repression.html (see note 50).
65 Subho Basu and Auritro Majumdar, 'Dilemmas of parliamentary communism: the rise and fall of the left in West Bengal', *Asian Studies*, vol. 45 no. 92, 2013, p. 196.

Part II
Parliamentary left in India

Articulating social democracy as a universal theoretical design

Of the two varieties of left radicalism in India, Maoism and parliamentary left, the latter became an ideological alternative once the erstwhile left extremists had adopted the parliamentary path for socio-economic and political changes. As is evident in the available literature, before India became free in 1947, the communist movement followed two different strategies: during the years 1935–9 and 1945–7, the communists endorsed bourgeois nationalism against imperialism and in other periods (1928–34 and 1948–50), they attacked bourgeois nationalism under the anti-capitalist strategy. There also emerged a third strategy of 'people's democracy' and 'new democracy', applied in Eastern Europe and China that was considered to be an effective strategy for the transition to socialism during which 'a communist-led regime completes the bourgeois democratic revolution and lays the basis for the subsequent achievement of socialism'.[1] This was evident when E.M.S. Namboodiripad, the first elected communist Chief Minister of Kerala asserted that the aim of the communist government was to form 'a united front … or a coalition, of all those parties and elements in our public life which accept the objective of socialism'.[2] He also announced a congenial line with respect to the ideological climate inside his party that his government was not going to bring about the socialism of Russia but through the parliamentary path his party in power in Kerala would try to implement the stated policies of Congress-led national government, which their state governments had failed to implement because of their class bias. The first experiment of the parliamentary left in Kerala did not last long because the Namboodiripad government was dismissed two years after its formation in 1957.[3] Nonetheless, this was a watershed in India's democratic politics with the parliamentary left becoming integral to the political processes. The trend that began in 1957 unfolded in the days to come. While Kerala set a new precedent in political governance the parliamentary left consolidated the gain by capturing power in two provinces in the eastern part of India, West Bengal and Tripura, in the 1970s. By holding power for more than three decades, the parliamentary left in West Bengal set a record of being the longest serving government to have captured power through democratic election. The trend is different in Kerala and Tripura where the left lost power intermittently to the opposition since their acceptance of the parliamentary path in the early 1950s.

The aim of Part II is to acquaint the readers with the distinctive nature of the parliamentary left in Tripura, West Bengal and Kerala. While in Kerala, the left radicals had captured power through democratic election as early as 1957, they became serious political forces in Tripura and West Bengal later. By analytically assessing the nature of left rule in these constituent Indian states, this part argues that the parliamentary left has not only become integral to India's political arithmetic, it has also articulated an ideology-driven alternative in India's distinctive liberal democracy. Left radicals, by adopting the parliamentary path, have, this part further argues, adapted social democracy in a non-European context. What is striking in the story is the fact that instead of being uniform, left radicalism has flourished differently in these Indian provinces: while, in Kerala and Tripura, left radicalism seems to have developed organic roots by adapting to the prevalent socio-economic environment, in West Bengal, the left's authoritarian iron-fist rule created a milieu in which left radicalism completely lost out to the opposition. The 2014 Lok Sabha poll is illustrative here. In West Bengal, the downfall of the left that had begun in the 2009 national poll seems to have been complete with almost a wash-out of the left in the election; the scene in Kerala is slightly better, though the loss was visible with the massive decline of its share of Lok Sabha seats and also share of popular votes in the state; by retaining both the parliamentary seats, the parliamentary left in Tripura seems to have shown that effective governance is a key to election victory. On the whole, this part underlines the point that left radicalism cannot be comprehended in a uniform conceptual framework given India's well-ingrained socio-economic and political diversity in which it is articulated and put to practice. So only by being sensitive to the contextual peculiarities of Kerala, West Bengal and Tripura, can one conceptualize the complex manifestation of left radicalism in India which, despite being appreciative of liberal democracy, appears to have reinvented its nature by reference to the critical importance of caste, ethnicity and other socio-economic features drawing on primordial loyalties. Here the fundamental tenets of Marxism-Leninism may help us understand the wider picture of class exploitation, but appears inadequate in grasping the context-dependent socio-economic circumstances in which class, as a category, may not be as critical an aid to comprehend a reality as in industrially advanced countries. The argument hinges around the assumption that a straitjacketed understanding of Marxism-Leninism can never provide an appropriate window through which to view India's peculiar socio-economic reality since the nature of contradiction is very context-specific; unless one is acquainted with the context, the analysis is bound to be faulty and thus futile.

In three chapters, the part analyses the distinctive characteristics of left radicalism in India. There are two questions that need serious attention: (a) despite being popular at the outset, why did the ideological appeal of left radicalism gradually wane? And (b) why did left radicalism fail to expand beyond Kerala, West Bengal and Tripura though the socio-economic conditions were also propitious for its growth and consolidation in various parts of India? A persuasive answer to these questions is contingent on a detailed contextual analysis of the forms of parliamentary left that have flourished in India in the midst of a peculiar blending of feudal and capitalistic values which necessitated a thorough re-looking at some of the fundamental conceptual pillars of the Indian variety of left radicalism. There lies the challenge.

Notes

1 Overstreet and Windmiller, *Communism in India*, p. 6.
2 The statement of EMS Namboodiripad is quoted in Overstreet and Windmiller, *Communism in India*, p. 548.
3 S. Gopal provides an analytical account of the nature of the first elected communist government and its dismissal by the union government in 1959 in his *Jawaharlal Nehru: a biography* (Harvard University Press, Cambridge, MA, 1984), pp. 52–74.

3 Parliamentary left in Tripura
Social democracy in a new mould

By retaining two parliamentary seats in the state in the 2014 national election, the left radicals in Tripura have proved once again that effective governance is a key to electoral success. Even in the context of a definite wave for the BJP in the entire country, the left support base remains as solid as in the past; the left juggernaut was unstoppable. This was not a mean achievement in the context of the failure of the left radicals to even sustain their support base in both Kerala and West Bengal, the left citadels. Despite lack of adequate support from the party high command, the CPI (M) candidates comfortably won both the seats in the state. A surface reading of the electoral victory suggests how effective the incumbent government was in utilizing the state machinery for common well-being regardless of class, caste or ethnicity. It was possible for the local state to fulfil its ideological mission because of the support that it had received from the local party unit which, by being most vigilant, never allowed the government to divert its way. Unlike its West Bengal counterpart, the CPI (M) party machinery remained most effective in pursuing the welfare schemes for the people at large since it was never allowed to be appropriated by the vested interests for partisan goals. The success of the left radicals in 2014 was thus attributed to a symbiotic network between the party and government which was missing in both Kerala and West Bengal.

The aim of this chapter is to narrate the growth and gradual consolidation of left radicalism in this tiny north-eastern state of Tripura. A former princely state, Tripura is also unique in terms of its demography comprising both the indigenous population and the erstwhile refugees from former East Pakistan. This was a source of tension in the state which was manifested often in violent skirmishes between the Bengali settlers and the sons of the soil. The left radicals, especially those with their allegiance initially to the CPI and later CPI (M) created circumstances in which both these groups agreed to work together for everybody's betterment. In other words, effective social engineering led to a situation in which the idea of the common good prevailed over other sectarian considerations. It is not surprising that in the consolidation of left radicalism, the role of the Bengali settlers was as critical as that of their indigenous counterparts. Given the unflinching popularity of the parliamentary left in Tripura in the midst of its debacle elsewhere in India, one is encouraged to pursue an argument defending the viability of Marxism-Leninism as an ideology. Not only has the electoral victory in Tripura firmly established the significance of left radicalism in sustaining the support base, it also proves beyond doubt that it has not been exhausted yet as an ideological alternative even in the midst of its collapse elsewhere. Besides defending the ideological validity of left radicalism, the chapter is an analytical elaboration of the processes leading to its consolidation since the state was founded in 1972. The comfortable victory of the left in the 2014 national poll also confirms that mere ideological rhetoric was not enough to garner votes; what seemed to have mattered most in voters' choice was the government's success in delivering the basic services for human existence to the people at large.

Evolution of Tripura as a constituent state in federal India

As a former princely state, Tripura joined the federal India in 1949 and it became a union territory in 1956. After much struggle in which the left radicals played key roles, it became a fully fledged state in 1972. The movement for statehood was spearheaded by an outfit called Janasiksha Samiti which was led by Dasarath Deb, one of the earliest prominent left radicals who fought hard for Tripura's merger with independent India. In this campaign, both the tribals and non-tribals participated wholeheartedly to fulfil their ideological goal. The first election in a democratic system was held in January 1952 in which a thirty-member electoral college was formed to elect a member to Rajya Sabha, the second chamber of India's parliament. The second general election was held in 1957, to the Tripura Territorial Council which was already constituted after the 1952 election. As per the 1956 Territorial Act, a referendum was held on 15 August 1959 and the Tripura Territorial Council started functioning as a unit of governance for Tripura under the administrative authority of the Chief Commissioner. Later in 1963, this tiny north-eastern state of India was recognized as a union territory which was to be ruled by a legislative assembly under the titular authority of a lieutenant governor. As soon as Tripura got its first legislative assembly, it also had a cabinet of five members to take care of local administration within the purview of the 1963 Union Territory Act. The relentless campaign for statehood that the left radicals had launched finally resulted in Tripura being recognized as a fully fledged state in 1972 according to the North-East Reorganization Act of 1971. Tripura got a legislative assembly of 60 members, and the first election to the assembly was held in 1972.

The electoral history of Tripura shows that in the initial stages of its existence as a constituent geographical unit of India, it was governed by the Indian National Congress: the Congress won the first three assembly elections and was in power from 1963 to 1971 and from 1972 to 1977. From 1977 to 1978 the state witnessed political instability. The short-lived Janata Dal and left coalition government gave two Chief Ministers within a span of eight months. In the elections held in 1978, the CPI (M) came to power for the first time. The left rule was followed by five years of Congress rule from 1988 to 1993. In the seventh assembly elections held in 1993, CPI (M) emerged victorious and has been in power in the state since then by winning all subsequent elections.

In the elections to the Lok Sabha, CPI won both seats in the 1952 and 1962 elections, while in the 1957 elections CPI and Congress won one seat each. Congress won both the seats in the fourth Lok Sabha elections held in 1967. The scene however changed with the victory of CPI (M) candidates who had captured both the seats in the fifth Lok Sabha poll; in the sixth Lok Sabha, the left failed to win a single seat; the seats which were divided between the Congress and a new political outfit known as Congress for Democracy, while in the seventh and eighth parliamentary polls, it was CPI (M) that recaptured both the seats from the state. The Congress was unstoppable in the ninth and tenth Lok Sabha polls in 1996. The left radicals have thus gradually become invincible; not only have they comfortably won both the parliamentary seats since the eleventh national poll in 1996, they have also increased their share of popular votes in successive elections since then. This is definitely an outcome of sustained efforts by the left radicals who, by remaining connected with the people at the grassroots, have firmly established the viability of left radicalism despite their political eclipse elsewhere.

March to victory

As is shown in the available literature, there are two major ideological forces in Tripura: on the one hand, there is a strong presence of the left radicals who have adopted the parliamentary path of socio-economic and political changes; there also exist, on the other hand, those old liberals who remain committed to the Congress for its revolutionary role during the freedom struggle. Besides these well-defined ideological groups, the local tribals continue to be critical players in politics. On most occasions, they prefer to support one of the groups; but given the growing popularity of the left, there are reasons to believe that the majority of the tribals have aligned with the parliamentary left notwithstanding the presence of some violence-prone tribal groups who are reportedly fighting for independence of Tripura. So, in Tripura's political chemistry, left radicals have definitely become unassailable, as the successive poll results show.

Until 1977, the state was governed by the Indian National Congress which was replaced by the left parties in 1978. After having ruled the state till 1988, it lost power to a coalition of Congress and its post-election partner, Tripura Upajati Juba Samiti (TUJS) which was completely defeated by the Left Front in 1993. The trend was undisturbed in the most recent state assembly election which was held in March 2013. With forty-nine assembly seats to its tally, the parliamentary left had won three more seats than its 2008 tally of forty-six and also registered a 1 per cent increase in its votes share to 51 per cent in 2008 which is significant because neither the Congress nor its allies had succeeded in denting its well-nurtured social base which is socio-culturally disparate due to a peculiar demographic composition of the state.

Since 1993, voters preferred the parliamentary left by giving them a mandate for rule. One of the factors that account for successive left victories was the failure of the opposition to fight unitedly against the most organized left. Nonetheless, one cannot undermine the sincerity of the left radicals in pursuing pro-people goals when in power, which explains the successive victories of the CPI (M)-led Front in Tripura. As Table 3.1 confirms, besides two terms of five years each, the parliamentary left has remained in power in Tripura since its inception as a constituent Indian state in 1972.

Table 3.1 reveals that not only has the Left Front increased its tally over its 2008 numerical strength, it has also enhanced its share of votes from 51 to 52 per cent which is a significant increase in a north-eastern state not entirely free from insurgency. The result is identical in the case of the national Lok Sabha poll since 1996. When the electorate almost rejected the parliamentary left in Kerala and West Bengal, in Tripura, there was hardly a crack in its social base: the left has held its bastion by winning two parliament seats in six successive Lok Sabha polls since 1996. A glance at the results of the state assembly elections also confirms the argument that the left support base remains solid and stable which helped the left radicals win the elections uninterruptedly since 1983 except in 1988 when the Congress captured power in alliance with the Tripura Upajati Samiti, as Table 3.2 illustrates.

Table 3.2 is self-explanatory. Over a period of time, not only have the left radicals developed organic roots in Tripura, they have also created circumstances by dint of their commitment to the underprivileged regardless of ideological preferences in which the opposition hardly remains a force to be reckoned with. The election results also prove beyond doubt that ethnic division never became a serious issue in elections except perhaps in 1988 when the Upajati Samiti managed to sway a section of the Tripura voters by reference to their ethnic

Table 3.1 Duration of the government

Duration of the government	Political parties/alliance
1972–7	Indian National Congress (41/60)
1977–83	Left Front (54/60)
1983–8	Left Front (39/60)
1988–93	Indian National Congress and Tripura Upajati Juba Samiti (31/60)
1993–8	Left Front (44/60)
1998–2003	Left Front (41/60)
2003–8	Left Front (41/60)
2008–13	Left Front (49/60)
2013–	Left Front (50/60)

Sources: for statistical input of elections till 2003, *Tripura Human Development Report*, Government of Tripura, Agartala, 2003, p. 117; for poll outcomes for 2008 and 2013 elections, *Frontline*, vol. 30, no. 5, 9–22 March 2013, pp. 1–2.

Note
Figures in parentheses show the number of seats won by the ruling coalition against the total number of seats in the legislative assembly.

Table 3.2 Performance of the contending parties in assembly elections, 1983–2008

Year	Left Front*	Congress
1983	39 (49.96%)	12 (30.51%)
1988	28 (45.82%)	25 (37.33%)
1993	47 (48.51%)	10 (32.73%)
1998	41 (49.08%)	13 (33.96%)
2003	41 (50.90%)	13 (32.84%)
2008	49 (49.49%)	10 (36.38%)

Sources: Prepared from the data, available from the Election Commission, Government of India, New Delhi.

Notes
Figures in parentheses show the share of total votes.
* The partners of the Left Front are CPI (M), CPI, RSP and All India Forward Bloc.

identity. That ethnicity is no longer a critical factor in political mobilization, especially during elections, is perhaps suggestive of the growing importance of class-based and ideology-driven politics in the state. This was no mean achievement in a state where ethnicity cannot so easily be dismissed since a section of the indigenous population always felt that they did not get what they deserved from the incumbent government led by the left. The trend continued in 2013 when the parliamentary left came back to power with a convincing victory in the assembly election while their bête noire, the Congress and its allies, was almost routed, as Table 3.3 highlights.

By winning fifty out of sixty assembly seats, the left radicals have proved again that they are invincible in Tripura in the foreseeable future. For the Congress party, it was a prestige fight as was evident in the poll campaign in which

Table 3.3 The results of the 2013 state assembly election

Name of the conglomeration/parties	Seats won	Vote share (in % points)	Vote swing since 2008 (in % points)
Left Front	50	52.3	+0.9
CPI (M)	49	48.1	+0.1
Communist Party of India	00	1.6	+0.1
All India Forward Bloc	00	0.7	+0.5
Revolutionary Socialist Party	00	1.9	+0.3
Front, led by Indian National Congress	10	44.1	+1.4
Indian National Congress	10	36.5	+0.2
Indigenous Nationalist Party of Twipra	00	7.6	+1.2
Bharatiya Janata Party	00	1.5	+0.05
Nationalist Congress Party	00	0.03	−0.07
Janata Dal (united)	00	0.02	−0.04

Source: prepared from the detailed constituency level results, made available by the Election Commission of India; *Economic and Political Weekly*, 15 June 2013, p. 79.

the members of its top leadership participated. By raising the issue of misgovernance, which resulted in discriminating against the local ethnic population, the Congress adopted perhaps a suicidal strategy which boomeranged and the performance of the Congress was the most dismal since 1983. The Congress lost about 8 per cent of popular votes which was translated into a massive loss of assembly seats in the 2013 election. For the left radicals, the thumping majority was also a testimony of the coming together of two conflicting ethnic groups, the Bengali migrants and the indigenous tribal population who constituted almost 31 per cent of the total state's demography. This was a noticeable change that led, as a commentator forcefully argued, to 'an environment of trust between the tribals and the Bengalis'.[1] By remaining connected with the local tribals in their daily struggle for existence, the left radicals strengthened the trust which has been translated in votes in successive polls. The election results also confirm the importance of Tripura Tribal Areas Autonomous Development District Council (TTAADC), formed in 1982, in which tribals were given constitutional rights for evolving plans and programmes for the development of their localities in accordance with their preferences. The principal objective behind the setting up of the council was to empower the indigenous people to govern themselves and also to entrust the tribals with the task of protecting and preserving their distinctive culture and traditions without interference from outside.

The parliamentary left has spread its popularity across the state while the Congress and its alliance partners have declined to a significant extent even in west Tripura where they had a stable support base in the past. This is a clear indication of the fact that, by adopting strategies for common well-being, the parliamentary left has not only created a base but also sustained it by consistently pursuing their pro-people agenda. The district-wise results of the 2013 assembly poll reconfirm the argument that the parliamentary left is an invincible political force in the state.

The analysis of the election results by district in Tables 3.4 and 3.5 shows that in three out of the eight districts in Tripura, not only have the Congress and its allies been outvoted in all the districts, they were denied a single seat in three districts of Sepahijala, Khowai and South. It was only in the West district that the Congress alliance gave a tough fight to the left radicals, winning six of the fourteen assembly seats. The 2013 assembly election also reveals that the Congress base in the West district was no longer as stable as in the past when a majority of the seats had always been won by the Congress. Nonetheless, even in the context of the Congress debacle, the West district provided 60 per cent of its total seats in the newly constituted assembly in 2013.

Along with its geographical spread, the left radicals have also established themselves firmly among the various strata of society. It will thus be wrong to identify the CPI (M) as a party representing just the interests of the Bengali migrants at the cost of the local tribals. Besides the TTAADC, the role of the government in redressing the tribal socio-economic grievances paid dividends in the election; the Congress strategy of parachuting in the star campaigners did not work at all, as Table 3.6a–b reveals.

Table 3.4 Left Front's share of seats and popular votes, 2013 assembly election

District	Seats won	Share of popular votes (%)
West	8	48.6
3.5Sepahijala	9	54.0
Khowal	6	56.8
Gomati	6	52.8
South	7	59.0
Dhalai	5	49.9
Unakoti	3	51.9
North	6	49.2
Total	50	52.3

Source: 'General Election 2013 to the Legislative Assembly of Tripura', *Economic and Political Weekly*, 15 June 2013, p. 80.

Table 3.5 Share of seats and popular votes of the Congress and its allies, 2013 assembly election

District	Seats won	Share of popular votes (%)
West	6	48.8
Sepahijala	0	43.9
Khowal	0	34.3
Gomati	1	44.5
South	0	38.8
Dhalai	1	46.4
Unakoti	1	44.8
North	1	45.0
Total	10	44.1

Source: 'General Election 2013 to the Legislative Assembly of Tripura', *Economic and Political Weekly*, 15 June 2013, p. 80.

The story is identical: the parliamentary left outperformed the opposition in all categories of seats, its best results came from the reserve constituencies for the scheduled tribes. Out of a total of twenty seats, the left candidates succeeded in nineteen seats, failing in one seat which went to the Congress. Similar to the 2008 assembly election, the left had retained the same number of seats though it had enhanced its share of popular votes by 1 per cent in 2013 in comparison with its share of 52.3 per cent of popular votes. In the reserved constituencies for scheduled castes, the performance of the Congress and its allies were far more satisfactory since they snatched two seats from the Left Front which had bagged all eight seats in this category in the assembly election, held in 2008. The Congress success in two seats was attributed to the nomination of outsiders by the left in Radhakishorepur and Karmachhara constituencies which reportedly alienated a large section of the left voters and result was evident.

92 Parliamentary left in India

Table 3.6a Share of seats and popular votes, Left Front in 2013 assembly election

Categories	Seats won	Share of popular votes (%)
Reserved constituencies (scheduled castes)	8	53.1
Reserved constituencies (scheduled tribes)	19	53.4
General	23	51.4
Total	50	52.3

Table 3.6b Share of seats and popular votes of the Congress and its allies in 2013 assembly election

Categories	Seats won	Share of popular votes (%)
Reserved constituencies (scheduled castes)	2	44.1
Reserved constituencies (scheduled tribes)	1	41.6
General	7	45.6
Total	10	44.1

Source: 'General Election 2013 to the Legislative Assembly of Tripura', *Economic and Political Weekly*, 15 June 2013, p. 80.

Lok Sabha polls

While the left radicals were fighting for their existence in two of their strongholds, Kerala and West Bengal, the voters in Tripura remained loyal to the parliamentary left in the last two national elections, held in 2009 and 2014 respectively. Not only did the left radicals retain the two Lok Sabha seats in 2009 and 2014, they have also expanded their support base across various castes and communities. What is also remarkable is the fact that the parliamentary left has continuously defeated their rivals since the eleventh Lok Sabha poll, held in 1996. The uninterrupted victory is attributed to the nomination of local candidates in the election which was almost absent in Kerala and certainly in West Bengal where some of the candidates for the Lok Sabha constituencies were parachuted in from outside, which did not go down well with the local party organizers. Tripura has a strategic advantage, given its small size and also the fact that it had emerged as an independent state just four decades ago out of the struggle involving both the Bengali migrants and local tribals that created a bonhomie among those struggling for a common cause. It is a society in which everybody is connected with each other. This feeling of being connected seems to have given a sense of belongingness which always worked favourably in the election and also in crises when togetherness was a key to strength and also provided a sense of solidarity. The success of the left in Lok Sabha elections since 1996 is thus attributed to their sustained work among the people in the state. As Table 3.7 shows, by securing more than half the popular votes in successive Lok Sabha polls, the left radicals have not only trounced the opposition, but also sustained their popularity despite being eclipsed elsewhere in the country.

Like the outcome of the assembly elections, especially since 1993, the Lok Sabha poll results also confirm the extent to which left radicalism continues to remain an effective ideological alternative. The results of the last two Lok Sabha polls show that the CPI (M) candidates have always had a comfortable margin of victory in relation to their competitors. The Congress registered victory over the parliamentary left four times since 1951 while CPI (M) maintained its grip over the voters in both these constituencies by winning in successive Lok Sabha

Table 3.7a Results of the 2009 Lok Sabha poll (Tripura West)

Name of the party	% of votes won	% of swing in relation to the 2004 Lok Sabha poll
CPI (M)	60.14	−10.72
Congress	33.63	+17.63

Table 3.7b Results of the 2014 Lok Sabha poll (Tripura West)

Name of the party	% of votes won	% swing in relation to the 2009 Lok Sabha poll
CPI (M	62.61	+2.67
Congress	15.68	−17.95

Note
For the first time, the AITMC candidate secured 10.97% of total popular votes which was an impressive performance since, in the 2009 election, it had secured only 0.59% of the popular votes.

Table 3.7c Results of the 2009 Lok Sabha poll (Tripura East)

Name of the party	% of votes won	% of swing in relation to the 2004 Lok Sabha poll
CPI (M)	63.47	−3.07
Congress	27.47	+15.12

Table 3.7d Results of the 2014 Lok Sabha poll (Tripura East)

Name of the party	% of votes won	% of swing in relation to 2009 Lok Sabha poll
CPI (M)	65.58	+2.11
Congress	14.66	−12.81

Note
For the first time, the AITMC candidate secured 8.10% of total popular votes which was an impressive performance since, in the 2009 election, it had secured only 0.51% of the popular votes.
Source: Tables prepared from the data made available by the Election Commission of India. www.eciresults.nic.in.

elections since 1996. It is also striking to note that in the reserved constituency of Tripura East, the CPI (M) candidate, Baju Ban Riyan, had never been defeated since 1996 parliamentary poll; he decided not to contest the 2014 national election in view of his failing health. This also shows the individual popularity of a left candidate who reportedly sustained his base by being connected with the electorate in their struggle for existence.

A scan of the social base also reveals that, besides their geographical expanse in the state, the left radicals seem to have built a solid organizational base across various sections of society. The parliamentary left is now socially widespread; it has built a strong base among the scheduled castes and scheduled tribes in the state where the indigenous population plays a critical role in the election. As a result, the conventional charge that the left radicals represent only the socio-economic interests of the Bengali migrants does not seem to be tenable in the light of their growing popularity among the various strata, especially among the underprivileged sections of society cutting across ethnic boundaries, as Table 3.8 confirms by showing votes by community in the context of the 2009 and 2014 Lok Sabha polls.

As is evident, the left candidates have further expanded their popularity across various social strata while the Congress lost its supporters from among the Tripuri scheduled tribes and other scheduled tribes. Interestingly, the Congress loss was not CPI (M)'s gain because those who shifted their allegiance supported the AITMC candidates in 2014 parliamentary election who, by securing almost 10 per cent of the popular votes in both the Lok Sabha constituencies in Tripura, have also shown that they are likely to be strong contenders for these parliamentary seats. Nonetheless, the scene is pretty clear: the left radicals remain as invincible as in the past not only because of the fragmented opposition, but also due to their ideological commitment to the result-driven activities in a sustained manner. This is what explains the continuity of the left in Tripura

Table 3.8 Percentage vote by community in 2009 and 2014 Lok Sabha poll

Caste	CPI (M) (%)	Congress (%)
Upper castes	64 (68)	26 (22)
Other backward castes	64 (64)	22 (22)
Rajbanshi (local indigenous people)	62 (70)	34 (28)
Other scheduled castes	72 (74)	22 (18)
Tripuri scheduled tribes	69 (68)	29 (14)
Other scheduled tribes	39 (41)	51 (38)
Others	60 (60)	37 (35)

Source: For data for 2009 Lok Sabha poll, Sukhendu Debbarma and Mousami Debbarma, 'Fifth victory in a row for CPI (M) in Tripura', *Economic and Political Weekly*, 26 September 2009, p. 173; the 2014 data are drawn from the website of the Election Commission of India: www.eciresults.nic.in.

Note
Figures in parentheses show the proportion in 2014 Lok Sabha poll calculated from local sources and the data made available by the Election Commission of India on its website, www.eciresults.nic.in.

in contrast with their ignominious failure in West Bengal and Kerala despite the electoral wave in favour of the BJP led by Narendra Modi which finally led to its landslide victory in the 2014 Lok Sabha poll.

Explaining the poll outcome

Undoubtedly, the parliamentary left is well entrenched in this tiny north-eastern state of India. What accounts for the success was the ability of the left radicals to bring about peace in a strife-torn state, like Tripura by building 'trust between the tribals and the Bengalis'.[2] This was not a mean achievement in the context of the terrible devastation in north-east India due to violent ethnic rivalries. While explaining the increasing popularity of the left in Tripura, a CPI (M) activist holding an important position in the party hierarchy thus argues that by following 'a three-pronged approach', it was possible to not only contain the insurgency, but also to consolidate the left in Tripura. The three-pronged approach is a creative blending of political means with coercive and institutional measures: in order to counter militancy, the left radicals were engaged in debates and discussions with the tribal insurgent groups to expose the limitation of their campaign when the state was ready to address their genuine socio-economic grievances; as a second part of the approach, the left government undertook coercive methods to combat the militants by deploying the para-military forces against them; and the third part of the approach was the creation of the TTAADC in 1982 which was made a powerful institutional forum for the tribals to govern in accordance with their own traditions with the support of the state government.[3] This approach yielded positive results. Militancy was significantly quelled. In the process, the tribals had an institutionalized forum of governance which allowed them to remain connected with the government and also democracy whereby they became integrally linked with the decision-making processes. By taking care of the basic needs of people in remote areas, the TTAADC gradually became very popular especially in those areas which were dens of insurgency. Besides the TTAADC, the left government took ample care in translating democratic decentralization in a true spirit. The state is divided into eight districts which are further subdivided into twenty-three subdivisions, and there are forty-five blocks which are the basic units of administration in which people from the localities elect their representatives to run the administration. In rural areas, *Panchayats* have regularly been constituted through democratic election which has caught the imagination of the people who participate spontaneously in local election to constitute the *Gram Panchayats, Panchayat Smaitis* and *Zila Parishads* (three tiers of governance under the *Panchayat* system of governance). By reserving 50 per cent of seats for women in *Panchayat* governance, the Left Front fulfilled the constitutional obligation that the Seventy-Third Amendment Act had bestowed. Two areas that had received utmost importance in *Panchayats* were health and education. With assistance from the Union government of India and also the state administration, these *Panchayats* play a critical role in providing healthcare to the rural populace. The scene is better in

Tripura than some of the Indian states, including the erstwhile left-ruled West Bengal, as Table 3.9 illustrates.

In comparison with the all-India figures, the situation in Tripura is better, especially in regard to infant mortality. This is evident if one's attention is drawn to the figures for neonatal mortality and under-five child mortality. In contrast with 39 per cent neonatal mortality at the national level, Tripura had only 33 per cent, and in case of under-five mortality, the figures from Tripura (59 per cent) were far below the all-India figure of 74 per cent during the 2010–11 period.[4] Similar to their endeavour in addressing the issue of health, the left radicals have also paid attention to improving literacy. The change is dramatic in just a decade: by 2011, the literacy rate had reached almost 88 per cent in the state which is better than the national figure of 75 per cent. The progress in literacy is uniformly distributed among the districts, as Table 3.10 demonstrates.

The figures in the tables are selective indicators showing the progress of the state in the last decade. What they reveal is the fact that Left Front government has brought about visible changes in both health and education which have helped build a solid support base for the left candidates who comfortably won in successive elections since 1996. The role of the political leadership was significant in sustaining the momentum of the government that the parliamentary left had been managing since 1993. By seeking to provide a corruption-free adminis-

Table 3.9 Health status of the people of Tripura (figures in percentages)

Indicator	Tripura	India
Birth rate	14.9	22.1
Death rate	7.2	5.0
Infant mortality rate	27	47
Total fertility rate	2.2	2.7
Natural growth rate	9.9	14.9

Source: *Economic Review of Tripura, 2010–11*, Directorate of Economics and Statistics, Planning (Statistics) Department, Government of Tripura, Agartala, p. 251.

Table 3.10 Literacy in districts of Tripura, 2011 (figures shown in percentages)

Name of the districts	Male	Female	Total
West Tripura	88.9	92.9	84.7
South Tripura	90.9	79.6	85.4
North Tripura	91.7	84.7	88.2
Dhalai	92.5	80.8	86.8
Tripura (total)	92.1	83.1	87.7

Source: Adapted from a table in *Economic Review of Tripura, 2010–11*, Directorate of Economics and Statistics, Planning (Statistics) Department, Government of Tripura, Agartala, p. 309.

tration, the incumbent Chief Minister and his colleagues have so far succeeded in consolidating a support base for the government which is relatively free from policy paralysis due to its organic connection with the ruled. This is what has contributed to the continuity of the parliamentary left even in the context of their failure to retain the base elsewhere. The most revealing description is available from the reminiscences of top government officers in the state secretariat who categorically mentioned that, by addressing the genuine socio-economic grievances of the people, especially the underprivileged sections, the present government of Tripura has shown how the governmental machinery can be utilized for meaningful changes in people's lives.[5] It was possible for the government to bring the militants to the mainstream also because of the success in projecting the image of the government as an instrument for ensuring the well-being of the people regardless of class, caste and ethnicity. The parliamentary left gave voice to the voiceless and their zeal for meaningful socio-economic changes consolidated the left social base in spite of well-entrenched ethnic division between the Bengali and tribals who constitute one-quarter of the total population. Here the left, seeking to champion the Gandhian goal of *Sarvadayo* (welfare to all), seems to have rewritten Marxism-Leninism by taking into account the specific socio-economic requirements of the people at the grassroots.

Concluding observations

Left radicalism is synonymous with good governance, as the Tripura story reveals. Being inspired by Marxism-Leninism, the left radicals have also shown how the state could effectively be utilized to bring about radical socio-economic changes. The leadership, despite being dominated by the Bengalis, seems to have been extra-sensitive to the peculiar ethnic texture of the state; it has also understood that militancy was fuelled by poverty which needed immediate attention. By creatively blending coercion with appropriate developmental schemes especially for those areas affected by insurgency, the parliamentary left contained the divisive forces in a manner which was followed later elsewhere in the country. In other words, Tripura has shown that militancy is not merely a law-and-order problem, but an obvious outcome of lack of development which needs to be addressed seriously to avoid further alienation of the affected people. In view of the ideological homogeneity of those in governance, it is possible for the Left Front to work as a unit while executing plans and programmes for development. The result was visible: while the parliamentary left is almost washed out elsewhere in the 2014 Lok Sabha poll, left radicals in Tripura have not only consolidated their social base, but also thrived across various communities. By being politically alert and socially sensitive, the parliamentary left has thus become invincible as an electoral force in a situation when its future elsewhere in India does not seem to be encouraging. The continuity of the left in power confirms that the key to success is not mere ideological beliefs, but the willingness and also the ability of the left radicals to translate them into practice by adopting appropriate schemes for development irrespective of discriminatory considerations. The government stands out for its distinct contribution to the mass well-being.

Tripura is not only a successful example of governance, but also an effective model of public administration drawing upon the fundamental ethos of social democracy. One of the biggest achievements of the incumbent Left Front is its success in maintaining a harmonious relationship between 'the indigenous people and the Bengali-speaking settlers and thereby helping the integration of the tribal population which accounts for 31 per cent of the total population of the state, into the mainstream'.[6] In his press interview immediately after the historic victory in the 2013 assembly election, the Chief Minister also attributed the successive electoral wins of the Left Front to 'the vigorous development work, undertaken by the government even in the interior tribal areas [that] has helped in countering the extremists with the help of the poor'.[7] Besides restoring peace, the left was also credited with empowering the tribals by recognizing their rights over forest produce; special steps were initiated to protect and develop their language, Kakabarak, by publishing school textbooks and dictionaries of the language which created a space for the government in the minds of the tribals. By recognizing and also seeking to retain the tribals' distinct socio-cultural characteristics, the parliamentary left sought to resolve the contradiction between class and ethnicity in a creative manner. The formation of the TTAADC represents a serious endeavour to create circumstances in which the aboriginal tribals will have adequate opportunities to develop themselves in accordance with their own distinctive cultural traits.[8]

Furthermore, the strategy that the incumbent government adopted to contain insurgency also paid off: instead of adopting 'an exclusive hawkish strategy', the government preferred a political solution which was translated into action by exposing the vacuous nature of the militancy. The organized campaign by the committed cadres highlighting the devastating impact of militancy on Tripura as a state resulted in persuading the local tribals to the idea that militants were not interested in development; their main objective was to disrupt the normal life for their own partisan gain. By building schools, primary health centres and roads connecting the remote areas with other towns and the city of Agartala, the government utilized state funds for visible welfare schemes. The state leadership, including the Chief Minister, Manik Sarkar, has an enviable reputation for probity. Sarkar, a son of a tailor and a government employee, is known as the poorest political leader in India; his frugal and simple lifestyle endeared him to the masses. So, by providing a people-centric public administration in Tripura, the parliamentary left reaffirms the importance of people in democratic governance. A CPI (M) activist thus exhorts that 'we may be a poor state with a lot of problems, but we recognize that our main asset is our people [and] it is in them that we invest our efforts and trust [which] will bring glory to Tripura'.[9] So, the parliamentary left in Tripura is not, at all, a uniquely textured political expression, but a reiteration of the fundamental ethos of liberal democracy by espousing the importance of people in its conceptualization and articulation.

Notes

1 Suhrid Sankar Chattapadhyay, 'The Tripura election', *Frontline*, vol. 30, no. 5, 9–22 March 2013, p. 7.
2 Chattopadhyay, 'The Tripura election', p. 7.
3 Prakash Karat, 'Towards a seventh left front government in Tripura', *People's Democracy*, 27 January 2013, pp. 17–8.
4 *Economic Review of Tripura, 2010–11*, Directorate of Economics and Statistics, Planning (Statistics) Department, Government of Tripura, Agartala, p. 320
5 Author's interview with top administrators in the state secretariat, 27–29 July 2013; these officers spoke on conditions of anonymity.
6 Chattopadhyay, 'The Tripura election', p. 9.
7 Press interview of Manik Sarkar, the Chief Minister of Tripura, on 9 March 2013; *The Hindu*, 10 March 2013.
8 Harihar Bhattacharyya and T.J. Nossiter, in their study of Tripura communists, have dealt with how the parliamentary left has sought to resolve the nationality question within the practical format of governance. Harihar Bhattacharyya and T.J. Nossiter, 'Communism in a micro state: Tripura and the nationalities question', in. Nossiter, *Marxist State Governments*, pp. 160–2.
9 The statement is quoted in Chattopadhyay, 'The Tripura election', p. 11.

4 Parliamentary left in West Bengal
The rise and fall of a hegemonic regime[1]

By concentrating on the distinctive nature of the parliamentary left in West Bengal, this chapter argues that it is difficult to provide a universal theoretical format to explain its growth and rising importance in India's democratic politics. This argument confirms the critical role that the prevalent socio-economic context plays in shaping a specific response. The trajectory of the parliamentary left in India thus hardly followed a pattern. Despite being broadly committed to social democratic goals, the left parties devised different strategies in different contexts. Undoubtedly, radical land reforms made the parliamentary left invincible in West Bengal and Kerala. It is also true that the left's failure to protect farmers' interests in the context of forcible land acquisition in West Bengal severely dented its social base that had remained stable till the 2006 assembly election when the CPI (M)-led Front obtained enviable two-thirds of the assembly seats. The aim here is to delineate the growth and evolution of the parliamentary left both in the overall Indian historical perspective and also in the specific context of each state in which it became a serious political force. By dwelling on the specific stories of the parliamentary left in West Bengal, this chapter will also focus on its distinctive context-dependent nature, demonstrating perhaps the peculiar texture of state-specific socio-economic realities in which ideologies other than social democracy do not appear to be acceptable.

West Bengal stands out because the parliamentary left ruled the state for more than three decades since 1977 when the Left Front came to power for the first time through democratic election by defeating its bête noire, the Congress. West Bengal also saw the rapid decline of the Left Front which lost power to a relatively new political outfit, the All India Trinamul Congress (AITMC) comprising dissident Congressmen in 2011, signalling perhaps a victory for democracy even in circumstances in which the left hegemony appeared invincible. This chapter has two broad sections: section I probes the factors leading to the consolidation of the left in West Bengal in the form of parliamentary politics; and section II mainly draws on the gradual disintegration of the Left Front[2] (the ruling alliance of several left and left-minded political parties which had been in power in West Bengal for more than thirty-four years) since the *Panchayat* election in 2008. From its phenomenal rise by clinching a record victory in the assembly election in 2006 to a near-routing in 2011, the history of the Left Front warrants serious intellectual introspection. Here several critical areas have been explored to decipher the sudden rebuttal of the left in West Bengal. This chapter makes three specific points while seeking to explain the rise and decline of the left in West Bengal: first, the debacle of the left in 2011 was anything but sudden. In fact, the signal, albeit unacknowledged, was there; second, though leftist organizational strength was often held responsible for the consolidation of the left in West Bengal, this chapter argues that organization alone can not sustain any regime for such a long time. Had this been the case, the left would not have lost so miserably in the assembly election in 2011 and in subsequent *Panchayat* and municipal elections in 2013 as there was no visible sign of receding left organizational strength in West Bengal in 2011. Third, the consistent downslide of left in consecutive *Panchayat* and municipal elections since 2011 should not be seen as the eclipse of leftist ideology in West Bengal. Rather, it would be safe to argue that the electoral defeat of the left in West Bengal may be a defeat for the parties and their infamous strategy of regimentation, but not the defeat of leftist ideology per se. If we take leftist ideology as a critical consciousness informed by equality and justice, it cannot die down. The occasional enamouring of the leftist constituencies and agenda by several non-left mainstream political parties, even after the historic defeat, is a case in point.

Evolution and consolidation of left radicalism

Unlike Kerala where the Communist Party formed the government, its counterpart in West Bengal became part of the ruling coalition, led by a dissident Congress leader, Ajoy Mukherjee, in 1969. The government collapsed in 1971 due to internal contradictions though it set in motion a new phase in India's political history, as evident in 1977 when the left parties attained political power in the state by winning a very convincing victory over the ruling Congress and other non-left parties. The election results from 1952 to 1971 indicate that the left was well entrenched in the industrial towns and adjacent areas. The Congress had strongholds in rural Bengal that ensured its victory. With the consolidation of the anti-Congress forces in the wake of the campaign against the 1975–7 Emergency, the situation radically changed in favour of the left in the state. Once in power, the Left Front government adopted radical agrarian policies to consolidate its support base in rural areas that held the key to political power because a majority of the state assembly seats came from rural areas. West Bengal had become the heart of 'parliamentary communism' that thrived due to circumstances in favour of the left parties. The continuity of the Left Front government in power in West Bengal for the last thirty years is a record not only in India but also in the context of electoral politics anywhere in the world. The reasons are not difficult to seek. Besides augmenting steady agricultural growth with effective land reforms, the left coalition maintained its strong presence in the state through a carefully managed organizational spread of disciplined left parties and their increasing mass base across the state. West Bengal is thus a unique example of democratic governance where political stability has not been the result of low levels of political mobilization,[3] but an outcome of sustained organizational efforts involving the stakeholders in both urban and rural areas. Parallel to the prevalent bureaucratic structure of the government, these organizations became facilitators for almost all public provision, from admission to hospitals to selection of beneficiaries in targeted government schemes. People, too, approached these organizations to settle private, even familial, disputes. It is therefore impossible to understand the durability of the government without appreciating the spread of the left organizations in the arteries of West Bengal's social sphere. While it gave society a sense of coherence, it also made the left – in its anxiety to be acceptable – socially conservative.[4] Nonetheless, it was the seventh time in a row that the Left Front had won the state assembly election since 1977; that itself was an exception in India's contemporary political landscape. The juggernaut of the Left Front seems to be unstoppable and the poll outcome was a continuity of the trend that had begun in 1977 when it captured power in the state for the first time. Besides almost completely destroying the opposition in the state, the Left Front constituents, especially its leading partner, CPI (M), had made significant inroads in Kolkata and other peripheral towns across various age groups. This election was a watershed in West Bengal politics with far-reaching political consequences not only for the Left Front leadership but also for the state that seems to have eschewed the orthodox Marxist state-directed development paradigm. In theoretical terms, the Left Front was closer to the West European social-democratic path, as some major policy decisions regarding industrial revival in the state of the newly elected government clearly indicated. This had not, by any chance, happened overnight. The aim of this exercise is to dwell on the changing nature of the Left Front leadership and its ideology which was not exactly the classical Marxism but its reinvented form.

Dwarfing of the parliamentary left

The parliamentary left is definitely on the decline, as the results of the 2014 Lok Sabha poll shows. The downfall is most revealing in West Bengal where the left radicals ruled the state uninterruptedly for more than three decades since 1977. What had begun in 2009's national election is further confirmed: the left radicals no longer remain as invincible as they were in the past. This is surprising for an ideologically well-knit group to have lost its grip over the masses so soon. Is this a decline of left radicalism or the failure of those left radicals who did not seem to gauge the popular mood under its hegemonic rule and, in the name of the masses, actually consolidated a clique for partisan interests? Interpretations may vary though the fact remains that left radicals have lost their appeal in West Bengal. Nonetheless, this is an occasion for introspection. As is evident, the wash-out of the parliamentary left from the grassroots is certainly indicative of the inability of the left radicals to sustain their base. This was undoubtedly an ideological failure, equally matched by an organizational vacuum that was responsible for the consolidation of dissent which was utilized effectively by the opposition to its benefit. There are two possible explanations for this: on the one hand, it shows ideological bankruptcy which means the intellectual limitations of the leadership to understand the new socio-economic issues in the context of the consolidation of neo-liberal ideological forces and to reap the electoral dividends by raising them, along with its failure to reframe its ideological priorities in the changed socio-economic milieu, so that left radicalism became almost irrelevant; on the other, the mass psyche which was never meaningfully addressed because of the weakening of the organization in view of the growing disenchantment of the cadres with the leadership. No effort was made, presumably because of the complacency of the leadership which felt that the effective land reforms of the past were sufficient to maintain the base even in 2014 when a new *Weltanschauung* gained prominence which did not appear to receive adequate attention while they prepared strategies for the election. The poll outcome was not surprising given the fact that the left radicals were believed to have taken the voters for granted even in the light of the consolidation of the opposition by a vigorous campaign highlighting the anti-people design of the left and the positive achievement of the incumbent government that trounced the Left Front in the 2011 state assembly election. Since the organization was no longer as strong as in the past, it was not possible for the left to match the momentum that the opposition had already generated over several months. In view of the instant popularity of the opposition in the 2014 Lok Sabha poll, in contrast with the left candidates, it would not be an exaggeration to suggest that the hegemonic rule of the Left Front, which has been ruthlessly partisan especially since the 2006 assembly election, not only alienated the genuine supporters but also caused massive disenchantment among the people who increasingly became assertive in their opposition to the ruling authority. This was a challenge that the left radicals had neither the intellectual capability nor the organizational resources to counter effectively. Furthermore, the declining importance of the parliamentary left was matched by the growing consolidation of the forces thriving on the mass disillusionment with the left. As a result, those who supported the left in the past came forward to strengthen the opposition that consolidated its base specifically by raising local issues which hardly figured in the left election campaign. By not adequately emphasizing the grassroots issues, the left radicals lost their support base in rural areas where the campaign for a secular democratic alternative never became effective in garnering support. This was therefore a strategic failure on the part of the parliamentary left which forgot that in the past it had gained mass support once it had addressed the sources of agrarian discontent by legally securing the rights of the tiller of the land. It was a revolutionary step in the early 1980s which made the left radicals invincible. A campaign around the achievements of the past is unlikely to give the same results in a new environment especially when the priority of the people has undergone radical changes while articulating their socio-economic preferences in the globalizing world. The downfall began in 2009 when the left lost its dominant role in the Lok Sabha poll. The leadership ignored the signals largely because of its overconfidence in its cadre-based organization which also, by then, had shown cracks with the growing disillusionment of its workers.

By taking stock of what led to the dissipation of the left radicals in West Bengal, the chapter narrativizes the evolution and also decline of the parliamentary left in West Bengal which was once a bastion of the left. The purpose here is to focus on the factors that contributed to its growth and gradual consolidation since 1977 when it captured power by defeating the Congress. With the arrival of the Left Front, consisting of political parties with left ideological beliefs, a new phase of governance had begun: it was an era of hope and aspiration which was guided by those leaders who had been through the grind in the trade unions and peasant struggles of the past. Ideologically well grounded and politically effective, these leaders helped build an organization to support their agenda when in governance. The result was obvious: the Left Front remained in power for more than three decades. By narrating the familiar story of the ascendancy of the left radicals in West Bengal, the aim here is to provide an analytical account by drawing on those factors which put the Left Front ahead of its political competitors. In a narrative mode, the chapter argues that what was evident in the 2014 Lok Sabha poll confirmed the processes that had their roots in the failure of the left radicals to remain connected with the grassroots. The chapter thus makes one major argument, supplemented by an assessment of the prevalent socio-economic and political circumstances in the state of West Bengal which underwent transformation as a result of the unavoidable consolidation of neoliberal values and preferences. In broad conceptual terms, the major argument of the chapter revolves around the predicament that the Left Front appeared to have been caught in, between the contrasting imperatives of adapting to the changing socio-economic conditions in liberalizing India while concurrently attempting to remain true to its traditional communist ideology and support base. The 2014 poll reversal also confirms that the Left Front has failed to address the changing socio-economic grievances of those of the grassroots. How the left radicals ultimately approach reconciling the contrasting imperatives remains to be seen. Despite the left debacle, what the 2014 epoch-making parliamentary poll confirms is the fact that democracy in India is organic in character and spirit.

Left radicalism has a long historical trajectory in West Bengal. As is shown in Chapter 2, left radicals became integrally connected with the trade union movements and peasant struggles in pre-partition Bengal; they also had a critical role in the Indian National Congress which accommodated some of their demands in order to expand the nationalist constituencies among the peasants and workers. Due to a peculiar unfolding of the historical processes, it was not possible for them to remain viable at the national level in post-independence India except in 2004–6 when the parliamentary left gave numerical support to the Congress-led coalition government at the national level for survival in case of a no-confidence motion against the government; their influence was confined to West Bengal, Tripura and Kerala. While in Kerala, the parliamentary left is definitely an ideological alternative, this cannot be said to be true with regard to West Bengal where the right-of-centre BJP appears to have replaced the left radicals, as the 2014 national poll outcome evinces. The situation is relatively stable in Tripura where the Left Front retained its tally of two seats despite the wave in favour of the BJP in the sixteenth Lok Sabha election, held in 2014. The rise and fall of left radicalism in West Bengal are indicative of the critical role of the organization in sustaining left radicalism: as long as the organization was strong, the parliamentary left remained unassailable, and its downfall started with its weakening in the state. This has been historically proved. One of the reasons for the decline of the Congress Party in the state was certainly the weakening of its organization following the breakdown of the Congress system of the earlier days. A contrasting example of the Left Front that rose to prominence and remained so for more than three decades since 1977 also shows the critical importance of the organization in sustaining and also consolidating its position in the state. The leading partner of the Left Front, CPI (M), never lost its hegemony in the Left Front presumably because it regularly reinvented its ideology by taking into account the changing social, economic and political circumstances. With its well-entrenched organization across the length and breadth of the state, it was possible for the parliamentary left to remain invincible for more than three decades. The fundamental point that comes out and is linked with the major argument is the idea that ideology, by itself, can never be a persuasive instrument unless it is backed by a cadres-supported organization with its tentacles spread around at the grassroots.

While providing an analytical account of the rise and fall of left radicalism in West Bengal, the chapter also draws our attention to the complex nature of India's democracy that always defies its classical description. By knocking out the parliamentary left, the sixteenth Lok Sabha poll firmly establishes that democracy articulates a voice which may not always be heard due to political repercussions in the state which also frequently witnesses vendetta by one group against another because of ideological differences. The role of elections in replacing one ruling party by another cannot thus be underestimated, though it is somewhat ironical that the Left Front, hailed as a saviour of the rural poor in the post Emergency era (1975–7) because of its large-scale land reforms which benefited the agrarian masses, had fallen out of favour with most sections of West Bengal society. If one goes by the 2014 election results, the parliamentary left in West Bengal seems to have been relegated to irrelevance, an outcome of a process that had begun with the victory of the AITMC in alliance with the Indian National Congress in the 2011 state assembly poll. The poll debacle is also illustrative of the declining importance of a political alternative that the left radicals pursued, in contrast with other contending ideological options. It is established beyond doubt that the clamour for development seems to have caught the imagination of the people across the country and the left campaign for strengthening the edifice of India's clichéd secular democracy did not seem to work at all. In the face of the BJP campaign in the 2014 national poll, the left radicals had run out of options when the idea of India was propagated, ignoring the multiple identities that seemed to have fractured the national persona: the idea is that we are first a nation and then Hindus or Muslims and so on. This is an indirect but powerful way of raising the point that being secular is not contrary to the idea of being religious. One can be a Hindu by being tolerant to Muslims and vice versa.

In the prevalent secularist view, religion per se is a taboo and hence it has no place in our regular discourse. In the perception of the so-called secularists, the argument runs that one cannot be religious without being communal. The whole majority, because of their specific religious identity, has thus become suspect in the so-called secular discourse! The outcome of the debate was evident in the 2014 election in which the left radicals, by championing the clichéd notion of secularism, lost to its bête noire, the BJP, which gained due to its tactful handling of mass sentiments against the pseudo secularists that yielded magnificent results. The radical left radicals had run out of steam largely because of its failure to comprehend the public mood in the changed socio-economic milieu. To the new voters, left radicalism, instead of being a creative alternative, had become ideologically vacuous. In an era of high expectation and instant results, the massive reversal that the parliamentary left witnessed in West Bengal was inevitable, given its failure to ideologically reinvent its approaches to the contemporary socio-economic and political issues confronting the underprivileged sections and also the middle classes in both urban and rural areas.

Ascendancy of left radicalism

The history of left radicalism in West Bengal can be divided into two phases: while the phase before 1977 was definitely a phase of struggle for the left radicals to establish themselves as a strong parliamentary force, the phase afterwards was the period when they not only held power in the state, but also consolidated their position in opposition to other contending political competitors. A glance at the poll outcome confirms that the left was far ahead of other political parties both in terms of the number of seats in the state legislature and the share of popular votes. The results also establish that the Left Front became increasingly popular to the extent of being unassailable by the 1990s, as Table 4.1 shows.

As Table 4.1 indicates, the left conglomeration enhanced its vote share in successive elections from 1996, though its share of seats dwindled in the 2001 assembly election. The left became invincible, though the most spectacular win was in 1987 when the Left Front won in 251 out of 294 constituencies and its leading partner, CPI (M), captured 187 assembly seats. Nonetheless, the 2006 assembly election stands out for two reasons: while it reconfirmed once again

Table 4.1 Seats and share of votes

Name of the conglomeration	1996	2001	2006
Left Front	203 (46.7)	199 (48.9)	235 (50.5)
Trinamul-led Alliance		60 (38.9)	30 (28.5)

Source, *Ananda Bazar Patrika*, 12 May 2006 and *The Telegraph*, 13 May 2006.

Note
Figures in parentheses show the percentage of votes obtained by the Left Front constituents.

the popularity of the Left Front in the state, it also established in power that section of the parliamentary left which was favourably inclined towards neo-liberal economic reforms for development and growth. The opposition was almost routed and the left radicals began another five-year stint in governance in West Bengal with two-thirds members in the assembly, as Table 4.2 illustrates.

Table 4.2 confirms not only the popularity of the parliamentary left but also the inability of the opposition to sway the masses in their favour. The left became unassailable largely because of the pro-people steps that the Left Front government undertook while in governance. Besides being backed by an organization, the ideology-driven parliamentary left utilized the government machinery to bring about radical changes in rural areas involving the hitherto peripheral sections of society in governance. Seeking to ameliorate the conditions of the rural poor, the left radicals were always insistent on radical agrarian reforms. Once in power in 1977, they had an opportunity to translate their ideological mission through specific legal directions. Although the left government failed to achieve what it proposed for the landless poor, it nonetheless adopted legal means, in the shape of Operation Barga, to formally recognize the rights of sharecroppers over the land that they tilled. This was a revolutionary step since it legalized the rights of the sharecroppers in a state where the proportion of absentee landlords was quite high. Before the acceptance of the Operation Barga, sharecroppers had rights over their share of the output, but, in practice, these rights were mostly denied, and in the absence of a clear legal

Table 4.2 The 2006 West Bengal assembly results

Parties	Seats won 2001	Seats won 2006	Percentage of votes, 2001	Percentage of votes, 2006
Left Front	*199*	*235*	*48.4*	*50.2*
CPI (M)	143	176	36.6	37.0
CPI	7	8	1.8	2.1
AIFB	25	23	5.6	5.7
RSP	17	20	3.4	3.7
WBSP	4	4	0.7	0.7
RJD	0	1	0.7	0.1
DSP		1	0.4	0.1
Independent (Left Front)		2	0.4	0.1
Congress	*26*	*21*	*7.9*	*15.0*
Trinamul Congress	*60*	*30*	*30.7*	*26.3*
GNLF	03	03	0.5	0.1
JKP (N)	00	01	0.2	0.2
Independent	09	04	5.0	3.8

Source: Drawn from *The Hindu*, 16 May 2006 and *Frontline*, 2 June 2006, p. 6.

Note
CPI: Communist Party of India; CPI (M): Communist Party of India (Marxist); AIFB: All India Forward Bloc; RSP: Revolutionary Socialist Party; WBSP: West Bengal Socialist Party; RJD: Rashtriya Janata Dal; DSP: Democratic Socialist Party; GNLF: Gorkha National Liberation Front; JKP (N): Jharkhand Party (Naren).

stipulation, their grievances remained unaddressed. Operation Barga,[5] initiated and implemented by the parliamentary left, radically altered the situation. The new enactment not only guaranteed sharecroppers the share of their labour, but also established that their claim could not be dismissed at the whim of their landlords. This legal change, along with party-led mobilization, created and also consolidated a solid base for the left in rural West Bengal. This was a useful strategy that paid off in the election. The sharecroppers, mostly the middle peasants with limited land at their disposal for cultivation, usually employed a large number of landless agricultural labourers who thus depended on them for livelihood. Out of a symbiotic network[6] between these labourers and the sharecropper emerged a bond which was utilized during election to garner votes for the left candidates. So, a mere legal enactment helped the left radicals to create a constituency of support in the election. As the election results since 1982, when Operation Barga was made constitutional, confirms, the growing importance of the Left Front in West Bengal was largely attributed to the guarantee of legal rights to the sharecroppers who held respect and authority in rural Bengal.

The other equally revolutionary step was the drive towards decentralization.[7] Elections to constitute local government (*Panchayat*) were first held in 1978, earlier than in any other state in India, and have been held regularly ever since. *Panchayats* were never instruments of dominant rural classes in view of the zealous participation of the poor peasants and the middle classes who got elected to the *Panchayats*. This step, along with the implementation of Operation Barga, ushered in a new era of democratic participation of the masses in governance which was inconceivable in the past. Although *Panchayati* governance was the outcome of the 1992 Seventy-Third Constitutional Amendment Act, it was not effectively implemented in any other state than West Bengal which endeared the Left Front government to the people. On the surface, the *Panchayat* governance was undoubtedly a definite step towards meaningful democratization of governance; however it became an instrument of the ruling classes in view of the hegemonic presence of the parliamentary left in the state. Despite being democratic, *Panchayats* gradually became a ladder for personal gain in aggrandizement. It was thus pointed out that,

> [n]o doubt, there emerged a new generation of leadership in rural West Bengal ... there developed a new institutional structure, decentralized in form but still dominated by the middle and rich peasants. The agricultural labourers and poor peasants, though not in proportion, have their representatives in the new structure but their participation in the decision making process is still a far cry.[8]

Nonetheless, these two steps consolidated the parliamentary left to a significant extent and the opposition seemed to run out of steam in rural areas where the well-entrenched party machinery sustained the base, even resorting to coercive tactics against the opposition, if necessary. Undoubtedly, the unparalleled success of the parliamentary left in successive elections is attributed to an all-pervasive party machine that mobilized mass support by drawing on the achievements of the government in power. The consistent performance of the Left Front 'has [thus] a great deal to do with elaborateness, intricacy and discipline of the CPI (M) organization in its campaign to mobilize votes'.[9] The party machine was always proactive in projecting the achievement of the incumbent government. This is probably one of the factors that ensured the parliamentary left its successive victories. The machine became effective because, as an analyst argues,

> it coincides at its nodal points with a regime that wields governmental power [and] ... the campaign machine works so effectively because it works in tandem with a regime of development [which was unique since it works by] coupling developmental regime with the organized mobilization and reproduction of political support.[10]

The result was inevitable. The parliamentary left had captured the majority of the seats in *Panchayats* in successive elections, as Table 4.3 shows.

A mere surface reading of these results suggests that *Panchayats* represented true instruments of democratic decentralization though the presence of a hegemonic party machinery tells a different story. Those opposing the ruling party were reportedly threatened and were thus scared to contest elections for the *Panchayats*. It was therefore not strange that a bulk of the candidates were elected unopposed since the first *Panchayat* election, held in 1978, as Table 4.4 highlights.

As Table 4.4 shows, the proportion of those elected unopposed expanded dramatically as time passed by. By 2003, more than one-tenth of the elected representatives had won the election even before the election took place. This was perhaps indicative of the fear that writ large in rural West Bengal because opposition was hardly allowed to operate politically. On most occasion, those holding views opposed to the parliamentary left restrained themselves because they did not dare 'to provoke a situation in which they would face the combined wrath of the [party] cadres and police'.[11] As a result, the *Panchayat* bodies, instead of becoming a forum for democratic deliberations and friendly discussions, became

Table 4.3 Percentage share of the Left Front votes in the *Panchayats* and *Zila Parishads*

Year	Gram Panchayat	Panchayat Samiti	Zila Parishad
1978	70.3	77.0	71.5
1983	61.2	66.2	62.2
1988	72.3	79.0	73.5
1993	64.4	72.8	65.7
1998	56.1	67.1	58.1
2003	65.8	74.1	67.2

Source: Computed from the data in *Paschim Banger Panchayat Nirvachan Tathya O Samiksha* (1978–2003), Bharater Communist Party, Paschim Banga Rajya Committee.

Table 4.4 The number of candidates who won unopposed

Year	Number of seats uncontested	Percentage of total seats
1978	338	0.73
1983	332	0.74
1988	4,200	8
1993	1,716	2.81
1998	600	1.35
2003	6,800	11

Source: D. Bandyopadhyay, 'Caucus and masses: West Bengal Panchayats', *Economic and Political Weekly*, vol. 38, no. 46, 15–21 November 2003, p. 4826.

'synonymous with the elected popular bureaucracy'.[12] For the party leadership, it never caused alarm because it conformed to the Leninist principle of democratic centralism in which the party always reigned supreme as a vanguard of the people. Not only did the party remain hegemonic, its role in guiding the masses for revolutionary transformation was also considered 'most appropriate' in a transitional society, as it was officially stated by admitting that:

> democratic participation [does] not mean acting at will. It means the activation of *Panchayats* in accordance with the principles of and ideals of the party. The basic issue involved here is giving party leadership to *Panchayats*. This leadership consists of (a) political leadership and (b) organizational leadership.... The political leadership of the party is established only when people in their own experience, accept the political perspective of the party as their own. Even though decisions may be correct, they are not automatically translated into actions. We need to activate our activists and the masses for carrying out our decisions.... The party has a definite aim. Panchayat activities should be conducted in such a way that they conform to the basic goals of the party.[13]

The directions are evidently clear. The party could not be bypassed; the so-called democratic forums for governance remained subservient to the party's directions since this was the ideological mandate of the parliamentary left. The system was streamlined further by the institution of *parichalan* committees (guiding cells) in each district under the care of the district party cell. In order to bring the *Panchayats* under the control of the concerned *parichalan* committees, the CPI (M) state committee further announced that:

> [a]ll elected party members of *Panchayat samiti* and *zila parishad* will act under the respective committees. Generally the local and zonal committees of the party will look after the *gram Panchayat samitis*. The final decision at each level will be taken by the Parichalan Committee of the party, although the elected members of the party may offer views if they are not satisfied with the decision.[14]

What is revealing is the fact that the party-driven parliamentary left was determined to execute its diktat regardless of the consequences. So at one level, these *Panchayat* institutions became harbingers of democratic decentralization, while at another level, they were instruments of party hegemony which, later on, accounted for its downfall in West Bengal where it appeared to be invincible till 2009. In other words, it was ironic that the processes purportedly encouraging decentralization of power led to massive centralization of power which was justified as appropriate in a transitional society. The *Panchayats* thus ended up being instruments for political patronage and populist policies. This pervaded the entire system of rural governance which doled out favour selectively, ignoring those who genuinely needed support for their survival. As a result, the planning process got politicized and those projects were reportedly implemented which gave the party electoral dividends. There were innumerable examples to show that the *Panchayats*, instead of being true to the principle of democratic decentralization, were reduced to another governmental instrument to pursue the personal aims and missions of those party functionaries who captured these instrument of authority in rural West Bengal.

Despite the obvious limitations of a party-guided local governance, there is no doubt that the effective implementation of the Seventy-Third Amendment Act (1992) radically altered the socio-economic texture of the grassroots in rural areas. Unlike in the past, the *Panchayats* had notionally given the rural poor a sense of empowerment which was inconceivable in any of the earlier regimes. The left radicals had empowered them to feel that they were as much part of the society as their relatively better-off rural counterparts. Similarly, Operation Barga placed the middle peasants in better stead by guaranteeing their legal rights over the land that they tilled. Besides recognizing their rights which now became inalienable, the Operation Barga legislation also became an instrument for dignity and respect for those associated with cultivation which was also socially empowering for them. On the whole, the story of the growing popularity of the parliamentary left in West Bengal, a state with a long history of left radicalism, confirms the critical role of developmental strategies in creating and also consolidating a support base that paid dividends in election after election since 1977. The story also reveals how a hegemonic Stalinist party sustained the support base by intelligently drawing on those governmental schemes that contributed to the well-being of the poor and also by scaring away those who had dared to challenge the party in the saddle.

As is evident, the parliamentary left was invincible in the 2006 state assembly election. It was also surprising that the Left Front had won majority of seats in urban West Bengal which was unprecedented. What was new in the 2006 poll was the proactive role of the incumbent Chief Minister, Buddhadeb Bhattacharjee, the new face of the Front and a symbol of both change and continuity. His clamour for industrialization and investment for development attracted the new voters who were disillusioned with the Left Front that, by being village-centric, had hardly paid any attention to urban areas. The message that the new leadership gave, by focusing more on industrialization, urban infrastructure and the urban middle classes, 'kindled the hopes and aspirations of the new voters'.[15] The electoral victory of the left candidates in towns and in the capital city of Kolkata also confirmed that the slogans for industrialization influenced the voters to a significant extent. For the left leadership, the poll outcome was thus an endorsement of their campaign based on the demand for rapid and quick industrialization in the state to generate employment for the youth. The leadership was fully convinced that the key to the landslide victory in 2006 was the change of strategy by the left which had so far neglected the urban voters. It was evident when the incumbent Chief Minister declared, while sharing his blueprint for developmental schemes for the state, that 'the message that the people have given us with their verdict is that we must give even more importance to what we are doing and we have to succeed'.[16] In this press meet, he identified three important tasks that the Front had to accomplish to fulfil the expectation of the voters: first, to continue to accord importance to the agriculture sector because that is what sustains the economy in a big way; second, to match the improvement in agriculture by similar growth in the industrial sector which would be possible if equal importance were given to industrial growth and investment in industries which create jobs and also contribute to the state's overall economic growth; third, to ensure the overall growth of the state and also to take care of those who still below the poverty line.[17] Despite his firm commitment to socialism, that he is a pragmatic leader was evident when he mentioned that 'we cannot avoid liberalization because we live in a time where we have to work according to the market conditions'.[18] He was in favour of inviting 'private capital' for industrial rejuvenation of West Bengal because 'this is the mandate [which] the Left Front cannot ignore'.[19] He wass critical of 'isolationism' which was, according to him, responsible for the breakdown of the former Soviet Union. In conformity with 'the Chinese reformist ideology', Bhattacharjee never found any contradiction between the private or even the foreign sector and the state sector when the primary mission is to 'ensure economic well-being of the people'.[20] The strategy worked and the parliamentary left emerged the gainer in the election: as the poll results show, in greater Kolkata, out of a total of forty-eight seats, the Left Front increased its tally to thirty-three in contrast with its tally of twenty-two seats in the 2001 election, defeating the AITMC in as many as twelve constituencies.[21]

The 2006 electoral victory was thus a significant turning-point for the left radicals for two important reasons: first, no longer appreciative of the classical Marxist-Leninist line of thinking, the left radicals appeared to have internalized new techniques for survival in the neo-liberal globalizing world. To remain in power, they had to expand their support base beyond the traditional groups of the peasantry and workers. The dramatic victory of the parliamentary left in 2006 is illustrative of how the left radicals successfully adapted their strategy to not only expand their support base in urban areas, but also to show their willingness for rapid industrialization with private help for generating employment. Second, the 2006 win was also symptomatic of a clear ideological change that the left radicals had witnessed. By being less catholic, the left radicals in West

Bengal agreed to explore various other strategies for development; furthermore, the fact that they were rewarded once they changed their strategies also confirms how limited the appeal of classical Marxism-Leninism was in the neo-liberal competitive world. So the left radicals had reasons to celebrate, despite the risk because the campaign for private investment for industrialization did not seem to go well with those committed workers who felt cheated by the leadership and thus preferred to withdraw from party activities. Since the consequences of such withdrawal were not immediately felt, the event did not even provoke discussions at any level of the party though it was to become manifest so strongly in 2011 when the parliamentary left was completely routed by the combined opposition of the AITMC and Indian National Congress in the state assembly election.

Shrinking of space

Left radicals experienced a dramatic poll reversal in the 2009 national election, just three years after the 2006 assembly election. The reversal is striking, but not entirely unanticipated given the growing opposition to the Left Front since the last state assembly election in 2006 in which the Left Front registered a landslide victory, comprehensively relegating the opposition parties to almost non-entities in the assembly. In Kerala the ruling Left Democratic Front was reduced to only four seats in comparison with its 2004 tally of eighteen seats while in West Bengal the incumbent Left Front lost more than half of the Lok Sabha seats. For the CPI (M) the decline in West Bengal was most dramatic: from twenty-six Lok Sabha seats that it had won in 2004 election, the number was reduced to only nine, while the opposition comprising mainly the AITMC and the Indian National Congress increased its tally from seven to twenty-five, as Table 4.5 shows.

The decrease in the tally of the constituent parties of the Left Front and the corresponding increase of opposition seats could be regarded as 'a near debacle' of the former which is also reflected in the significant decline of their share of popular votes. What, in broad terms, accounts for the near debacle of the Left Front was probably the failure of the government to meaningfully address the

Table 4.5 Share of parliamentary seats and share of popular votes, 2004 and 2009

Year	CPI (M)	CPI	RSP	AIFB	AITMC	Indian National Congress
2004	26 (38.57)	03 (4.01)	03 (4.48)	03 (3.66)	01 (21.04)	06 (14.56)
2009	09 (33.10)	02 (3.60)	02 (3.56)	02 (3.04)	19 (31.17)	06 (13.45)

Source: for 2004 figures, *Statistical Report on General Elections, 2004 to the 14th Lok Sabha*, vol. 1, Election Commission of India, New Delhi, pp. 160–1; for 2009 figures, http://eci.nic.in/results.

Notes
CPI (M): Communist Party of India (Marxist); CPI: Communist Party of India; RSP: Revolutionary Socialist Party; AIFB: All India Forward Bloc; AITMC: All India Trinamul Congress.
Figures in parentheses show the percentage share of votes of political parties.

socio-economic grievances at the grassroots. As a former CPI (M) activist laments, 'despite constant warning, the CPI (M) leadership never bothered to take us seriously often "dismissing" our apprehension as entirely "overstretched" and also reflective of "political immaturity".[22] Nonetheless, the poll outcome registered left radicals' decline in the state which was evident in the vote swing: for instance, an 8 per cent vote swing against the ruling coalition in West Bengal cost them more than half of the seats they had won in the 2004 Lok Sabha poll while almost 10 per cent vote swing for the AITMC increased their seats from one to nineteen in the present Lok Sabha. The shift in voters' preference was thus quite visible. Interestingly, the issues – security in land rights and livelihood – that catapulted the Left Front onto the centre stage in 1977 seemed to have swayed the West Bengal voters in the 2009 Lok Sabha poll, especially in rural areas, in favour of the AITMC and Indian National Congress as against the ruling Left Front. In other words, what became critical in the victory of the AITMC–Congress combine was the successful application of the pro-people 'leftist' rhetoric to galvanize opposition against the parliamentary left.

The probable explanations

The outcome of the 2009 Lok Sabha poll was a clear testimony of the decline of the Left Front in West Bengal. This was most striking given its massive electoral victory in the 2006 state assembly election. While the key to the consolidation of the Left Front in West Bengal in the past was undoubtedly meaningful land reforms and decentralization, the decline was due to its inability to address popular grievances in the changing economic conditions of the state and the country. In the face of these changes, the Left Front failed to comprehend 'the new class equations in which the ethical stock of land reforms [and also decentralization] was fast depleting'.[23]

In 2006, the Left Front reduced the opposition parties to almost a nonentity in the state assembly by winning more than two-third of the assembly seats. Within just three years, the Left Front lost more than half of the Lok Sabha seats that it had won in 2004 parliamentary poll. While seeking an explanation for this 'near debacle' of the Left Front, one cannot possibly ignore the weakening of its social base since the 2006 assembly elections which was linked with the complete failure of the left radicals to gauge the popular mood, especially in the light of the their decision to grab land for private gain in Nandigram and Singur in 2007–8.

As was evident, the West Bengal voters seemed to have rejected the Left Front for its zeal for quick industrialization with the help of private operators. The trouble started with the acceptance of neo-liberal development policies by the incumbent Chief Minister, Buddhadeb Bhattacharjee, that gave credibility to the argument that the Front government was likely to drift away from the ideological goal that had accounted for a massive popular mandate in its favour in the past. With the left zeal for capturing large tracts of fertile land for setting factories and establishing SEZs,[24] the rural population that relied on the left parties for radical land reforms felt cheated. As a result, the left was increasingly 'perceived as an ally of capital's surging spree for primitive accumulation, for dislocating the close tie between labour and the means of production in the countryside'.[25] There was also the fear of 'ideological distortion', given the unassailable majority for the ruling coalition; in its closed-door meetings, debates broke out between those following the 'orthodox' line of thinking and their counterparts redefining Marxism, underlining the Trotskyite observation that 'socialism cannot strike roots in one corner of the country'. Furthermore, the opposition of the CPI (M) labour union, CITU, to 'economic reforms' from the very beginning revealed the tension among those who mattered in decision-making. In such a charged environment, the Front decision to allot agricultural land for factories caused serious consternation among those who lost their land and also those who derived sustenance from the land. Hence it was sarcastically argued in the local press that the Front tempted the majority by giving them Operation Barga and now they were deceived when the Front government was assured of its continuity in power in the Writers' Buildings (the state secretariat). The Left Front ignored them since it would hardly affect its political viability in the state.[26] There were dissenting voices questioning the orthodox Leninist-Stalinist method of running a communist party along conspiratorial lines that suspect every voice of dissent.[27] The schism within the CPI (M) leadership came out in the open in regard to the decision of its Politburo to withdraw support from the UPA government. The removal of the former speaker of Lok Sabha, Somnath Chatterjee, from the party because he declined to resign from the post when he was asked to do so by the CPI (M) general secretary, caused consternation particularly among those belonging to its West Bengal unit. This episode revealed that the left were not as united as was usually assumed. Their constituent parties never arrived at a consensus on the 123 Agreement with the USA for nuclear fuel. The chasm between the West Bengal unit of CPI (M) and its central committee on the issue of withdrawal of support from the government in 2008 on the nuclear deal had shown clear differences within the party which never got meaningfully addressed. So while the left radicals were handicapped due to an internal feud within the organization, they also lost their base to the AITMC–Congress conglomeration due to their enthusiastic backing for the grabbing of private land for rapid industrialization.

The 2011 state assembly election

What was seen in the 2009 parliamentary poll when the left radicals were trounced badly loomed large in the 2011 state assembly election when they were replaced by the AITMC–Congress combination in the state secretariat, as Table 4.6 shows.

As the table shows, the parliamentary left lost miserably and was replaced by the coalition of AITMC–Congress in most constituencies. Not only did the winning combination of parties register victory in a majority of assembly constituencies, they also enhanced their share of popular votes. Along with the

116 *Parliamentary left in India*

Table 4.6 Comparing the 2011 and 2006 West Bengal assembly results

Parties	Seats won 2011	Seats, won 2006	Percentage of votes, 2011	Percentage of votes, 2006
AITMC–Congress*	226	0	42.9	0
Left Front	62	235	39.1	50.2
CPI (M)	40	176	39.1	41.9
CPI	2	8	1.8	2.1
AIFB	11	23	5.6	5.7
RSP	7	20	3.4	3.7
West Bengal Socialist Party	1	4	0.7	0.7
Rashtriya Janata Dal	0	1	0.1	0.7
Congress	*42*	*21*	*15.0*	*7.9*
AITMC	*184*	*30*	*44.1*	*26.3*
Gorkha Janmukti Morcha	3		0.5	
Others	7	18	5.0	3.8

Source: Drawn on *The Hindu*, 16 May 2011; *Hindustan Times*, 17 May, 2011; *Ananda Bazar Patrika*, 16 and 18 May 2011; *Bartaman*, 18 May 2011.

Note
* All India Trinamul Congress (AITMC)–Congress alliance.

leading partner of the Left Front, CPI (M), the constituents also suffered electoral defeat in constituencies in which they had won in the 2006 assembly election. The rout was spread across the state which confirmed the shrinking of the left's support base. This is also reinforced from the detailed poll results from the districts which also show the failure of the left radicals to remain electable despite the presence of a widespread organizational network to support their candidates. Table 4.7 also illustrates the increasing importance of the AITMC as a parliamentary party that had neither the organizational backing nor able local leadership in recent past.

The dramatic poll reversal is an expression of accumulated mass anger against the outrages committed by the Left Front, particularly arrogant CPI (M) leaders, cadres and *Panchayat* heads in rural areas who ignored the genuine grievances of those allegedly belonging to the opposition camps. The writing on the wall was clear. The left radicals became discredited by their failure to halt the decline by adopting appropriate steps.

What significantly dented the social base of the Left Front was the anti-farmer land acquisition policy for industrialization. The decision to acquire land provoked severe criticism from within the Left Front, it also led to serious dissent within the CPI (M) which forced the central leadership to bring out a communiqué defending land acquisition as perhaps the only option to rejuvenate the economy. Justifying the transfer of land to private investors for industrialization, the central leadership defended the decision because it would surely create jobs and thus produce income for the state. As the state was debarred in the prevalent federal arrangement from augmenting its income by way of fresh taxation, the Left Front government had no alternative but to bring in private investment for

Table 4.7 District-wise West Bengal assembly election results 2011

District	Left Front†	AITMC alliance‡	Others
Bankura (12)	3	9	0
Bardhaman (25)	14	11	0
Birbhum (11)	3	8	0
Cooch Behar (9)	6	3	0
Darjeeling (6)	0	3	3**
East Midnapore (16)	1	15	0
Hooghly (18)	2	16	0
Howrah (16)	0	16	0
Jalpaiguri (12)	5	6	1*
Kolkata (11)	0	11	0
Malda (12)	2	9	1*
Murshidabad (22)	9	13	0
Nadia (17)	3	14	0
North 24 Parganas (33)	2	31	0
North Dinajpur (9)	3	6	0
Purulia (9)	4	5	0
South 24 Parganas (31)	4	27	0
South Dinajpur (6)	1	5	0
West Midnapore (19)	8	11	0

Source: Prepared from *Ananda Bazar Patrika*, 14 May 2011; *Bartaman*, 14 May 2011; and *The Telegraph*, 14 May, 2011.

Notes
Figures in parentheses show the total number of seats in the districts.
* Independent
** Gorkha Janamukti Morcha
† Left Front comprises Communist Party of India (Marxist), Communist Party of India, Revolutionary Socialist Party of India, All India Forward Bloc, Revolutionary Communist Party, Samajwadi Party, Democratic Socialist Party, Biplabi Bangla Congress and Workers Party of India.
‡ AITMC alliance consists of All India Trinamul Congress, Indian National Congress and Socialist Unity Centre.

industrial growth. With its acceptance of private investment, the parliamentary left consciously opted for a choice which, despite being antithetical to its ideological belief, was justified as perhaps the only realistic option to bring about development.[28] Critical of such 'an anti-people decision',[29] a sizeable section of the traditional supporters was reported to have walked away because of the crass insensitivity that the Left Front exhibited on the issue of land acquisition for industrialization under private patronage. For the opposition, it was a grand opportunity to mobilize the aggrieved sections of the local population who lost their land. The result was obvious: the AITMC reaped rich electoral dividends by leading protests against the land acquisition for industry. For the first time in three decades, the left radicals faced stiff opposition which was consolidated further by the mass discontent over the insensitive ruling authority. In the process, the anti-incumbency sentiments also gained ground. Instead of addressing the new challenges, the left radicals continued to support their clamour for industrialization as the only option for development in the state. There were hardly any serious attempts to understand the growing mass alienation in this changed environment. The leadership reportedly ignored the consequences of mass disenchantment with the Left Front especially in rural areas, dismissing it as a mere ripple, given the benefit of Operation Barga in the past.[30]

In the context of mass disillusionment with the incumbent government, the 2007 decisions to forcibly acquire land for a car factory in Singur in the vicinity of Kolkata and for the SEZ in Nandigram seem to have added fuel to the AITMC-led opposition in West Bengal.[31] Not only did these decisions alienate a significant section of grassroots supporters who were drawn to the Left Front primarily because of the radical land reform measures that the state government undertook since it came to power, they also consolidated the civil society activists, especially in Kolkata and its satellite towns. For the party activists, the land acquisition policy was suicidal for the party which came to power by championing the agrarian issues. As a bewildered supporter articulated his disenchantment, 'the only party we have known all our life is CPM. For years, we heard leaders spew anti-industry speeches. Now, there is a sudden turnaround. I don't understand.'[32] Bewilderment led to anger when the state police resorted to violence, killing fourteen protestors in Nandigram on the occasion of a protest march opposing the SEZ on 14 March 2007. Justifying the SEZ as the only effective economic instrument to 'reverse the process of de-industrialization', the Left Front leadership dismissed the incident as 'a stray-one, engineered by outsiders'.[33] The situation however took a radical turn when the Nandigram firing hogged the limelight and also caused a fissure among the Front partners. None of the constituents, including the three major partners, Revolutionary Socialist Party, CPI, and Forward Bloc, supported the government's uncritical endorsement of the SEZ. Describing the incident as 'unexpected, unbelievable and traumatic', the CPI squarely blamed Bhattacharjee for running the Left Front government as 'a government of CPM [sic] alone keeping the allies in the dark'.[34] Critical of land acquisition by force, even a former CPI (M) minister expressed disappointment over the Left Front strategy of quick industrialization based on private capital with large state subsidies without taking the landowners into its confidence.[35] The people's tribunal that looked into the 14 March police firing in Nandigram also came out sharply against the government by insinuating that 'the motive behind this massacre seemed to be the ruling party's wish to teach a lesson to the poor villagers by terrorizing them for opposing the proposed SEZ'.[36] The police firing on the innocent villagers was reflective of 'the arrogance of a party in power' which along with 'a massive wave of anger and resentment against the state government ... resulted in the unprecedented electoral debacle [of the parliamentary left] in West Bengal'.[37] This is reinforced in a survey conducted recently to find out what prompted the voters to oppose the Left Front. The survey confirms that 'higher dissatisfaction with local leaders in the left-dominated gram *Panchayats* and with non-local leaders accounts for the decline of the left in West Bengal' and there is also evidence to argue that 'the Singur–Nandigram effects diminish in strength in areas away from them'.[38] What is thus fundamental in the story is the fact that the left debacle was inevitable regardless of the Singur–Nandigram fiasco, in view of the lackadaisical party activists who, being arrogant of their acquired authority by being linked with the party's higher echelons, became completely alienated from the people at the grassroots. The 2011 election epitomized the disgruntlement of the mass of voters who expressed their dissatisfaction by casting votes against the incumbent Left Front candidates.

The situation remained unchanged in the 2013 local election. The electorate had handed 'a third consecutive defeat to the Left Front, led by the CPI (M)'.[39] In the 2013 election, the Front only won one of seventeen *Zila Parishads*, the same as the Congress, while the AITMC bagged thirteen of them, as the left radicals did five years previously. The poll outcome reveals that the share of the Left Front seats had shrunk from 68.7 per cent in 2008 to staggeringly low 24.8 per cent. The Front's loss was AITMC's gain, as it enhanced its share of seats from 16 per cent to as high as 61.6 per cent. The defeat was most glaring in the left citadels in central Bengal: Bardhaman, Birbhum, West and East Medinipur, Bankura and Purulia. Tables 4.8 and 4.9 show the results of the 2008 and 2013

Table 4.8 Results of the *Panchayat Samiti* election, 2008

	AITMC	Left Front	Total
Bolpur-Sriniketan (Birbhum)	0	24	25
Labpur (Birbhum)	5	19	33
Ilambazar (Birbhum)	0	19	25
Goghat 1 (Hooghly)	0	19	27
Goghat II (Hooghly)	0	24	28
Arambagh (Hooghly)	0	44	47
Khanakul (Hooghly)	0	36	39
Garbeta II (West Medinipur)	0	30	36
Garbeta III (West Medinipur)	0	21	26

Sources: www.epw.in-exclusives/2013-panchayat-elections-west-bengal-role-reversal.html; Kumar Rana, '2013 *Panchayat* elections in West Bengal: a role reversal?' *Economic and Political Weekly*, 30 July, 2013, pp. 3–4.

Table 4.9 Results of the *Panchayat Samiti* election, 2013

	AITMC	Left Front	Total
Bolpur-Sriniketan (Birbhum)	24	1	25
Labpur (Birbhum)	32	0	33
Ilambazar (Birbhum)	25	0	25
Goghat 1 (Hooghly)	20	7	27
Goghat II (Hooghly)	25	3	28
Arambagh (Hooghly)	45	2	47
Khanakul (Hooghly)	39	0	39
Garbeta II (West Medinipur)	33	3	36
Garbeta III (West Medinipur)	21	5	26

Sources: www.epw.in-exclusives/2013-panchayat-elections-west-bengal-role-reversal.html; Kumar Rana, '2013 *Panchayat* elections in West Bengal: a role reversal?' *Economic and Political Weekly*, 30 July, 2013, pp. 3–4.

elections to the *Panchayat samitis* from the district of Birbhum, Hooghly and West Medinipur and illustrate the complete poll reversal for the left radicals in the district.

The tables show the large-scale defeat of the Left Front in 2013 though it was a different story in 2008 when the slide was not so visible in rural areas. Reasons are not difficult to locate. The 2013 local election took place when the AITMC held power in the state and voters shifted their loyalty to the party in power, which is not unusual as the past precedent shows. The left radicals failed to retain their supporters, which also directs our attention to the widely hyped strength of the cadre-based organization that sustained the party for so many decades. In the changed environment, the party organization collapsed like a house of cards. One commentator noted that CPI (M), which has always been distinctive for its political organizational skill, 'appears to have been reduced to a timid organization, something foreign to its political culture developed through its being in power for more than three decades'.[40] The successive defeats are also indicative of the fact that the parliamentary left failed to arrest its slide since the Singur (2006) and Nandigram (2007–8) crises which instantaneously created a base for the AITMC-led opposition against the incumbent Left Front government. In view of the weakening of the organization, it was not possible for the left radicals to capitalize on the failure of the government in power; the voice of opposition was so feeble that it hardly had any impact on those governing the state. The defeat reveals that the popular discontent against the Left Front was hardly quelled. The voters expressed their disenchantment by switching over to the AITMC as perhaps the only option to get out of the party-driven authoritarian rule in West Bengal. This was therefore a comment on the abuse of the governmental authority by the party cadres who barely remained connected with the people at the grassroots. The outcome was thus not sudden, but the upshot of the long-drawn-out processes leading to the dwindling of left radicalism in West Bengal as an ideological force.

The parliamentary poll in 2014

The parliamentary left has almost lost its viability as a political force in the sixteenth Lok Sabha, as the 2014 poll results show. The decline of both the CPI and the CPI (M) has been most prominent: besides the dwindling of their vote share, they have also failed to retain the number of seats in the Lok Sabha to keep their status as national parties. The vote share of the CPI was reduced from 1.4 per cent in 2009 to mere 0.8 per cent in 2014 while CPI (M) lost almost 2 per cent of their popular votes in comparison with what they got in 2009. The CPI that had four seats in the fifteenth Lok Sabha has won only in one constituency (Thrissur in Kerala) and its ideological partner, CPI (M) retained nationally nine of the sixteen Lok Sabha seats that it had won in 2009. The set-back is most glaring in West Bengal, the traditional citadel of the parliamentary left since 1977. In the fifteenth national poll, CPI (M), the leading partner of the Left Front, had nine seats which was less than what it got in the 2004 Lok Sabha election; in the 2014 parliamentary poll, the CPI failed to win a single seat from West Bengal, and its big brother, CPI (M), was reduced to only two seats and was also forced to abdicate its space to the newly resurgent BJP in a majority of the constituencies. In the 2011 state assembly election, the Left Front, including its leading partner, CPI (M), lost to the AITMC–Congress combine with only a meagre share of sixty-two seats in the state assembly of 294 members though it had 235 seats in the assembly that was constituted after 2006 assembly election. The slide of CPI (M) seats was most prominent: from an enviable number of winning candidates (176) in the 2006 election, the CPI (M) managed to retain only forty seats in the 2011 assembly poll. Reports on the 2014 election suggest that they recorded a lead in a mere twenty-seven assembly segments: if an assembly election had been held in 2014, the left radicals would have won only in twenty-seven assembly constituencies. The vote share of the Front was now reduced from 41 per cent in 2009 to mere 29 per cent in the latest national poll, held in 2014.

What is most striking was the fact that the left radicals had reportedly lost their grip among the agrarian masses and also factory workers. The march of the AITMC was simply unstoppable in rural Bengal for a variety of reasons, including the high-handed behaviour of the left cadres in dealing with the genuine socio-economic grievances of the people at the grassroots. Except Raiganj in north Bengal and Murshidabad in the western part of the state, where the CPI (M) won, the left candidates were defeated by a huge margin by the AITMC candidates. In the industrial hub of Asansol, with a significant organised working class, the BJP won, the AITMC came second and a veteran CPI (M) activist managed to win an adequate number of votes to save his deposit. Even in Kolkata and its satellite towns, the parliamentary left was rejected by the voters; in the capital city of Kolkata, the pavement and slum dwellers, the street hawkers, and also those evicted to accommodate the ambitious urban development project of the incumbent government, deserted the left, as the poll results show. Despite attempts by the left radicals to blame widespread rigging by the AITMC supporters, the steady decline of the left since 2009 confirms that 'the real reason for the fall of the party is definitely a total estrangement of the party from its core constituencies'.[41] The left's loss was AITMC's gain; one should also not miss the point that the 2014 election also registered the firm arrival of the BJP on the political scene. The growing importance of the BJP was indicative of a visible change in the mindset of the voters who seemed inclined towards this north-India based party; the fact that the BJP no longer remained as orthodox as in the past might have endeared the party to the voters in West Bengal which had not, so far, endorsed a BJP candidate so enthusiastically in the past.

The slide that began in 2009 with the national poll continued unabated in the 2014 Lok Sabha poll. The left radicals seem to have lost not only their momentum but also their ideological direction, given their failure to adapt to the changed socio-economic environment in the context of the globalizing India. Despite the change of guard, the new leadership continued to draw on classical Marxism-Leninism without realizing that it had lost its ideological validity in the new milieu. By holding on to Stalinistic modes of authoritarian leadership, the left leadership never felt hesitant in applying the strong-fist rule while grabbing land for industrialization in 2007; the Singur and Nandigram crises could have been averted had the left radicals been sympathetic to the demands of those who lost their land because of governmental designs for rapid growth at the cost of the poor. So, it was a clear failure of the leadership to reinvent a meaningful strategy to take care of those new social and economic demands which were rooted in the transformed circumstances. The shifting of loyalty of erstwhile left voters and sympathisers was largely attributed to the anti-people image of the parliamentary left in West Bengal, especially in the aftermath of the Singur–Nandigram fiasco. Furthermore, the half-hearted land reforms through Operation Barga which benefited only a specific section of the peasantry did not enable the Left Front to expand their base among the landless peasants. As a result, Operation Barga, instead of sustaining the base in rural areas, created a schism among the farmers, and those who had to reluctantly abdicate their rights of eviction of the *bargadars* (cultivators) joined the AITMC to push the left out of power. If the government in power had continued distributing land to the landless farmers and giving them legal rights over land (*patta*), thereby making them eligible for financial assistance from the banks through creation of cooperatives, then the party could have continued to rule the state. But by pursuing Operation Barga which protected the middle peasants at the cost of the other sections in rural West Bengal, the leadership failed to carry forward their agrarian reforms towards their logical conclusion. As a result, the efforts of the left radicals to expand their social base were largely aborted when they were already dubbed as being partisan to the middle peasants. In addition, the plans to acquire vast tracts of farm land in Nandigram and Singur without really consulting the grassroots activists of the party were responsible for the erosion of the social base among the small and landless farmers which the party had created by dint of hard work over the last few decades. Landless peasants, the vast majority of whom are Muslims, were affected once the land was taken forcibly for the state's industrial growth. Muslims remain one of the most backward communities in West Bengal, as the 2005 Sachar Committee[42] confirms, refuting the claim of the Front government that it had brought about uniform development across the communities. It is clear that in the 2014 Lok Sabha poll, the Muslims, who constituted about 20 per cent of the state's voters, had almost entirely gone against the Left Front and, by extending its support base among the Muslims, the AITMC had won convincingly in those constituencies where Muslims were a critical factor in the poll outcome. By seeking to address their grievances, the AITMC supremo, Mamata Banerjee, the incumbent Chief Minister of the state, translated the Muslim support into votes in the 2014 election. It is ironical that she, by not acquiring farm land, not fixing urban land-ceiling and blocking multi-brand retail giants, had 'virtually hijacked the Left agenda'[43] which led to the AITMC landslide victory and the consequent ignominious defeat of the parliamentary left in the 2014 Lok Sabha poll. What was most demoralizing for the cadres who held the Front in power by their sustained hard work at the grassroots was the fact that 'the party seems to have lost its will to fight back'.[44] The decrease of the left vote surely confirms the popularity of the Banerjee-led Trinamul Congress which the organized parliamentary left failed to scuttle.

The failure of the left to retain its base in rural West Bengal seems to have exposed the weaknesses of the so-called cadre-based invincible organization of the left which was largely 'mythical' and also unnecessarily hyped in public eyes.[45] The avalanche of downfall that had begun in 2009 went unabated, as the successive poll verdicts confirm. Not only did the left radicals become politically irrelevant in the national parliament, they also failed to rejuvenate the party in the state that was likely to affect the future of the parliamentary left in India. Whether the dramatic downfall of the left radicals in West Bengal is illustrative of the decline of the ideology or the failure of those who remained incapable of reconceptualizing Marxism–Leninism in the neo-liberal context is difficult to answer. What it reveals is the fact that the gradual downslide of the parliamentary left in less than five years since 2009 is the outcome of complex processes that were at work in the state, cutting across communities, classes and various social segments. The rise of the AITMC is attributed to the left's failure to remain viable in the popular psyche; what has consolidated the AITMC grip among the masses, rather ironically, is its concern for those basic issues of human survival which the left radicals had championed in the 1970s while opposing the ruling Congress; the 1977 historical victory of the left established a regime that lasted till 2011 when the AITMC–Congress combination electorally slaughtered the ruling left by drastically reducing its numerical strength to just sixty-two out of a total of 294 assembly seats.

The left radicals failed to sustain their base and the result was evident in the 2011 state assembly elections and 2014 Lok Sabha poll. This is usually explained in terms of the failure of the left constituents to remain connected with the people; they no longer attracted supporters who were willing to work for them as cadres. As is evident from the reports that were presented in the 2012 West Bengal CPI (M) state congregation, they suffered a significant loss in a number of districts which were considered left citadels in immediate past. Table 4.10, showing the decline of members of CPI (M), is revealing.

Besides the lack of enthusiasm for membership in CPI (M) from among the people which is visible in Table 4.10, the decline was also noticeable in specific segments of its supporters, namely the workers and agricultural labourers who had previously remained strong pillars of its support base. Once the party became a hostage of the vested interests in both urban and rural areas, it was difficult for the leadership to halt its downfall. This was admitted by the party in the 2012 State Committee Congregation by referring to its failure to consolidate its appeal among the workers and agricultural labourers, a failure which is evident in Tables 4.11 and 4.12.

What was most disturbing to the State Committee was also the declining number of women in the local party units. Initially when the parliamentary left captured power, it was the women cadres who played a critical role. Even in sustaining its rule in the state, these women cadres also remained critical. Their

Table 4.10 Increase and decrease of CPI (M) members in the districts of West Bengal, 2008–11

District committee	2008	2009	2010	2011
Coochbihar	19,691	19,522	20,312	17,225 (−18.5)
Jalpaiguri	9,561	9,182	9,086	9,370 (4.4)
Darjeeling	6,945	6,531	5,911	6,602 (4.5)
North Dinajpur	3,909	3,690	3,859	3,654 (2.6)
South Dinajpur	4,474	4,813	4,622	4,948 (3.6)
Maldaha	9,531	8,981	8,825	8,607 (4.8)
Murshidabad	15,132	14,992	14,592	16,701 (4.8)
Nadia	10,032	9,323	9,030	9,287 (−2.3)
North 24 Parganas	22,220	22,285	20,875	21,045 (−0.2)
South 24 Parganas	14,740	13,423	12,805	13,976 (12.2)
Kolkata	23,117	23,578	22,730	21,281 (−1.6)
Howrah	16,521	15,648	14,889	15,461 (3.2)
Hooghly	13,296	13,949	12,764	13,559 (2..6)
East Midnapur	23,743	22,979	20,342	20,980 (4.9)
West Midnapur	32,228	34,438	34,829	34,291 (−1.6)
Purulia	20,428	20,500	20,229	20,925 (3.2)
Bankura	22,638	22,655	20,865	22,608 (0.3)
Bardhaman	21,276	21,130	20,528	21,348 (1.7)
Birbhum	12,923	12,257	10,980	10,123 (0.4)
Total	302,405	298,976	288,073	292,048 (0.5)

Sources: Adapted from the table, given in the draft notes for the congregation of the CPI (M) State Committee of West Bengal, 2012, District Committee, Kolkata, 16–19 February 2012.

Note
Figures in parentheses indicate the percentage of decrease or increase of members during this period.

Table 4.11 Decrease in members from among the workers in CPI (M) in selected districts in West Bengal, 2008–11

District committee	2008	2011
Jalpaiguri	1,172	946 (−19.3)
Darjeeling	1,706	1,287 (−24.6)
South 24 Parganas	2,435	1,961 (−19.5)
Kolkata	5,047	4,589 (−9.1)
Howrah	5,339	5,125 (−4.1)
East Midnapur	3,053	2,803 (−8.2)
Birbhum	911	728 (−20.1)

Source: Adapted from the table given in the draft notes for the congregation of the CPI (M) State Committee of West Bengal, 2012, District Committee, Kolkata, 16–19 February 2012.

Note
Figures in parentheses indicate the percentage decrease in the number of members in three years.

Table 4.12 Decrease of agricultural labourers in CPI (M) in selected districts in West Bengal, 2008–11

District committee	2008	2011
Jalpaiguri	722	621 (−14.0)
Darjeeling	439	310 (−29.4)
North Dinajpur	564	540 (−4.3)
South 24 Parganas	724	705 (−2.6)
Maldaha	785	575 (−26.7)
Nadia	1,192	1,149 (−3.6)
North 24 Parganas	1,907	1,524 (−20.1)
South 24 Parganas	1,957	1,376 (−29.7)
East Midnapur	6,298	5,282 (−16.1)
Bankura	6,924	6,694 (−3.3)
Bardhaman	3,830	3,790 (−1.4)
Birbhum	5,015	3,970 (−20.8)

Source: Adapted from the table given in the draft notes for the congregation of the CPI (M) State Committee of West Bengal, 2012, District Committee, Kolkata, 16–19 February 2012.

Note
Figures in parentheses indicate the percentage decrease in the number of members in three years.

alienation from the party was never seriously addressed, presumably because of the hegemonic grip of those party functionaries who did not seem to be sensitive to gender issues. The scene was far from satisfactory as the decline was evident in nine out of nineteen districts in West Bengal, as Table 4.13 shows.

The decline is most dramatic in the districts of Darjeeling, Birbhum, Maldaha, East Midnapur and North Dinajpur which always supported the parliamentary left in the earlier elections. That it had affected poll outcomes in both the 2009

Table 4.13 Decrease of women members in CPI (M) in selected districts in West Bengal, 2008–11

District committee	2008	2009	2010	2011
Darjeeling	1,295	1,211	1,081	717 (−88.6)
North Dinajpur	282	224	254	217 (−23.1)
Maldaha	861	614	662	621 (−26.5)
Nadia	1,392	1,301	1,223	1,289 (−7.4)
South 24 Parganas	1,624	1,548	1,278	1,370 (−15.6)
Kolkata	2,163	2,259	2,207	2,122 (−1.9)
East Midnapur	2,986	2,741	2,366	2,287 (−23.4)
Birbhum	1,173	1,103	926	803 (−31.5)
Howrah	1,894	1,812	1,763	1,770 (−6.5)
Total	32,466	32,389	31,743	31,666 (−2.5)

Source: Adapted from the table given in the draft notes for the congregation of the CPI (M) State Committee of West Bengal, 2012, District Committee, Kolkata, 16–19 February 2012.

Note
Figures in parentheses indicate the percentage decrease in the number of members in three years.

national and 2011 state assembly elections was evident in the massive defeat of the left candidates in these districts which always stood by the parliamentary communists in the past.

Explaining the decline

The decline of the parliamentary left in West Bengal began long before the 2014 poll debacle. The organization that made the left invincible in the state had shown signs of cracks which neither the leadership not its cadres ever recognized. For the left, it was more or less a foregone conclusion that the Left Front would recapture power in the 2011 election. Though the writing on the wall was clear, the left ideologues would never admit it, which was ironic for a party that had had its tentacles in every nook and corner of West Bengal. An analysis of how it was possible for the AITMC to replace the thirty-four year Left Front rule provides basic cues to understanding the phenomenon.

Rising party aristocracy

When Marx cautioned the working class against labour aristocracy, he had virtually no inkling of party aristocracy, which seems to have damaged the left parties that formed the Left Front beyond repair. A.K. Gopalan had expressed his apprehension regarding the corrosive nature of parliamentary politics as it had the potential to spoil party workers by indulging them in the seductive world of luxury. Gopalan wrote in his memoir:

> I found myself in an environment calculated to ruin a man. First class travel, comfortable chambers in parliament, a surfeit of money, magnificent quarters and a life free of heavy responsibilities – all circumstances favourable to a life of pleasure. Is anything more necessary to turn a man's head?... Communists like me who had suffered for want of a change of clothes to wear, for want of shelter for a night's sleep, for want of money to pay for our tea and bus fare, and who were scoffed at by the elite society, were particularly liable to be spoilt by this sudden onset of luxury.[46]

After thirty-four years of parliamentary politics, Gopalan's worst fear appears to be tragically true. From the central committee to local committees, aristocracy seems to have enveloped the entire party structure.

Decline of 'bhadralok *(gentleman)*[47] *political culture' within the party leadership*

The decline of *bhadralok* political culture within the party leadership also contributed to the degeneration of the left in West Bengal. The left party leadership in West Bengal has been known for its refined quintessential *bhadralok* culture. But of late, a sudden decline in this culture in the form of character assassination of the opposition leaders had its repercussion among Bengali society. Even the CPI (M) state committee in its special electoral analysis issue of *Party Chiti* (explanatory notes from the party) in the wake of the 15th assembly election in West Bengal has accepted it. The central committee document read:

> In the entire campaign phase a typical lack of humility was observed among the party leaders. The derogatory and sexist comment of a senior central committee member just before the second phase of the assembly election had serious repercussion among the masses especially among women. Our party cadres were equally embarrassed due to such comment. Though the state committee took immediate steps to condemn the comment, it failed to have any impact on the people.[48]

Rise of mediocrity in the party hierarchy

Merit was the basis of party composition of left during its formative phase. P.C. Joshi was among others who took the initiative to recruit the best talents from different academic circles. But of late in West Bengal, probably after the split between CPI and CPI (M), CPI (M) primarily relied on mediocrity for running the party organization. There were two reasons behind it: one, due to the split in the communist camp in India, most of the talented people decide to remain with CPI and consequently, the nascent party CPI-M had to rely willy nilly on the mediocrity; two, the mediocre leaders have always remained faithful and docile to their creator for the want of adequate talent.

Ideological bankruptcy

Sudden tactical shifts in the avowed ideological positions also cost the left in West Bengal very dearly. With the intention of putting the industry-starved West Bengal into a high-growth trajectory, the Left Front government wooed the big industrial houses so long forsaken by it on ideological grounds. Piggybacking on its unprecedented electoral mandate in 2006, the Left Front government shook off its ideological inhibition and began to negotiate with both national and international business bigwigs for investment in the state. However, barring a few occasional appreciations by industry people, such a dramatic turnaround in the ideological position failed to bring any credible change in the overall investment atmosphere. In fact, in a hurry to catch prospective investments, the Left Front government antagonized its traditional support base in the villages by adopting a pro-industry stand. The government's alleged role in the land acquisitions in Singur and Nandigram further deteriorated the left vote bank.

Fragility of the Left Front coalition

The fragility of Left Front was another factor that seems to have accelerated the decline of the left in West Bengal. However, it would be a gross oversimplification to consider the Left Front as a closely knit ideological alliance of several left-minded political parties in West Bengal. In fact, from the very beginning this alliance was marked by bossism of the single majority party, and mutual squabbling. Interestingly though, the constituent parties of the Left Front, despite occasional verbal exchanges, remained within the alliance. Even, the incidents of violent clashes were not rare. History stands testimony of it.[49]

Denial mode

The left leadership, thanks to being in power for an uninterrupted three decades, had grown an attitude of denying the signals of popular anguish. Though the party occasionally sounded cautions on the increasing gap between party and the masses, the party leadership at every stage seemed to be in a denial mode. For example, the comment of the central committee member after the unexpected electoral disaster in the *Panchayat* elections in 2008 was indicative of such a denial mode among the leadership. Instead of going for detailed introspection, which is supposed to be the hallmark of the left, that leader had gone on record characterizing the electoral defeat 'as grave mistake for which the people of West Bengal have to pay a heavy price'.[50] In addition to denial, the statement smacked of an audacious attitude of the left leadership in questioning the collective conscience. But the left leadership seems to have learnt very little from the recent electoral reversal. Instead of having introspection at every level of the party machinery, the party appears to have dodged any such attempt, even if that came from well-known party sympathisers and erstwhile party ideologues. Just before the 2014 Lok Sabha poll, the debate between the noted economist and the former Finance Minister of the Jyoti Basu cabinet, Ashok Mitra, and the former Housing Minister, Goutam Deb, is a case in point, where the party, in a desperate attempt to put a brave face on the serial electoral defeats in the recent past, reportedly disowned the critique as 'erudite quips'.[51]

Concluding observations

The meteoric rise of the parliamentary left in West Bengal was a testimony to the success of democracy in India. By exercising their franchise, the voters ousted the Congress-led political regime that ruled the state with an iron fist, especially after the imposition of the 1975–7 National Emergency. The success of the Congress was largely attributed to the chaotic rule in West Bengal that immediately preceded the 1972 Congress victory. It was not possible for the ruling party to sustain its rule as the voters did not seem to have been persuaded by its electoral pledge for welfare measures. The left ascendancy in 1977 was a welcome relief for the people of the state. It was an overwhelming victory for the left parties since the voters trounced the Congress Party by supporting the opposition spontaneously. In their election pledges, the left parties laid out a blueprint for effective governance to bring about radical agrarian changes by executing meaningful legislations benefiting the poor and marginalized sections of the population. This worked miracles, especially in rural West Bengal. The landless and those surviving as agricultural labourers came forward spontaneously to vote for constituents of the Front to seemingly fulfil their long-cherished goals.

As is shown above, the Left Front remained a significant ideological force in West Bengal until the 2009 Lok Sabha poll largely because it had brought about radical changes in the socio-economic profile of the state through significant land reforms and meaningful devolution of power by taking advantage of the available legal mechanisms and machineries for democratic decentralization. The overwhelming popularity of the parliamentary left had gradually shown cracks which the leadership either ignored or did not seem to pay adequate attention to, confirming the old dictum that 'power corrupts and absolute power corrupts absolutely'. There had emerged a parallel party-led administration to supplant the institutionalized form of governance at every levels of the government which was effectively utilized to weed out those opposing the party hegemony. The Stalinist iron-fist rule worked temporarily so long as the opposition was confined to a minority; however it collapsed once it became a general rule for the government in power: there was hardly a space for an opposition and the party became an instrument for self-aggrandizement at every levels of its existence. There were clear signs of the erosion of its social base which the party leadership never addressed meaningfully. In fact, it was also not admitted by the top leaders, presumably because of their uncritical acceptance of the partisan inputs of the local cadres that sealed the channels of communication from the non-party activists, but sympathizers to the left cause, at the grassroots. So, it was a failure of the leadership and also the inability of the organization to understand the changing mind-set that finally accounted for the left debacle in the state.

The quick unfolding of left radicalism in West Bengal is also matched by its quick disintegration in just five years after it had captured two-thirds of assembly seats in the 2006 election. The Left Front treated its electoral successes in the 2004 Lok Sabha election and the 2006 state assembly election as an endorsement for rapid industrialization. It took its rural support base for granted in its 'grand plan to seize large tracts of fertile land for setting up factories, establishing special economic zone [and] expanding urban territories'.[52] Yet, by attempting to procure land for factories or SEZs at any cost, the Left Front tarnished its pro-people image, including in the urban areas. Similarly, the new leadership that emerged in the aftermath of the 2001 assembly elections seems to have been favourably inclined towards disinvestment to reduce the fiscal burden on the already crippled state economy. In concrete policy terms, the parliamentary left endorsed the principle of closing down the non-viable public sector units and agreed to have joint ventures with private companies, taking as much as 74 per cent of the shares in them. Not only is this a radical shift from the familiar ideological position of the Left Front government, this is also an indication of a consequential change underlining probably the decline of the so-called 'old guard' who insist on ideological purity even at the cost of losing significant constituencies of support. The outcome was that the parliamentary communists who caught the imagination of the people not so long ago lost their credibility to a significant extent. The simmering discontent spurred the 2009 Lok Sabha election poll debacle in the face of an emboldened and united AITMC–Congress electoral alliance that reaped the benefit of the estrangement of the left radicals from the people.

In the end, it was an Orwellian truth that resurfaced with the decline of the parliamentary left following the consolidation of the forces, opposed to its hegemonic politics. The tight Napoleonic control of the animal farm was ephemeral since it was coercive and brutal and the plot was eventually exposed. In a similar vein, the pace of the decline of the left in West Bengal was as dramatic as its rise in the 1970s following the withdrawal of the 1975–7 Emergency. The left parties became victims of their ideological bankruptcy: on the one hand, they abdicated classical Marxism in favour of Bernsteinian revisionism which was considered politically correct in a transitional society like India, but, on the other, they had behaved, rather strangely, in an authoritarian Stalinist manner while dealing with their opponents. They thus became victims of their own folly by not being adequately sensitive to the democratic ethos that had evolved in India out of the struggles that people had, in a sustained manner, waged to protect their basic democratic rights. This is an irony because by neglecting people as it protected the left temporarily, the left in West Bengal repeated the historical mistake that Napoleon made in the *Animal Farm*[53] by initially undermining and later finishing-off Snowball since the latter was the farm's conscience-keeper and was therefore undesirable for the fulfilment of his partisan aims.

Notes

1 I am indebted to my graduate student, Mr Arindam Roy of the department of Political Science, Burdwan University, West Bengal (India), for his inputs which were very useful in articulating my thought on the parliamentary left in West Bengal.
2 The constituent parties of the Left Front in West Bengal were: the Communist Party of India (M), Communist Party of India, Revolutionary Socialist Party, All India Forward Bloc, Revolutionary Communist Party of India, Samajwadi Party, Democratic Socialist Party, Biplabi Bangla Congress, Workers Party of India.
3 Atul Kohli, *Democracy and Discontent: India's growing crisis of governability*, Cambridge University Press, Cambridge, 1990, p. 267.
4 Dwaipayan Bhattacharya pursues this argument in his, 'Road to revolution: land reform to industrialization', *Hindustan Times*, 21 June 2007.
5 The best though slightly dated account of the redistributive programmes is articulated in Atul Kohli, *The State and Poverty in India: the politics of reform*, Cambridge University Press, Cambridge, 1987.
6 For an in-depth study of this symbiotic network underling the agrarian changes in West Bengal in a comparative perspective, see Ben Rogaly, Barbara Harris-White and Sugata Bose (eds), *Sonar Bangla: agricultural growth and agrarian change in West Bengal and Bangladesh*, Sage, New Delhi, 1999.
7 For details of the system of decentralization, Maitreesh Ghatak and Maitrea Ghatak, 'Recent reforms in the *Panchayat* system in West Bengal: towards greater participatory governance', *Economic and Political Weekly*, 5 January 2002, pp. 45–58.

8 Poromesh Acharya, '*Panchayats* and left politics in West Bengal', *Economic and Political Weekly*, 29 May 1993, p. 1080.
9 Partha Chatterjee, *The Present History of West Bengal: essays in political criticism*, Oxford University Press, Delhi, 1997, p. 141.
10 Chatterjee, *The Present History of West Bengal*, pp. 153–4.
11 D. Bandyopadhyay, 'Caucus and masses: West Bengal *Panchayats*', *Economic and Political Weekly*, vol. 38, no. 46, 15–21 November 2003, p. 4826.
12 Dwaipayan Bhattacharyya, 'Limits to legal radicalism: land reform and the Left Front in West Bengal', *Calcutta Historical Journal*, vol. 16, no. 1, January–June 1994, p. 86.
13 The West Bengal CPI (M) State Committee directives on *Panchayats*, CPI (M) State Committee, 31 January 1994 (unpublished), courtesy of the late B.T. Ranadive.
14 The West Bengal CPI (M) State Committee directives on *Panchayats*.
15 Suhrid Sankar Chattopadhyay, 'Left landslide', *Frontline*, 2 June 2006, p. 10.
16 Press conference addressed by Buddhadeb Bhattacharjee on 12 May 2006. *Ananda Bazaar Patrika*, 13 May 2006.
17 This summary of the press conference addressed by Bhattacharjee is drawn from Chattopadhyay, 'Left landslide', p. 10.
18 *Ananda Bazaar Patrika*, 13 May 2006.
19 Buddhadeb Bhattacharjee's press meet reported in *The Statesman*, 12 May 2006.
20 Buddhadeb Bhattacharjee's press meet on 15 May 2006. *Ananda Bazar Patrika* reproduced the views in its edition of 16 May 2006.
21 The figures are drawn on Yogendra Yadav, 'The opportunities and the challenges', *The Hindu*, 16 May 2006.
22 Interview with a former CPI (M) member of local committee in the district of Birbhum. He expressed his views on condition of anonymity.
23 Dwaipayan Bhattacharyya, 'Left in the lurch: the demise of the world's longest elected regime?' *Economic and Political Weekly*, 16 January 2010, p. 52.
24 Seeking to create an environment conducive for private business, the Left Front government adopted the SEZ Act in 2003, two years before it was accepted by the Union Government. SEZs are generally defined as specially demarcated zones that are exempt from various duties and tariffs by virtue of their treatment as a foreign territory for the purposes of trade operations. The scheme offers a vast range of economic activities including manufacturing, services, trading, reconditioning, labelling, repacking and warehousing.
25 Bhattacharyya, 'Left in the lurch', p. 52.
26 Bolan Bandyopadhyay, 'The left front does not require the poor peasants' (Bengali), *Ananda Bazar Patrika*, 7 September 2006.
27 Sumanta Banerjee, 'Beyond the debacle', *Economic and Political Weekly*, 27 June 2009, pp. 23–6.
28 Jurgen Dige Pedersen elaborates this argument in his 'India's industrial dilemmas in West Bengal', *Asian Survey*, vol. 41, no. 4, 2001, pp. 600–3.
29 In various district committee meetings, the land acquisition policy was dubbed as being 'anti-people' and hence was 'contrary to the fundamental ideological ethos of Marxism-Leninism'. *Ananda Bazar Patrika*, 7 July 2008.
30 The issue of mass resentment over land acquisition was never seriously discussed at any of the meetings of local or district committees of CPI (M). Those who raised the issue were shunted out by the dominant section within the party in a very thoughtful way. As a result, the party meetings became mere forums for discussion of those issues which were endorsed by the top leadership. The consequences were disastrous: not only did the party become an instrument of personal aggrandizement, it also failed to discharge the role of a vanguard of the people. The poll debacle in 2011 is thus attributed to the organizational failure to sustain the support base which was no longer as stable as in the past.

31 This discussion draws on my 'The Left Front's 2009 Lok Sabha poll debacle in West Bengal, India: prospective causes and future implications'. *Asian Survey*, vol. 51, no. 2, March–April 2011, pp. 290–310.
32 Author's interview with Haran Mondal, a Nandigram farmer, 29 March 2007.
33 Press statement of Prakash Karat, CPI (M) General Secretary, *The Times of India*, 24 March 2007.
34 Press statement of A.B. Bardhan, CPI General Secretary, *The Times of India*, 23 March 2007.
35 Press interview of Abdur Rezzak Molla, the former CPI (M) Land and Land Reforms Minister, *The Times of India*, 14 May 2011. While explaining the left debacle, Molla angrily stated that 'had they paid heed to my words earlier then we wouldn't have faced such a situation. I have heard that all big leaders of our party lost. He [Buddhadeb Bhattacharjee, the incumbent Chief Minister] cannot catch a benign snake and he went to catch a poisonous cobra. Industry is a poisonous snake and they did not listen to my words.' Molla retained his Canning (east) seat defeating his rival with a huge margin while his ministerial colleagues, including the Chief Minister, bit the dust.
36 Dipanjan Rai Chaudhuri and Satya Sivaraman, 'Nandigram: six months later', *Economic and Political Weekly*, 13 October 2007, p. 4103.
37 Dipankar Basu, 'The left and the 15th Lok Sabha elections', *Economic and Political Weekly*, 30 May 2009, p. 13.
38 Pranab Bardhan *et al.*, 'Changing voting patterns in rural West Bengal: role of clientelism and local public goods', *Economic and Political Weekly*, 15 March 2014, p. 62.
39 Praful Bidwai, 'The retreat of the Indian left', *The News*, 18 August 2013.
40 Kumar Rana, '2013 Panchayat Elections in West Bengal: a role reversal?' *Economic and Political Weekly* (web version), 30 July 2013, p. 1. Online at www.epw.in-exclusives/2013-*Panchayat*-elections-west-bengal-role-reversal.html.
41 'Fall of the Left', editorial in the *Economic and Political Weekly*, 7 June 2014, p. 8.
42 Headed by the former Chief Justice of Delhi High Court, Rajinder Sachar, the Sachar Committee was appointed in 2005 to look into the social, economic and educational condition of the Muslim community in India. The report was placed before the parliament in November 2006.
43 Suvojit Bagchi, 'Red star fading over Bengal', *The Hindu*, 15 April 2014.
44 Anita Joshua, 'The waning influence of the left', *The Hindu*, 15 April 2014.
45 Dwaipayan Bhattacharya and Kumar Rana, 'West Bengal Panchayat elections: what does it mean for the left?' *Economic and Political Weekly*, 14 September 2013, p. 11.
46 Quoted from B.T. Ranadive, 'In Memory of A.K. Gopalan', *People's Democracy*, vol. 28, no. 41, 10 October 2004.
47 *Bhadralok*, referring to those belonging to the upper-caste educated middle class, is a conceptual category that gained currency in the literature on the nationalist movement in pre-partitioned Bengal.
48 State Committee, CPI (M), *Party Chiti*, Analysis of Fifteenth Assembly Election-2011, 29th Convention 2011, p. 13.
49 Partha Sarathi Banerjee, 'The party and the *Panchayats* of West Bengal', *Economic and Political Weekly*, 14 June 2008, p. 819.
50 Bhattacharaya, 'Left in the lurch', p. 51.
51 The 'Turn Around' debate between Ashok Mitra and Goutam Deb, source: *Bartaman*, 17 October 2013, Kolkata edition.
52 Bhattacharya, 'Left in the lurch', p. 52.
53 George Orwell, *Animal Farm*, Signet, New York, 1946.

5 Parliamentary left in Kerala

Redesigning parliamentary democracy amidst ideological elasticity[1]

The communist parties in India were able to withstand the cataclysmic events faced by Marxist parties in many socialist states in the 1990s. Even after the collapse of the former Soviet Union, Marxism-Leninism continues to inspire resistance movements in India. The parliamentary left remains a powerful ideological alternative in three major states – West Bengal, Kerala and Tripura – of federal India. Of all these states, Kerala stands out since this is where the Communist Party of India captured power for the first time in the history of communism through democratic election. Besides resorting to the parliamentary path, the parliamentary left in Kerala has also shown how to run a coalition government comprising the left and left-minded political parties in highly diverse socio-economic circumstances. This is a unique experiment, showing how an ideology-driven government fulfils its socio-economic mission in a liberal democratic set-up. A look into the history of communism in Kerala points out three major challenges for the left parties forming the conglomeration of the parliamentary left: *first*, how the communists who were persuaded to pursue a revolutionary path of socio-economic changes adapted to the practices and principles of parliamentary democracy and a multi-party system; *second*, how the CPI and later CPI (M) defended their ideological faith in class politics within the constraints of coalition politics wherein non-left parties were also occasionally included. The third challenge of left politics in Kerala is how to remain viable in a left political front along with the pluralistic social left, which is a very recent phenomenon.

By concentrating on the evolution and functioning of the parliamentary left in Kerala, this chapter is an attempt to identify the possible factors that account for its organic growth in a milieu which was not exactly in its favour. The story that follows aims to draw out the distinctive nature of such an experiment which is both theoretically innovative and intellectually refreshing. The fact that the parliamentary left in Kerala always remains in the reckoning as a powerful political entity unlike its counterpart in West Bengal provokes a further debate when attempts are made to explain the phenomenon in one-size-fits-all format.

The importance of social movements in politics

In the first half of the twentieth century – the preparatory phase of contemporary Kerala politics – three kinds of movements were found to be crucial. They are caste/community-based social reform movements, the national freedom movement and class movements. Each of them has great imperative for politicizing social identities relevant to the political struggles, identifying issues and groups for political mobilization and defining the ideological perspective of various social and economic demands. All these movements held a worldview which was very close to the value system of modernity. Most of them resembled the ambitions of the modernizing western-educated middle class emerging as a social force from each and every community with varying strength. Probably, this common framework of modernity provided them with a shared opinion, but each of them was also divergent on many social and economic questions confronting the people. Nationalism, modernization, linguistic sub-nationalism, preference for democracy and self-rule over any other forms of government, etc. were the threads that united these movements though each of these ideas varied in strength and proportions in different movements. The contributions of the three types of movements are worth mentioning to understand the main currents of Kerala politics and society. All of them signify different phases of the slow and steady process of democratization of Kerala society, evolution of the public sphere, the politicization of social groups and classes and the setting of political objectives for the future. The gradual evolution of many left political leaders' careers shows their involvement in the three types of movement: beginning as social reformers, maturing through roles as national freedom fighters and culminating as revolutionary vanguards. Current Kerala politics is mainly composed of the remnants of various sorts of such movements of this period.

Social reform movements, otherwise known as caste/community movements, were relatively newer to Kerala when compared with similar ones in Bengal and Maharashtra. Even though the society was outside the reach of the pure *varna* system of caste hierarchy, the stringency of caste was no less here than north India. In addition to untouchability, the caste system in Kerala incorporated another barrier – the unseeability – between people of different castes. It prevented people from coming together to constitute a common public sphere. Humanism inspired by modern education and the slow process of modernization was gaining currency across the newly emerging middle class of that time. Under the leadership of the educated middle class, several movements were organized against the age-old ritualistic life, superstitions and many injustices related to caste hierarchy. All these movements, which will be broadly described as social reform movements, were mobilizing people based on their ascribed social identity, mainly against caste practices. Their impact cut across the higher, lower and middle castes of that time. The higher-caste social reform movements were inward-looking for reform, espousing, for example, an end to polygamy, the importance of widow remarriage and women's education, the abolition of intra-caste inequalities based on sub-caste, etc. The caste-based social movements from the upper, middle and lower castes, respectively Brahmins and Nairs, Ezhavas and Dalits, represented values of modernity such as equality, freedom, human dignity and equal social opportunity in their struggles. The lower- and middle-caste movements were more outward-oriented in their reformist project. They were the first to question the relevance of the caste system and the denial of opportunity for eligible people on the basis of their ascribed identity of caste. The modernized middle class remained most critical in all these movements for social reforms.

It is also important that there existed a great degree of consensus among the groups for social reform irrespective of their difference in focus. Besides consensus among the new middle-class leadership, the messages of their spiritual gurus were much more progressive when compared to the value system of the previous social order which was fortified by a forced consensus among the different caste groups for the religiously justified caste-based discrimination. At the level of ideas, there was a consensus that existed among the caste-based social movements. However there were hardly any concrete grounds for all of them to represent any common material interest in the economic and social life, mainly because of their different location in the caste hierarchy. This is indicative of the fact that the social reform movements paved the way for a modern Kerala which contributed parallel campaigns against discrimination linked with the prevalent socio-economic circumstances. In the course of time, this resulted in the rise and consolidation of competing social groups with specific political aims which also led to rivalry among these groups, despite their having more or less the same roots of origin.

Impact of the freedom struggle

The Gandhi-led freedom struggle remained critical in political mobilization against social atrocities, linked especially with the caste system. The Indian National Congress of Malabar took up the cause of lower castes along with the social reform movements following the Gandhian non-violence since the 1920s. In the 1930s, the Congress with the help of a vast number of activists and like-minded reformers took part in Guruvayoor Satyagraha (the successful non-violent protest to open up the temple of Guruvayoor for the untouchables). In spite of Gandhi's intervention and the participation of reformers from outside the state like the Dalit leader Periyar (E.V. Ramasamy Naicker), the movement was suddenly withdrawn when it gained momentum, due to differences of opinion among the participants. The Congress Party faced a real division inside the organization over the method of agitation. The moderate sections withdrew their support when the radicals (a majority of them became the leaders of the CSP and the CPI later) decided to picket the temple until it was opened to all Hindus. The Congress Party's wavering position as to whether or not to support lower-caste agitation and its vacillating stance towards the land question disenchanted a large number of young radicals who joined the nationalist organization to pursue their political mission.

In 1934, when the CSP was formed at the national level, based on an ideological division between moderate and radical sections within the Congress, a large number of youth in Malabar were attracted to the new outfit. The CSP activists and units under the leadership of P. Krishna Pillai, A.K. Gopalan and E.M.S. Namboodiripad spread the message of socialism all over Malabar with vibrant militant activities. This left leaning in the Indian National Congress of Malabar district was crucial for the future consolidation of communism in Kerala's northern region. The leftists were able to build their strong support base among the peasants and the working class in the industries. By 1938 the CSP in Kerala became in all sense inseparable from the CPI. The events of the 1930s in Malabar are thus important to finding out the root of left politics in Malabar and the findings are helpful to understanding the changes between the evolution of politics in north and south. Compared to the south, the north (Malabar) is noted for a leftward change which is reflected in those events such as a slow and steady transition of Congress into CSP and finally to CPI.

As Nossiter and many others remark,[2] various upper-caste Christian denominations, Nair Service Society (NSS) and Shree Narayana Dharma Paripalana Yogam (SNDP), were expressions of caste/communal rivalry which were slightly susceptible to national or class mobilization. The policy of non-intervention in the princely states by the INC caused a delay to the arrival of cross-caste/community secular organizations to Travancore and Cochin. When the Congress started its units in the two princely states after the Haripura session in 1938, the political terrain was deeply divided on communal lines. Nationalism in the south was growing as an assemblage of caste/community organizations at the initiative of the conservative leadership of Travancore and Cochin units of the Congress. In future democratic politics, the chances of success for left politics in south Kerala were mainly based on the weakness of its rival, Congress, to manage the political coalition of the major caste groups. Namboodiripad described the approach of Congress Socialists/communists towards the Congress state units in Travancore and Cochin in the following way:

> As for politics proper, the first political organization to be formed in Travancore (with anti-autocracy demand for a government responsible to the elected legislature) was called a Joint Political Congress. This was a caste coalition of three caste-communal groups – Ezhavas, Muslims and Christians. It was this organization which was got converted into Travancore State Congress. By that time, of course, the leaders of other communities (mainly Nairs) joined the organization in sizeable numbers. While the right wing congress leaders of Malabar opposed any support to the Travancore State Congress due to its communal character as reactionary organization. In Cochin also similar Cochin Congress was formed as a non-Hindu and non-caste Hindu alliance. The Congress socialists assessed the situation from a historical angle of class struggle. Analyzing the class character of Malabar Congress and the caste communal organizations in the South the socialists found that all of them were representatives and leaders of the rising bourgeoisie. The socialists as the representatives of the working class and equally interested in the struggle of the Malabar Congress against

imperialism and the fight of non-caste organizations against the princely administration were obliged to support the Congress movement in Malabar and the anti-administration agitations in Travancore and Cochin.... [They understood that] even though in the beginning the Travancore Congress assumed the form of a caste-communal movement, but its *essence* was secular and democratic. The demand for the protection of non-Hindus and non-caste Hindus from caste oppression was, therefore, basically democratic, even if, for the time being, it was couched in caste and communal terminology.[3]

However, the ambitions of the communists to promote class polarization within each of the communally consolidated groupings to build up a unified support base of the lower class from all the communities did not always work well, even though Namboodiripad felt that the socialists, as an independent political group, popularized a basic class approach, which was in fact the real political opponent of casteism and communalism and pitted the poor belonging to all castes and communities against the rich, cutting across caste and communal barriers.[4]

In the north, class politics following the secular national movement against the colonial state had a different trajectory than from the south. While the common people in Malabar were roused by ideas of Swaraj and direct action to secure Swaraj, the people in Travancore and Cochin seem to have been motivated by the demands of non-Hindus and non-caste Hindus for protection against the domination of caste Hindus. Except in the Muslim-dominated Malabar, where the Muslim League claimed control over the geographically concentrated community, in the democratic electoral competitions the left succeeded in forming political fronts based on cross-caste mobilization of the lower class, led mainly by the upper- and middle-class radicals.

The geographical differences in the caste nature of Kerala politics proved to be a more formidable challenge to the left parties than it was for the Congress. Besides the division of lower-caste votes, the cross-class unity of upper-caste votes in favour of the Congress was a source of irritation for the left seeking to garner support for democratic elections. However, the question of caste was important for the left political parties in deciding their candidates in elections. Probably the CPI would not have been very serious about it when compared with the Congress when deciding on the candidates and dividing the spoils after elections and government formation. Yet, it is important to point out that the left parties, in spite of their concerns for secular practices and the economic causes, were forced to argue for the proportional representation of caste and communities in their government and party organization. To put it briefly, in Kerala politics, the political parties, Congress and communist, which were formed during more or less the same period of the pre-state reorganization phase, were under pressure from the contemporary caste/community organizations though the extent of caste influence varied.

Ideological metamorphosis

Under the influence of modernity, changing patterns of administration and the emerging new economy, the old power structure of feudalism in the princely states started to crumble. In fact the consolidation of royal power in the two princely states went against the feudal power and wealth of the Nairs and other Malayalee Brahmins. The Travancore kings slowly avoided the help of traditional feudal lords in administration. They encouraged non-Hindu wealthy families to start business and commerce and invited Tamil Brahmins (who had no interest in power struggles inside the palace) to civil service posts. There were instances of the kings relocating Christian families and Muslims from rural villages to the newly built towns to start industry and commerce as part of their efforts at modernization. The feudal order based on the caste system thus faced a severe blow from many sides – collapse of feudalism, beginning of colonialism and spread of modernization, royal power consolidation, and above all, the rise of the educated middle class from every caste/community seeking to empower the lower castes by instilling values of socio-cultural awakening among them.

Simultaneously with the struggle against caste atrocities, peasants and workers had launched an offensive campaign for land rights and wages respectively. In certain parts of Kerala, the workers in plantations, ports, and the coir, wood and cashew industries established and managed by the colonial power and indigenous businessmen, also undertook effective campaigns. The peasant workers were organized by the Pulaya leader Ayyankali in Travancore. They called for the first known peasant workers' strike in Kerala for social dignity and economic justice. As was pointed out earlier, the recruitment of the downtrodden to the Congress and the emergence of a radical youth leadership helped the formation of the CSP and CPI in Kerala. In the words of Namboodiripad,

> the Malabar portion of the state at that time was under the powerful influence, political and cultural, of the British rulers, while Travancore and Cochin had no 'politics' other than the doings of palace cliques at the top and caste organisations below.[5]

The Kerala Pradesh Congress, which was formally constituted in 1920–1, was, for all practical purposes, a Malabar Congress Committee. Until the formation of the CSP in the 1930s the Congress followed a policy of non-intervention in the affairs of the princely states. When A.K. Gopalan undertook a tour in his capacity as the secretary of the first left-led Congress committee in Travancore and Cochin, the Diwan of Travancore put restrictions on Congress activities in his state. However Congress activities and the policies of the British raj were discussed by the literate public across the princely states.

Many communist leaders in Kerala emerged in the pre-state reorganization phase as social reformers, activists in caste organizations, and leaders of the INC and CSP. It was a common career graph for a majority of the first generation leaders of Kerala communism. Namboodiripad thus remarked that the emergence of class struggle in Kerala in the form of a political struggle for equality was not due to any systematic understanding of Marxian ideology or penetration of the idea from the outside. Until the 1930s Marxism or Soviet socialism was not a serious issue for debates among the intellectuals and in public meetings. Many progressive left activists who were engaged in social reform movements and national movements were convinced of the evils they had to fight out in their surroundings and when they were introduced to the thought patterns of Marxism, success stories of the Soviet socialism and rising unrest on the industrial front on the eve of the World War years, Marxism and revolution became the desirable strategies to establish an egalitarian and modern social order. Their affinity to Marxism was not a matter of theoretical or ideological attraction, but was a practical option to fight the moderate wing of the Congress leadership and the unwillingness of the caste organizations' leadership to reject the influence of the elite interests while they were negotiating with the states.[6] According to Namboodiripad, the novelty of class movement led by socialists-communists was its ability to bring together various social and economic issues in the form of a struggle against *feudal-janmi-landlordism*. It intertwined effectively the issues of caste and class and charted a path of social transformation. While the struggle for the modernization of Kerala society was certainly a positive trend, the prevalent social texture did not appear to have undergone a radical metamorphosis given the well-entrenched caste tilt in interpersonal interactions among the Malayalees.

Democratic politics in Travancore and Cochin

The roots of democratic politics are usually traced back to the period before the 1947 transfer of power from the colonial power. Travancore and Cochin were no exceptions. Besides the rising popularity and spread of anti-imperialist and anti-landlord movements the elections held under 1935 Government of India Act also helped the people of Malabar to be drawn to democratic politics of representation. Malabar had a Kerala Pradesh Congress Committee well before the other two princely states. The passing of the Malabar Tenancy Act in 1929, though it was very moderate in outlook, was instrumental for the leaders and activists in Malabar to think about the utility of representative democracy as a tool for change in the prevalent socio-economic circumstances.

Ideological fissures that developed in the Indian National Congress during the 1930s had made a decisive impact on its unit in Malabar. In 1937 the organizational elections re-established the non-left groups because many Congress moderates who had left Congress due to their differences with the extremists returned after the national leadership gave a green signal for contesting the provincial elections under the 1935 Government of India Act. They gained an advantage over the socialists initially in the organizational elections. But the volunteers of the Congress district unit of Malabar were with the socialists. This led to the decline of organizational discipline in the Malabar unit of the party due to the differences between the Congress workers who were following the socialist national leadership, and their provincial leadership which declined to toe the socialist line of thinking. In 1939 and in 1940 organizational elections in the Kerala Pradesh Congress Committee (KPCC), the leaders who represented both Congress socialists and the nationalist Muslims won.[7] The militant advocates of socialism and left extremism gradually expanded their influence in Malabar, which was not tolerated even by the pro-socialist national leadership. The KPCC, dominated by the left, was dismissed due to non-compliance with the principle of non-violence in 1938. The split came into the open when the left-led KPCC supported Subhas Chandra Bose against Gandhi's candidate, Pattabhi Sitaramayya, in the 1939 presidential election at the Tripuri Congress.

The dominance of the left leadership in the KPCC also helped the Congress to strike deeper roots among the masses in Malabar, mainly among the peasant population. Quite naturally, when they formed the Communist Party, the official Congress lacked mass support in Malabar which was garnered by the leftists through Kisan Sabha, trade unions and the progressive writers' and intellectuals' associations. Meanwhile, the Congress Socialists who led the KPCC of Malabar were officially supporting and popularizing the pro-people programmes and policies of the Madras provincial government headed by C. Rajagopalachari. When Subhas Chandra Bose resigned from Congress and started a new political party, Forward Bloc,[8] Abdul Rehman, the leader of nationalist Muslims and the then president of KPCC, joined his party. This led to the development of another left organization in Kerala, though it failed to gain any durable public support. Following this event in the 1940s, Malabar and parts of Travancore and Cochin witnessed a proliferation of left parties, such as the socialists, RSP and Kerala Socialist Party (KSP), that weakened the unity of the political left to a great extent vis-à-vis the Congress which thus gradually regained its lost strength based on the weakness of its opponents, mainly CPI, during the 1942 Quit India movement because of its withdrawal from the campaign.

Even though, during 1940s, the unity of the left had deteriorated, which was evident from the ideological differences between the socialists and the communists, it helped the rise of CPI as the most prominent and most popular left party for the future. The CPI, born in the aftermath of the maturing left–right divide in Kerala, especially in Malabar, was facing both opportunities and hurdles in establishing the party organization. Since the KPCC was dismissed by the Congress leadership, the communists and socialists were deprived of an institution to openly interact with people and to disseminate their views. The colonial apparatus was repressive towards them and the Congress volunteers, especially those in Travancore and Cochin, became police informers about communist leaders' underground activities. However, the decision of the communists to remain aloof in the 1942 Quit India movement enabled them to gain a legal recognition for the political activities in the open. This helped them to build up the organization and continue the propaganda against landlordism and the effects of war on the working class, mainly in Malabar.

Electoral politics in Malabar, 1947–57

When India became independent in 1947 and the colonial authority transferred power to the interim government, Malabar became part of the Indian Union. The communists were involved in organizing armed rebellion against the state while the Congress and Socialists found the democratic state an effective instrument for nation building. There was little possibility for the Muslim League in Malabar to join Pakistan. The ultra-loyalists and the rich people among the Muslims migrated to Pakistan, though their number was meagre. In October 1951, a special committee of the CPI adopted the party programme and statement of policy and decided to fight elections in democratic politics.

The first general election held in independent India in 1951–2 saw a spectacular victory for the non-Congress parties in the assembly seats in Madras state. The Congress won only four out of thirty seats. The alliance of CPI and Kishan Mazdoor Praja Party (KMPP)[9] founded by a group of ex-Congress socialists won fifteen seats[10] and the Muslim League and Socialist Party won the rest of the seats. In Travancore–Cochin, Andhra districts of Madras and the state of Hyderabad, West Bengal and Tripura, communists defeated Congress in large numbers of seats. In the opinion of Namboodiripad, for a party that had been politically isolated from the anti-imperialist masses during the Quit India struggle and whose organization was weakened and divided after the second party congress, this was indeed a worthy achievement. The Muslim League, which was not part of the left alliance, was against the Congress in Madras.[11] The Muslim League's communal politics limited the left's prospects in Malabar to a certain extent even though the national Muslims stood in alliance with the left against the Congress.[12]

In Madras, the governor invited Congress, the single largest party in the assembly, to form the government. The Congress was able to manage the majority with the support of independents. C. Rajagopalachari became the first Chief Minister of Madras. Later when Rajagopalachari resigned, Congress was able to secure the support from KMPP leader T. Prakasham (the leader of allied left opposition) and the Muslim League in the mid-term election after the bifurcation of Andhra from Madras. The KMPP leader in Malabar, K. Kelappan, switched his allegiance to the Congress. The remaining members of the Socialist Party and KMPP formed a new party called Praja Socialist Party. In 1953 the CPI fought alone in the elections to the Malabar district board. It won the elections and the party held the post of president of the board. It was the first administrative position held by the party through democratic election.

Electoral politics in Travancore–Cochin: 1948–57

In Travancore, Pattom Thanu Pillai from Congress became the first Chief Minister of the responsible government formed in 1948 following the first general election in the princely state based on adult suffrage. Out of a total of 120 seats, the Congress won ninety-seven, Travancore Tamil Congress fourteen,

Muslim League eight and independents one. The CPI fielded candidates in seventeen seats and KSP in eight, but all of them failed to win. The elected body was recognized by the king of Travancore as the first legislative assembly. Like their counterparts in Telangana, the communists launched an armed rebellion in several parts of Travancore. The struggles in Punnapra and Vayalar remain most memorable in the history of communist struggles in south Kerala. Following the internal differences and power struggle among the party leaders in Travancore, the Congress ministry, headed by Pattom Thanu Pillai, fell within a year and T.K. Narayana Pillai succeeded him to the post. The government continued in power when the Union government decided to merge Cochin with Travancore on 1 July 1949. The ministry accommodated Congress leaders from Cochin. But power struggles based on the regional identity of leaders from the two princely states remained a bone of contention which did not allow the ministry to function as efficiently as was expected.

In Travancore–Cochin the CPI formed an alliance with RSP and KSP against the Congress. The Congress was not able to forge a unity between the three crucial caste/communities – Ezhavas, Nairs and Christians. Besides this, the Congress in south Travancore (present Nagarcoil and Kanyakumari districts) was divided on the linguistic issue between Tamils and Malayalees. The Congress failed to win a majority in the state assemblies of Travancore–Cochin though it was able to form a government because the *Rajapramukh* (the king) of Travancore–Cochin invited Congress leaders to form the government on the basis of its status as the single largest political party in the assembly. A.J. John became the Chief Minister in Travancore–Cochin with the support of independents. Congress was able to rule even though it did not have the majority to form a one-party government. The divisions between the Congress and the Travancore Tamil Nadu Congress led to the resignation of the A.J. John cabinet in 1953.

In Travancore many socialist leaders had left the socialist party during 1947–52 and formed the KSP. Some of them joined the RSP. In Malabar and Travancore–Cochin, the CPI lost its credibility, seemingly due to the vacillation of its partners, KMPP, KSP and RSP towards the Congress. The KSP under Pattom Thanu Pillai merged with Praja Socialist Party (PSP) and he became its chief. When Pattom Thanu Pillai joined PSP, he was guided by the consideration of personal gain which did not augur well with the masses. One of the inevitable outcomes of the split within the left radicals was the weakening of their social bases across the region. This adversely affected, on the one hand, the political struggle that they wished to carry on and, on the other, the growth of a united platform to pursue the left radical ideological mission.

In the second assembly election in 1954 in Travancore–Cochin, the left front (CPI, KSP and RSP) made a tactical understanding with PSP against the Congress. The formation of the Travancore Tamil Nadu Congress (TTNC) by those who were disillusioned with the Congress weakened the latter to a significant extent. The Catholic Church opposed the left alliance tooth and nail in the 1952 and 1954 assembly elections. The NSS had a strong dislike for the Ezhava–Christian leadership of the Congress which resulted in the resignation of Pattom

Thanu Pillai (the favourite of the NSS in Congress leadership) from the Congress (he immediately joined PSP). After the election the Congress became the single largest party though it was short of a majority in the assembly. The possibility of the formation of a PSP–Left Front government was aborted by the offer from the Congress to support the PSP if it would form a single-party government. The pre-election coalition broke down and Pattom Thanu Pillai from PSP, which had only nineteen seats in the assembly, became the Chief Minister with Congress support from outside. The PSP government resigned after eleven months in power following a no-confidence motion moved in the house by the TTNC in 1955. The TTNC, aided by the Congress, was instrumental in defeating the PSP in power. The communists abstained from voting. Following the resignation of Pattom, the Congress formed the government with Panampilly Govinda Menon as the Chief Minister in March 1955.

New phase in the history of parliamentary left

With the dismissal of the democratically elected communist government in Kerala in 1959, a new phase began in its political history.[13] The CPI-led single-party government was a victim not of any internal dissension or loss of majority in the assembly but of its own failure to come to terms with the demands of the conflicting interests of the dominant caste groups.[14] Socio-politically unique, this southernmost state of India is distinct in its demographic profile. Not only are there Hindus; Muslims and Christians also have significant shares in Kerala's population. The politics of Kerala is in fact 'the making of permutations and combination of the four communities'[15] of Ezhavas (22.1 per cent), Christians (22.1 per cent), Muslims (19.1 per cent) and upper-caste Hindus belonging to the Nair community (14.4 per cent).[16] The different religious groups are not evenly distributed throughout the state. Muslims are, for instance, concentrated in the north Malabar, especially in the Malappuram district, while Christians are numerically preponderant in south central Kerala (Ernakulam, Kottayam and Idukki districts). This peculiar demographic arithmetic is important in conceptualizing coalition politics in Kerala. Since Muslims are a preponderant minority, they hold not only the electoral balance in the district but also provide the required numerical support to a coalition of parties endorsing their demands. As the electoral outcome shows, the Kerala Muslims remain a critical factor in the formation of coalition in the state. The Muslim League always reaps the dividends since, in almost all state assembly elections held so far, it succeeded in winning a considerable number of seats which were critical in cobbling together a majority to form the government. Similarly, the Christians also act as a solid vote bank, divided between the Congress and other splinter groups representing the 'sons of the soil'. In order to understand the dynamics of government formation in Kerala meaningfully, one has thus to be sensitive to this peculiar religious composition of the demography.

Since 1980, Kerala has been ruled by two different coalitions of parties: the CPI (M)-led Left Democratic Front (LDF) and the Congress-dominated United

Democratic Front (UDF). Besides the three major communist parties, CPI (M), CPI and RSP, the LDF also included the Mani and Pillai faction of the Kerala Congress and the rebel Muslim League and the vacillating Congress (led by Devaraj Urs) so long as it existed. Like the LDF, the UDF is equally heterogeneous because, apart from the Congress, the other constituents were Muslim League, a faction of Kerala Congress, Janata Party, Praja Socialist Party, the (Nair) National Democratic Party and the (Ezhava) Socialist Revolutionary Party (SRP). Although the major parties in both these conglomerations remained firm, the constituents kept changing affiliations for political expediency. Kerala's peculiar communal profile, with no religious or caste groups ever being numerically dominant and the obvious conflicting interests of different social groups, seems to have contributed to the multiplicity of political parties that perhaps made coalition government inevitable.

The disintegration of the Congress system in 1967 coincided with the formation of the non-Congress government in Kerala. Under the leadership of E.M.S. Namboodiripad, the United Front came to power. Defending the United Front as ideologically most appropriate, B.T. Ranadive thus argued that:

> the necessity of a united front including a united front ministry, arises out of the needs of class struggle, out of the awareness of the people that without their combined efforts they cannot move forward. Leaders of opportunist parties may look upon the United Front as an electoral machine, but the masses attach more basic importance to it as their weapon of struggle.[17]

In order to ensure smooth functioning of the coalition government, a coordination committee was set up by representatives of the coalition partners including the CPI (M). From the very outset, the Namboodiripad ministry had to sail through rough weather. The United Front's essential problem was primarily due to internal rivalries which in turn provoked conflicts within as well as between its constituents. The coordination committee failed to mitigate the tensions within the coalition and its existence virtually became ornamental. Its failure was attributed to the prevalence of conflicting opinions that never led to a consensus. There were three shades of opinions: the Chief Minister's views that invariably represented those of CPI (M) of which he was a leader; the cabinet decisions which reflected the diverse views of the constituent partners; and finally the views of the partners usually representing their socio-political constituencies.[18] So, the coordination committee was practically ineffective. One of the reasons for its gradual decline was the reluctance of the major partner, CPI (M), to endorse the decisions arrived at after deliberations in the committee. For instance, the CPI (M) openly opposed decisions of the committee regarding the procurement of the entire surplus of paddy from those holding more than ten acres of land and vesting the responsibility for wholesale trade in food grains in the Food Corporation of India. Such a clear violation by the major partner created a fissure within the ruling coalition which made the committee redundant.

Corruption was rampant. The government was hardly effective in this regard presumably because of the rivalry between the CPI and CPI (M). It was a tragedy, argues a Kerala expert, that 'the government that pledged to provide a clean administration finally went down on charges of corruption against all the thirteen of its ministers'.[19] The role of the coordination committee was insignificant. In fact, it was alleged that the committee always acted as a shield for the CPI (M) since it was headed by a member of this party and this was the reason for its virtual non-existence. The discussion in the committee was thus merely academic, with hardly any consequence. As a result, the coalition partners were always suspicious of one another and the government machinery was utilized to improve their political fortune rather than strengthening the coalition government in the interest of the people. Even the major partners, CPI and CPI (M), seemed to have paid less attention to administration since, according to them, 'nothing could be done under the present bourgeois framework of the Indian constitution'.[20]

What drove the coalition government was not the spirit of accommodation and consensus, but compromise, on most occasions. In view of the acrimonious relationship between CPI and CPI (M), the Muslim League, that was key to the coalitions' survival, managed to squeeze maximum benefits in exchange for their support. In order to isolate the CPI, the League emerged as the most acceptable strategic partner to the CPI (M) in its opposition to the former. In the process, the League gained most and the government conceded its demand for a Muslim majority district in Malappuram and a new university at Calicut. The non-League partners in the coalition characterized this as 'abject surrender to the communal demand of the Muslim League'.[21] Given its numerical strength in the assembly which was short of a majority, the League's support was crucial for the coalition's survival. It was therefore strategically suicidal for the CPI (M) to ignore the League. The position of the CPI (M) was most vulnerable when the League joined hands with other coalition partners in demanding an interim enquiry into corruption charges against CPI (M) ministers. The Chief Minister declined and suggested to move a no-confidence motion against the government. The motion was carried and Namboodiripad resigned. His calculation that the governor would impose Article 356 was wrong and the CPI leader, Achutha Menon, was invited to form a minority ministry comprising the Muslim League, Indian Socialist Party and Kerala Congress which was also supported by the RSP, and tacitly by the Congress. The Menon ministry was a unique example of coalition where the CPI (M) was totally excluded.[22]

The CPI (M) seemed to have been edged out by the CPI and other non-CPI (M) political parties. On the eve of the historic 1977 assembly election, the CPI (M) forged an alliance of seven parties – the Janata Party, the Congress Radicals the Opposition Muslim League, the RSP National, the Kerala Socialist Party and the Kerala Congress (Pillai) – that came together in their hostility to Indira Gandhi. Because of its impressive track record when in power, the Congress-led ruling front won 'handsomely with fifty three per cent of the votes and 111 of the 140 Legislative assembly seats'.[23] The worst sufferer was CPI (M) that was reduced to an insignificant political entity in the assembly with just seventeen seats and managed only 22 per cent of the popular votes.

What emerged in 1967 gradually became a pattern with the consolidation of the LDF with the CPI (M) as its dominant partner and UDF with the Congress as its nucleus, as forms of coalition in Kerala. The pattern remains unchanged since the 1982 election to the state assembly. Apart from the respective dominant partners in the Fronts – the Congress and CPI (M) – the constituents cross floors more than once. It would not be wrong to suggest that what was initiated in 1967 with the formation of the United Front under Namboodiripad's stewardship has become an important feature in political articulation in Kerala. The Fronts have gradually become more ideologically oriented and less politically expedient. Hence, by 1987, the CPI (M)-led LDF decided not to include the Muslim League because of its 'explicit' communal ideology to develop 'a fairly genuine LDF, [based on] the socialist ideas of coalition-building'.[24] Notwithstanding the ideological metamorphosis of the respective Fronts, their importance in redefining Kerala politics in coalition terms can never be underplayed. The assembly elections since 1982 corroborate the trend, as Table 5.1 shows.

Unlike other states in India where the coalition experiment did not last beyond 1969 – except perhaps West Bengal where an ideologically inspired coalition has survived since 1977 – Kerala is the only state to have been continuously governed by a coalition of parties irrespective of ideology. Crucial to coalition in this densely populated state on the south-western coast of India is not ideology but the success of the political parties/groups in mustering the support of the major communities of Ezhavas, Nairs, Christians and Muslims. The declining importance of ideology-driven political choice seems to have created a vacuum in which the community-based choices have become critical both in the formation of ministry and its survival. It is therefore not surprising that the Catholics, despite being ideologically opposed to the atheists, support the communist-led coalition. Similarly, both the Congress and the communists forge alliances with the Muslim League notwithstanding its communal character. Class-based ideology seems to have lost its resilience in Kerala and political parties tend to be community-based, presumably because of the importance of communities in the assembly and Lok Sabha elections.

Bipolar coalitions: LDF and UDF

In the 1980 state assembly election CPI (M)-led LDF secured ninety-three out of 140 seats, but the government led by E.K. Nayanar fell in October 1981. The CPI (M), CPI and RSP were truly the left political partners of the front. But the inclusion of two major fractions of Kerala Congress led by K.R. Mani and Balakrishna Pillai raised criticism about the quality of the front to be labelled as a left alliance. The Congress (Urs) led in Kerala by the opponents of Karunakaran also joined the LDF. In the formative stage of the LDF, its success against the rival UDF did not give any indication that its share in vote was the consolidation of left voters in Kerala. While the LDF had rightist allies, the UDF had

Table 5.1 Elections in Kerala, 1982–2011

Front	1982 Assembly	1984 Lok Sabha	1987 Assembly	1989 Lok Sabha	1991 Assembly	1991 Lok Sabha	1996 Assembly	1996 Lok Sabha	1999 Lok Sabha	2004 Lok Sabha	2006 Assembly	2009 Lok Sabha	2011 Assembly	2001 Assembly
UDF contested	140	20	138	20	140	20	140	20	20	20	140	20	140	140
Won	77	17	60	17	92	16	59	10	11	3	42	16	72	99
% of votes	48.2	50.9	43.6	49.3	48.1	48.6	48.6	46.6	46.7	32.1	42.7	47.7	45.8	49.0
LDF contested	140	20	140	20	140	20	140	20	20	20	140	20	140	140
Won	63	3	78	3	48	4	80	10	9	17	98	4	68	40
% of votes	47.2	42.3	45.0	44.4	45.9	44.3	46.7	44.6	43.7	44.5	49.1	41.9	44.9	42.2

Source: James Chiriyankandath, 'Bounded nationalism: Kerala and the social and regional limits of Hindutva', in Thomas Blom Hansen and Christophe Jaffrelot (eds), *The BJP and the Compulsions of Politics in India*, Oxford University Press, Delhi, 1998, p. 223. Figures for 1999 Lok Sabha poll and 2001 Assembly poll: *Indian Express*, 14 May 200; figures for 2004 Lok Sabha election are drawn from the website of the Election Commission of India (eci.nic.in); for 2006 assembly election, the website of the Election Commission of India (eci.nic.in); for 2009 Lok Sabha pool, K.M. Sajjad Ibrahim, 'Kerala: a negative verdict on LDF government', *Economic and Political Weekly*, 26 September 2009, p. 118; for 2011 Assembly poll, 'Fourteenth assembly election in Kerala', *Economic and Political Weekly*, 18 June 2011, p. 135.

Note
In the 2001 assembly election, Congress won 62 out 88 seats contested while the CPI (M) had only 23 out of 77 seats contested. *The Hindu*, 14 May 2001.

the support of certain socialist groupings. But, comparing the nature of political parties in each front, the UDF was more communal and depended more fully on the caste/communal vote banks than the LDF. Such a combination would have been a winnable one if the LDF had not received the support from factions of Congress, Kerala Congress and Muslim League. Interestingly the two caste-based political parties, NDP of NSS and SRP of Ezhava, joined the UDF. It has been argued by the spokespersons of the LDF that the factions from the rightist parties that associated with them were comparatively left-oriented in outlook. However, by the 1980s the ideological differences were not a reason for the left parties to join their hands after two decade-long mutual competitions. The communists started to justify political alliances based on a flexible and ill-defined right–left divide in Kerala politics. It was a transition: Kerala communists from confrontation to political adaptation which scholars like Nossiter had identified.[25] Very soon further troubles developed within the practical line of the left parties. Throughout 1950s and 1960s ideology was identified with the means of achieving the fruits of revolution, call it socialism. But in the 1980s, the left political parties had almost got accustomed to the inconclusive stages of the inner-party debates and inter-party conflicts over the last two decades. Since 1980 the two major partners of left politics, CPI (M) and CPI, have not faced any major organizational split. There were instances of disciplinary actions against certain popular leaders from the CPI (M), such as M.V. Raghavan and K.R. Gouri. But the separate political parties formed under these two leaders (Communist Marxist Party and Janathipathiya Samrakshana Samithy (Association for Defence of Democracy) respectively) hardly became a major force to threaten their parent organization.

Left politics in Kerala since the 1980s provide us with a different picture which shows striking contrasts with the past. Left politics has been divided between two major parties (CPI (M) and CPI) and a handful of socialists mainly RSP. After sixteen years of the split in united CPI and ten years of its alliance with Congress 1980, it was evident that the CPI (M) outnumbered the CPI and other left forces in Kerala politics. Their political strength is rooted in their solid social base which the CPI (M) cadres built by dint of their pro-people activities through various frontal organizations scattered all over the state. This feature of CPI (M) was the reason for their occupying the leadership role in left politics, even though there may be reservations about the way in which they manage other left parties inside the front. On such occasions of conflicts between the left parties within the LDF, none of them point out ideological differences as a reason. It shows, on the one hand, that the CPI (M) has become critical in contemporary left radicalism in India and on the other hand, that the nature of politics based on ideological differences has changed the socio-political texture of the bipolar coalition that has been ruling the state interchangeably since 1982. The Kerala coalition is thus drawn not on clear ideological preferences, but on broad generic divisions along a left–right axis.

The rise and fall of the parliamentary left

A perusal of Kerala's recent political history shows that the parliamentary left does not seem to be ideologically rigid in choosing its partners in coalition: the partners come together on the basis of some common minimum programmes for welfare, irrespective of religion, ethnicity and socio-economic location. This is evident in the acceptance by the left of Janata Dal (Secular) and NCP, which are not at all drawn on Marxism-Leninism, as constituents of the LDF despite the fact that these political parties have always supported the Congress-led United Progressive Alliance at the federal level since 1999. So, Kerala's coalition experiment is a pragmatic solution to governance in the context of new socio-political circumstances in which no single party, irrespective of its organizational strength or ideological appeal, is capable of winning a majority in the assembly election. Nonetheless, the left in Kerala had increased its share of popular votes consistently till the 2006 election when it had obtained more than 49 per cent of total votes polled, but never became a dominant political force as was the case in West Bengal and Tripura. One of the reasons for its growing popularity was surely the adoption of meaningful pro-people programmes: for instance, in 1987, the parliamentary left collaborated with Kerala Shastra Sahitya Parishad (a literary organization) to conduct the 'total literacy campaign' and during 1997–2001, the left launched, in collaboration with several grassroots socio-political outfits and also faith-driven organizations, the People's Plan Campaign (PPC) through the newly constituted local self-government institutions which was specifically conceived as 'a vehicle for deepening democracy',[26] 'taking the State ... toward building genuine and sustainable institutions of local self-government to a higher level infused with principles of sustainable progress towards genuine autonomy'.[27] As a set of far-reaching institutional reforms, the campaign evolved from a comprehensive critique of 'the inefficacies of top-down, insulated, command-and-control bureaucracies and of the myriad problems, both practical and normative, of the local participation deficit'.[28] PPC became an empowering mechanism by making the very nature and institutions of the state itself

> an object of contestation with the goal of deepening and widening democracy ... the ordinary citizens who have never been afforded an opportunity to effectively engage the state outside of campaign-oriented social movements now routinely deliberate and cooperate with elected representatives and local officials in deciding how to spend large sums of money.[29]

The purpose was to extend the practice of democracy by promoting participation and creating new, local, public spheres. As a vehicle for deepening democracy, the PPC remained a key institution for involving stakeholders in the decision-making processes at the grassroots. According to an analyst, the nested design of the campaign's core institutions, *Gram Sabhas* (ward-level assemblies), development seminars, task forces and local governments, 'represent a deliberate attempt to broaden avenues for citizen participation ... [in local planning, which] takes shape through a multi-stage process of iterated deliberation between elected representatives, local and higher level government officials, civil society experts and activists and ordinary citizens'.[30] With the *gram sabha* being the nucleus, the entire process of planning was now 'to start from the village up, going through many phases and tiers of co-ordination to final approval at the district level'.[31] The design shows that the entire cycle of planning was basically 'an extended exercise in practical problem solving' since the plans were usually the outcome of intensive deliberations involving people at various levels of their formulation and implementation.[32] In such an exercise, the role of the Kerala Shastra Sahitya Parishad (KSSP), a 50,000 member organization with a long history of engagement in local-level development, continued to remain critical by engaging citizens at every step. There is no doubt that it had a significant role in Kerala's social transformation through its motto of 'science of social revolution'.[33] This was a unique design of cooperation between the state and civil society. It was possible simply because of the existence of a cadre-based and disciplined CPI (M) that, despite being occasionally plagued by internal factional feuds, pursued with determination its ideological commitment for democratic decentralization. So, along with a supportive state planning board, aided by the KSSP, the ruling party easily carried its ideological mission that sustained the LDF social base so long as it remained in power. In other words, as a result of coming together, these three agents seemed to have created a synergy of action which brought about substantial changes at the grassroots in Kerala. This also explains why the parliamentary left continues to remain a respectable political force with a substantial hold in the state, unlike its counterpart in West Bengal where the left ruled uninterruptedly for more than three decades. There is a flipside too. Notwithstanding its role of radical social transformation at the grassroots, the PPC was basically 'the product of a state-led initiative under a left wing government, headed by the CPI (M)'[34] which was also criticized for being prejudiced against the voices of opposition. Nonetheless, the achievement was remarkable. As an extensive report shows, in five out of thirteen categories, from primary healthcare and housing for the poor to income and job generation, 'more than 40% of the respondents, across the political spectrum found that there was a significant improvement in service delivery and development, the biggest success being road construction, child care and housing for the poor'.[35] Almost all the respondents supported the view that 'the main beneficiaries of the plan were the socially and economically disadvantaged [which] demonstrates that elite interests were not able to subvert the Plan'.[36] On the whole, the PPC was an innovative design of economic planning in which stakeholders were involved in a meaningful manner. Since it was supported by the party in power, most of the difficulties that it had encountered were addressed conclusively. It was also an innovative design of how a democratic system was utilized to fulfil the social democratic aims of the parliamentary left. The PPC is said to have 'rescaled the political geography of the state by creating substantial, well-resourced and democratically accountable local governments [which, because of its utility in governance,] ... survived two changes of government and now enjoys support for all political formations'.[37] Even the critics have appreciated the campaign by saying that it has not only created 'a public platform for a vigilant civil society' but has also ensured 'an enabling environment for development'.[38] So, the fact that the LDF remains a strong political force in Kerala, despite losing power to the opposition at regular intervals, is attributed to the institutionalization of developmental programmes and schemes which were seriously pursued when in power to attack the sources of class imbalances.

Besides the PPC which naturally helped the left to strengthen their base, the parliamentary communists, in order to reach out to people with different political predilections, also undertook various steps towards recruiting members to local parish committees, temple trusts and Islamic mosque committees. So, it was an all-out campaign to expand its social base regardless of ideological considerations which was evident in the 2006 election results.

As Table 5.2 shows, the LDF registered a record win in 2006 through its mass campaign involving people from various strata underplaying, if not disregarding, ideological compatibility. The internecine factional feud between V. Achuthanandan and the party general secretary reached a deplorable height which adversely affected the organization. The result was evident in the 2009 Lok Sabha poll outcome in which the parliamentary left lost its grip over the masses to a significant extent as was witnessed in the 2009 national poll, as Table 5.3 shows.

It was a massive blow to the parliamentary left which lost a large number of seats due a significant erosion of its social bases across classes. While seeking to

Table 5.2 The results of the 2006 Kerala state assembly election

LDF (98 seats/49% popular votes)	Number of seats	UDF (42 seats/42, 7% popular votes)	Number of seats
CPI (M)	61 (30.5%)	INC	24 (24/2%)
CPI	17 (9.1%)	Kerala State Muslim League	7 (7.3%)
NCP	1 (0.64%)	Democratic Indira Congress (Karunakaran);	1 (4.27%)
Janata Dal (Secular);	5 (2.4%)	Kerala Congress (Mani);	7 (3.3%)
RSP	3 (1.4%)	Janadhipathiya Samrekshna Samiti	1 (1.51%)
Indian National League	1 ((0.90%)	Kerala Congress (Balakrishna Pillai).	1 (0.62%)
Kerala Environment Congress	4 (1.75%)	Independent	1 (0.76%)
Konattumatam Chidrmbara Subrahmanaia	1 (0.30%)		
Congress (S)	1 (0.47%)		
Independent	1 (2.1%)		

Source: prepared on the basis of data made available by the Election Commission of India.
Notes
Figures in parentheses show the share of total popular votes.

Table 5.3 Results of the 2009 Lok Sabha election

Party	Seats won	% of votes
UDF	16 (2)	47.7
LDF	4 (18)	41.9
BJP	0 (0)	6.3
Others	0 (0)	4.1

Source: K.M. Sajad Ibrahim, 'Kerala: a negative verdict on LDF government', *Economic and Political Weekly*, 26 September 2009, p. 118.

Note
Figures in parentheses show the number of seats won in the 2004 Lok Sabha poll.

explain such a loss, the CPI (M) leadership attributed the defeat 'to internal squabbles, inability to project its governance record due to never-ending controversies within the leadership and non-implementation of promises, made in the 2006 assembly elections'.[39] Despite its remarkable achievement in Kerala, the parliamentary left does not seem to be independent of factional feud which is linked with the loosening of organizational control over the leaders and their cadres. In the last ten years the internal squabbles of CPI (M) were highly personified in two leaders of the party – V.S. Achuthanandan (former Chief Minister) and Pinarayi Vijayan (former state secretary of the party). Group war in CPI (M) also affected party decisions related to candidature in the parliamentary election. The factionalism in CPI (M), cloaked in ideological debates, took a heavy toll in the Lok Sabha poll in 2009. The setback faced by the LDF in the *Panchayat* election in 2010 was also unprecedented in the history of Kerala. In addition to factionalism, the consolidation of minority votes in favour of UDF through the regenerated Muslim League and reunited factions of Kerala Congress played a crucial role in the dismal failure of LDF in those elections. The official faction miserably failed to convince a section of the cadres and sympathizers that their non-class approach is not essentially anti-poor. Besides, the undesirable consequences of non-class approaches, such as corruption, tainted the public image of the official line. The official faction is capable of constructing a political formula to win (as well as to lose) the elections and to develop the physical and financial infrastructures of the organization. That may also be a reason for their strength inside the organization. However, the social mobilization strategy of the CPI (M) leadership in Kerala is relatively stagnant when compared to their ability to design political alliances to win the election. This strategy to capture parliamentary power prevent the left from being actively engaged in non-class politics.

Within a year, in 2010, when elections to the local bodies were held, the results were identical: the parliamentary left failed and its bête noire, the UDF, captured the majority of seats in the civic bodies in ten out of fourteen Kerala districts. Despite being in power for almost four years, the LDF seemed to have ignored mass discontent over its failure to implement the promises that were made in the

2006 election. There were many welfare measures which the government, led by V.S. Achuthanandan, had adopted, though their implementation was far from satisfactory. What might have alienated a large number of Christian voters was the LDF campaign against the interference of the church in politics, which provoked a counter-movement in which the UDF activists in the localities participated to reap the benefit from the discontent of a significant section of 'disgruntled Christian voters'.[40] The change was evident in the gradual decline of the LDF in local elections in 2010 in comparison with its tally of seats in the 2005 poll.

As Tables 5.4 and 5.5 demonstrate, the LDF failed to maintain its hegemony in local bodies while the UDF registered a convincing victory.[41] This was a testimony to the gradual decline of the parliamentary left that was also visible in the 2011 state assembly election.

It was clear by 2010 that the social base that the left had assiduously built and was sustained by the cadres by dint of their hard work at the grassroots had shown cracks which were beyond repair. Furthermore, the organization did not appear to be as strong as it was before presumably because of the factional feud among the top leaders. The party remained non-committal and the differences between the two top leaders, V. Achuthanandan and Pinarayi Vijayan, caused a severe dent in the organization which was evident in the 2011 state assembly

Table 5.4 Comparative assessment of the poll outcome of local elections, 2005 and 2010

The Front/Party	Votes secured in 2005	Votes secured in 2010
LDF	7,697,151 (45.3)	7,763,495 (42.3)
UDF	6,882,314 (40.5)	8,447,977 (46.1)
BJP	964,133 (5.7)	1,147,297 (6.3)
Others	1,440,538 (8.5)	967,598 (5.3)

Source: S. Ramchandran Nair, M.T. Narayanan and V. Assa Kumari, *Democracy and Power: electoral politics in Kerala*, Manak, New Delhi, 2013, p. 107.

Note
Figures in parentheses show the percentage of the total votes polled.

Table 5.5 Comparative assessment of seats, won by the UDF and LDF in 2010 local elections

Institutions	UDF	LDF
Gram *Panchayat*	565 (54.8)	348 (35.6)
Block *Panchayat*	92 (60.5)	60 (39.5)
District *Panchayat*	8 (57.1)	6 (42.9)
Municipalities	40 (7.2)	17 (29.8)
Corporations	2 (40.1)	3 (60.1)

Source: Ramchandran Nair *et al.*, *Democracy and Power*, p. 107.

Note
Figures in parentheses show the percentage of the total votes polled.

election. While explaining the gradual downfall of the parliamentary left, it was thus succinctly stated that 'the deficit of governance, the absence of a vision for the state's development and the internal bickering of the partners of the LDF have earned the wrath of the voters'.[42] The defeat in the local polls was thus a continuation of the trend that had begun with the poor performance of the LDF candidates in the 2009 Lok Sabha poll.

The poll outcome of the 2011 state assembly election

The final outcome of the election followed a pattern of change of government every five years. The incumbent government lost power to the opposition with a margin of victory that is the smallest in Kerala's recent political history. Despite factional squabbles, the CPI (M) emerged as the single largest party in the assembly, as the detailed results in Table 5.6 demonstrate.

In the light of the massive seat losses in the 2010 *Panchayat* polls, the performance of the parliamentary left was very impressive in terms of winning seats in the assembly election though there was an almost 4 per cent swing of votes away from the LDF. As a poll survey indicates, neither of the conglomeration of parties witnessed a major shift in its social base: the UDF enjoyed a big lead

Table 5.6 The outcome of 2011 state assembly election

Name of the coalition/party	Seats won	Share of votes (%)	Vote swing since 2006 assembly elections (%)
LDF	**68**	**44.9**	**−3.7**
CPI	13	8.7	+0.6
CPI (M)	45	28.1	−2.3
NCP	2	1.2	+0.6
Janata Dal (S)	4	1.5	−0.9
RSP	2	0.33	−0.1
Kerala Congress Party (anti-merger)	0	0.5	+0.5
Indian National League	0	0.2	−0.6
LDF-supported Independents	2	3.2	+1.1
UDF	**72**	**45.8**	**+3.2**
INC	38	26.4	+2.3
Muslim League Kerala State Committee	20	7.9	+0.6
Kerala Congress (Mani)	9	4.9	+1.7
Socialist Janata Democratic	2	1.6	+1.6
Communist Marxist Party	0	0.6	−0.2
Janadhipathiya Samrakshana Samithy	0	1.3	−0.2
Kerala Congress (Bal murlikrishna)	1	0.7	+0.1
Kerala Congress (Jacob)	1	0.9	+0.9
Kerala Revolutionary Socialist Party (Baby John)	1	0.4	+4
UDF-supported independents	0	0.1	+0.2

Source: 'Fourteenth Assembly Elections in Kerala', *Economic and Political Weekly*, 18 June 2011, p. 135.

among the Christians and Muslims (constituting 45 per cent of the total population) whereas the LDF made up the loss by securing a lead among the Ezhavas (who are Dalits), the rest of the other backward classes and the scheduled castes. Despite having a solid base among Ezhavas, the parliamentary left was also charged with its failure to politically involve the Dalit women who are part of 'most of the visible forms of public action (such as mass demonstration, strike and sit-ins) … they remained invisible in both the discourses and the organizational structure of leftist politics at all levels'.[43] Nonetheless, there appears to have emerged a pattern: the LDF continued to hold its support among the poorer and less educated while the UDF held a lead among the better-off and more educated.[44] What accounted for massive Christian support for the UDF was 'the pronouncement emanating from the religious leadership in its favor'.[45] Muslims were alienated because the erstwhile LDF government 'adopted a simplistic rationalist approach … incognisant of the specific religious atmosphere in those communities'.[46] This was certainly a strategic limitation for a party that, by seeking to understand the question of minority in the classical Marxist class formula, failed to gauge the contextual appeal of Islam in Muslims' identity formation. Hence, there were hardly any serious endeavours to ideologically counter clearly religious appeals for political mobilization. The other significant factor that helped the LDF to do well in the poll was certainly the dynamic leadership and also clean image of V.S. Achuthanandan, the LDF Chief Minister. In the midst of the unearthing of several scams involving the political bigwigs irrespective of party affiliations, this was a great resource for the party which was significantly crippled due to internal squabbles involving the top leadership.

Concluding observations

In this period of seven decades, left politics in Kerala shows several signs of transition: first, the past ideological debates have paved the way to the present form of coalition; second, elections do not appear to be instruments for massive structural change or socialism; and third, there is not much to be expected from the left parties other than their raising avoice for meaningful welfare schemes and programmes for the underprivileged. The meaning of communism in Kerala in the 1990s changed under the shifts that took place in the international arena after the collapse of the Soviet Union and the transformation of China as a market socialist country. Moreover, the social texture in which the parliamentary left had its organic roots when it emerged on the scene in the state had undergone a sea-change. Hence the characterization of Kerala as a class-ridden and left-leaning society demands a revision against the backdrop of its current cultural settings. The bourgeoning middle class cannot be undervalued in our analysis. The middle class in Kerala denotes a cultural feature more than an economic occurrence. Its influence across all social strata irrespective of the class/caste/religious identity of individuals is a political and cultural challenge to the left. Rancorous remarks from such individuals in mundane conversations usually show their strong dissatisfaction with politics in general, and left politics in particular. Similarly, the changing class pattern of Kerala, the stagnant productive sector and the greater apprehensions of the educated unemployed youth and the consumerist middle class about trade union rights were strong reasons for the party to underplay class mobilization.[47] The new middle class is uncertain over their political choice and regards all forms of political process with disdain. Their aspirations for jobs, soft communalism, mixed nostalgia about left radicalism and feudal privileges, and consumerist inclination appear significant in formulating left strategies especially during and after elections, since the poll outcome is a determinant of whether the parliamentary left remains in the reckoning or not. Even though the new middle class does not seem to be keen on direct political activities, their importance is greater in Kerala politics because of their crucial role as opinion-makers and also its ability to swing voters in election.

Nonetheless, the left governments and the movements led by the left party organizations had a significant role in designing the Kerala model of development which provided for effective and wider distribution of entitlements, mainly at the initiative of the state. Such a model was possible in the context of a mixed economy. But the continuity of the state-led development was negatively affected due to the emerging market economy which was further aggravated by the low productivity in the state economy. However, unlike the UDF, the LDF cannot get rid of this model. It has limitations in its ability to alter the primacy of distributive principles in policy-making. The LDF under CPI (M) tried to reinvent the Kerala model through the PPC in 1997. It aimed at the penetration of the welfare state into the local level with a participatory outlook. It also aimed at substituting class-based political programmes with those focusing on non-class identities such as gender and community, among others, for empowerment and development.

The success of the Kerala model is partly attributed to the application of the right strategies to achieve the goal by those who held power. As Sen has forcefully argued, 'the political process ... has played an extremely important role in Kerala's development supplementing or supplanting [the] inherited characteristics'.[48] Less catholic in their approach, the political leaders evolved a platform undermining ideological compatibility while choosing partners. The goal was far more important than those contributing to it. The adoption of mass mobilization strategies by the parliamentary left in Kerala was visible on two occasions when it was in power. In 1987, it collaborated with Kerala Shastra Sahitya Parishad to successfully conduct the total literacy campaign, and during 1997–2001 it went for collaboration with NGOs and faith-based organizations to implement the PPC through the newly constituted local self-government institutions. The party has shown interest in formulating non-class strategies for election victory. The changing approach of the party towards religion and faith was visible from the increasing recruitment of party members to local parish committees, temple trusts and Islamic mosque committees. The CPI (M) leadership was enthusiastic about inviting the Muslim League, a coalition partner of UDF, to the LDF in the 1990s. The party has also changed its adamant opposition to private investment, Asian Development Bank loans, self-financing professional education and administrative reforms advised by the multi-lateral lending agencies. In the midst of controversies and internal squabbles the PPC was branded as a project of the World Bank. From the history of Communist Party and the political left in Kerala, what is most visible is the constant tension between the agency (party) and the socio-economic system and parliamentary politics (structure), wherein, on most occasions, the latter overcame the former. This does not mean that the party was totally changing in accordance with the structure. The party's involvement had made changes in the structure though it was very little compared with the original promise. Efforts were made in the past to show that the party continued to remain an agency for social change. But now the nature of the struggles in which the competing parties are involved have become substantially different, and in the changed environment of globalization giving precedence to the market, the strategies of the parliamentary left need to be more pragmatic than in the past, when adherence to the tenets of the ideology was always preferred, even at the cost of losing constituencies of support. With the growing importance of a pro-active middle class in Kerala politics, it will be theoretically debilitating and empirically myopic unless one takes into account its transformed socio-economic texture. In order to capture the changed socio-political reality in which the parliamentary communists are located, one is thus required to develop a different theoretical framework, since the received wisdom in this regard may not be adequate to understand the nature of its contemporary version; otherwise, attempts at analysing the rise, consolidation and the relative fall of the parliamentary left in Kerala will be anything but analytical.

Notes

1 I warmly acknowledge the contribution made by Dr B.L. Biju of the Department of Political Science, University of Hyderabad, in giving a concrete shape to this chapter. His written notes and verbal communication were of tremendous help in conceptualizing some of the intricate issues relating to the consolidation of the parliamentary left in Kerala.
2 T.J. Nossiter, *Communism in Kerala: a study of political adaptation*, Oxford University Press, Delhi, 1982; Victor M. Fic, *Kerala, Yenan of India: rise of communist power (1937–1969)*, Nichiketa Publications, Bombay, 1970; R. Jeffrey, *Politics, Women and Well-Being: how Kerala became a model*, Macmillan Press, Basingstoke, 1992; T.M. Thomas Isaac and Richard Franke, *Local Democracy and Development*, Leftword Books, New Delhi, 2000; Manali Desai, *State Formation and Radical Politics in Kerala*, Routledge, Oxford, 2007.
3 E.M.S. Namboodiripad, *The Communist Party in Kerala: six decades of struggle and advancement*, National Book Centre, New Delhi, 1994, pp. 24–6.
4 Ibid., p. 26.
5 Ibid., p. 22.
6 Ibid., pp. 26–31.
7 This alliance between socialists/communists and the nationalist Muslims were ridiculed as the Mecca–Moscow league by its opponents. In the newly constituted KPCC, E.M.S. Namboodiripad was the secretary, and Muhammad Abdul Rehman was the president. N.E. Balaram, *Communist Movement in Kerala* (in Malayalam), vol. 1, Prabhat, Trivandrum, 1973, p. 96.
8 I have elaborated on the events that led to the formation of the Forward Bloc in 1939

in my *Subhas Chandra Bose and Middle Class Radicalism: a study of Indian nationalism, 1928–1940*, Oxford University Press, Delhi, 1990.
9. The KMPP was founded by the erstwhile Congress leaders of socialist and Gandhian orientation such as Acharya Kripalani and T. Prakasham in Andhra and Kelappan in Kerala on the eve of first general election. It was considered the second incarnation of the Congress Socialist Party. Later, when Kelappan and Prakasham rejoined Congress, those who were left in the organization united with the rest of socialist party leaders to form the PSP, which is the third incarnation of the Congress Socialist Party; Namboodiripad, *The Communist Party in Kerala*, p. 129.
10. It was the first left coalition formed by the communists to fight elections. This brought together the communists and socialists in Malabar against the Congress. RSP, Forward Bloc and the Peasant Workers' party of Maharashtra also joined hands with communists all over India. The socialist party under Jaya Prakash Narayan kept out of the alliance from the left of the political spectrum.
11. The caste groups and their organizations which were not much stronger in Malabar when compared with those in south Kerala were more loyal to the British rule through their affiliation with the Madras-centred Justice Party. The Justice Party contested the 1937 election and faced no big success from Malabar.
12. The Muslim population in Malabar, especially after the communal riots of 1921, was insulated by all the secular forces including the left and Congress was mobilized politically by the communal party, the Muslim League. The significance of geographically concentrated Muslims in Malabar became a significant force in Kerala politics and remains so today which has given a decisive power to the Muslim League in Kerala. Namboodiripad, *The Communist Party in Kerala*, p. 134.
13. For a detailed exposition of this experiment, see H. Austin, *Anatomy of the Kerala coup*, People's Publishing House, New Delhi, 1959; Victor M. Fic, *Painful Transition to Communism in India: strategy of the Communist Party*, Nachiketa Publications, Bombay, 1969; Fic, *Kerala*; Georges K. Lieten, *The First Communist Ministry in Kerala*, K.P. Bagchi & Co, Calcutta, 1982.
14. For details, see M.K. Das and N.P. Che Kutty, 'Coalition government-Kerala experiment', in Lakshmi Krishnamurti *et al.* (eds), *Making a Success of Coalitions*, East West Books, Chennai, 2000, pp. 134–5.
15. S.N. Sadsivan, *Administration and Social Development in Kerala: a study in administrative sociology*, IIPA, New Delhi, 1988, p. 16.
16. These demographic figures are taken from Nossiter, *Marxist State Governments*, p. 61.
17. B.T. Ranadive, *Lessons of the Break-up of Kerala United Front*, Communist Party of India (Marxist), Calcutta, 1970, p. 18.
18. For details see Dr P. John John, *Coalition Government in Kerala*, The Institute of Public Policy and Management, Trivandrum, 1983, pp. 129, 134–42.
19. John John, *Coalition Government in Kerala*, p. 142.
20. E.M.S. Namboodiripad, *Anti-Communist Gang-Up in Kerala: betrayers of UF set-up anti-people government*, Communist Party of India (Marxist), Calcutta, 1970, p. 28.
21. 'The trouble in Kerala', *Economic and Political Weekly*, 18 November 1967, p. 1973; E.J. Thomas, *Coalition Game Politics in Kerala after Independence*, Intellectual publishing, New Delhi, 1985, pp. 134–6.
22. For details, see Nossiter, *Communism in Kerala*, chapters 3 and 4.
23. Nossiter, *Marxist State Governments*, p. 101.
24. Nossiter, *Marxist State Governments*, p. 107.
25. Nossiter, *Communism in Kerala*; Nossiter, *Marxist State Governments*.
26. Isaac and Franke, *Local Democracy and Development*, p. 5.
27. *Report of the Committee on Decentralization of Powers*, preface, Part A, vol. 1, p. iv.
28. Patrick Heller, 'Building local democracy: lessons from Kerala', paper presented for the workshop on poverty and democracy, Duke University, North Carolina, 17–18 February 2006 (unpublished), p. 6.

29 T.M. Thomas Isaac and Patrick Heller, 'Democracy and development: decentralized planning in Kerala', in A. Fung and E.O. Wright (eds), *Deepening Democracy: institutional innovations in empowered participatory democracy*, Verso Press, London, 2003, pp. 107–8.
30 Heller, 'Building local democracy', p. 9.
31 Nissim Mannathukkaren, 'The poverty of political society: Partha Chatterjee and the people's plan campaign in Kerala, India', *Third World Quarterly*, vol. 31, no. 2, 2010, p. 302.
32 Heller, 'Building local democracy', p. 9.
33 Tornquist, Olle and P.K. Michael Tharakan, *The Next Left: democratization and attempts to renew the radical political development project: case of Kerala*, Copenhagen: NIAS Books, 1994, p. 70.
34 Mannathukkaren, 'The poverty of political society', p. 301.
35 Heller, 'Building local democracy', pp. 31–2.
36 Mannathukkaren, 'The poverty of political society', p. 306.
37 Patrick Heller, 'Making citizens from below and above: the prospects and challenges of decentralization in India', in Sanjay Ruparelia, Sanjay Reddy, John Harriss and Stuart Corbridge (eds), *Understanding India's New Political Economy: a great transformation*, Routledge, Abingdon, 2011, p. 165.
38 K.P. Kannon and V.N. Pillai, 'Development as freedom: an interpretation of the Kerala model', working paper 361, Centre for Development Studies, Trivandrum, 2004 – quoted in Heller, 'Making citizens from below and above', p. 165.
39 K.M. Sajad Ibrahim, 'Kerala: a negative verdict on LDF Government', *Economic and Political Weekly*, 26 September 2009, p. 120.
40 *The Mathrubhumi*, 3 November 2010.
41
Seats won by the political parties in local elections, 2010

Party	Gram Panchayat	Block Panchayat	District Panchayat	Municipalities	Corporations
UDF	**8,501**	**1,230**	**194**	**1,097**	**178**
Congress	5,729	873	123	746	144
Muslim League	1,717	220	35	248	15
Kerala Congress	643	95	21	55	4
Janata (S)	127	19	8	11	9
Kerala Congress (B)	31	4	2	0	0
Kerala Congress (Jacob)	30	9	1	2	0
Indian National League	32	4	3	7	0
ISS	27	1	0	2	2
CMP	18	5	1	7	3
KRSP (B)	12	0	0	0	1
Independents	135	0	0	19	0
LDF	**6,607**	**828**	**134**	**801**	**155**
CPI (M)	5,431	680	106	661	123
CPI	778	122	24	77	16
RSP	51	5	4	2	9
NCP	34	8	0	2	2
JD (S)	14	03	0	2	0
Kerala Congress (Thomas)	14	3	0	2	0
Congress (S)	6	0	0	4	1
Independents	279	7	0	51	4

Source: Ramchandran Nair *et al.*, *Democracy and Power*, p. 109.

42 Ramchandran Nair et al., *Democracy and Power*, p. 111.
43 Rekha Raj, 'Dalit women as political agents: a Kerala experience', *Economic and Political Weekly*, 4 May 2013, p. 56.
44 'Fourteenth Assembly Elections in Kerala', *Economic and Political Weekly*, 18 June 2011, p. 136.
45 Subin Dennis, 'Kerala Elections: nothing mysterious', *Economic and Political Weekly*, 18 June 2011, p. 128.
46 T.M. Thomas Isaac, 'The left position in Ponnani', online at www.pragoti.org/node/3293, accessed on 21 October 2013.
47 Patrick Heller, 'From class struggle to class compromise: redistribution and growth in a South Indian state', *Journal of Development Studies*, vol. 31, no. 5, pp. 484–519.
48 Amartya Sen and Jean Dreze, 'India: economic development and social opportunity', in *The Amartya Sen and Jean Dreze Omnibus*, Oxford University Press, New Delhi, 1999, p. 55.

Part III
Left-wing extremism in India

An indigenous endeavour at ideological innovation(?)

written in collaboration with Rajat Kujur

Unlike their parliamentary counterpart, the left-wing extremists continue to believe in violent revolution as perhaps the only available means to change the prevalent class basis of the Indian polity. Inspired by a reinvented version of Marxism of the Maoist variety, the Indian counterpart is a creative intervention in an ideological domain that seems to have lost its appeal following the disintegration of the former Soviet Union and her satellite Eastern European states. Based on the idea that organic complementarities between agriculture and industry and between town and country are critical to development, Maoism actually reiterates an old dictum that a deep bond between these two sectors of the economy is what holds the nation together. Maoism is also an outcome of disillusionment with the state-led development paradigm that was zealously pursued by independent India's political leadership immediately after political independence in 1947 as perhaps the most appropriate strategy for economic development. In other words, given the socio-economic roots, it can safely be argued that, besides its ideological appeal, Maoism is also a contextual response to 'mal governance' or 'lack of governance' in the affected areas. The chapters in this part therefore dwell on those factors that provide a plausible explanation for the growing significance of the 'red corridor' or 'red belt' in contemporary India. Since 'compact revolutionary zones' or the 'red corridor', as characterized by the Home Ministry are an articulation of obvious mass discontent, one cannot dismiss Maoism as 'an infantile disorder'. Instead, it has raised serious questions not only about India's development strategies, but also on the state that seems to have failed to gauge 'the erosion of state' at the grassroots due to its uncritical faith in the planning-driven economic model. One should not also lose sight of the contemporary context of globalization that, by linking domestic capital with its global counterpart, theoretically substantiates the major Marxist formulation that market-driven capitalism is borderless and hence is naturally expansive for its survival. Maoism is thus not merely an innovative political experiment involving 'the wretched of the earth', but also a creative theoretical endeavour to understand the processes that are critical in making people rebel against a coercive state. For the marginalized, left radicalism of the Maoist variety is a powerful voice to press for genuine socio-economic demands which have so far escaped serious attention from those presiding over their destiny. An empowering ideology, Maoism, despite being derivative, remains inspirational to the historically underprivileged, notwithstanding the adverse consequences. By focusing on this experiment, the chapters in this part are an endeavour both to understand the phenomenon and to seek to evolve a framework of analysis in conceptually dealing with ideologically charged mass resistance in adverse circumstances.

6 Historical roots and gradual consolidation of the Maoist left radicalism[1]

India is a unique polity in which both forms of left radicalism are visible: while the parliamentary left seeks to bring about socio-economic changes through liberal democratic means, the left-wing extremists remain committed to violent revolution as the only available means to radically alter the prevalent class structure in a meaningful manner. For the latter, violence cannot be dispensed with in a class-divided society although the parliamentary left, despite having drawn ideological inspiration from classical Marxism-Leninism, prefers the available democratic means to fulfil its fundamental ideological mission of human emancipation. In tracing the historical roots of left-wing radicalism in India, also known as Maoism, this chapter focuses on the context and also its distinctive ideological character to understand the phenomenon which is not merely a ripple, but a powerful voice of those in the periphery for meaningful socio-economic changes. There are two arguments that the chapter makes: first, the contemporary Indian variety of left-wing radicalism is a context-driven ideological endeavour seeking to chart a specific course of history by involving the marginalized as integral to the entire processes of social, economic and political changes; and second, what is also striking is the unstinting faith of the left radicals in the revolutionary ideology of Marxism, Leninism and Maoism despite the brutal state repression. So in its new avatar of left radicalism, Maoism is not merely a conceptual category, but an appropriate description of India's socio-economic reality supporting the prevalent class balances to benefit a selected few.

Evolution and consolidation of Maoism

Maoism is a continuity of the ultra-left wing radicalism that was ideologically articulated in the form of the Naxalbari movement[2] in the late 1960s in India. Drawing on classical Marxism, Leninism and Maoism, the left radicals of the Maoist variety spearheaded a politically meaningful campaign in the subcontinent of India that has undoubtedly put forward a new development discourse by challenging both the state- and market-led development paradigms. Unlike the Naxalbari movement of the past, the Maoist movement is not only geographically well spread out; it also has provided a powerful voice to the peripheral

164 *Left-wing extremism in India*

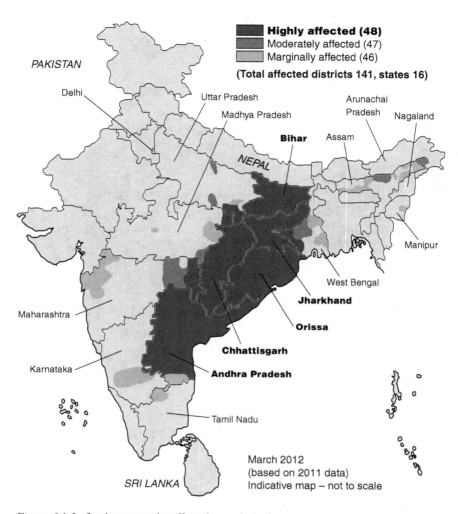

Figure 6.1 Left-wing extremist affected areas in India.

sections of Indian society. In view of its ideological correspondence with the 'Spring Thunder' which became famous as the Naxalbari movement, Maoism can be said to have articulated Marxism in the changed socio-economic and political environment of a globalizing world. The expressions, Naxalites and Maoists, are therefore used interchangeably to denote the same ultra-left-wing radical movement, especially in the official records and contemporary visual and print media. It is true that differences between the two movements in two completely different historical phases are merely cosmetic, given the clear ideological compatibility between these two movements representing serious endeavours in pursuing an ideological purpose based on 'the 'reinvention' of

Marxism in the non-industrialized world. In the industrially developed countries, Marxism articulated its ideological responses keeping in the mind the adverse impact of mechanical industrialization subjecting the producers of services and goods to alienation. Maoism is a Marxist formulation to address the basic contradiction in an agricultural society where feudal land relations are still well entrenched. Maoism is not a revisionist doctrine, but an extension of Marxism that is being interpreted and also reinterpreted to make the doctrine contextually relevant. This is a creative exercise because, given the growing complexities of Indian society due to an equally complex unfolding of her development trajectory since independence in 1947, it is difficult, if not impossible, to comprehend India's socio-economic reality in a strait-jacketed formula. Furthermore, because of colonialism and its obvious devastating role for more than two centuries, India's growth was skewed and was naturally tuned to the consolidation of British power in India. So the political authority was neither responsible for a uniform development of the country nor was accountable to the governed. In independent India, political authority was transferred. But the euphoria over this shift was short-lived since the planned economic development programme that independent India pursued did not appear to be appropriate to fulfil the aspired goal of a socialistic pattern of society. Instead, by creating severe economic imbalances across the country, the Nehruvian development planning completely lost its viability, especially when the market-compliant development programme was introduced following the adoption of the 1991 New Economic Programme by India's political elite. The phase that began by officially accepting economic liberalization is different from its past on a variety of counts. Besides projecting the obvious adversities of market-drawn development plans, this phase also witnessed the mass mobilization over numerous new macro issues, particularly the environment and the displacement of people due to indiscriminate industrialization. The indigenous population seem to be hard hit as a result and it is therefore not surprising that Maoism has struck an emotional chord with the tribal populations in areas where the forest land is being taken away for industrial purposes at the cost of the habitat. By challenging the land-grabbing by the industrial houses and also the government, the Maoists in these areas have become 'the true saviour' of the tribal populations. In fact, this is a major factor explaining the growing consolidation of Maoism in large number of constituent Indian states. Besides attacking feudal forces, Maoism has thus raised those issues which do not belong to its ideological fold in the classical Marxist sense. Broadly speaking, Maoism is a politico-ideological platform seeking to articulate the neglected voice of the peripheral sections of Indian society that have become critical to India's contemporary development trajectory. One has to be careful while assessing its future because the story of Maoism is also one of factional feuds, personal rivalry and also of corrupt practices that perhaps account for its slow success in building a united platform for espousing the cause of 'the wretched of the earth'.

Maoism is an outcome of the steady democratization of the political processes with the participation of the masses not only during elections, but also in the interim period. In other words, sustained participation by the people in the democratic processes has unleashed a process that has gone beyond mere voting by empowering people in a manner which radically changed the contour of Indian politics. The process is getting translated as rage and revolt, making India 'a country of a million little mutinies'.[3] But these mutinies created tangible space for the democratic aspiration to flourish. And also they make the state available for those who hitherto remained peripheral for any political transactions. The process is significant for another related reason, namely, that the democratic empowerment of the lower strata of society and formerly excluded groups led to articulation of voices that always remained feeble in the past. Since these groups interpreted 'their disadvantage and dignity in caste terms, social antagonism and competition for state benefits expressed themselves increasingly in the form of intense caste rivalries'.[4] So the growing importance of caste in contemporary Indian politics is essentially a modern phenomenon and not a mere continuity of the past. This is theoretically puzzling since caste action in India, articulated in modern political vocabulary, cannot be comprehended within the available liberal democratic parameters unless one is drawn to the empirical context that radically differs from the typical liberal society in the west. In the changed socio-economic context, caste has gained salience because of its 'encashability in politics [which] is now dominated by the numerically stronger lower and middle castes [and] the upper castes are now facing a very real reverse discrimination'.[5] So democratization seems to have set in motion a process whereby peripheral sections of society who remained peripheral because of well-entrenched caste prejudices have become politically significant due to their demographic preponderance. This may sound paradoxical since democratization, as an empowering process, has made the numerically stronger sections aware of their importance in contemporary politics without undermining their caste identity that brings people together irrespective of class differences. In this sense, democratization seems to have legitimized caste by reaffirming its role in cementing a bond among various social groups who, despite being differently placed in class terms, are drawn to each other because of their caste affiliation.

Roots of Maoism

In order to understand the current phase of Maoism, we need to understand different aspects of organizational transformation that occurred within the Naxal movement during the last decade or so, because the Naxal movement is a reflection of continuity and change. Drawn on Marxism and Leninism and Mao's political thought, the present incarnation of this movement is undoubtedly a continuity, at least in ideological terms. That the nature of the movement differs from one district to another is also suggestive of the extent to which the local socio-economic circumstances remain critical in its articulation. For instance, in the tribal districts of Orissa, Maoism consolidates its support by concentrating on tribal rights over forest products. In non-tribal districts, the movement builds support by challenging the feudal land relations. In other words, Maoism is adapted to the prevalent socio-economic issues while setting its agenda for 'the downtrodden'.

Despite having drawn ideological impetus from the same source, Maoists are highly fragmented and are prone to factional squabbles to settle personal scores among themselves. The fragmented character of the movement has given rise to all possible trends and groupings and thereby paved the way for new avenues of organizational conflict. Due to its fragmented character, the movement witnessed many past leaders and cadres making a comeback as though from oblivion. This aspect of Naxal organizational politics is very important to understand as it also enabled the re-emergence of a whole range of questions that were supposed to have been already resolved once and for all.

A prelude to the growth of the Naxal movement in India

To understand the genesis of the Naxal movement one needs to locate it within the framework of the communist movement in India. To be more specific, any study on the Naxal movement cannot overlook the importance of the rise and fall of the Telangana movement (1946–51). For Indian communists, the peasant movement in Telangana will always remain the glorious chapter in the history of peasant struggles. It was 'a simple peasant movement against feudal oppression and Nizam's autocracy [that] had grown into a partisan struggle for liberation'.[6] In that sense, the Telangana movement was the first serious effort by sections of the Communist Party leadership to learn from the experiences of the Chinese revolution and to develop a comprehensive line for India's democratic revolution. Despite the role of the committed activists, the movement remained confined to districts of Warangal and Nalgonda, where the communist leadership implemented the ideological programme. This limited success seemed to have 'convinced the CPI leadership that Telangana was soon going to be the pattern all over the Nizam's state and then for the rest of the country'.[7] That these signals were too deceptive to take seriously was evident when the movement was finally withdrawn in 1951, just two years after it began, for parliamentary politics in which CPI enthusiastically participated. Nonetheless, the Telangana experiment facilitated the growth of three distinct lines in the Indian communist movement. First, the line promoted by Ranadive and his followers rejected the significance of the Chinese revolution, and advocated the simultaneous accomplishment of the democratic and the socialist revolutions based on city-based working-class insurrections. The group drew inspiration from Stalin and fiercely attacked Mao as another Tito.

The second line mainly professed and propagated by the Andhra secretariat drew heavily from the Chinese experiences and the teachings of Mao in building up the struggle of Telangana. The Andhra leadership successfully spearheaded the movement against the Nizam; however, it failed to tackle the complex question of meeting the challenge of the government of India. The Nehru government embarked on the road to parliamentary democracy, conditioning it with reforms like the abolition of Zamindari system. All these objective conditions facilitated the dominance of a centrist line put forward by Ajay Ghosh and Dange. This line characteristically pointed out the differences between Chinese and Indian conditions and pushed the party along the parliamentary road which articulated the third line in the Indian communist movement.

The third ideological line was translated in 1957 when the communists succeeded in forming a government in Kerala, which however, was soon overthrown and, following the India–China war, in 1964 the party split into two, the CPI and the CPI (M). While the CPI preached the theory of a 'peaceful road to non-capitalist development', the CPI (M), went ahead with the centrist line. Though there were serious differences on ideological and tactical lines both the parties went ahead with their parliamentary exercises and formed the United Front government in West Bengal.

Assessment of past movements

One can draw two conclusions on the basis of careful reading of the socio-political processes by which Telangana and Tebhaga (discussed later in the chapter – a radical peasant movement organized by the CPI to fulful long-standing peasant demands for a one-third share of crop proceeds) were organized.[8] First, these movements were organized by political parties drawn on Marxism-Leninism and Maoism. It is true that these movements failed to attain the goal of radical agrarian reforms for a variety of reasons. Yet, by raising a powerful voice against feudal exploitation, they seem to have begun a process of social churning that became critical for future movements. Second, these movements also articulated an alternative to the state-led development paradigm which was hardly adequate to get rid of well-entrenched feudalism. These movements were watersheds in independent India's political history and also powerful statements on the failure of the state to redress peasant grievances due to reasons connected with the ideological priority of the ruling authority that replaced the colonial power following the 1947 transfer of power. Despite their failure, these movements had undoubtedly sensitized Indian society to the desperate efforts made by the rural poor to escape the intolerable conditions of economic oppression and social humiliation. There is also no doubt that Naxalbari movement served as a catalyst in West Bengal, where it made its first appearance, for the introduction of land reforms by the Left Front state government that ruled West Bengal uninterruptedly for more than three decades since 1977.

In the backdrop of political uncertainty of far-reaching consequences, one particular incident that took place in an little-known location involving some hitherto unknown people, hugely transformed the history of left-wing extremism in India. In a remote village called Naxalbari in West Bengal one tribal youth named Bimal Kissan, having obtained a judicial order, went to plough his land on 2 March 1967. The local landlords attacked him through their goons. Tribal people of the area retaliated and started forcefully capturing back their lands. What followed was a rebellion, which left one police sub-inspector and nine tribal people dead. This particular incident acquired a larger appeal in about two months on the basis of the open support it garnered from cross-sections of communist revolutionaries belonging to the state units of the CPI (M) in West Bengal, Bihar, Orissa, Andhra Pradesh, Tamil Nadu, Kerala, Uttar Pradesh and Jammu and Kashmir. Though the United Front government of West Bengal, steered by two communist parties, CPI and CPI (M), with all repressive measures, was able to contain the rebellion within seventy-two days, these ultra radical units finally regrouped in May 1968 and formed the All-India Coordination Committee of Communist Revolutionaries (AICCCR). 'Allegiance to the armed struggle' and 'non-participation in the elections' were the two cardinal principles that the AICCCR adopted for its operations. However, differences cropped up over how armed struggle should be advanced and this led to the exclusion of a section of activists from Andhra Pradesh and West Bengal, led respectively by T. Nagi Reddy and Kanai Chatterjee.

On the issue of annihilation of the class enemy the Kanai Chatterjee group had serious objections as they were of the view that this project should only be taken up after a build-up of mass agitations. However the majority in the AICCCR rejected this and the AICCCR went ahead with the formation of the Communist Party of India (Marxist-Leninist) in May 1969. This led Chatterjee to join the Maoist Communist Centre (MCC). The CPI (ML) held its first congress in 1970 in Kolkata and Charu Mazumdar was formally elected its general secretary.

The Naxalbari movement (1969–72): a review

The Naxalbari movement was a short-lived 'Spring Thunder' that helped reconceptualize political discourses in India. It was primarily an agrarian struggle against brutal feudal exploitation that led to a massive anti-state confrontation. Hailing the Naxalbari movement, the *People's Daily*, the mouthpiece of the Chinese Communist Party, commented that,

> a peal of spring thunder has crashed over the land of India. Revolutionary peasants in the Darjeeling area [in West Bengal] have risen in rebellion. Under the leadership of a revolutionary group of the Indian Communist Party, a red area of rural revolutionary armed struggle has been established in India. This is a development of tremendous significance for the Indian people's revolutionary struggle.[9]

Challenging the *status-quo*ist state, the movement inspired a large section of Indian youth to undertake even armed struggle for seizure of political power. When it was launched, the centre of gravity of the movement was rural West Bengal; it later shifted also to urban areas in various Indian states. In terms of its geographical expanse, the movement was not as widespread as its contemporary incarnation, namely Maoism. Nonetheless, there is no doubt that the Naxalbari movement provided the ideological impetus to Maoism that is a contemporary response to the prevalent socio-economic imbalances in the globalizing India.

The Naxalbari movement was not 'suddenly created in 1967, [nor] did it fall from heaven by the grace of God, not was it a spontaneous outburst'.[10] It was the culmination of long-drawn-out anti-feudal struggles in the Indian state of West Bengal that began with movements against 'illegal extortion' of *jotedars* (landlords). It was therefore argued in the *People's Daily* that the Naxalbari movement was 'an inevitability ... because the reactionary rule has left [the people] with no alternative'.[11] At the outset, this was an agrarian struggle that 'combined both institutional and non-institutional means of exercising power as [the participants] developed some kind of a disciplined peasant militia, comprised mainly tribal Santal, Oraon and Munda communities, with traditional arms like bows and arrows'.[12] In the course of time, the movement that was considered to be a 'prairie fire' lost its momentum for a variety of reasons: primary among them was the failure of the leadership to sustain the revolutionary enthusiasm of the masses, as Kanu Sanyal, one of the top Naxal leaders, admitted by saying:

> [a]fter we went underground during 1967–68 and later during 1969–72, most of us lost touch with the reality of the situation on the ground; unfortunately we learnt much later that what was being dished out by our top leaders and others including the party organs were either distorted or highly exaggerated accounts which suited 'the high command's dictates' and in the process the revolutionary potential suffered incalculable damage.[13]

There are two important reasons for the gradual decline of the Naxalbari movement, as Sanyal underlines. First, what caused the breakdown of the movement was a tactical failure to build an ideology-driven organization of the exploited classes. Unable to form 'a revolutionary front of all revolutionary classes' comprising 'poor and landless peasants and also the workers', the CPI (ML) leadership insisted on guerilla war for 'the seizure of power'. Emphasizing guerilla warfare waged by the peasantry 'as the only form of struggle in the present stage of revolution', the party ignored 'the need for mass organizations or for an agrarian programme as a concomitant of peasant struggle'.[14] Holding Charu Majumdar, the main ideologue of the party, responsible for such a futile tactical line, Sanyal further argues that not only did Majumdar reject 'the ideas of a mass organization', he also advocated 'the building of a secret organization through which the poor and landless peasants can establish their leadership of the peasant movement'.[15] Despite strong opposition by his colleagues, Majumdar was hardly persuaded because, in his opinion, revolution was possible only 'by organizing guerilla war by poor and landless peasants.... Guerilla war is the only tactic of the peasants' revolutionary struggle [that] cannot be achieved by any mass organization through open struggle.'[16] The second tactical line that caused irreparable damage to the movement was 'the battle of annihilation' as Majumdar characterized. Appreciating this battle as 'both a higher form of class struggle and the starting point of guerilla war', Majumdar supported the annihilation campaign even to the extent of alienating his colleagues by arguing:

> [o]nly by waging class struggle – the battle of annihilation – the new man will be created, the new man who will defy death and will be free from all

thought of self-interests. And with this death-defying spirit he will go close to the enemy, snatch his rifle, avenge the martyrs and the people's army will emerge. To go close to the enemy, it is necessary to conquer all thought of self. And this can be achieved only by the blood of martyrs. That inspires and creates new men out of the fighters, fills them with class hatred and makes them close to the enemy [to] snatch his rifle with bare hands.[17]

The annihilation line caused consternation among the leaders and also the rank and file of the movement. Characterizing the annihilation line as 'a terrorism of a very low kind', Ashim Chatterjee critiqued Majumdar by saying that 'this was nothing more than secret assassination by small armed groups. He further argued that such actions do not, in any way

raise the class consciousness of workers and peasants or enthuse them to organize on a class basis. Rather they inhibit their natural feelings of class hatred within the bounds of individual revenge and retribution.... All communists recognize that by ... annihilating individual capitalists or individual landlords, the capital or the system of feudal exploitation will not be eliminated, nor will a proletarian dictatorship or the rule of workers and peasants be created. It is natural for those at a low level of political consciousness to go for the apparently simple solution of annihilating the individual capitalist or the individual landlord.[18]

Not only was the annihilation line criticized by Chatterjee, it was condemned by the Naxal activists at the grassroots. In his appraisal of the Naxalbari movement, Prabhat Jana, an activist in Orissa, found annihilation totally incompatible with Marxism-Leninism. As he argued,

individual terror – secret assassination of individuals – does tremendous harm to the cause of revolution instead of helping it in two significant ways: first, it diverts the Party from the path of class struggle, from the path of people's war. It is petty-bourgeois subjectivism [dreaming] to create mass upsurge through individual terror by a handful of militants.[19]

Second, annihilation line is suicidal because 'a handful of militants isolated from the people can easily be suppressed by the enemy'. So 'it belittles the enemies' strength from the tactical point of view'.[20] The annihilation campaign, instead of contributing to the cause of the movement, damaged its future to a significant extent. A large section of the people were 'antagonized, thousands of cadres tortured, maimed and imprisoned and several hundred – both leaders and cadres – died'.[21]

Besides clear tactical failures, the movement was also handicapped due to lack of proper ideological guidance. For instance, in order to do away with the bourgeois cultural traditions, the party instructed the cadres to burn the portraits and deface and destroy the statues of 'the heroes' of the Bengal Renaissance in Kolkata and elsewhere. This step, instead of fulfilling the ideological aim of the movement, alienated the urban middle class to a significant extent. Supporters were bewildered because, instead of ideologically combating the influence of bourgeois cultural traditions, the party resorted to easy means that shocked 'the middle class that [was] brought up to revere the pro-imperialist and cultural leaders'.[22]

Besides the ideological bankruptcy, the Naxalbari movement received a serious jolt when its ideological mentor, the Chinese Communist Party, threatened to withdraw support and came out strongly against the Naxal leadership for having deviated from Marxism-Leninism. As the present stage of revolution in India was 'people's democratic revolution' in which the principal task was to overthrow feudalism and the domination of imperialism and to distribute land among the peasants, the Chinese leadership, particularly Chou En-lai, insisted that the Indian revolutionaries should, as a strategy, build a united front even with some of the exploiting classes, including the capitalists. It was also pointed out that the Naxalbari movement had lost its vitality because it failed to mobilize the peasant masses since it lacked a well-defined agrarian programme. The Indian leadership was also criticized for mechanical application of the Chinese model of revolution to contemporary India that was undoubtedly a failure to creatively articulate Marxism-Leninism, disregarding the prevalent socio-economic milieu. Peeved with the annihilation line that drew on Charu Majumdar's dictum that 'one who has not smeared his hands red with blood of the class enemy is not fit to be called a communist', Chou En-lai was reported to have asked the Indian communist leadership to withdraw the campaign for such secret assassinations. And also, the slogan that 'China's chairman is our chairman' displeased the Chinese leadership to a significant extent since it meant that the movement was controlled and guided by a foreign power which was certain to alienate 'any sensible human being with self-dignity and pride in one's national identity'.[23] Although this slogan never became so popular, it appears to have reflected a genuine weakness of the left-radical movements in India since the formation of the Communist Party in 1923 by those charged in the Meerut Conspiracy Case. Initially, it was the Communist Party of Great Britain that, through its emissaries, almost dictated the Communist Party of India during the nationalist struggle. The most disappointing course of action by the Communist Party was undertaken during the Second World War. So long as former Soviet Union had a pact with Hitler's Germany, the war was an 'imperialist war'. Following Hitler's attack on Moscow, the war became a 'people's war'. As the Soviet Union joined hands with Britain against Hitler, the Indian communists found it ideologically appropriate not to oppose the British war effort in India. As a result, they did not participate in the Congress-led Quit India movement in 1942 since it would weaken the British government (and thus the people's war) that was involved in a historic battle against fascism in the Second World War. The stance that the Indian communists had adopted in this context was perhaps ideologically tenable though it was 'a betrayal' for the nationalists fighting for independence despite adverse consequences. The Indian communists later realized that by supporting the colonial government, they alienated the masses. Nonetheless, history was repeated and those involved in the 'Spring Thunder' almost two and a half decades after the 1942 open rebellion uncritically accepted the hegemonic role of a foreign communist leadership until the Chinese Communist Party strongly voiced its annoyance and later disapproval.

The Naxalbari movement after Charu Majumdar

The history of the post-Charu Majumdar Naxal movement is characterized by a number of splits brought about by personalized and narrow perceptions about the Maoist revolutionary line and attempts at course correction by some of the major groups. Even Kanu Sanyal, one of the founders of the movement, was not free from this trend. He gave up the path of dedicated armed struggle by 1977 and accepted parliamentary practice as one form of revolutionary activity.

It was during 1974 that one influential group of CPI (ML), led by Jauhar (Subrata Dutt), Nagbhushan Pattnaik and Vinod Mishra, launched a major initiative that they termed 'course correction'. This group renamed itself as CPI (ML) Liberation in 1974, and in 1976, during the Emergency, it adopted a new line that called for the continuation of armed guerilla struggles along with efforts to form a broad anti-Congress democratic front, consisting even of non-communist parties. The group also suggested that pure military armed struggle should be limited and that there should be greater emphasis on mass peasant struggles in an attempt to provide an Indianized version of Marxism-Leninism-Maoism. However, during the next three years the movement suffered further splits with leaders, such as Kondapalli Seetharamaiah (Andhra Pradesh) and N. Prasad (Bihar) dissociating themselves from the activities of the party. This led to Prasad forming the CPI (ML) (Unity Organization) and Seetharamaiah starting the People's War Group (PWG) in 1980. Seetharamaiah's line also sought to restrict 'annihilation of class enemies' but the PWG's emphasis was on building up mass organizations, not on developing a broad democratic front. Since then, the principal division in the Naxalite movement has been between the two line of thought and action, as advanced by the CPI (ML) Liberation and the PWG. While Liberation branded PWG a group of 'left adventurists', the PWG castigated the Liberation group as one of the 'revisionists' imitating the CPI (M). On the other hand the growth of MCC as a major armed group in the same areas created scope for multifarious organizational conflicts among the Naxal groups. Liberation took a theoretical stand of correcting the past mistakes by 'completely rejecting parliamentary politics'. On the other hand PWG and MCC completely rejected the parliamentary democratic system of governance and vowed to wage 'people's war for people's government'. In the process while the Liberation group registered its first electoral victory in Bihar in 1989, more Naxalite factions such as the CPI (ML) New Democracy, the CPI (ML) S.R. Bhajjee Group and the CPI (ML) Unity Initiative were formed in that state.

The Naxalbari movement saw different turns and twists in the 1990s. First, the intra-organizational conflict and rivalry among different groups touched several low points resulting in the loss of considerable number of cadres of rival groups. Second, despite the large-scale inner conflicts there was always an exercise going, at various levels, attempting at the unity. Third, in the 1990s the affected state registered a considerable growth in violent incidents and at the same time a considerable change in policy approach at the government level was also witnessed. If the Naxal movement is mostly characterized by fragmented groups and innumerable splits; successive governments at the national and state level were never able to follow a uniform approach to deal with the problem of Naxalism. All these have had a marked impact in the growth of the Naxal movement.

Maoism is a contemporary manifestation of the ultra-left movement in India although it would not be wrong to characterize the movement as a historical continuity simply because of its broad ideological compatibility with the past movements which drew on Marxism-Leninism and also Maoism. Besides the Naxalbari movement in the late 1960s and early 1970s, the Telangana Liberation struggle (1946–51) and Tebhaga movement (1946–9) had also mobilized the marginalized against the so-called 'feudal forces', stalling land reforms and promoting other ameliorating social and economic measures for the majority.

What distinguishes the Tebhaga and Telangana upsurges from the past movements was that these were politically inspired and supported by a well-entrenched organization, under the guidance of the undivided CPI. The Tebhaga movement, as its nomenclature suggests, demanded the reduction of the share of the landlord from one-half of the crop to one-third. The leadership came from the Kisan Sabha, a peasant-front of the CPI. This Bengal-based movement gradually spread in Dinajpur and Rangpur in north Bengal and 24 Parganas in south Bengal. Despite its temporary success, the movement petered out gradually in the face of an organized government-sponsored counter-offensive. Yet, the movement forced the ruling authority to introduce the Bargadar Act that legalized the demand of the sharecroppers for two-thirds of the harvested crop. Unlike the Tebhaga movement, which mobilized Bengal peasants in selective districts for enhancing their share of the produce, the Telangana movement was a genuine agrarian liberation struggle to get rid of feudal landlordism and the dynastic rule of the Nizam in Hyderabad. The movement however lost its momentum with the 1947 independence when the Nizam's rule came to an end. There were some in the Communist Party who wanted to continue the movement against the Indian government, but a majority of them were in favour of withdrawal. In 1951, the movement was formally withdrawn. In a rather superficial sense, the Telangana movement succeeded because the Nizam lost his authority in the changed environment of free India after the 1947 transfer of power. Yet, it would be appropriate to suggest that the movement raised a voice against feudal atrocities which was articulated differently in independent India, resulting in ameliorating land reform measures.

The Naxalbari movement was an ideological continuity of the past movements that sought to organize peasants against feudal exploitation. The name is derived from Naxalbari, a non-discript place in the northern part of West Bengal. Mobilized by those who formed CPI (ML) in 1969, one of the primary aims of the 'Spring Thunder' as it is metaphorically characterized, was to bring about radical changes in the prevalent agrarian structure that endorsed feudal exploitation of perhaps a very primitive nature. As a 1969 political resolution of the party suggests,

The increasing concentration of land in the hands of a few landlords, the expropriation of almost the total surplus produced by the toiling peasantry in the form of rent, the complete landlessness of about 40% of the rural population, the back-breaking usurious exploitation, the ever-growing evictions of the poor peasantry coupled with the brutal social oppression – including lynching of '*harijans*', reminiscent of the medieval ages – and the complete backwardness of the technique of production clearly demonstrate the semi-feudal character of our society.[24]

What is distinctive about Naxalbari is that a majority of peasants are tribal people. Exploited by the landlords and their agents, they were employed on a contractual basis and in most case, they did not get even the government fixed wage for their work in the fields. The movement failed to attain its goal. Nonetheless, it left a far-reaching impact on the entire agrarian scene throughout India. It was like a 'premeditated throw of a pebble bringing forth a series of ripples in the water'.[25] The uprising, though ephemeral in existence, was widely publicized and inspired the rural poor in other parts of the country to launch militant struggles against feudal exploitation and the failure of the state to evolve an equitable economy. While the immediate and spontaneous demand of the peasants involved in the Naxalbari movement was the fulfilment of some economic demands, it led to a long-range struggle for the ultimate seizure of political power that not only survived but also expanded, despite internal factional squabbles and also the organized state counter-offensive.

Consolidation of Maoism in 2004

Following the merger of the three major outfits, the Maoist Communist Centre, the CPI (ML) and the PWG, a new outfit, known as the Communist Party of India (Maoist) was formed in 2004. According to an official report, the CPI (Maoist) is active in thirteen Indian states,[26] including Andhra Pradesh, Chhattisgarh, Jharkhand, Bihar, Orissa, Uttar Pradesh, Madhya Pradesh, Maharashtra, West Bengal, Karnataka, Tamil Nadu, Uttaranchal and Kerala. The merger makes the Maoist group a pan-Indian entity with its tentacles in what they call 'the compact revolutionary zone' which extends from Nepal through Bihar in the north to Dandakaranya region (forest areas of central India) and Andhra Pradesh. Maoism is thus not a mere descriptive category but an organized revolutionary movement for seizure of political power in India.

Maoism is an ideological continuity with the past, and yet this is a contextual response to the peculiar Indian reality that differs radically from one place to another. In the past, ultra-left movements seem to have uncritically accepted 'the one size fits all' approach by accepting the classical Marxism-Leninism as sacrosanct. Given the socio-economic and cultural diversity of the subcontinent, India can never be comprehended in a single axis. By being sensitive to this well-entrenched diversity, Maoism has reinvented Marxism-Leninism in a non-European milieu. Even within India, the issues that Maoists raise differ radically from one state to another. In Andhra Pradesh, Maoism draws, for instance, on anti-feudal sentiments whereas in the tribal belt of Orissa and also Chhattisgarh, rights over forest produce remain the most effective demand for political mobilization. This context-driven articulation of Maoism is certainly a critical factor in its rise as perhaps the most effective ideological voice of the downtrodden, notwithstanding the adverse consequences.

Despite obvious similarities, the Maoist movement differs from the 'Spring Thunder' of the 1969–72 period on a variety of counts: first, Maoism seems to have struck an emotional chord with the tribal population, unlike the Naxalbari movement that shifted its centre of gravity to the urban and semi-urban areas and drew on the support of the educated middle-class youth. It is difficult to clearly identify the class background of the Maoists though there is no doubt that the participants are 'not romantic, middle class babus, as was the case generally during Charu Majumdar's quixotic misadventure of 1969–72 period especially in West Bengal'.[27] Second, unlike their Naxal counterparts, Maoists are better organized and also well equipped with sophisticated fire power, as was evident in the series of successful attacks on the police and paramilitary armed forces in Bihar, Chhatisgarh and Orissa. There are official reports that Maoists are regularly trained in a military style in areas where the government seems to have lost its control. Finally, Maoists are ideologically better-knit than those involved in the Naxalbari movement. One of the major factors that led to the collapse of the Naxalbari movement was internecine feud, not only among the leaders but also among the grassroots activists. According to Kanu Sanyal, one of the top Naxal leaders, what led to the downfall of the Naxalbari movement was 'an atmosphere of disrespect and expression of arrogance by the leaders that [resulted in] reducing the Communist revolutionaries in India to groups and sub-groups'.[28] What crippled the Naxalbari movement was the emergence and consolidation of two contradictory trends: On the one hand 'the urban-based leadership, cloaked in a more sophisticated ideology, claimed superior knowledge and status with regard to the manner in which the movement should be conducted'.[29] Opposed to it was, on the other hand, 'the co-opted indigenous leadership'[30] that followed the principle of democratic consultation at every levels of the organization before arriving at a decision. While the first trend is illustrative of an elitist leadership that Charu Majumdar consolidated by evolving a centralized organization with concentration of power at the top, the Kanu Sanyal-led rural wing of the leadership sought to democratize the organization by meaningfully involving the activists at various levels of the leadership. The movement considerably lost its momentum, largely due to the division among the leaders that not only weakened the organization but also caused confusion among the followers. The present-day Maoists seem to have learnt a lesson from the past that was translated into reality, when out of four different Maoist groups emerged the CPI (Maoist) in 2005. Undoubtedly, this merger is a milestone in India's left-wing movements since most of the radical outfits fizzled out in the past due to factional fights. The formation of the CPI (Maoist) is therefore a watershed in so far as the consolidation of those clinging to Maoism is concerned. The gradual but steady expansion of the 'red corridor' since the 2005 merger is also a powerful testimony to the growing importance of Maoism as a political means to get rid of the well-entrenched socio-economic imbalances at the grassroots.

In spite of severe state repression, Maoism is reported to have succeeded in expanding the 'red corridor' by involving mainly the peripheral sections of society in an area stretching across almost half of India. This itself is suggestive of the historical limitations of the state-led development programmes that miserably failed to take care of the basic needs of a vast population. The situation seems to have worsened following the acceptance of neo-liberal economic reforms in the wake of serious domestic fiscal crisis in the early 1990. The government design for rapid industrialization seems to have received a serious blow because of an organized opposition by those who lost their land for industries. The idea of SEZs did not go down well with the people at the grassroots who felt betrayed by the government policy of transferring land owned by many small peasants to a single, privately owned company. In areas where Maoism was hardly a force, the forcible eviction of peasants from land for SEZs led to circumstances in which Maoists are accepted as a natural ally by those fighting for their rights. In other words, the economic reforms, despite being middle-class friendly, seem to have consolidated the class division in India's rural areas by pursuing a path of development that is surely tilted towards foreign capital and its Indian collaborators. Given the appalling socio-economic circumstances in which the vast majority of the Indian population stays alive, it will not be an exaggeration to suggest that Maoism is likely to strike roots since it provides the struggling masses with a powerful voice defending their rights for survival. Maoism is therefore not merely an articulation of ultra-extremist ideology, it is also a well-designed scheme for mobilizing those who remain historically underprivileged for reasons connected with India's interventionist economic strategies under the state-led development planning since independence. As is evident in a 2007 report of the Planning Commission, Maoism has gained momentum mostly in tribal-dominated, forested and mineral-rich states of India because

> despite being resource-rich, the local population has remained poor; forest wealth and minerals have been exploited by outsiders with almost no local value addition. Administration has been thin and weak, connectivity poor and more difficult areas can only be reached on foot. There is also near absence of education and health facilities.[31]

Hence it was admitted that 'there is a consensus that [Maoism] is not primarily a security problem, but has its roots in the feeling of oppression and depression fuelled by poverty and lack of development'.[32] It was thus not surprising that within a span of five years since 2002, Maoism was reported to have affected almost 20 per cent of a total of 604 districts in thirteen out of twenty-nine Indian states which were declared as 'the Naxal-hit districts'.[33] The steady expansion of what is characterized as 'the single biggest internal security threat' to the Indian state[34] is thus indicative of the clear failure of the state-led planned development paradigm to fulfil the ideological mission of India's founding fathers of creating an India free from poverty, hunger and displacement. In this sense, Maoism not only is a powerful critique of post-independent India's development strategy, but also exposes the limitations of a top-driven strategy of socio-economic changes.

Nature of Maoism

Maoism is thus not an academic expression. This is an ideological movement seeking to replace the semi-feudal and semi-colonial state that has flourished in India since independence. Maoism in India is both a continuity and break with the past: continuity because it has elements of those Marxist-Leninist movements of the past which sought to mobilize the peasants and workers; it is also a break with the past simply because of its approach drawing on the 'revisionist' interpretation of Marxism-Leninism in the context of a typical agrarian society which is articulated as Maoism. Furthermore, there is one unique feature: unlike their counterparts in the past, Maoists, instead of rejecting the indigenous ideological traditions, seems to have provided adequate space for these traditions while mobilizing masses for a political caus. It is not therefore surprising that Gandhi is also appreciated for his concerted effort to eradicate social evils, justified in the name of religion and long-drawn-out traditions. This suggests that 'Indian Maoism' cannot be comprehended in the 'derivative discourse' format. Nepal Maoism may have ideological affinity with its Indian counterpart, though the movement crystallized largely against a feudal monarchy that was, for obvious reasons, clearly opposed to the ideas of peoples' empowerment. In two major ways, the Indian example is different: socio-economic indicators (reflective of distorted state-led planned development) and deepening of democracy since the 1947 independence, when a democratic form of polity was inaugurated in India. The historical legacy of the freedom struggle in which several ideological streams coalesced with Gandhian non-violence remains critically important in the articulation of democracy involving different layers of Indian society. Maoism is a contextual response to the socio-economic grievances of the peripheral sections of society that, despite the euphoria over the state-directed Soviet model of planned economic development, remain impoverished. In the changed socio-economic environment following the acceptance of neo-liberal economic reforms by the Indian state, Maoism is Marxism-Leninism in an agricultural context, where national and global capital are strongly resisted by drawing upon an ideological discourse that has been creatively articulated by taking into account the indigenous socio-economic and political forces besides local traditions.

Maoism is an ideological movement challenging the so-called democratic state in India that miserably failed to address the genuine socio-economic grievances of the poor. It has thus been argued that,

> despite a relatively progressive Constitution what came into practice was a potpourri of democratic symbolism with highly reactionary and repressive system of patronage and power sharing. For all practical purposes, the poor

and the Dalits were driven out to the margin of the everyday existence of the nation.[35]

As a nation, India is thus genuinely fractured: while the elites have access to all comforts of life, the poor, the dispossessed and the marginalized continue to remain mere statistical details in the annual census reports. What is striking is the pace at which the Maoists have been growing. No longer confined to dense forests of Orissa, Bihar, Jharkhand or Andhra Pradesh, the Maoists cadres are reported to have expanded their domain of influence in other states as well. A government report suggests that as many as 170 districts, located in fifteen Indian states, have already been affected by 'the red terror'.[36] Maoism continues to attract millions of the impoverished and oppressed masses, presumably because it is not only ideologically empowering, but also meaningful conceptually in projecting an exploitation-free human society. The conditions of the poor are getting precarious day-by-day with the massive transfer of forest and agricultural land for developing industry, mining, infrastructure as well as agro-business. Those dependent on agriculture find it less and less remunerative. Tribals are dispossessed of sources of livelihood by their shrinking access to forest resources and large-scale displacement due to mega-mining projects. As the novelist Amitav Ghosh comments,

> [i]n effect, over many decades, there has been a kind of 'ethnic cleansing' of India's forests: indigenous groups have been evicted or marginalized and hotel chains and urban tourists have moved in. In other words, the costs of protecting Nature have been the thrust of some of the poorest people in the country, while the rewards have been reaped by certain segments of the urban middle class. Is it reasonable to expect that the disinherited groups will not find ways of resisting, whether it be through arms or [otherwise]?[37]

The ideological appeal of the Naxalites has thus, comments an analyst, 'a material basis in the Indian environment and that explains their expanding social base'.[38] The increasing presence of the Naxalites in large areas speaks of their success in building a base for Maoism. The growing popularity of the ultra-left forces in Indian villages is largely due to their involvement in various kinds developmental works in those areas. With their sustained work for the villagers, they become part of the community, sharing their joy and sorrow. The aim is to create a sense of belonging to the community that is the only insurance against government neglect and indifference. This was articulated very clearly by Ganapathy, the CPI (Maoist) general secretary, when the only available bicycle was not given up for transporting a person with fever to the nearby health centre. Condemning the owner of the bicycle, Ganapathy did not conceal his anger when he said that the refusal to take the ailing villager to the health centre was 'inhuman' and could never be justified.[39] This is a lone incident which is suggestive of seeking to create a sense of collectivity among the villagers. While explaining 'the natural inclination' of the villagers for Maoism an eye-witness account suggests that the attraction to Maoism is less ideological and more due to the involvement of the Naxalite cadres in those activities that contribute to the well-being of the villagers. This is a part of a well-planned strategy, as the following report suggests:

> Instead of carrying out a recruitment drive, the Maoist leaders wander through the remotest villages, talking to people. In areas where the government has hardly any presence, the Maoists help the villagers in constructing irrigation canals. They also educate the villagers against the problem faced by them. This makes an impact. And, through this process, they become a part of the village. Once inside a village, the extremists offer instant justice for internal problems like theft, cheating, vandalism and land disputes in the area, drawing villagers closer to them. It is at this stage that the villagers develop a trust in them and are ready to protect the Maoists from the police.[40]

It is not therefore surprising that the Maoists take, as a police report confirms, 'advantage of the jungles, inaccessible hamlets, poor roads and the tribal population where the government is all but absent'.[41] Besides the logistic difficulties, the government apathy towards the indigenous population seems to have created a natural space for the Maoists, presumably because of their sincere effort in improving the conditions for the poor by their deeds. The Maoists have gained a mass base among the *adivasis* 'by taking up cudgels on their behalf against corrupt government functionaries, exploitative traders and money-lenders'.[42] Through their ideological campaign, the Naxalites have also given the villagers in remote areas a sense of identity and dignified existence. It is thus argued that the historical failure of the Indian state forced the tribal population to join the Maoists since they have gained 'least and lost most from 60 years of political independence'.[43] In remote upland areas, the tribals have hardly any access to facilities which are so basic to human existence, like minimum medical care or primary education. Most of the villages are not accessible throughout the year because there is hardly any road. Undoubtedly the living conditions are appallingly poor. The government officials, appointed for these areas are not available when needed. 'In the absence of any government support and the apathetic attitude of [the government departments] towards the [local] communities', a forest official laments, 'the Naxalites have found fertile ground to proliferate'.[44] Their increasing presence in inaccessible terrain is partly due to their commitment to the downtrodden and partly due to the failure of the government to reach out to the tribals in remote areas. Whatever may be the reason, the fact remains that Maoism has become a formidable ideological force in those districts which remain neglected for a variety of historical and contextual factors.

The Naxalites no longer remain outsiders; they are organically linked with the people by their involvement in developmental projects and also in such activities which help the villagers combat superstitions and blind faith in black magic and witchcraft. On one occasion, the CPI (Maoist) secretary, Ganapathy was reported to have blamed the villagers for their appreciation for black magic when an

Roots and consolidation of Maoist radicalism 181

infant was brutally sacrificed or a widow was publicly lynched to propitiate god. As he stated,

> there are no gods, you are your own god and even if there is one, he shall not be pleased to accept an infant as a gift because that infant would have been his latest and finest creation. Moreover, sacrifice means departing with something of your own. Only your life is your own, not the infant's.[45]

On the lynching of the widow, Ganapathy further added that 'my foolish friends, there are no witches, children die due to malnutrition and due to mosquito bites'.[46] As part of the awareness campaign, the Naxalites insist that hospitals should be built and modern medicine should be made available to the indigenous people. The purpose is twofold: (a) to provide proper medical care and (b) also to convince the people that medicine is always preferable to witchcraft, for instance, to cure an ailment. In his address to the villagers in an undisclosed location, Ganapathy exhorted them:

> the medicines should not be avoided when there is ailment. The medicines, which the doctors give you, should not be stored, but should be consumed. These are precautionary dose; you should consume them even if there is no fever. If there is fever, wait for a day or two, then rush to the primary health centre.[47]

On the question as to whether the villages should have hospital and schools, there is near unanimity among the Maoist leaders except for a group of cadres who are not comfortable with the building of school blocks in the Naxalite areas because 'the government builds a school block and uses it for the police. So the people do not want schools.'[48] On building roads for better connectivity, the Maoists are not appreciative because 'roads are built for the police to [gain] access to our villages and tyrannize us'.[49] There is no doubt that roads will ensure easy movement for the police and paramilitary forces and hence a significant section of the Maoist cadres are vehemently opposed to this idea, though there are voices within the group in its favour because roads are synonymous with development. Hence they argue:

> Naxalites do not want development. They, for instance, are opposed to construction of metalled roads [which] are synonymous to development.... But as the network of metalled roads is increasing, the police accessibility is also improving. So, now the COC [Central Organization Committee] wants us to lay ambush on the metalled roads to discourage the government from building metalled roads. Is this not a contradiction? [This is a] clear case of confused state of leadership.[50]

The cadres at the grassroots are also bewildered at the decision of the Naxalites to utilize the government facilities when the aim is the seizure of power. As a Maoist was constrained to admit:

> we exhort the villagers to pick up arms and overthrow the tyrant government but how the government is tyrant that we are not able to explain. The Naxalites tell the tribals to use these government facilities and at the same time exhort them to boycott the government and elections. Either Naxals should say that they are [a] pressure group forcing the government to spend money for development in sparsely populated tribal areas. Or they should say they are revolutionaries trying to overthrow the democratic system of government.[51]

Ideally speaking, the differences of opinion should not lead to splits within the party. But as the past shows, Naxalites became divided on both ideological and leadership issues. What is striking in regard to the CPI (Maoist) is the success of a group of ultra-left extremists in bringing together various splinter groups under one platform. Differences were sorted out, claimed Ganapathy, at the 2007 Ninth Congress, through 'politico-ideological debates' among the participants. Such debates are 'the sources of strength of the party' underlining

> the democratic credentials of the party which allows freedom of expression for all kinds of opinions and viewpoints, and its ability to digest various opinions if they are expressed in a constructive way to enrich the Party line and not with a malafide intention to wreck the Party.[52]

Serious differences over major contradictions in the globalizing world were resolved through 'sharp debates' among those appreciative of the Leninist principle of democratic centralism.

Concluding observations

Maoism is a powerful ideological movement with organic roots in India's socio-economic reality. The spread of the movement shows that the ideology of Maoism is well conceived and the tactic is sound. There is no doubt that Maoism has struck an emotional chord with a significant section of India's indigenous population. For those suffering due to abysmal poverty, Maoism is an empowering ideology inspiring them to launch an assault on the state power, notwithstanding the adverse consequences. The state appears to have failed in providing the basic facilities for human existence to the forest-dependent tribals. It seems that they are destined to suffer because the state is either invisible or, where it exists, it is just a mute observer, and appears to be absolutely crippled and unable to meaningfully attack the age-old system of exploitation at the behest of the government-sponsored agents. Unless a long-term solution to the endemic poverty is meaningfully pursued by the state, the objective conditions supportive of left-wing extremism continue to thrive. A long-term solution lies in an honest attempt to address the basic causes arising out of poverty, land alienation, unemployment, corruption, displacement and dispossession of tribals and poor governance. True, these problems cannot be solved overnight. But if the state could at least give an impression that 'their severity is being mitigated every year, that itself would go a long way in building confidence among [the affected] people'.[53]

So, the movement, backed by effective striking power, has the effect of 'sharpening inequity which many see as the biggest danger facing India in the next few years and which is the Naxalites' recruiting sergeant'.[54] In its submission to the Supreme Court of India in November 2013, the Home Ministry of the government of India also confirms the critical role that the ideologues and sympathizers play in keeping the Maoist movement alive by mentioning that

> the ideologues and supporters of CPI (Maoist) in cities and towns have undertaken a concerted and systematic propaganda against the state to project it in a poor light and also malign it through dis-information.... In fact, it is these ideologues who have kept the ... movement alive and are in many ways more dangerous than the cadres of People's Liberation Guerrilla Army.[55]

Explaining the dynamics of 'the Maoist insurgency', it was further stated in the same report that in order to overthrow the democratically elected parliamentary form of government in India, the Maoists are reported to have adopted 'a three pronged strategy' involving 'a combination of armed insurrection, mass mobilization of certain sections of the society and tactical partnership with other insurgent groups operating in different parts of the country'.[56] So, the Maoists do not appear to be directionless, as the Home Ministry confesses. The inevitable outcome is the growing ascendancy of Maoism in areas which so far remain unaffected. It is true that the Maoists cannot match the government of India in providing what is required to ameliorate the conditions of the poor, but their endeavour to extend support to the villagers whenever need arises has resulted in a symbiotic bond between the Maoists and the local people. The belief that the Maoists are fighting for the tribals has gained ground particularly in areas where they are being forced by the state to give their land for private capital. *Adivasis* gruelling in a state of penury are persuaded to accept that the left radicals are their saviours in distress. So, the success of left-wing extremism can safely be attributed to the stark poverty in which tribals are forced to survive, if that is possible. The aggrieved tribals gravitate towards Maoists who hold out the promise of fighting their cause.

Maoism is thus not a passing phase, as was the case in the past with regard to left radical assaults on the Indian state. It has acquired a base and also a capability to hit the Indian state where it is weakest. Thriving on the government failure to deliver basic services to those who need them most, the Maoists appear to have created a space for themselves in India's recent political history. The possibility of Maoists capturing the state power is certainly remote though they have the power to deter investment and development in some of India's poorest regions, which also happen to be among the richest in some vital resources – notably, coal, iron and other useful mineral resources. In such circumstances, the principal losers are those hapless local inhabitants who are supposedly the main beneficiaries of both the Maoist revolutionary sacrifice and the developmental endeavour of the state, and are caught in the crossfire

> between two maximalist positions – one adopted by the revolutionaries who are determined in their well-meaning goal of smashing the present iniquitous socio-economic order and replacing it with a peoples' democratic order, and the other taken by a stubborn ruling class equally determined to continue with the status quo and suppress any resistance to it.[57]

This is the most tragic consequence of what is happening in the so-called 'red corridor' in the name of fulfilling the ideological mission of the Maoists and their bête noire, the Indian state.

Notes

1 I have drawn on my *Maoism in India: reincarnation of ultra-left-wing extremism in the twenty-first century* (Routledge, London, 2010) which I wrote in collaboration with Dr Rajat Kumar Kujur of the Department of Political Science, Sambalpur University, Orissa, India.
2 The expressions, Maoist and Naxalites, are used interchangeably in the book to denote the left-wing extremist movement in contemporary India.
3 V.S. Naipaul, *A Million Mutinies*, William Heinemann, London, 1991, p. 106. According to Naipaul, every protest movement strengthens the state 'defining it as the source of law and civility and reasonableness'. The institutionalization of power in the form of ademocratic state gives

> people a second chance, calling them back from the excesses with which, in another century, or in other circumstances (as neighbouring countries showed), they might have had to live: the destructive chauvinism of the *Shiv Sena*, the tyranny of many kinds of religious fundamentalism ... the film-star corruption and the racial politics of the South, the pious Marxist idleness and nullity of Bengal.

4 Sudipta Kaviraj, 'Modernity and politics in India', *Daedalus*, Winter 2000, pp. 156–7.
5 Satish Despande, *Contemporary India: a sociological view*, Penguin, New Delhi, 2003, p. 103.
6 Javeed Alam, 'Communist politics in search of hegemony', in Partha Chatterjee (ed.), *Wages of Freedom: fifty years of Indian nation-state*, Oxford University Press, New Delhi, 1998, p. 183.
7 Alam, 'Communist politics in search of hegemony', p. 184.
8 For details of these movements, see Sumanta Banerjee, *India's Simmering Revolution: the Naxalite uprising*, Selection Service Syndicate, New Delhi, 1984, pp. 18–28.
9 'Spring thunder over India', editorial in the *People's Daily*, 5 July 1967 – reproduced in Samar Sen, Debabrata Panda and Ashis Lahiri (ed.), *Naxalbari and After: a frontier anthology*, vol. 2, Kathashilpa, Calcutta, 1978, p. 188.
10 Kanu Sanyal, 'More about Naxalbari', April 1973, in Sen *et al.*, *Naxalbari and After*, p. 330.
11 'Spring thunder over India' in Sen *et al.*, *Naxalbari and After*, p. 188.
12 Partha N. Mukherji, 'Class and ethnic movements in India: in search of a pertinent paradigm for democracy and nation building in the third world', in Lars Rudebeck (ed.), *When Democracy Makes Sense*, Akut, Sweden, 1992, p. 19.
13 Interview with Kanu Sanyal on 16 January 1991, quoted in Arun Prasad Mukherjee, *Maoist Spring Thunder*, K.P. Bagchi, Calcutta, 2007, p. 3.

Roots and consolidation of Maoist radicalism 185

14 Charu Majumdra, 'On the political-organization report', 13 September 1070, reproduced in Sen et al., Naxalbari and After, p. 293.
15 Kanu Sanyal quoted in Sen et al., Naxalbari and After, p. 5.
16 Charu Majumdar, 'Why guerilla war?' in Ghatana Prabaha, vol. 2, no. 1, quoted in Sen et al., Naxalbari and After, p. 6.
17 Charu Majumdar, 'On the political-organization report', 13 September 1970, reproduced in Sen et al., Naxalbari and After, pp. 293–4.
18 Ashim Chatterjee, 'Hold high the genuine lessons of Naxalbari', in Sen et al., Naxalbari and After, pp. 388–89.
19 Prabhat Jana, 'Naxalbari and after: an appraisal', 12–19 May 1973, reproduced in Sen et al., Naxalbari and After, pp. 121–8.
20 Jana, 'Naxalbari and after: an appraisal', p. 123.
21 Jana, 'Naxalbari and after: an appraisal', p. 124.
22 Jana, 'Naxalbari and after: an appraisal', p. 125.
23 This paragraph is based on the testimonial of Souren Bose, one of the top Naxal leaders, who was sent to China during the heyday of the movement to ascertain the support of the Chinese Communist Party and also government. Bose's statements were recorded while he was in custody on 11, 20 and 24 April 1972. These statements are quoted from Mukherjee, Maoist Spring Thunder, pp. 232–5.
24 Political resolution of the Communist Party of India (ML), 1969.
25 Banerjee, India's Simmering Revolution, p. 92.
26 Times of India, 27 October 2007.
27 Mukherjee, Maoist Spring Thunder, p. 30.
28 Sanyal, 'More about Naxalbari'; Sen et al., Naxalbari and After, p. 347.
29 Partha N. Mukherji, 'Naxalbari Movement and the peasant revolt in north Bengal', in M.S.A. Rao (ed.), Social Movements in India, Manohar, New Delhi, 2008 (reprint), p. 75.
30 Mukherji 'Naxalbari Movement', p. 76.
31 The Planning Commission Report is reproduced in the Times of India, 27 September 2007.
32 The Planning Commission Report.
33

The 'Naxal-hit districts' in India

State	Number of districts affected
Bihar	25
Jharkhand	20
Andhra Pradesh	19
Orissa	14
Chhattisgarh	10
West Bengal	9
Madhya Pradesh	6
Uttar Pradesh	6
Maharashtra	6
Karnataka	5
Kerala	2
Uttarakhand	2
Tamil Nadu	1

Source: Times of India, 27 September, 2007.

34 Prime Minister's speech at the Chief Ministers' meeting on Naxalism, Prime Minister's Office, Government of India, August 2006, available at http://pmindia.gov.in/speech-details.php?

35 Arun Kumar, 'Violence and political culture: politics of the ultra-left in Bihar', *Economic and Political Weekly*, 22 November 2003, p. 4979.
36 Figures are quoted in the *Times of India*, 30 June 2008.
37 Amitav Ghosh *Two New Essays: confessions of a xenophile and wild fictions*, Outlook, New Delhi, 2008, p. 64.
38 Manoranjan Mohanty, 'Changes of revolutionary violence: the Naxalite movement in perspective', *Economic and Political Weekly*, 22 July 2006, p. 3163.
39 The address by Ganapathy is quoted in Vineet Agarwal, *Romance of a Naxalite*, National Paperbacks, New Delhi, 2008, p. 67.
40 A report prepared by a journalist after having travelled the difficult terrain of Orissa–Andhra Pradesh border. This report was published in the *Times of India*, 30 June 2008.
41 The police report was quoted in a news item published in the *Times of India*, 30 June 2008.
42 The report of the fact-finding team to Chhattisgarh in 2006 was quoted in Sagar, 'The spring and its thunder', *Economic and Political Weekly*, 22 July 2006, p. 3177.
43 Ramchandra Guha, 'Adivasis, Naxalites and Democracy', in Rajesh M. Basrur, *Challenges to Democracy in India*, Oxford University Press, New Delhi, 2009, p. 179.
44 The statement of a senior forest official was quoted in Guha, 'Advasis, Naxalites and Democracy', p. 179.
45 Ganapathy quoted in Agarwal, *Romance of a Naxalite*, p. 66.
46 Ganapathy quoted in Agarwal, *Romance of a Naxalite*, p. 67.
47 Ganapathy quoted in Agarwal, *Romance of a Naxalite*, p. 67.
48 Interview by the Naxal commander, Rangam of Bijapur: *Tehelka*, vol. 6, no. 13, April 2009.
49 Interview by Kunjam, the Naxal commander in Dantewada in Chhattisgarh, date not known, *Tehelka*, vol. 6, no. 13, April 2009.
50 The anonymous interview is in Agarwal, *Romance of a Naxalite*, pp. 94–5.
51 This interview is quoted in Agarwal, *Romance of a Naxalite*, p. 94.
52 Text of the interview of Muppala Lakshman Rao alias Ganapathy, General Secretary, CPI (Maoist), in April 2007; available at http://satp.org/satporgtp/countries/india/terroristoutfits/CPI_M.htm, accessed on 20 November 2012.
53 Prakash Singh, 'Terror won't work: both government and Naxalites suffer from delusions', *Times of India*, 6 July 2007.
54 'India's Naxalites: a spectre haunting India', *The Economist*, 17 August 2006, available at www.economist.com/world/asia/displaystroy.cfm, accessed in 12 November 2013.
55 The report of the Home Ministry is reproduced in *The Hindu*, 16 November 2013 with the title 'Maoist ideologues keeping Naxal movement alive'.
56 Report of the Home Ministry in *The Hindu*, 16 November 2013.
57 Sumanta Banerjee, 'Beyond Naxalbari', *Economic and Political Weekly*, 22 July 2006, p. 3162.

7 Left-wing radicalism in practice in Orissa
A field-based analysis[1]

Contrary to popular belief, Maoism in Orissa is not a recent phenomenon. For long, Orissa's tryst with left-wing extremism was reduced as a spillover effect from the neighbouring Andhra Pradesh. However, Orissa has a long history of communist movement, peasant mobilizations and labour unrest. Left-wing extremism in Orissa is altogether a different experience from that of West Bengal, Andhra Pradesh or Bihar. The long history of left radicalism in Orissa does not have a Naxalbari (as in West Bengal) or Telangana (as in Andhra Pradesh) movement to boast about, and yet this Indian province has a separate and distinct place in the consolidation of the left-wing extremist movement from the very beginning. Led by the maverick Nagbhushan Pattnaik, the echoes of 'Spring Thunder' were felt in different pockets of Orissa as early as 1968. Even his worst critics would agree that if the Naxal movement got recognition in Orissa it was due to the revolutionary leadership and charismatic appeal that Nagbhushan commanded among the cross-sections of the society. However, it is during the past two decades that the Naxal movement gained momentum and strengthened its position. Prior to their merger, the Peoples War Group (PWG) was already a significant political force in the districts of Koraput, Malkangiri, Nabarangapur, Rayagada, Gajapati, and Ganjam; whereas the Maoist Communist Centre (MCC) was largely visible in Sundargarh, Mayurbhanj and Keonjhar. After the formation of the CPI (Maoist), the Naxal movement spread to different parts of Sambalpur, Kandhamal, Deogarh, Jharsuguda, Jajpur and Angul. The ultra-left ideology seems to have gripped a large part of the state due largely to socio-economic deprivation of the people who found a powerful voice in Maoism. The aim of this chapter is thus two-fold: (a) to draw out the socio-economic characteristics of those districts where Maoism is a serious political force and (b) to indicate the importance of mass-scale economic deprivation in bringing people together for a cause.

Maoism is the latest incarnation of left-wing radicalism in Orissa. It had its organic roots in the past movements which drew on Marxism-Leninism and Mao's socio-political ideas. Given its geographical spread in the 'red corridor', it would be incorrect to describe Maoism as a region-specific movement, though there are some specific socio-political agendas which are only meaningful to Orissa. In other words, since Maoism attracts a large number of tribals in Orissa, the Maoist leadership cannot avoid tribal-specific issues to sustain and expand the organization. Unlike their counterparts elsewhere in India, the Orissa Maoists have played significant roles in redefining Maoism by reference to the peculiar socio-political milieu of Orissa and its vicinity. By contextualizing Marxism, not only have the Orissa Maoists indigenized the ideology, they have also sought to universalize its role as a liberating ideology for 'the wretched of the earth'. In this sense, a critical study of Maoism in Orissa is also a useful theoretical exercise by challenging the idea that Marxism is merely a derivative discourse, since it is being constantly reinterpreted and redesigned contextually. Hence it is not surprising that a grassroots response always remains critical to the leadership while seeking to understand the reality which may not conform to the conventional copy-book description. Two critical points have therefore emerged: (a) Maoism in Orissa is a historical phenomenon drawing its ideological roots from a variety of ultra-left extremist movements of the past; and (b) despite being rooted in Orissa, Maoists are inspired primarily by the Maoist variety of Marxism which is not merely a meaningful analytical device to understand a transitional society, but also articulates a powerful ideological voice for radical socio-economic and political transformation.

In the following pages, we will trace the roots of Maoism in Orissa by looking at its evolution chronologically. The aim of this discussion is two-fold: first, it will acquaint the readers with the circumstances in which the ultra left ideology rose as a meaningful voice, and second, by elaborating its growing consolidation among the poorest of the poor, this will perhaps reconfirm the success of Maoism, a twentieth-century version of Marxism that was articulated in the context of colonialism in China for mobilizing the peripheral sections of society for a political battle, despite adverse consequences.

The growth and spread of the Naxal brand of politics in Orissa has been mostly shaped by the inter-organizational and intra-organizational conflict dynamics within the larger gamut of the communist movement. The Naxalbari movement of 1967 started with a romantic slogan of 'land to tillers' and the subsequent *modus operandi* of different Naxal groups in Orissa suggests that the slogan still has not lost its vigour. Issues pertaining to control over land and other natural resources have so far remained a primary cause of conflict, which have considerably helped the growth of the Naxal movement in the remote corners of the state. Similarly industrialization, mining, displacement and rehabilitation are other dynamics of conflict, which have substantially affected the course of the Naxal movement in the state. The targeted Naxal attacks on security forces and other symbols of state authority have become an inseparable feature of left-wing extremism in Orissa.

To understand the genesis of the Naxal movement in Orissa one has to go back to pre-independence India. During colonial days, the undivided Koraput district was under Jaipur Zamindari and the undivided Ganjam was with the Vishkhapattanam district of the Madras presidency.[2] It was during this period a number of *sahukars* (moneylenders) and 'king's men' from neighbouring Andhra Pradesh settled in these areas. They not only settled down but, taking advantage of the simplicity of local tribal people, they became their masters by virtue of taking their lands. The rural people of these areas were subjected to severe oppression and exploitation by the *sahukars* and king's men. Alluri Sitaram Raju led a massive popular movement during 1930, in Malkangiri area, to protest against injustice to the local rural tribal people.[3] Later on, people of these areas responded to the call of Mahatma Gandhi and joined the national movement because they understood independence would make them free from the evils of monarchy, oppression and exploitation. When independence came the British were gone; but oppression, exploitation, underdevelopment, starvation, illiteracy and poverty all refused to go and the struggle continued there after.

Phase 1: Consolidation of left extremism in Orissa

In the post-independence scenario, Orissa has always remained a prime target of left-wing extremism right from 1951. For long it was confined to the southern part of the state before engulfing more than half of the geographical territory of the state. The armed peasant insurrection of Telengana during 1947–51 had a far-reaching impact on the consolidation of communist forces in Orissa. During this period, under the leadership of CPI, Orissa witnessed several people's resistance movements in different parts of the state. The people's movement in Nilagiri and Ranapur, the abolition of *bethi* (slavery) in Koraput, the movement against the moneylenders in Ganjam and Koraput, the protest movement against the forest police–official nexus: these are but a few low-scale protest programmes which were successfully implemented by the communist cadres and leaders and were instrumental in creating a space for communist ideology and movement in the map of Orissa politics.

The withdrawal of the armed method from the Telengana struggle by one group of the communist leadership in 1951 created a nationwide polarization among the communists. The impact of this polarization was strongly felt among the communist leaders from the Koraput and Gajapati regions of the state. For this particular reason the battery of communist leaders from these areas, Bhuban Mohan Pattnaik, Nagbhushan Pattnaik, Purna Chandra Gomang, Purushottam Pali and Jaganath Mishra, were in constant touch with their counterparts from Srikakullam. As a result, by 1952, under the leadership of the Communist Party, organizations of local tribals were formed, called *Adivashi Sanghs*. By 1961, mostly under the leadership of Nagbhushan Pattnaik, communists were able to launch a large-scale programme in the name of 'food liberation' in the Gunupur subdivision of the Koraput district.[4]

The communist movement in Orissa received a major setback in 1962, when, on the verge of the Indo-China war, a majority of its leaders were arrested and put behind bars under the Defence of India Act. The year 1964 is an important landmark in the history of the Indian communist movement as it was in the same year that the CPI suffered a major split, resulting in the birth of the CPI (Marxist). The architect of the Naxal movement in Orissa, Nagbhushan Pattnaik, and a number of his communist comrades joined CPI (M) in Orissa. However, from the beginning, Nagbhushan was not so convinced with the ideology and programmes of CPI (M). In one of his rare interview, he said 'after the division of CPI, I joined CPI (M), but somehow I was not able to believe the party'.[5]

However, Nagbhushan was arrested during 1964 under the Defence of India Act and was sent to the Tihar jail and it was during his two-year stay in Tihar he came in contact of P. Sundaray and reinvented his principles of socialist revolution. After his return in 1966, Nagbhushan played an instrumental role in connecting the activists of Koraput and Paralakhemundi with those of Srikakulam. During this period they formed the Jaipur Motor Shramik Sangha, J.K. Kagaja Kala Shramik Sangha, and Balimela Power Project Power Sangha and then successfully linked the trade union activists to the tribal movement. In 1967, when the seeds of the Naxal movement were sown in Naxalbari, one important development was taking place within the communist movement of Orissa. CPI (M) central leadership, concerned by the revolutionary activities of Nagbhushan and his colleagues, instructed them to immediately suspend all revolutionary programmes and join electoral politics. This was the turning-point in the decades-old Naxal history of Orissa as, not impressed by the party directives, Nagbhushan led his colleagues to form the Orissa State Coordination Committee (OSCC) and expressed solidarity with Charu Majumdar's All-India Coordination Committee of Communist Revolutionaries (AICCCR) which later on came to be known as the CPI (ML). The other members of the OSCC were D.B.M. Pattnaik (convener), Jaladhara Nanda, Rabi Das, Kundan Ram, Nagbhushan Pattnaik, Dinabandhu Samal and Jagannath Tripathy.

After the formal split and the formation of OSCC, its members got themselves involved with the violent programmes and propagandist activities. With the active support from Purushittam Pali, Hashnar, Jagannath Tripathy, Bidyadhar Patra, Yudhisthira Gouda, Shibram Panda and A.K Biswas, Nagbhushan was able to take the Chitrakonda movement to a new reach. A new conflict dynamics emerged from Naxalite politics in Orissa when, on 1 May 1968, under the leadership of Nagbhushan, nearly 5,000 workers raided Chitrakonda police station and looted all the arms and ammunitions from there. This was the beginning of the integration of the politics of organized violence with the brand politics of Naxalism in Orissa.

> It's not advisable to kill the exploiter at once. Rather we should kill him slowly as his exploitation is like a slow poison for the society. We should torture the devil to death everyday so that he experiences the pain of death every day. Political power flows from the barrel of gun to eliminate the class structure.[6]

Because of their revolutionary programmes, by 1968 the communists belonging to CPI (ML) were able to make their presence felt throughout the state. During this period, trade union leader Manmohan Mishra was attached to the Bengal–Bihar–Orissa Border Committee and, with his involvement in the labour politics of the Biramitrapur iron mines in Sundargarh district, Naxalism fast reached western Orissa. As a part of the Naxalbari line, at the beginning of 1968 the Revolutionary Student Front was formed in Berhampur by Santosh Mohapatra and Ramesh Sahu. Jaladhar Nanda, Rabi Singh and Rabi Das took the leadership of the movement in the coastal region of the state. During this period Dr Gananath Patra left his lecturership at the Paralekmundi College to join the CPI (ML) ranks. In a week-long secret meeting of the Orissa leadership as Kapilapur near Gunupur the participants agreed to adopt the revolutionary path of Naxalbari.

This period, particularly 1960 to 1968, could be seen as the formative phase of the Naxal movement in Orissa. It was during this phase that the Naxal movement as a whole carved a place for itself in the political map of the state and this was made possible mostly because of the organizational changes that took place within the communist movement. This phase witnessed a couple of splits: first the split of CPI resulting in the birth of CPI (M) and then the split resulting in the birth of CPI (ML). Both these splits had an electrifying impact on the left extremists of Orissa, which was not at all negative. Due to the organizational conflict, the extremists successfully managed to prove their viability in the prevailing situation of that time and this enabled them to reach different parts of the state. The extreme poverty conditions of southern Orissa provided the CPI (ML) with a perfect Maoist setting to organize protracted armed struggle against the system. Lack of political involvement and recurring bureaucratic apathy never really allowed development to take place in these areas and in such geo-political condition Nagbhushan Pattnaik led his brand of left extremists to newer heights. It was as early as 28 February 1969 that the then Chief Minister of Orissa, Rajendra Narayan Sighadeo, informed the state assembly that 'There are 32 guerilla squads operating in the Berhampur region of the state'.[7]

It was in these conditions that Charu Majumdar visited Andhra Pradesh in 1969, which had a far-reaching impact on the Naxalite politics of Orissa also. In a significant decision on 29 March 1969, the OSCC was dissolved according to the instructions of Charu Majumdar. After dissolving the OSCC, Charu Majumdar also effectively attached different regions of Orissa to the extremist organizations of the neighbouring states. Obviously, he was aiming at giving a concrete shape to his ideas of formulating a guerrilla zone. As a result the undivided Koraput and Ganjam districts of southern Orissa were attached to the Srikakulam regional committee. Similarly, the northern Orissa districts of Mayurbhanj and Balasore were attached to the coordination committee of West Bengal. On the other hand the Sambalpur and Sundargarh districts of western Orissa were linked to the South Bihar committee. 'These committees instigated the tribals to commit various acts of violence. They also held classes, distributed leaflets and organized arms training.'[8] This decision of Charu Majumdar marked the beginning of a new phase, the formation of guerrilla zones in the border districts of Orissa. Majumdar was quick to understand the ethnic, linguistic and cultural similarities between the people of Koraput/Ganjam and Andhra Pradesh, Mayurbhanj/Balasore and West Bengal, Sundargarh/Sambalpur and South Bihar. The tribal people belonging to Sambalpur, Sundargarh and South Bihar use one common language, Sadri, for their day-to-day interaction; similarly Telugu is the common language among the people in the Andhra bordering districts. It was part of a well-thought-out strategy to link these bordering areas to give the concept of guerrilla zone a concrete shape. The later turn of events prove that Charu Majumdar was not wrong as in subsequent years the emergence of armed action in the border areas became more violent. Northern Orissa witnessed the first spark of Naxalite violence on 26 February 1971, when extremists killed a schoolteacher and Gram Rakhshi, a low-level police functionary. Again on 5 June 1971, the Naxalites attacked a police post at Bholla, stabbed one *havildar* and set fire to a police van.[9]

This decision of Charu Majumdar also gave a new dimension to the organizational politics of the Naxal movement. It marked the beginning of the dominance of Andhra leadership over the course of Orissa Naxal movement. This was not a small development as it resulted in more competition among the Orissa leadership of the movement. Of course the then Orissa leadership never had an adverse reaction over the decision to dissolve the OSCC, but 'several times in the history of the Naxal movement in Orissa the Oriya leaders like Nagbhushan Pattnaik, and Sabyasachi Panda engaged themselves in a tussle with the Andhra leadership over several issues including leadership issue'.[10] On the other hand, because of this tussle, the Orissa leadership engaged themselves more in the activity of party-building which in turn strengthened the Naxal movement in different parts of the state.

The then government of Orissa took strong exception to the recurring violent activities of the Naxal groups. Between 1969 and 1971 the government of Orissa, actively backed by the Union government, followed a concentrated anti-Naxal strategy. In the execution of this strategy the state police force received adequate support from their Andhra counterparts. The Chitrakonda Conspiracy Case came for hearing at the Jaipur court in 1969, where Naxal leaders like Nagbhushan Pattnaik, Purna Gomango, Purushottam Pali, Yudhisthir Goud, Shivaram Panda, Jagannath Tripathy, D.B.M. Pattnaik and many others were sentenced to five years' imprisonment. The verdict of the Gunupur Conspiracy Case also came up in 1969, where seventy-one Naxalites, including leaders like Manmohan Mishra, were sent to jail. Similarly in the Paralekhamundi Conspiracy Case, eighty-seven Naxalite cadres, including Bidyadhar Patra and Navin Bauri, were sentenced to two years' imprisonment. Police arrested Naxal leaders like Parimal Pal, Tapan Ray, Ashok Chowdhury, Surendra Panigrahi and Ireshu Achari as a fallout of the Chatrapur Conspiracy Case. Between 1969 and 1972 the state police arrested nearly 300 Naxal cadres, including leaders like Sarat Panda, Dandapani Mohanty, Bhagirathi Mishra and Surya Patra. Nagbhushan was arrested on 15 July 1969 from the Vishakahpattanam University campus. But in a daring jailbreak episode Nagbhushan along with his eleven comrade associates fled from the Vihakhapattanam jail on 9 October 1969. Thereafter he took charge of the party organization in the Andhra–Orissa border area. On the other hand, Subarao Panigrahi was given the charge of party building in Uddan and Paralakhemundi. Subsequently Nagbhushan was arrested in Kolkata on 14 July 1970, after which Subbarao Panigrahi was also arrested. Because of the severity of police action, the movement lost its momentum during 1972.[11]

The founding father of the Naxal movement in India, Charu Majumdar, died in 1972. After his death, the Naxalites were divided over tactical issues, besides the factional feud that had already started to cripple the organization. The intra-organizational conflict that accompanied Charu Majumdar's death had a far-reaching impact on the course of the Naxal movement in Orissa. The post-1972 inner-group conflict and split within CPI (ML) created large-scale confusion and frustration among the CPI (ML) rank and file in Orissa due to which many of them rejoined CPI (M) and some preferred to remain aloof.

> By 1975 the first phase of the Naxal movement in Orissa came to an end. As many leaders like Nagbhushan were in Jail and some other Ideologues of Orissa Naxals were killed by the police. The period between 1975 to 1985 may be said the 'dumb period' in the history of Naxal Movement in Orissa.[12]

Also the movement received several jolts during the Emergency. The movement might have been pushed back but it was not finished. During 1981, Nagbhushan Pattnaik was released from jail after he was granted a presidential reprieve from a death sentence. After being released, Nagbhushan was instrumental in the formation of Indian Peoples Front (IPF). The same year he got himself elected to the politburo of CPI (ML) Liberation. But things were not the same for Nagbhushan any more. His old colleague and comrade of many programmes, D. Bhuban Mohan Pattnaik, developed serious differences and joined the Unity Centre of Communist Revolutonaries of India (Marxist-Leninist) after leaving IPF. However, Nagbhushan was still assisted by Vidyadhar Patra, Purna Gomango, and K.M.M Rao to reorganize the party in southern Orissa. The death of Purna Gomango in 1982 created a major vacuum in Koraput.

New polarization among the communist force was taking place during this period. The formation of People's War (PW) in Andhra Pradesh during 1980 had its impact on the course of the Naxal movement in Orissa. 'During 1985–86 Sabyasachi Panda came in the contact of Nagbhushan Pattnaik and his association with Nagbhushan marks the beginning of the second phase of Naxal Movement in Orissa.'[13] By the end of 1991, the CPI (M), Orissa suffered another split and hundreds of its cadres led by Dandapani Mohanty, Sabyasachi Panda, Budha Gomango, Hitinga Majhi and Tirupati Gomango joined CPI (ML) Liberation. However, by that time Nagbhushan's tryst with violent revolutionary technique (annihilation of the class enemy) was complete and it was on this issue that serious differences started to come up between him and Sabyasachi Panda. These differences further proved to be vital in the context of the growth of the Naxal movement in Orissa.

Under the new leadership in CPI (ML) Liberation, the Naxal movement again tried to consolidate its position. Led by Dandapani Mohanty, Sabyasachi Panda and Khitij Biswal, CPI (ML) Liberation organized the people's movement in different parts of Puri, Kalahandi and Sundargarh. CPI (ML) organized Pipalapanka agitation in Sorada, the land capture movement in Gunupur region, the bamboo-cutters' rights movement in Gajapati, Raygada and Ramanaguda. However, as said above, by that time PW was slowly but steadily gaining strength in different parts of Malkangiri and other areas bordering Andhra Pradesh. A group of CPI (ML) Liberation, under the leadership of Sabyasachi Panda, was in constant touch with the Andhra leadership of PW. 'Sabyasachi Panda started baseless allegations against Nagbhushan Pattnaik. Instead of spreading party programme and ideology he wanted to impose PW line of functioning on CPI (ML) Liberation.'[14] Finally during 1996 Sabyasachi Panda revolted against the party and formed Kui Labanga Sangha and Chashi Mulia Samiti. Soon Daku Majhi, Abraham Gomango, Budha Gomango, Kamal Sabar and Bhalu Chandra Sarangi joined him. 'Due to the opportunist politics of Nagbhushan and Vinod Mishra, Sabyasachi Panda declared that gun fight and guerrilla war is the only technique to attain revolutionary goals.'[15] With the death of Nagbhushan Pattnaik on 9 October 1998 an era of the Naxal movement in Orissa came to an end.

The period from 1951 to 1996 can be seen as the formative phase in the history of the Naxal movement in Orissa. As mentioned above, during this phase the several splits that occurred within the larger communist movement had really given a direction to the consolidation of left extremist forces in Orissa. What started with small-scale revolutionary communist programmes during 1951 in the limited pockets of south Orissa really took shape of a violent Maoist movement by the end of 1996.

Phase 2: Emergence of splinter groups and their impact on the Naxal movement in Orissa

This second phase of the growth of the Naxal movement in Orissa is characterized by the emergence of different Naxalite splinter groups in the map of red politics in Orissa. By the time Nagbhushan Pattnaik died in 1998 different Naxal groups like People's War Group (PWG) and Maoist Communist Centre (MCC) were already a force to reckon with in different parts of Orissa. Prior to their merger, PWG was successful enough to establish substantial guerrilla network in the districts of Koraput, Malkangiri, Nabarangapur, Rayagada, Gajapati and Ganjam; whereas the MCC was largely visible in Sundargarh, Mayurbhanj and Keonjhar. Other than these two prime groups, CPI (Red Flag) and CPI (ML) Liberation do have a nominal presence in the Gajapati and Rayagada districts of southern Orissa.

A The People's War Group (PWG)

It was during 1989 that one armed battalion of PWG under the leadership of K. Punam Chand moved into Motu, MV 79, and Kalimela, areas of the then undivided district of Koraput, and established their control over Girkanpali, Kunanpali and Anantapali villages.[16] However, the PWG got a real shot in its arm when Sabyasachi Panda and group came to its fold during 1996. After that a new pattern of guerrilla warfare emerged in the Naxal brand of politics in Orissa. To carry out its armed operations in Orissa, PWG formed a number of *Dalams* (action squads) namely, Jhanjhavati Dalam, Nagavali Dalam, Nagalkonda Dalam, Kalimela Dalam, Motu Dalam, Mahila Dalam, Korkonda Dalam, Uddanam Dalam, Vasdhara Dalam and Anantagiri Dalam.[17] PWG also formed several guerilla *Mandals* to strengthen its network and to give a concrete shape to its concept of guerrilla zone and liberated zone. Dandakaranya Guerilla Mandal, North Telengana Guerilla Mandal (Koraput, Raygada, Gajapati and Vijaynagaram, Srikakulam of Andhra), South Telengana Guerilla Mandal and North Andhra Guerilla Mandal all proved vital to strengthen the power and strength of PWG in the Andhra-bordering parts of southern Orissa.

Over the years, the PWG have managed to develop a number of frontal organizations of tribal people, women and cultural artists. Some of them are the Kui Labanga Sangh, the Lok Shakti Manch, the Nari Shakti Bahini, the Kui Sanskrutika Sangathan, the Chasi Mulia Royat Samiti, the Radical Students Organization, the Rajanaitika Bandi Mukti Committee, the Jana Natya Mandali and the Royat Kuli Sangram Manch.[18] Those frontal organizations of PWG were entrusted to carry on propaganda work, posting posters, distributing leaflets, conducting meetings, organizing cultural programmes, etc. The importance of these organizations cannot be underestimated, as they were instrumental in establishing a chord with the local tribal people. They worked as agencies of recruitment. It was through these frontal organizations that PWG reached out to the masses and used them as a platform to justify its armed operations.

> The expansion of the Naxalite activities in Orissa intensified after the PWG formed the Andhra–Orissa Border Special Zonal Committee (AOBSZC) in 2001. The AOBSZC covers the four north coastal districts of Andhra Pradesh–East Godavari, Vishakhapattanam, Vijayanagaram and Srikakulam – and five districts of southern Orissa Koraput, Malkangiri, Rayagada, Nabarabgpur and Gajapati.[19]

The *modus operandi* of the PWG proved to be more militarized than the earlier Naxalites and with its guerrilla attacks and lethal capability in the use of landmines and explosives it proved to be a resilient outfit. The integration of military activities and cultural activities done by its frontal organizations gave a new dimension to organizational aspect of Naxalite politics in Orissa. The decade-old experience of PWG leading the Naxal movement in Orissa proved to be largely successful because, through the works of its frontal organizations that work among various marginalized groups in a non-violent manner through mass mobilization and cultural events like street plays, it sufficiently radicalized the local population to support the activities of the military units. Following these organizational formulas, the PWG actually aimed to make the state redundant and come up with 'liberated zones'. This has brought the PWG into conflict with structures of the state like the security forces. Even elected leaders and members of organized political parties were targeted. The larger aim behind the attacks on political leaders at the grassroots meant to make democratic political activities impossible and to put pressure on the elected leaders to go slow on a counter-strategy.

The PWG mainly targeted the security personnel and political activists to spread terror in the region. By attacking security personnel, PWG intended to make it loud and clear that protracted armed struggle is the only way to attain the revolutionary goals, and for the attainment of the same it never minded killing the poor policemen.

> Going by the class structure an ordinary policeman should be our friends. But where government is working for the imperialist and capitalist class, executing the order of such a government means helping them in their anti poor agenda and the policemen are doing the same mistake. It's true that they are working to earn their livelihood but they cannot be allowed to spread state terror.[20]

By attacking the police force the PWG was working on a multi-pronged strategy. First, it wanted to demoralize the police force, as it knew that the only credible presence of government in the Naxal-infested areas was the presence of the police force. By attacking them, PWG was successful enough to create a Robin Hood image for its cadres. It was a well-thought-out guerrilla strategy applied by the PWG to lead systematic attacks on the police force as it knew that a demoralized police force will allow them to operate freely among the masses and it would also earn them respect and fear among the masses. Second, PWG, by leading attacks on the security personnel, was working towards its larger aim of establishing parallel government and liberated zones in its operational areas. Subsequent developments in Orissa prove that PWG was largely successful in its game plan. After the 9 August 2001 PWG attack on the Motu and Kalimela police station the then officer in charge of Motu said in an interview that 'If the Naxalites attack us again then we will surrender to them immediately. To save our life we are even ready to lick their foot.'[21] A demoralized police force in Orissa has provided more opportunities of growth for the Naxal movement. On the other hand, by attacking political leaders PWG wanted to spread the message that it aims at the replacement of the prevailing system of parliamentary democracy and for this purpose it draws inspiration from the 'annihilation theory' of Charu Majumdar.

B *The Maoist Communist Centre (MCC)*

For long the Jharkhand bordering districts of Orissa, namely, Sundargarh, Mayurbhanj, and Keonjhar, served as a base area for the erstwhile MCC. Since the late 1990s several villages belonging to Gorumahisani, Jharpokharia, Bangiriposhi, Bisoi and Chiranga police stations of Mayrbhanj district have remained under the influence of MCC. Similarly it has been close to a decade now that the MCC cadres from neighbouring Jharkhand have consolidated their position in the villages under Bisra, Bolang, Banki, Podia, Gurundia and Tikayatpali police station of Sundargarh district. On the other hand, the mining-rich pockets of Joda and Badbil in Keonjhar are known to be Naxal-prone.

The history of MCC in Orissa can be traced back to its activities in Mayurbhanj. It was not accidental but was part of one well-thought-out strategy.

> The border districts of three states – Bengal, Bihar and Orissa – were selected as a prospective area to wage and advance the class struggle to higher stage. To achieve this, revolutionary propaganda and contacting people of this remote backward Adivasi district of Mayurbhanj of Orissa began. At first one centre, Bangriposhi, was started; and later it was expanded to two areas i.e., Badampahar and Gurumoshani. In the process of our work, Badampahar and Bangriposhi were merged and the area was called the Bangriposhi area.[22]

With its rich forest cover, hilly terrains and dominant tribal (Santhal) population the underdeveloped backward region of Mayurbhanj provided a natural environment for the growth of MCC. By the end of 1997 the state police started taking cognizance of the growing Maoist activity in the state. The MCC organizer in Bangriposhi, Ajoy, along with fellow member Monica, was arrested in Jamtoria village of Simlipal forests on 1 August 1999.[23] The MCC in Mayurbhanj for long operated through several area party committees.

However, it is not Mayurbhanj but Sundargarh, which is known for a spurt of Maoist-related activities in recent times. Though in recent past the MCC cadres managed to put forth some daring attacks on the security forces, the police for long were clueless about the organizational *modus operandi* of MCC.

> Sundargarh was always in the Maoist map. By 1999 we managed to form the Krantikari Kisan Committee (KKC, the Revolutionary Farmers' Committee), and Jungle Surakhya Committee (JSC, Forest Protection Committee) in the Jharkhand bordering villages of Bisra, Bhalulata, Jharbeda, Kaliaposh, Tulsikani, Makaranda, Sanramloi, Badramloi, Jareikela.[24]

These committees were entrusted to mobilize villagers and to recruit unemployed girls and boys. Each KKC consists of thirty members and the JSCs have twenty members. By now the Maoist ultras have carved a space for them in the social structure of this remote corner of Orissa.

> MCC members from Jharkhand are regular visitors of our area. They attend every marriage, festivals in the area; eat and go. They come to the market. They visit different villages in the night. They have their members in every border village.[25]

As of now Naxals are functioning through the Krantikari Kissan Sangh, the Local Regular Guerrilla Squad (LRGS) and the Special Regular Guerrilla Squad

(SRGS), above which there is a military platoon that effectively takes all the important decisions.

> The LRGS is at the bottom of the Military command which consists of 15-armed cadres and, above which there is the SRGS consisting of 15 to 30 armed cadres. At the apex we have the 'military platoons' consisting of 30 armed cadres.[26]

In sharp contrast to their PWG counterparts the MCC in this part of the state never operated through organized peasant insurrection. Despite chronic poverty and miserable living conditions, people from this side of the border have never been inclined to join MCC out of any ideological belongingness. Several allegations of forced recruitment have been levelled against the MCC in the recent past.

> Due to the sheer negligence of police the area has become Naxal infested. The absence of credible mechanisms of governance has encouraged the growth of Maoist forces in this area. The security forces never really operate in a concentrated manner to eliminate Maoist forces. The area has become so unsafe that we had to send our daughters and sisters away from home to save them from forced recruitment in MCC.[27]

For long the Jharkhand cadres of MCC were using these border villages as their hide-out and during this time they managed to give shape to their revolutionary designs in these tribal-dominated villages.

> The first incidence of violence was noticed on 17th January 2002 when they attacked a forest beat house and murdered the Forest Guard. Again on 18th January they murdered another person near Jaraikela. On 4th April 2003, around 30–40 armed MCC activist entered into Orissa from the Jharkhand side of the Sarnda forest through Chiruguda village. First they visited Sanramloi village in Monko Gram *Panchayat* of Bisra Block. Forcibly they drove out villagers from their house and arranged a public meeting there. To generate fear among the masses the MCC activists burnt a *Tendu* leaf loaded truck and a forest beat house. During October 2003 some armed MCC activists managed to cross the border and enter into Orissa. They stopped a bus near Bhalulata; forcibly made the passengers get down and took them a place nearby to conduct a public meeting. On 6th June 2004, again some MCC activists crossed into this side of Orissa and visited Sanramloi and Badramloi villages in Bisra Block. They arranged one public meeting in Badramloi village. The message in the meeting was to hamper the entire road and bridge works in the area. The motive behind was to destroy all means of communication in order to enable guerilla warfare.[28]

This statement of a local police officer from Jaraikela covers the high points of MCC operations in the Sundargarh district.

However, the government of Orissa made the biggest blunder of reducing the MCC activity in Sundargarh and other Jharkhand bordering districts as a spillover effect from the neighbouring state. This allowed the Jharkhand-based guerilla leaders to spread their network in forest-covered areas of Sundargarh, Sambalpur, Keonjhar and Mayurbhanj. This development became more visible after the formation of CPI (Maoist) in 2004. Due to administrative and security negligence, the Maoists have now managed to link the Sarnda forest in Jharkhand–Orissa border with the Redhakhol forest in Sambalpur with a strong guerilla network. The details of all this will find a place in the subsequent parts of this chapter.

Phase 3: Formation of the Communist Party of India (Maoist) and after

The Naxal movement in Orissa entered yet another phase with the merger of PWG and MCC and the formation of CPI (Maoist) on 21 September 2004. The merger proved to be vital in terms of metamorphic growth of violence and inclusion of newer areas in the Maoist map of Orissa. Prior to the merger, Naxal activities in Orissa were limited to the nine districts, but after the merger the Naxal movement managed to reach to newer areas and, as of now, fourteen districts of Orissa are under the influence of the Naxal movement. Sambalpur, Jharsuguda, Deogarh, Jajpur and Kandhamal were relatively untouched by the growth of the Naxal movement; however as the post-merger story goes, these areas have now become the worst affected.

Despite their organizational and ideological differences, there were no instances of enmity as far as the Orissa operations of PWG and MCC were concerned. 'Ideologically PWG is quite nearer to MCC. Talks are going on for the merger of these two parties and if it materializes then there it will be a huge opportunity for the revolutionary forces in India.'[29] What Sabyasachi Panda spoke in the context of India became true for Orissa also. By merging into a single outfit, PWG and MCC managed to link their base areas of south Orissa and western Orissa and in the process also it included newer areas to their road map. At present, there are two zonal committees of CPI (Maoist) functioning in Orissa: the Andhra–Orissa Border Special Zonal Committee and the Jharkhand–Bihar–Orissa Special Zonal Committee.[30] There are also media reports that in the first quarter of 2006, the CPI (Maoist) Central Committee formed a state committee in Orissa with Sabyasachi Panda as its head.[31] However, as far as the ground conditions are concerned, both PWG and MCC have so far maintained the same organizational structure. Since the area of operation for both the groups was clearly distinct, there is absolutely no confusion as far as the ground operations are concerned. Despite all these committees, the Orissa operations are mostly taken care of by the Andhra–Orissa Border Special Zonal Committee of CPI (Maoist).

After the formation of CPI (Maoist), a lot of changes have been noticed in the *modus operandi* of the Naxalites in the state. So far they have shown more organizational capability and more accuracy in attack and they have become more ruthless. After the formation of CPI (Maoist) the Naxals in Orissa have been able to make impressive inroads into the newer areas. This unification phase was a period of relative calm. However, the beginning of 2005 witnessed some major incidents in different parts of Orissa. In February 2005, the Naxals masterminded a major landmine blast in the Badigeta village of Malkangiri district in which two policemen were seriously injured, in retaliation for the killing of two Naxalites and imprisoning of four cadres by state police. Similarly, in late March, the Naxalites killed a police informer at his home near Rayagada. On 1 April, the district Congress president of Rayagada, Satyanarayan Doki, became the victim of this growing 'red terror' when the Naxalites looted and attacked his house with explosives. In another daredevil act the Naxalites engineered a landmine blast to destroy the Sheshakhol police outpost in the Rayagada district. These are not only specific incidents of violence but are also the clear signals of a dangerous Naxal game plan. Naxal threats like abduction and formation of guerilla squads have cropped up in other districts too. Most recently, in early 2005 an incident came to light in which Naxals abducted eighteen labourers from Pudamal and Phulkusum villages of Sambalpur. According to Sushant Nath, the then superintendent of police of Sambalpur, the Maoists have been desperately trying to create a corridor from Jharkhand's Sarnda forest to the Rairakhol forest in Orissa. Similarly, the then police chief of Sundargarh, Yashowant Jethua, confirmed in February 2005 that the Naxals have been able to form local guerilla squads in different areas of Sambalpur and Deogarh.

Sambalpur district of Orissa, in particular, which was nowhere on the earlier Naxal map, now became a hotbed for Naxal activities. In 2005 the Naxals managed to strike terror in the interior areas of the district by killing civilians. On 27 May of that year, the Naxals went on the rampage and killed three villagers and injured several others in Burda village under Jujumura police station. Prior to this the Maoist activities were only confined to abductions followed by ransom. The incident came as a shock as the Maoists generally target the police, forest officials, contractors and other businessmen. This incident has been considered important with regard to the course of Naxal growth in the underdeveloped and tribal-dominated western Orissa. The timing of the incident speaks volumes about the greater aims and ambitions of Naxals in the region. The incident came barely nine hours after an important meeting of high-level police officers held at Sambalpur district headquarters to discuss problems related to left-wing extremism in the area. It clearly signals the Naxal game plan of defying the government and creating an environment of terror and suspicion. Earlier in May, the village headman of Chhamunda village council was abducted and was released only after he signed a bond paper to pay Rs 4 to the rebels. With the daring jail break incident in the Gajapati district of Orissa, the Naxals sent a loud and clear message that they were capable enough to strike anywhere at will. On 24 March 2006, a 200-member armed contingent of the CPI (Maoist) seized the small town of R Udayagiri and went on a rampage that left three security personnel dead. The Naxals kidnapped the R Udayagiri police station officer-in-charge, Ranjan Mallick, and sub-jail superintendent, Rabindra Narayan Sethi, ransacked

Left-wing radicalism in Orissa 201

the *tehsil* building and an inspection bungalow, and damaged phone company tower. The administration was caught unawares of the Naxal game plan. The Gajapati district magistrate, Binod Bihari Mohanty, had to run for his life when the Naxalites approached the inspection bungalow. Not finding him there, they ransacked the inspection bungalow. The Naxals also attacked the sub-treasury and burnt stamp papers worth nearly Rs40 *lakh*. They looted a huge quantity of arms and ammunition from the police camp. According to the government reports, the police killed three Naxals, including one woman. However, the three bodies were taken away by the Naxals as they retreated. This Naxal attack brings back disconcerting memories of the November 2005 Jehanabad Jail raid. In 2003 the Naxals had displayed their capabilities in Orissa in the most dramatic way when they raided the district headquarters town of Koraput and looted arms and ammunitions from the district armoury.

If the September 2004 merger of several Naxal groups signalled a new beginning in terms of the direction of Maoist movement in India, the beginning of 2007 signaled the Naxal movement's entry into yet another phase in the cycle of Maoist insurgencies in India. The merger of CPI (ML-PW) and MCC-I which resulted in the birth of CPI (Maoist) also successfully brought the dominant fraction of CPI (ML-Janashakti) to its fold. However, the honeymoon between the CPI (Maoist) and Janashakti could not last beyond one year and in 2006 it became apparent that both were clearly going different ways to occupy operational areas. During the open session of CPI (Maoist) held in December 2006, Janashakti was asked to clear its stand on its political aims and programmes; however, Janashakti chose not to attend the session. Consequently CPI (Maoist) withdrew the partner status from Janashakti and decided to provide needs-based support only in the case of police actions.[32] The conflict between CPI (Maoist) and Janashakti became public when the Orissa Janashakti group, led by Anna Reddy, killed three forest officials on 31 January 2007.[33] Immediately the CPI (Maoist) state leadership distanced itself from the killings and the subsequent police enquiry confirmed the involvement of the Janashakti group in the gruesome act.

The beginning of 2008 witnessed increasing use of mobile war technology by the Naxalites in the state. Orissa, with a total death toll of 132 in Naxal-related incidents, remained a hotbed of Maoist activity. On 17 February 2008, a date which would always remain a special entry in the Naxal record-book, armed cadres of CPI (Maoist) raided a police training school, the district armoury and district police station in coordinated attacks at Nayagarh in Orissa, killing at least fourteen police personnel and a civilian before fleeing with a huge cache of arms, including AK-47s and light machine-guns.[34] The Nayagarh attack was certainly an attempt by the Naxals to woo the middle class, and particularly the lower middle classes, which seem to be caught between the rich and poor. It signalled that the Naxals in the state are attempting to spread beyond the tribal belt and venture out to non-tribal areas with a sizeable middle-class population. Again, on 29 June 2008, the Naxals for the first time showcased their ability in the tricks of marine warfare when they chose to attack a motor launch inside the Balimela reservoir in the Malkangiri district of Orissa, which left thirty-four security personnel dead. Malkangiri is separated from Andhra by the Sileru River and from Chhattisgarh by the Saberi River. Besides the Sileru and Saberi, there is another inter-state river, the Mahendrataneya, between Orissa and Andhra. This is the area where, in 2005, Naxals raised a boat wing to facilitate faster movement of their cadres and weapons.[35] On 23 August Swami Laxmananda Saraswati, a Vishwa Hindu Parishad leader, and four others were killed by the Naxal cadres in the Kandhamal district of Orissa. Eyebrows were raised when Sabyasachi Panda claimed a Naxal hand in the assassination.[36] There were many who suspected Panda's claim on the grounds that Naxals have no history of interfering in religious matters. However generalizations are deceptive in the studies of movements; Naxals may not have interfered in religious issues in the past but that does not prevent them from entering into the arena of communal politics. The Kandhamal operation was well in the line with deliberations of the 2007 party congress of CPI (Maoist) wherein fundamentalism was considered the second biggest threat, after globalization.[37] The Kandhamal incident led to two distinct Maoist formulations in Orissa. First, a split of CPI (Maoist) on religious grounds which led to the formation of a new outfit called 'Idealize of Democrat Guerrilla Army – Maoist (IDGA-Maoist)'. Second, in a related development, the Central Committee of the CPI (Maoist) expelled Sabyasachi Panda, secretary of the CPI (Maoist)'s Orissa unit, from the party. Undeniably Panda was the pillar of the Naxal movement in Orissa. These two developments brought in significant changes in the Maoist strategies in the state.

The growth of the Naxal movement in Orissa is undoubtedly an interesting story of twists and turns in ultra-left-wing extremism in a rather economically backward constituent state of India. It also shows that Naxalism in Orissa was textured in accordance with Orissa's peculiar socio-economic dynamics; it followed different courses by reinterpreting (or rather adapting) Marxism-Leninism to articulate its opposition to the prevalent state power in different times of the history. However, one can safely argue that Maoism in Orissa essentially is a result of several conflicting dynamics – be it inter-organizational conflict or intra-organizational conflict or natural resource conflict or a conflict involving the internal security of the country. What is striking, however, is the fact that, despite having been ideologically inspired by an identical thought-process, Maoists in Orissa seem to have become faction-ridden except for a temporary period after the formation of CPI (Maoist) in 2004 following the merger of three major Maoist groups. In this respect, Maoism seems to be a continuity with the past when the Indian communist movement suffered due to splits over ideological disagreements that invariably resulted in the formation of competing political outfits claiming to be pursuing 'true Marxism-Leninism'.

Socio-economic context and the growing consolidation of left-wing extremism in Orissa

Orissa is a paradox: on the one hand, it is one of the well-endowed Indian states in natural resources but the state stands out, on the other, as one of the poorest in terms of basic human development index. Orissa figures predominantly in the list of underdeveloped states in India and is a victim of the state-led development strategy that contributed to a sluggish economic growth in India.[38] Since independence, several mega industrial and mining projects have come up in areas which were under the occupation of tribal communities. Originally, before the emergence of the state and ruling class, customary rights were more or less the statutory rights under the state. When the British occupied India they could not understand and appreciate the customary rights of the people of India, particularly those of tribal communities. Earlier, customary rights were recognized in India because they concerned not only the tribals but also the village communities. The UN document of 1966 defines customary rights as the rights to use or dispose of the rights over land. In the past, most of the tribal settlements comprised members of a single clan who held land and forest resources as their own, in their habitat. Land for others may be an object for agriculture but land for tribals is a part of larger socio-economic structure of society, which is handed over from one generation to another as sources of life sustenance. Scheduled tribes, which constitute 22 per cent of Orissa's population, are the most marginalized and poor social group in the state, with over 72 per cent living below the poverty line. Though land and land-based resources are central to the livelihoods of tribal people, they have poor access to land and forests. Most tribal communities in Orissa have strong cultural and social relationships with land, with many practising communal ownership of land, especially hill-slope land. During the last two centuries, tribal communities have been affected by land loss through alienation of plain lands to non-tribals and the hill-slope lands to the state, which has categorized these areas as forest land or revenue waste lands. The loss of private landholdings by tribals has been a cause of concern, with a number of laws being passed by both the pre-independence state and the postcolonial state to check land alienation. These laws suffered from many shortcomings and were unable to check the transfer of land from tribals to non-tribals.

Despite being a rich state in terms of its mines and minerals and natural resources, Orissa has not made any real progress as far as the development of the state and its people are concerned. This is ironic that a state which is floating on rich mineral resources remains one of the most economically backward states in India. The reasons are not difficult to seek. Besides the general failure of the statist model of development, the mismatch between India's development strategy and 'the limited capacity of the state to guide social and economic change' seems to be a critical factor.[39] As the evolution of Orissa as a constituent state in independent India shows, the development strategy that the political leadership undertook was drawn on certain meta-considerations, ignoring, to a large extent, the inherent economic strength of the region by virtue of its minerals and other natural resources. This neglect was partly political and partly due to lack of proper planning for utilizing the resources for a balanced growth of the state. As a result, the state remained economically backward, and people suffered miserably despite the euphoria associated with planned economic development since India's independence in 1947. The aim here is not to elaborate the processes that led to a lopsided growth in Orissa, but simply to show the economic richness of the state because of the vast mineral reserves that have remained underutilized. Orissa belongs to that region of India which is a rich repository of mineral resources, as Table 7.1 illustrates

Despite having such mineral resources Orissa is infamous for poverty, starvation and underdevelopment. Ironically, the underdeveloped, Maoism-affected western and southern belts of Orissa are the storehouse of most of the state's mines and mineral deposits. Besides small irrigation projects, there have been hardly any attempts to explore these mineral resources for development. The ongoing development process in these areas has not benefited the rural mass, which suffers socio-economic injustice. The state-sponsored development in Orissa remains largely divorced from people's participation in decision-making. The nexus between Maoism and lopsided development has considerably damaged the democratic values and institutions.

Over forty-two steel plants are poised to come up in Orissa requiring 1,600 million tonnes of iron ore in the next twenty-five years. Multinational giants like BHP-Billiton, Vedanta Resources, Rio Tinto Mining, Alcan, Aditya Birla Group, Tata Group and Saudi Arabian companies have started queuing up to exploit the state's resources. The state government has already leased 1,000 million tons of bauxite ore to different companies. These are but misguiding signs of development in Orissa.[40] One cannot take this massive industrialization and mining activity as the scale to judge the case of human development among the people in the remote areas of southern and western Orissa. Exploitation, zero healthcare and educational facilities, malnutrition, inhuman torture, rising unemployment, inordinate delay in disposal of land cases and unwillingness to undertake land reforms seem to have plagued considerably the development aims and programmes.

Table 7.1 Mineral resources of Orissa

Mineral ore	Reserves in Orissa (in million tons)	Reserves in India (in million tons)	State share of country's reserves (%)
Bauxite	1,733	2,911	59.5
Chromite	183	186	98.4
China clay	311	986	31.5
Coal	49,406	199,282	24.8
Dolomite	889	4,967	17.9
Fire clay	178	696	25.6
Graphite	2.2	3.1	71.0
Iron ore	4,200	12,745	32.9
Managanese ore	119	176	67.6
Mineral sands	82	266	30.8
Pyrophyllite	8.6	13.2	65.1
Nickel ore	270	294	91.8

Source: http://orissagov.nic.in/e-magazine/orissaannualreference/ORA-2004/pdf/mineral_resource_of_orissa.pdf, accessed on 27 September 2012.

Tribal exploitation and suffering have become the destiny of many with the establishment of the Rourkela Steel Plant. The Steel Authority of India acquired about 35,000 acres for this plant and another 12,000 acres for its reservoir Mandira dam. As per one *Gazette of Orissa* notification, over thirty-three villages covering 2,503,524 acres of land had been acquired by the Orissa government in 1954 to set up the Rourkela Steel Plant. Another thirty-one villages spreading over 1,192,398 acres were acquired for the construction of the Mandira dam in 1956–7. In both projects, a total 3,695,912 acres had been acquired for the plant and the Mandira dam, resulting in the uprooting of 4,251 families.[41] Both the Steel Authority of India and the state government have failed miserably to rehabilitate and resettle the evacuees of the last fifty years. This has caused considerable damage to the socio-economic conditions of the local tribal.

In recent years, hundreds of sponge iron factories have mushroomed all over in the district of Sundargarh, where the Maoists have a stronghold. Existing environmental laws have been flouted openly by the industrialists who have no concern for pollution and environment degradation. They have been dumping their waste everywhere, so that most agricultural land of the area has lost its fertility. Local people have witnessed and complained about the polluted air and water being emitted from the plant of Rexon Strips in Kumarkela village of Gurundia Block. The polluting units are emitting ammonia fumes strong enough to corrode tin sheets and burn paddy and green vegetables, which have become a major threat to life. Thousands of people who live in the villages of Ramabahar, Jampali, Jhagarpur, Bargaon, Vedvyas, Balanda, Kuarmunda, Kalunga, Rajgangpur, Birkera, Koira, Bonai, Tensa, Birmitrapur, Bijabahal, Tensa, Bersuan, Bonai, Lahunipada and Gurundia in Sundargarh are suffering from various skin diseases, tuberculosis and allergies. Similar is the case of people in the Barbil and Joda region of Keonjhar district.[42] The failure of government to take the local tribals into the development map was successfully exploited by the erstwhile MCC in establishing a strong Naxal support base in the tribal districts of Sundargarh and Keonjhar.

Now let us turn our focus to Malkangiri where Maoism seems to have developed an emotional chord with local inhabitants. Poverty, rampant corruption and failed government mechanisms and programmes are some of characteristics associated with this area. The CPI (Maoist), under the banner of erstwhile PWG has created a red bastion in the remote areas in Malkangiri. In the 1970s the government of Orissa constructed the Balimela Dam Project in Chitrakonda at Malkangiri. Villagers from more then 250 villages were displaced and a number of villages of Kudugulugumma Block remained cut off from the mainland and from most of supplies of the government system.[43] The government performance on the rehabilitation front can be simply termed as disastrous. Thousands of people are still living in tiny islands within the dam area, which the government terms the 'cut-off area'. One would find hardly any sign of governance in these areas of Janbai, Panasput, Jodamba, and Andrapali *Panchayats*; where there is no school, no hospital and no public distribution system.[44] To visit other parts of the district, the villagers depend solely on a motorboat which runs twice a week. The cut-off areas are not even interconnected by road. Government-sanctioned development projects in these areas are just completed on paper; residents of these areas complain of gross financial irregularities because of an unholy nexus between contractors and government officials. It is an irony that inhabitants of these areas have sacrificed everything for the dam but to date they have not seen the electricity produced by the dam. Who says big dams bring prosperity? For the people of Malkangiri the Balimela Dam has only brought broken dreams. Extreme poverty and lack of the basic requirements of life among the people in most areas of Malkangiri have made people move closer to Naxals.

Another affected southern district of Orissa is Rayagada, which bears the same signature of extreme poverty, rampant corruption and a chaotic but violent social atmosphere. It has a dominant tribal population and a total of 72.03 per cent of them in the district are living below the poverty line.[45] To the outside world the area is known for its backwardness and death from starvation. Between 1990 and 2000, more than Rs 100 crores were spent, but a large part of this amount was appropriated by the political leaders, bureaucrats, contractors and traders. The state government, as part of its development activity, started planting eucalyptus and this only helped the J.K. paper mill to get cheap raw material. A concrete road was constructed from Tikiri to Kashipur via Maikanch only to welcome the Utkal Alumina Industries Ltd. To sum up, all these so-called development projects in no way helped the majority tribal people of the region. This has alienated the rural tribal people and created a natural support base for Maoism. The area is blessed with a huge content of bauxite: 1957.3 lakh tons in Baphli Mali, 810 lakh tons in Sasubahu Mali, 860 lakh tons in Siji Mali near Kasipur. The Utkal Alumina International Ltd (a joint enterprise of Aditya Birla Group, and ALCAN, a Canadian company) is constructing a Rs 4,500 crores aluminum plant site at Doraguda near Kasipur. The project threatens displacement of over 20,000 people, and would adversely affect eighty-two villages.[46] Since 1994, the local communities in Rayagada have been protesting bauxite mining, condemning the breach of constitutional provisions barring the sale or lease of tribal lands without consent. People protest the devastation of their ecosystems, histories and futures, the destruction of forests, agricultural lands, mountains, perennial water-streams, the water-retention capacity of mountains, which are integral to their life and livelihood. So far, the government has not been able to come out with an answer to people's apprehension; instead it uses police methods to suppress people's voices. And this lackadaisical government attitude creates conditions in which Maoism succeeds in building a support base among the tribes in this area.

The story is similar in the case of another affected district, Koraput, which has a poverty ratio of 78.65 per cent and the literacy rate is miserably at 36.2 per cent. With a tribal population of 585,830[47] this district has remained a hotbed of ultra-left extremist activities for decades. The government's insensitivity towards basic problems of poverty-stricken rural and tribal people is the main cause for the growth of Maoism in Koraput. It is a sad reality in Koraput that the government programmes never really reach the people for whom they were really made. It was in March 2000 that the state government made a declaration that the tribal people would have the right to collect minor forest products though it has not been implemented to date.[48] The government strategy on development has been mostly limited to lip service only, without really understanding the problems typical of the lifestyle of the majority tribal people of Koraput. There is no market for minor forest products in Koraput, and tribals do not even have access to financial institutions to get loans for investments. It is surprising as well as shocking that the government has never thought of developing self-help groups for the forest-dependent communities in Koraput, an area that has no dearth of mineral deposits, but the government's failure to take proper steps to utilize these resources in favour of local people has really worsened the situation. Taking advantage of this alienation among the masses, the Maoists have shown them the dream of a revolution; a Maoist revolution. In the name of revolution the Maoists now control over 400 villages in Koraput, where they collect tax (extortion) and have established a sort of parallel administration.

Rehabilitation of people displaced by dams like Hirakud in Sambalpur district, built way back in the 1950s, is not yet complete. Compensation amounting to Rs154,146,994 was not paid for years. Finally, when some compensation was paid to some people, it was a saga of gross financial irregularity, as many displaced persons complained.[49] People still have not forgotten this sense of humiliation and this has pushed them to the Maoist fold in different parts of Sambalpur. According to the Ghadei committee report, published in 2006, among nine blocks of the district, three are grossly underdeveloped, three are underdeveloped and three are developing. Hirakud is the world's largest dam, but only 28 per cent of the district's area is irrigated whereas the remaining 72 per cent has no sign of irrigaton. Except in some areas of Rengali, Maneswar and Jujumura Block, the remaining six blocks are not linked with a canal system. What is most deplorable is that in all these nine blocks of Kuchinda, Jamankira, Jujumura, Naktideul, Bamra, Maneswar, Rengali, Rairakhol, and Dhankauda there is an acute shortage of drinking water.[50] The electricity requirements of the state are mostly catered by the Hirakud Dam, but most villages in the district have yet to get proper electricity connection and supply. The government neglect of the poor and the downtrodden is successfully exploited by the Maoists.

The mishandling of the Kalinga Nagar incident in the Jajpur district has now created another red bastion in the state. In an ugly incident on 2 January 2006, during a tribal protest meeting, the police fired on and killed at least twelve innocent tribals, which again gave Maoists an issue to prove their point. For TISCO's Kalinga Nagar project, industrial distributor cooperatives acquired the land at Rs35,000 per acre during 1992–4 and are now selling it at Rs350,000 to the company. The decision of the government to sell land at a price higher than what they fixed while purchasing land from the local owners led to frustration among the people. For the original owners of the land, this was 'unacceptable' because 'the state government is doing business with us instead of helping us in the development process. It is making huge profits from our land. When we ask for our share they offer us bullets.'[51] In and around Kalinga Nagar, people complained that the industries set up in the region, (the Neelachal Ispat Nigam Ltd, Jindal Steels, Mesco Steels) only brought miseries and humiliations; it has crushed them, the proud tribals, and they hate it. The people earlier were independent, poor but with self-dignity; now they have been reduced to outsiders in their own homeland, daily wage labourers or beggars. Not only in Kalinga Nagar have the tribal people repeatedly expressed their dissatisfaction; in many places like Kashipur and Lanjigarh the tribals are also struggling for daily existence.

The inevitable outcome of a thoughtless and also inappropriate development strategy in Orissa is that, in all of the resettlement operations, the majority of those ousted have ended up with lower incomes, less land than before; fewer work opportunities, inferior housing, less access to the resources of the commons such as fuel-wood and fodder, and worse nutrition and physical and mental health. It is estimated that about three to five million people have been displaced since 1950 in Orissa on account of various development projects of which more than 50 per cent are tribal. The tenth Five Year Plan (2002–7)[52] made a very special mention of different poverty alleviation schemes and programmes; however their impact on rural poverty, particularly in Orissa, remains dubious. When it comes to implementation, the government agenda is grossly mismanaged, and it mostly comes with a package of corruption, which raises serious doubts over government's commitment to human rights and social security. These failed efforts so far have been successfully exploited by ultra-leftist groups to win over the local tribal people as their formidable support base. Asymmetrical development in Orissa causes different kinds of conflict between values of democratic governance and aspirations of the people. Maoism in Orissa has succeeded because it moves around the life of marginalized people in these areas. It has established a link between underdevelopment, regional imbalance, economic disparity and gun culture. In the name of ameliorating the displaced tribals, the movement also endorses the use of excessive violence and counter-violence that gains an easy acceptance, given the failure of the government to adopt adequate steps for implementing the developmental programmes.

In view of the pauperization of the local tribals, due to the taking away of their land for private capital, the left radicals continue to mobilize their support around issues of land since it immediately strikes an emotional chord with those who lost their possessions. The PWG, for instance, never ignored this aspect of deprivation for obvious strategic importance. Particularly the Chashi Mulia Samiti and the Kui Labanga Sangh, which Sabyasachi Panda led, were instrumental in leading the land recapture programme. During 1996, the Chashi Mulia Samiti organized its first land recapture programme at Anugur *Panchayat* of Gajapati district, to reoccupy six acres of land. In 1997 tribals of Raba village of Mohana block of Gajpati district occupied fifty acres of tribal land, which had been under the control of non-tribals for the last three to four decades. Four cadres of PWG were arrested in this struggle and cases were foisted on many. Finally the tribals won the battle. About 400 to 500 peasants participated in this land struggle. In 1998, the movement for land reclamation occurred in Mandrabaju and Sindhba of

Mohana block, Murising-Tabarda of Naugada block and in many other places of Gajapati district.[53] However, 'these were all small scale programmes with little mass support'[54] which collapsed soon though they had emotionally inspired the victims of the mindless policy of industrialization.

On the other hand, though the Naxal leadership makes strong claims to fight for the rights of the poor, they have so far remained apathetic in enhancing the quality of life in villages, arguing that all reforms have to follow revolution. To them development is adversary to revolutionary consciousness. In fact Naxal groups in these areas are vehemently opposed to any type of construction work. It seems that they are afraid of the fact that the government will win over the poor ignorant tribals to its side once they allow the development process to start.

Concluding observations

As is evident, Maoism is the latest incarnation of ultra-left extremism in India. The movement remained confined to West Bengal, part of Bihar and Andhra Pradesh at the outset. In the course of time, as the above narrative shows, it has spread its tentacles to more than half of Indian provinces. This is suggestive of a failed state which has neglected, for a variety of historical reasons, the peripheral sections of Indian society. The sustained growth of ultra-left extremism is a powerful comment on the failure of the state-led development paradigm. This is one part of the story. The other part is about the application of a correct strategy by the Maoist leadership to articulate their ideological faith in terms of a dream of fulfilling basic human requirements. By itself, an ideology is hardly a force unless backed by a strong organization. The evolution of Maoism as a strong political force in India is illustrative of the fact that a strong organization sustains an ideological campaign against all odds. What is most striking in contemporary Maoism is the successful efforts by the leadership to unify splinter groups drawing on the Maoist variety of Marxism. By amalgamating in 2004 three major groups – CPI (ML), MCC and PWG – the CPI (Maoist) has emerged as perhaps the strongest ever ultra-extremist political outfit in India that cannot be wished away easily, given its well-entrenched organization in rural areas in those affected Indian provinces, though one must not gloss over the internal tension due largely to the interpretation of the ideological texts. What is evident in Orissa, especially after the 2008 Kandhmal incident in which a Hindu religious priest was allegedly murdered by the Maoists, is illustrative here. For those clinging to the orthodox Marxist ideological line of thinking, religion is a debilitating force and has therefore no place in healthy human existence. Contrary to the classical Marxist position, there is a powerful voice championing the context-driven interpretation of Marxism-Leninism that instead of outrightly rejecting the importance of religion in transitional societies, prefers to set in motion a thorough debate on this issue to alert the masses to the adverse consequences of submitting to religion for 'supernatural gain'. The debate will, for obvious reasons, remain inconclusive since it involves a radical shift in the prevalent mindset in reconceptualizing one's social-political existence in societies which are in transition. This also requires a meaningful adaptation of Maoism to the Indian context which is radically different from its place of origin. Unless this is pursued with the utmost seriousness, Maoism in India will result in an ideological package with no meaningful substance and, in this sense, the debate that began over the Kandhmal incident has undoubtedly instilled a new political dynamics in the movement with clear socio-economic aims.

A study of the Maoist movement in Orissa thus reveals that today's explosive situation is largely designed by a continuous process of mal-development. But violence itself is no means to attain development; rather it is the extreme form of exploitation. To meaningfully address mal-development, and to replace this atmosphere of chaos and terror, what is required is to create appropriate institutions, systems and relations. The need of the hour is to free the system of exploitation and corruption which would surely bring down societal tension by ensuring equality of status and opportunity. To deal with the rising tide of ultra-left extremism, what is needed is not only an increase of allocation of funds but also its proper management in the field of healthcare, education, nutrition programmes, disease control, irrigation, rural electrification, rural roads and other basic requirements, especially in those affected rural areas. The state must ensure that its institutions do not breed exploitation. It must work on a formula where there is larger democratic participation in the processes of decision-making and development. So, besides having raised a powerful voice for change, the extremist left radicals have posed new challenges for the state and other stakeholders which were conveniently ignored in the past. This is the most significant outcome of Maoism in India which cannot be bypassed as a mere law-and-order problem, precisely because of the organic roots that it has developed over the last few decades by being intimately connected with the day-to-day struggle of the people at the grassroots. Maoism has thus not only become a struggle for empowerment, but a powerful critique of the state-directed development paradigm which India's founding fathers so zealously pursued once India became free.

The Orissa experience also confirms that mindless industrialization does not seem to be a panacea for those in penury. As land is emotionally connected with the indigenous people, it was easier for the left radicals to mobilize them when efforts were made by the state to forcefully take possession of their land for mining and other industrial projects. The unanimous vote by twelve *gram sabhas* (village councils) in Orissa's Rayagada and Kalahandi districts over two months in the first half of 2013 rejecting Vedanta Aluminum and Orissa Mining Corporation's plan to extract bauxite from the Niyamgiri hills is a historic and significant precedent that could determine the course of similar developments in other tribal areas in India.[56] For the tribals, 'Niyamgiri is [their] God [and] they won't give it to anyone'.[57] Not only will the government effort deprive the tribals of their land, it will also make them 'bonded labour [and] subservient to those with resources'.[58] This was most blasphemous for them since they draw their emotional resources from the Niyamgiri hill which is the natural abode of the tribal god, Niyam Raj. The Supreme Court of India also supported them by declaring that, under the 2006 Forest Regulation Act, since the primitive tribal groups have a customary right to worship the mountains, villagers in and around the Niyamgiri hill would decide whether mining would cause harm to their religious rights of worshipping the hill.[59] The Indian state however thinks otherwise. The former Home Minister of the government of India, P. Chidambaram, thus counters the argument by saying that

> no country can develop unless it uses its natural and human resources ... we can respect the fact that they worship the Niyamgiri hill, but will that put shoes on their feet or their children in school; or [will] that solve the problem of malnourishment?[60]

This is a no-win situation for the tribals who will also be deprived of free access to the forest products once the excavation of the hill begins. It is therefore not difficult to understand why they are so easily organized by the Maoists against the state snatching their land for private gain. So, left radicalism of the Maoist variety consolidates and thrives in this area since the deprived masses have nowhere to go to ventilate their grievances against a coercive state power. The battle, though uneven, is a testimony of how ruthless a neo-liberal state can be in fulfilling its ideological mission of protecting a few at the cost of many. As a result, a peculiar situation has emerged, as the Orissa story illustrates. In the crossfire, neither the Maoists, who are ideologically indoctrinated to destroy India's parliamentary system of governance, nor those holding the state power suffer; the hapless victims are the tribals who, in such adverse circumstances, have become pawns without realizing the devastating consequences of their identification with either the state or Maoists. Their only fault is the desire to survive with dignity that has thus a very high premium in a situation where the state and the left radicals have, for obvious reasons, become staunch enemies for their respective socio-economic and political goals. There is hardly an escape route for the victims since they are not only born and raised there, but also emotionally attached to the land which they worship as divine. Given India's lopsided development, and the failure of the state to halt the process, it is easy to comprehend why the Maoists become the natural tribal ally in circumstances where private capital is allowed free play, bypassing conveniently the basic constitutional values for human honour and dignity. Despite its failure elsewhere in the globe, Indian left-wing extremism does not thus appear to be just another ideological shot in India's long history of mass struggle, but a sustained and adequately organized violent campaign with organic roots in the prevalent socio-economic circumstances. The Orissa narrative just confirms that left radicalism has flourished in a specific socio-economic milieu in which the state's zeal for private capital has contributed to a massive displacement of the indigenous population which has drawn them to the Maoists, presumably because of their ideological commitment to human emancipation and complementary efforts at removing the agents and also sources of exploitation of human beings by their fellow counterparts. This is what sustains the Maoist popularity among the indigenous tribals in the 'red corridor' where the Indian state, which, to them, is just an instrument of coercive power, has failed to emerge as a dependable ally for its partisan role in defending private capital for rapid industrialization at their cost.

Notes

1 This chapter is a joint venture since it draws upon material written in collaboration with my student-cum-colleague, Dr Rajat Kujur, which came out in our jointly authored book, *Maoism in India: the reincarnation of left-wing extremism in the twenty-first century* (Routledge, London and New York, 2010). I warmly acknowledge the significant contribution of Dr Kujur in shaping the chapter in its present form and thank him for having supported the project since it was mooted.
2 In a measure to check the growing Naxalite influence and to make the administration more accessible the then Chief Minister Biju Pattnaik, divided the Koraput and Ganjam districts in 1992. Four new district were created, Malkangiri, Nabarangpur, Raygagada and Gajapati.
3 Raghunath Patnaik, 'Naxal Problem', *Samaja (Oriya Daily)*, 1 September 2004 Raghunath Patnaik is a former minister of the state government who hails from the Naxal-infested Koraput district.
4 The 'food liberation' programme which originally started from Gunupur (now in Rayagada district) soon spread to some pockets of Berhampur, Chhatrapur, Phulbani and Koraput. Under this programme the peasants and tribals were successfully persuaded by the communist leadership to attack the landlords and Zamindars and forcibly distribute food grains among the villagers.
5 The full text of the interview given by Nagbhushan Pattnaik was first published in *Onlooker* Magazine, 15 February 1986. After that it was reproduced numerous times in various languages.
6 Nagbhushan Pattnaik, as quoted by Dandapani Mohanty and Mundimkhola Ru Satya Nagar Samshan, in *Biplaba Sari Nahin, Biplabi Mari Nahin* (Revolution not finished, revolutionary not died), an undated Oriya publication of CPI (ML), Andhra–Orissa Border Committee.
7 As recorded in *Andhra–Odisha Simanta Re Naxalbad* (Another Current of Naxalism: People's War), an undated Maoist publication published in Oriya by CPI (ML).
8 Prakash Singh, *The Naxalite Movement in India*, Rupa, New Delhi, 1995, p. 61.
9 Singh, *The Naxalite Movement*, p. 62.
10 Statement of M.M. Praharaj, IPS, Director General of Police, Orissa, 27 Februray 2006, during one of my several meetings with him.
11 Most of this analysis is based on narratives of present and former activists of the Naxal movement in Orissa. We cannot disclose the names of many of them as they believe it would create security problems for them. In the process we also accessed several Maoist documents. To get the other side of the story I have discussed many things with M.M. Praharaj, Director General, Orissa Police.
12 Anadi Sahu, 'Naxals in Orissa: Then and Now', translated from his original Oriya article published in *Shatabdi* (Oriya monthly), 15 September 2001. Mr Sahu is the retired Inspector General of Orissa Police. During his tenure in the police he supervised many anti-Naxal campaigns in the state. He is also a former member of Lok Sabha from Orissa.
13 Interview with M.M. Praharaj, 27 February 2006.
14 Mohanty and Samshan, *Biplaba Sari Nahin, Biplabi Mari Nahin*.
15 Dandapani Mohanty, in an interview given to us on 2 June 2005 at his Berhampur residence. This statement is in sharp contrast with his earlier stand as mentioned in his earlier article *Biplaba Sari Nahin, Biplabi Mari Nahin*. This makes it clear that after

the death of Nagbhushan Pattnaik, Sabyasachi Panda has established himself as the undisputed leader of the Naxal movement in Orissa.
16 *Andhra Odisha Simanta Re Naxalbad.*
17 Based on several reports of Orissa police and personal interviews with several police officers taken during the course of the fieldwork.
18 Dandapani Mohany, convener, Daman Pratirodh Manch, a banned Naxal front organization in Orissa, in an interview given to me during the Jana Garjan Samabesh, the first-ever Naxal show of strength in the state capital of Bhubaneswar on 14 Sepember 2004. During this convention I interviewed twenty-five people who were members of different frontal organizations of PWG as well as of MCC.
19 Sanjay Kumar Jha, 'Naxalite consolidation in Orissa', *South Asia Intelligence Review*, vol. 2, no. 3, 4 August 2003, South Asia Terrorism Portal, www.satp.org.
20 Sabyasachi Panda, the then secretary of the Bansdhara Divisional Committee of PWG, in a rare interview given to *Sambad* (Oriya daily), published on 19 September 2004.
21 Indramani Behera, officer in charge of Motu police station of Malkangiri district, in an interview published in *Shatabdi*, 15 September 2001.
22 Sukanta, 'Arrests in Mayurbhanj District, Orissa', *People's March*, November–December 2001.
23 Dr Rajat Kujur's interview with M.M. Praharaj on 27 February 2006.
24 Dr Kujur's interview with Ajit Baxla, 20 June 2005.
25 Dr Kujur's interview with Mahesh Singh, a businessman from the Naxal-hit town of Bisra on 19 June 2005.
26 Dr Kujur's interview with Ajit Baxla on 20 June 2005.
27 Subdar Badaik, one contractor based in Jaraikela made this point in his conversation with Dr Kujur on 22 June 2005.
28 C.S. Rout, assistant sub-inspector of police, Jaraikela police outpost, in an interview with Dr Kujur on 22 June 2005.
29 Sabyasachi Panda, secretary, CPI (Maoist), Orissa state committee, in a rare interview, given to *Sambad* on 19 September 2004.
30 Dandapani Mohanty, convener, Daman Pratirodh Manch, in an interview conducted as a part of our fieldwork, 22 June 2005.
31 Nihar Nayak, 'Maoist consolidation intensifies in Orissa', Article no. 70, www.sspconline.org, accessed on 16 May 2006.
32 Information obtained from a number of senior Naxal leaders of Orissa whom we interviewed in June–August 2005.
33 Bomai Narsimhulu, also known as Anna Reddy, hails from Nalgonda district of Andhra Pradesh and was operating under the name of Naresh in Uttar Pradesh and Rasul in Andhra Pradesh. He was deputed to take control of the outfit in Orissa in 2005. Anna was asked by his central leadership to prop up anti-displacement movement in the state. The Janashakti group established their base within about a 5,000-sq km area of the bordering forest region of Jajpur, Keonjhar and Dhenkanal. He was arrested by Orissa police in 2008.
34 Nayagarh is 87 km west of Bhubaneswar, the state capital. This was the first time that the Naxals showcased their ability to strike in the vicinity of the state capital.
35 One Maoist area commander belonging to Dandakaranya area met Dr Kujur soon after the incident in a place near Malkangiri. However we cannot disclose his name.
36 Sabyasachi Panda, at an undisclosed destination, told reporters from private Oriya channels that the Maoists decided to eliminate Saraswati as he was 'spreading social unrest' in the tribal-dominated district.
37 The ninth Congress of CPI (Maoist) held sometime in January–February 2007 at some undisclosed location is believed to have infused newer tricks among Indian Maoists. This information was obtained from a Maoist leader whom we met in Kandhamal in November 2008.

38 India's economic growth, 1950–2000

	1950–64 %	1965–179 %	1980–2000 %
GDP growth	3.7	2.9	5.8
Industrial growth	7.4	3.8	6.2
Agricultural growth	3.1	2.3	3.0
Gross investment	13	18	23

Source: Kohli, *State-Directed Development*, p. 258.

39 Kohli, *State-Directed Development*, p. 258.
40 Jatindra Dash, 'Mining threatens Orissa's environment', *Indo-Asian News Service*, 5 November 2004.
41 Dr K. Nayak, 'Rourkela: a historical perspective', www.rourkela.com/history.htm. As a part of our fieldwork Dr Kujur met the president of the Rourkela Displaced Persons Association in August 2005.
42 Based on the field interview conducted by Dr RKujur during June–August 2005.
43 Kishore Kumar Das, Lecturer in Botany, Balimela College of Science and Technology, in his unpublished article, 'Life on the Other Side of the Reservoir'.
44 Interview with the villagers, conducted during June–August 2005.
45 *Census Report*, Orissa, 2001.
46 Information obtained from the *Prakrutik Sampad Surakshya Parishad*, Raygada. Interviews conducted among a cross-section of the population in and around Rayagada during June–August 2005.
47 *Census Report*, Orissa 2001.
48 *Sambad*, December 25, 2005.
49 Amrita Patwardhan, 'Dams and tribal people in India', www.dams.org/, accessed 22 June 2005.
50 Interviews with the residents of the villages during June–August 2005.
51 Statement of Debendra Jarika, a resident of Kalinga Nagar, on 18 June 2005.
52 planningcommission.nic.in/plans/planrel/pl49ndc/orissa.htm, accessed on 27 September September 2009.
53 'Revolutionary Adivasi movement spreads to southern Orissa', *People's March*, November–December 1999. www.peoplesmarch.com was an unofficial website of CPI (Maoist). The website was closed by the order of the government of India from 15 May 2006. However, the editor of the site was kind enough to provide me with all the content of the website on a CD.
54 Statement of Sri Krishna Chandra Mangaraj, a senior journalist from Rayagada, who has been covering the Naxal movement in the local media for the past two decades, during an interview conducted on 15 May 2005.
55 planningcommission.nic.in/plans/planrel/pl49ndc/orissa.htm, accessed on 27 September 2009.
56 For details of this story, see Manipadma Jena, 'Voices from Niyamgiri', *Economic and Political Weekly*, 7 September 2013, pp. 14–16.
57 Quoted in Jena, 'Voices from Niyamgiri', p. 14.
58 Quoted in Manipadma Jena, 'Voices from Niyamgiri', p. 14.
59 For details, see Kailas Sarap, Tapan Kumar Sarangi and Jogindra Naik, 'Implementation of Forest Rights Act 2006 in Odisha: process, constraints and outcome', *Economic and Political Weekly*, 7 September 2013, pp. 61–7.
60 The statement of P. Chidambaram, the home minister of the Union government of India is quoted in Gautam Navlakha, *Days and Nights in the Heartland of Rebellion*, Penguin, New Delhi, 2012, pp. 84–5.

Conclusion

I

A thorough scan of the two varieties of left radicalism in the Indian context is intellectually useful in two interrelated ways: first, it has enabled us to grasp the manner in which the left radicals steered a clear ideological line of thinking to justify a politically viable mode of action for significant socio-economic transformation. It also helps us understand circumstances in which a section of the left radicals preferred social democracy to the acceptable interpretation of Marxism and Leninism. For them, the liberal parliamentary path seems to be most appropriate for human emancipation in a transitional society like India. This was an effective strategy in a particular context which was not conducive to violent revolution. Second, the text is an aid to clearly identifying the social bases of these respective versions of left radicalism in India. As has already been shown, the parliamentary left became a strong political force since the 1950s, following the adoption of meaningful socio-economic programmes benefiting the majority of those who remained very significant in rural life. The left-devised agrarian programme, the Operation Barga, did not benefit the poor, but a section in the villages which held the key to socio-economic balances. While this section of the rural gentry consolidated the left base in West Bengal at the outset, it was also responsible for its gradual downfall in the course of time, following the failure of the leadership to contain this section of the rural gentry in accordance with what the left rule meant for the people at large. Similarly, the chapters on left-wing extremism have shown how the successful Maoist mobilization of the marginalized led to its consolidation, notwithstanding massive state repression. By their sustained work among those suffering due to structural inequalities, the Maoists created a base for themselves which was a key to their growing popularity in the 'red corridor'.

Left radicalism is thus not a mere descriptive category, but an ideological device for mobilization around relevant socio-economic and political issues. In an instrumental sense, left radicalism is a goal-driven endeavour seeking to articulate a different brand of politics. With very well-defined ideological postulates, the left radicals chart a course of action which is usually tuned to the goal that they strive to achieve. In contemporary parlance, it is generally associated with that variety of organization that evolves out of movements for specific causes. As is evident in the preceding text, the Indian version of left radicalism is first and foremost a movement-centric ideological expression. This is true of the parliamentary left and its bête noire, the left-wing extremists, popularly known as the Naxalites or Maoists in contemporary India. Before it was drawn to liberal democratic politics in the early 1950s, those who later became flag-bearers of the parliamentary left were engaged in a violent revolution to bring about meaningful socio-economic transformation. Over a period time, the party ideologues fiercely debated the plausibility of peaceful parliamentary means in fulfilling the Marxist-Leninist objective of human emancipation. Finally, it was accepted as perhaps the best option in a post-colonial society which was not prepared for a violent break with its feudal past. One should therefore factor in the importance of the context in shaping the ideological response which is a creative blending of derivative inspiration and the contextual inputs highlighting the specific socio-economic characteristics. Similarly, the contemporary Maoists and their predecessors, the Naxalites, developed their ideological leaning towards violence on the basis of their understanding of Marxism, Leninism and Maoism. For them, India, despite being a transitional society, was a perfect socio-economic context for violent seizure of power. It was possible for them to develop and consolidate constituencies of support in the context of endemic poverty in which victims had minimal chances even of survival. The situation became worse with the onset of globalization supportive of indiscriminate exploitation of natural resources even at the cost of displacing the natural habitat in areas which attracted private capital for precious mineral deposits. So, left extremism was an outcome of the prevalent socio-economic circumstances in which the minimum human needs remained unfulfilled. With their success in politically mobilizing the underprivileged, the Maoists have certainly created a niche in Indian politics by being ideologically different, if not innovative in conceptualizing the socio-economic issues that did not appear to have received adequate attention. This was an important factor in sustaining and expanding the Maoist sphere of influence across the 'red corridor'. Left radicalism is thus both an ideological construct and a context-drawn strategy for political mobilization against injustice. This is a construct with specific ideological tenors which are usually derived from non-liberal theoretical discourses. As history demonstrates, given its specific contextual roots, the nature of left radicalism differs from one place to another. There cannot thus be a universal model of left radicalism which can be applied anywhere regardless of socio-economic and political circumstances.

II

The nature of left radicalism underwent significant changes. Issues for mobilization also became different: While, for the Naxalites of the 1960s, the agrarian issues remained most critical in political mobilization, their contemporary counterpart, the Maoists, drew on the ruthless endeavour at extracting mineral resources by private capital at the cost of the displacement of the local tribals across India's forest land, besides attacking feudal land relations. Maoism was thus a powerful voice for the marginalized who remained peripheral in the erstwhile state-led development scheme because of its obvious class prejudices. Drawing on the identical ideological sources of Marxism, Leninism and Maoism as their contemporary counterpart, the Naxalites never became as expansive as the Maoists, suggesting perhaps their failure as an ideologically engineered version of left radicalism. There are two critical issues that need elaboration: for the Naxalites, India was a semi-colonial and semi-feudal society where national democracy was an unavoidable stage for socialist revolution. What was thus needed was a multi-class political unity involving even the petty bourgeoisie who were never accepted as dependable allies in struggles for genuine human emancipation. In the Maoist perception, besides the semi-colonial and semi-feudal social forces, the role of the comprador bourgeoisie remained most critical, especially with the onset of globalization following the collapse of the former Soviet Union; the latter, by defending the state-centric approach to socio-economic problems, had articulated an alternative ideological voice in contrast to global capital. It was possible for this voice to strike roots in India since the majority of the poor were those who suffered most because of the specific developmental strategy which was tilted heavily in favour of the private capital. The poor merely became pawns in the prevalent scheme of things, in which their needs were conveniently bypassed, if not entirely ignored, to accommodate the global capital which operated through their indigenous counterparts for partisan gains. A situation was thus created in which the poor and socio-economically marginalized felt cheated in their own country; they were, in other words, in a no-win situation which created circumstances in which Maoism seems to have struck an emotional chord with the victims of mindless and prejudiced development strategies. It is now clear that Maoism is not, at all, a law-and-order problem, but an outcome of the state-led development paradigm which failed to effectively address India's class imbalances.

Like its left-wing extremist counterpart, the parliamentary left rose to prominence in contemporary India largely due to an intelligent mixing of social democratic means with the available liberal strategies. Once they captured political power through democratic elections, the parliamentary communists found out how effective the parliamentary institutions were in fulfilling some of their basic socio-economic goals. It was possible for the left to strike roots in Kerala, West Bengal and Tripura largely because of the stringent application of those progressive legislations that radically altered the rural texture, which was not a mean achievement given the lack of sincerity of the past regimes in fulfilling their constitutional obligation to the people of India, especially those on the lower rung of the social order. The strategy was to extend the benefit to the genuinely deprived section of the masses thorough various institutionalized mechanisms. Without substantially disturbing the prevalent class balances, the left regimes in contemporary India devised an effective strategy towards fulfilling, on the one hand, the basic social democratic goals and, on the other, creating and consolidating a social base by drawing on the class prejudices against the disprivileged. This was a key to the success of the parliamentary left which, despite having failed to expand its influence beyond Kerala, West Bengal and Tripura, has remained a significant ideological force in India's recent political history. In the context of the growing importance of coalition politics, when neither of the pan-India political parties, the Congress and Bharatiya Janata Party, is able to cobble up a majority in the national Parliament, the role of the parliamentary communists is likely to be far more critical, as was evident in 2004 when the Congress-led United Progressive Alliance sought their support to form the government at the centre. Once they became part of the alliance, it was possible for them to steer the government policies towards those socio-economic goals which did not receive adequate attention in the past, as shown in Part II.

III

Left radicalism in India represents two contrasting versions of socio-economic transformation: the parliamentary left seeks to fulfil the ideological goal through liberal democratic means while its counterpart, the left-wing extremists, continue to appreciate violent revolutionary methods for eradicating human exploitation and class differences once and for all. As is evident in West Bengal, Kerala and Tripura, the parliamentary left brought about significant socio-economic changes even within India's democratic framework through liberal means. The growing expansion of the 'red corridor' also reveals that left-wing extremism no longer remains a mere academic expression, but is a political movement that has caught the imagination of the people in large parts of the country. It is no exaggeration that Maoism has engulfed a long stretch of India, between Pashupati in Nepal and Tirupati in Tamil Nadu. While explaining the increasing popularity of left-wing extremist politics in India, a former Maoist thus admits that:

> the Maoist movement ... articulates the deep sense of estrangement that pervades the vast backwater of the country – the alienation of peasantry from land; the rupture between the oppressed indigenous people and depressed castes on the one hand and the oppressive upper caste/class feudal vested interests on the other; the uprooting of the urban poor from their socio-cultural moorings.[1]

Maoism is thus a context-driven ideological response seeking to redress the genuine socio-economic grievances of the peripheral sections who never became 'true citizens' of the country. Even in the face of massive state repression, it was possible for the Maoists to mobilize the majority of the disprivileged segments of India's demography simply because they empowered them 'with moral and military strength to recover their land, assert their right and reinvent themselves as dignified human beings in their quotidian existence'.[2] With their involvement in the daily struggle for human dignity, the Maoists succeeded in changing 'power relationships in village society by overturning the patron–client network, and enabling the rural poor and oppressed marginalized groups (i.e. indigenous people, women) to rediscover their collective self and reassert their rights'.[3] There is no denying that the left-wing extremist movement acted as a catalyst agent in rural society that gave the poor a voice which was powerful enough to challenge the age-old system of exploitation to establish their claim for human dignity.

Nonetheless, there are hurdles which the Maoists confront while pursuing their revolutionary zeal for change. The poor do not seem to be instinctively revolutionary; if the basic needs of food, clothing and shelter are taken care of, a large section of the poor may not be persuaded to resort to armed struggle. According to a former Maoist,

> if the immediate economic and social benefits (like a plot of land, a home, higher returns from labour, improvement in civic facilities, schooling for their children, better medical facilities, end to casteist discrimination and oppression) are offered in their everyday life by any government – irrespective of its political hue – [a significant section of the underprivileged] may rather opt for that in exchange of a distant ideological dream of people's democratic state.[4]

This was evident in the case of the earlier left-wing extremist campaign, known as the Naxalbari movement, that despite having rocked the nation in the 1960s gradually waned since it failed to sustain the support base that it had built, especially in West Bengal, Bihar and Andhra Pradesh, among the marginalized sections. The result was almost a miracle in West Bengal, where those who took part in the movement for seizure of power withdrew to appreciate the parliamentary path of socio-economic changes. The movement lost its momentum to a significant extent with the assumption of power by the parliamentary left in West Bengal in 1977. As is shown in Chapter 4, the growing popularity of the parliamentary communists in the state is attributed to their success in fulfilling the basic human requirements of the majority located in rural areas which included small plots of land, higher wages for labour and a partial voice in local decision-making through self-government institutions, known as *Panchayats*.

While the Maoists empowered the underprivileged communities across India's rural areas, the parliamentary left evolved itself as invincible in West Bengal and Tripura by extending significant economic benefits through constitutional means. There is no doubt that the Operation Barga (ensuring legal entitlement to the tiller of the soil) and the formation of the *Panchayati* system of governance consolidated the left in the state which was later supplemented by a strong party organization. With the institutionalization of benefits, it was possible for the left to sustain its hegemony for more than three decades from 1977. What explains the gradual decline of the social democratic parliamentary left was its failure to extend these benefits to the poor, especially the tribal and Dalit (depressed) sections who never had access to the facilities that the Left Front government made available for the intermediary sections in rural West Bengal. This was neither seriously addressed nor were there attempts to map out the sources of their grievances. The left-devised land reforms or other pro-people welfare schemes did not benefit the marginalized sections, including the tribal people and Dalits. Thus the Left Front in West Bengal never became popular among the tribals who were located in the backward areas of the districts of Bankura, Purulia and Midnapur. It is not surprising that Maoism is a critical political force in these areas though its influence elsewhere in the state does not seem to be as significant as it was in the past. What it demonstrates is the fact that Maoism is a powerful voice of opposition in areas which are inhabited by the most deprived sections of the Indian rural poor, including the tribals who always remain left out from the government-sponsored developmental packages. The Maoists stepped into the vacuum by mobilizing the poor against oppressive landlords, moneylenders and forest contractors. With its support to the oppressors, the state also became a predator and thus provoked challenges by those who remained at the periphery. In this sense, Maoism, instead of being a derivative ideological endeavour, is largely a context-dependent political response highlighting the nature and sources of exploitation in a semi-feudal and semi-colonial society in the context of globalization.

IV

Rural India is now a tinderbox. With the onset of globalization, the situation has become far more complicated because of the support that private indigenous capital extends to its global counterpart for mutual benefit. India's tribal belt has attracted the global economic players, not for any benevolent objective but for the deposit of rich mineral resources in these areas. So the local inhabitants need to be displaced to allow the excavation of these precious mineral resources to ensure India's rapid economic development. The outcome is most devastating because there has emerged a clear gap between those seeking quick economic development and the bulk of those living in these areas who are dependent for their livelihood and well-being on a healthy base of natural resources. Instead of being people-centric, the state has become a partner with the mindless endeavour of industrialization amounting to the creation of 'an economy of violence [which] is promoting grabbing and spoiling land, water, mineral and forest resources to benefit the few, at the cost of the larger society'.[5] Rather than addressing the adverse consequences of 'the economy of violence', the parliamentary left seems to have been sucked into the processes of neo-liberal economic development, appreciative of the Darwinian principle of the survival of the fittest. The point is well illustrated in Chapter 4, showing the decline of the parliamentary left in West Bengal following the forcible acquisition of land for an automobile factory. This was most ironical since the regime that sustained its popularity by legalizing rights of the tillers over land which they cultivated struck at its very foundation with the decision to coercively acquire land for private capital. As is demonstrated in Chapter 4, this was one of the major reasons for the downfall of the Left Front regime that failed to withstand the popular wrath in the 2009 Lok Sabha poll, followed by the 2011 state assembly election. This was admitted by the Front leadership while seeking to explain the massive electoral defeat by saying that

> [a] the forcible acquisition of land [for private capital] was suicidal for the party and the government; the damage was irreparable in two ways: while it resulted in alienating a large chunk of the supporters it also provided the opposition with a persuasive argument to cement a bond among the forces opposed to the Left Front.

This event had a snowballing effect which got worse following the

> indiscriminate police firing in Nandigram to disperse those who stood against the government policy of forcible land acquisition [which] also led the educated middle class to withdraw support to the government'; and [b] the decline of the organization due to indiscipline, corruption, bureaucratization and hegemonic and dictatorial style of leadership at the grassroots resulting in the weakening of the *Panchayat* bodies which, instead of being people-centric, remained busy in fulfilling the partisan and whimsical desire of those holding authority.[6]

It is clear that the parliamentary left gradually deviated from the pro-people perspective while in governance which allowed the opposition to stake its claim. Was this a failure of social democracy as an ideology or was it the failure of the Left Front to effectively utilize the social democratic means to accomplish the fundamental ideological goal of human emancipation? It was perhaps both. The rise and fall of the Front in West Bengal 'exposes the limits of social democratic experiment within the institutions of parliamentary democracy'.[7] And the long duration of the left regime was also responsible for the vested interests being able to strike roots which were reflected in the growth and consolidation of arrogant party functionaries who were not questioned nor challenged by the top leadership, presumably because of their critical role in sustaining social bases in rural areas. In the long run, they did not only become a liability for the party, but had also caused a serious dent in the organization. This was admitted by the ideologues who felt that 'the defeat could have been avoided had the party activists at the grassroots been alert in effectively addressing people's genuine socio-economic grievances'.[8] Hence it was advised that 'they should not only reorganize themselves but also remain integral to the rural life in order bring the left back to power'.[9] It is clear to the leadership that the Stalinist iron fist rule does not seem to work in the changed political environment of mass empowerment. In order to regain power, the left, it was strongly felt, needs to redefine its strategy since the party, as a hegemon, became a liability, as was evident in Nandigram and Singur where the Left Front government forcibly took land from the farmers for private capital.

This is also true of the left-wing extremists in India. Instead of contextually comprehending the socio-economic reality, the Indian left radicals of the extremist variety appear to have been governed by the classical Marxist-Leninist analysis of class struggle and new democratic revolution. Their ideological responses do not seem to have taken into account the changing context of the twenty-first century when global capital has become far more intimate with domestic capital than in the past. While understanding the context, one cannot ignore the rising importance of global capital supporting neo-liberal economic forces. It is thus increasingly felt that the old tools to fight capitalism that were effective in the twentieth century seem to have become redundant. Several countries in Latin America – Venezuela, Bolivia, Columbia, among others – have already tried to evolve alternatives to the classical Marxist line of thinking by simultaneously waging armed struggle and participating in parliamentary elections. The Indian left radicals have also had an opportunity to reconceptualize some of the fundamental tenets of the Marxist socialist alternative in the light of the Indian context which is distinctively different in both texture and manifestation.

Two important points stand out in the discussion: first, historically speaking, left radicalism in India has not expanded its sphere of influence to the extent it was expected when it emerged on the political scene during the nationalist struggle. There are multiple reasons for its failure. One of the fundamental reasons was certainly its failure to contextually understand the Indian reality. As shown in this book, Indian left radicals hardly ever made an independent endeavour to conceptualize the reality in which they were located; instead, it was generally direction from outside which stuck with the local comrades. The communist withdrawal from the 1942 August revolution caused irreparable damage to the organization. Despite their meteoric rise in West Bengal in 1977, the parliamentary left collapsed in 2011 largely due to its failure to comprehend the basic needs of the majority of the people who were hapless, due to the whimsical policy decisions of the so-called people's government. Second, this is also applicable to the left-wing extremists, known as the Naxalites and also Maoists in contemporary India. Being inspired by the Maoist doctrine of 'new democracy', the Naxalites rocked the country in the 1960s and continue to ideologically inspire those who believe in violent revolution as perhaps the only means to eradicate the sources of the present class imbalances defending vested interests. The derivative nature of the movement was responsible for its decline, as Kanu Sanyal, one of the top Naxalite leaders, explained, saying

> the failure to keep in view the specific features of Indian society and the inability to solve the problems of Indian revolution from the traditions of struggles of the Indian people led to subjective super-imposing of the experiences of other countries mechanically.[10]

Unlike their predecessors, the Maoists do not appear to have blindly followed the derivative ideological line of thinking though they are substantially tuned to classical Marxism, Leninism and Maoism. It is true that efforts are made by the Maoists to ensure human dignity and higher value for labour in those areas where they are effective. But their failure to provide a well-argued socialist design of development, as the Maoist documents and other complementary sources reveal, is very striking which perhaps suggests their inability to comprehend the changing Indian reality or simple lack of interest. This is a source of weakness for the movement because a battle for state power does not attract support in the long run unless and until an alternative is devised and pursued. In this sense, left-wing extremism, despite being ideologically challenging, does not appear to be a serious threat to the prevalent liberal democratic class-prejudiced state of India.

V

One fundamental question that seems to be bothering activists and analysts of left radicalism alike is what its future is. There is no straightforward answer to the question since it is a contextual socio-political phenomenon that gains ground in specific contexts. So long as the sources of exploitation are embedded in the prevalent socio-economic system, left radicalism will continue to give voice to those seeking to challenge and also alter the structure creating and consolidating divisions among human beings. This is a basic lesson of history. As history unfolded, the left radicalism always remained a source of inspiration, simply because it ignited hopes and the desire not to accept the present social order as given. During the nationalist phase, the Congress, led by Mahatma Gandhi, was most prominent in the battle against colonialism for historical reasons. But the role of the Congress socialists and later communists was equally important in reconceptualizing the nationalist goal and objectives by expanding the nationalist reach among the peasantry and workers in the late 1920s and early 1930s. It was possible for the Congress to accommodate the left radicals because it was primarily a multi-class and multi-ethnic political platform to pursue the nationalist goal of independence. Although the Congress socialists remained with the Congress, the communists always maintained a separate existence especially when it came to the fights for workers' and peasants' rights. As is shown in Chapter 2, there are innumerable instances when the Congress violently opposed the communists since the former was reluctant to participate in movements harming the Indian industrialists or local landlords. Instead, the Congress was keen for negotiation when the communists were willing to continue the struggle till their demands were met.

The rising importance of the left radicals was largely due to their success in nurturing specific constituencies. After India's independence in 1947, the communists resorted to an armed struggle in West Bengal and Telangana to bring about human emancipation; it was aborted for a variety of strategic reasons. Once the ban was withdrawn in 1950, the communists came out and decided to participate in parliamentary politics. This was a watershed in the history of left radicalism which was now beginning to be articulated in the spirit of social democracy. Parliament thus became an instrument of change. Nonetheless, there were individuals who continued to hold on to the classical Marxist-Leninist method of violent revolution as perhaps the only effective means of fulfilling their ideological goal. This means that left radicalism was conceptualized in two diametrically opposite ways: on the one hand, it was appreciative of parliamentary democracy which was believed to be capable of contributing to significant socio-economic changes; on the other, it was manifested differently at the hands of those who strongly felt that there was hardly a substitute for violent revolution so long as society was divided by class.

The trajectory of left radicalism – in its two differently textured avatars, the parliamentary left and its bête noire, the left-wing extremists – is also a useful narrative to understand its context-dependent nature. As argued in Part II, the parliamentary left was a refreshing input in a situation when the Congress lost its appeal to the people largely because of its failure to effectively address people's genuine socio-economic grievances. This was the story in West Bengal, Kerala and Tripura. Of these three Indian provinces, West Bengal is the only state where the parliamentary left appears to have lost its credibility among the people to a significant extent, as is evident in the outcome of the 2009 Lok Sabha poll, followed by the 2011 state assembly election, the recent 2013 elections to the local bodies in rural areas and the 2014 Lok Sabha poll. In Tripura, the left maintained its grip by winning the 2013 assembly election while in Kerala, notwithstanding their defeat in the 2011 assembly election, the left parties continue to remain a significant political force in the state. Nonetheless, what is most striking is the failure of the parliamentary communists to expand beyond those areas where they have traditionally been well entrenched. In other words, that the parliamentary left remains confined to Kerala, West Bengal and Tripura is also illustrative of their inability to ideologically inspire the rest of the country even more than six decades after their arrival on the political scene since the ban was withdrawn in 1950. Unlike the parliamentary left, that is confined to a southern state (Kerala), an eastern state (West Bengal) and a north-eastern state (Tripura), the Maoists have a larger support base in what is defined in government parlance as a 'red corridor' covering parts of Maharashtra and the entire tribal belt of Chhattisgarh, Andhra Pradesh, Orissa, Bihar, Jharkhand and West Bengal. What catapulted the Maoists to the centre-stage of ultra-left-wing extremism was their success in giving the desperately poor tribal people, living in conditions of chronic hunger, a dream for a better life free from hunger and indignity. Left-wing extremism is thus unlikely 'to disappear because the root causes that feed it are unlikely to disappear for the next few decades'.[11] The increasing expansion of Maoism also reinforces the fact that this is not mere political adventurism by a group of dedicated 'foot soldiers', but an articulation of an ideological voice, drawn on genuine socio-economic grievances[12] and supported by an equally powerful and well-entrenched organization involving people from various social strata and regions of India. The new version of ultra-left-wing extremism has become integral to contemporary Indian politics, and, by seeking to grasp its transformed texture in a different fashion, it has not only redefined India's political discourse, but has also challenged the so-called universal appeal of liberal democracy as perhaps the most acceptable political form of governance in postcolonial India.

VI

As the discussion reveals, there can hardly be a conclusive narrative on left radicalism which is both a contextual ideological response and a well-argued theoretical design to understand India's socio-economic reality. It is also a movement with clear historical antecedents. Ideologically inspiring and politically meaningful, left radicalism is also a documentary history chronicling the past, in which efforts were made to pursue an alternative path of development involving the stakeholders who usually remained left out. This study is a testimony to the multifaceted nature of left radicalism, especially in a country like India which is neither capitalistic nor feudal but a unique blending of both. Given its distinct ideological character, the Indian version of left radicalism cannot thus be comprehended as a derivative discourse. In other words, in view of its distinctive contextual roots, there cannot be a universal model of left radicalism and in that respect, *Left Radicalism in India* not only is a useful contribution to understanding the Indian version, but also reinforces the argument challenging the one-size-fits-all formula in comprehending socio-political movements with clear organic roots. As is evident, despite having been inspired by the classical Marxism, Leninism and Maoism, both the parliamentary communists and their extremist counterparts charted a course of action by taking into account India's distinct socio-economic conditions. In West Bengal and Kerala, the constitutional left lost power to the non-left political forces due largely to the arrogant functioning of the party functionaries; similarly, the downfall of the Naxalite movement in the early 1970s was linked with a variety of factors including the failure of its leaders to inspire the victims of state-led-development adequately for a sustained campaign against the state. The relevance of Maoism is attributed to its success in movements for human dignity, especially among the tribals who historically remained disconnected from the mainstream. These are all illustrative of the argument defending the context-dependent nature of the Indian variety of left radicalism which is not merely an academic expression or a conceptual category, but epitomizes the lived experiences of those sections of the Indian masses that historically remain marginalized and vulnerable for all practical purposes.

Notes

1 Sumanta Banerjee, 'Reflections of a one-time Maoist activist', *Dialectical Anthropology*, vol. 33, 2009, p. 253.
2 Banerjee, 'Reflections', p. 253.
3 Banerjee, 'Reflections', p. 254.
4 Banerjee, 'Reflections', p. 260.
5 Madhav Gadgil, 'Towards an economy of mutualism', *The Hindu*, 4 December 2013.
6 'Analysis of the 2011 assembly election', *Party Letters, meant for the party members* (in Bengali), CPI (Marxist), West Bengal State Committee, 29th congregation, 16–17 July 2011, pp. 17–18.
7 Subho Basu and Auritro Majumdar, 'Dilemmas of parliamentary communism: the rise and fall of the left in west Bengal', *Asian Studies*, vol. 45, no. 2, 2013, p. 196.
8 'Analysis of the 2011 assembly election', p. 21.

9 'Analysis of the 2011 assembly election', p. 28.
10 Sanyal, 'More about Naxalbari', p. 344.
11 Sudeep Chakravarti, 'Naxalism in India: thriving or surviving', *Hindustan Times*, 2 June 2013.
12 In their commentary on *India since 1980* (Cambridge University Press, Cambridge, 2011), Sumit Ganguly and Rahul Mukherjee make the argument by saying that what accounts for the Maoists' increasing popularity is their success in 'the mobilization of extant grievances in India's more remote areas, which have not benefitted much from the country's surge of economic growth' (p. 177).

Select bibliography

Left radicalism is a constantly expanding field of enquiry. So is the literature. Hence no bibliography can be exhaustive. While preparing this bibliography, I am guided by two of the following considerations: first, I have identified some basic conceptual texts which are useful to understand the complexities that usually go with the conceptualization of left radicalism. As shown in the book, left radicalism is a context-driven phenomenon. The bibliography therefore contains texts that use various contexts to build and defend specific arguments. Second, left radicalism is also an indigenous articulation. Hence the rich section of the relevant literature is in the vernacular. After having located them, I have utilized them while analysing the peculiar nature of the Indian variety of left radicalism. The other important source of the narrative is the party literature supporting parliamentary communism and left-wing extremism respectively. Some of the texts were collected during the field trip, and some were from websites maintained by the political outfits pursuing specific ideological courses. There is less difficulty in procuring written materials on the parliamentary left because they are generally in the public domain. This is not true of texts regarding Maoism since CPI (Maoist) is an outlawed organization in India. Nonetheless, an extensive field trip in Orissa which belongs to the 'red corridor' allowed me access to literature which would not have otherwise been available.

There are three types of texts which figure in the bibliography: first, like any conventional bibliography, this is a select bibliography comprising the basic books, both in vernacular and English languages, which are useful to grasp the phenomenon of left radicalism. The available literature is a guide through the complex alleys of left radicalism in a transitional society like India. Second, since the text has drawn on inputs from websites, the bibliography has also included those websites which are now frequently used in academic discourse. There are areas in our discussion which benefited from the web inputs. For instance, statements on the inner functioning of Maoism would have been less persuasive without such inputs. The third type of text that is also very critical to comprehend the varieties of left radicalism in India is the daily newspapers, both national and local and in vernacular and English languages. Despite obvious methodological limitations, the inputs from the fourth estate cannot be avoided, especially since this is a study of an organic politico-ideological movement that has clear historical antecedents.

Select bibliography

Given the space constraints, it is difficult to include the plethora of literature on the topic. The aim here is to incorporate those texts which are pertinent in making and also defending the argument that has been pursued in the text. So, it is a select bibliography which will act as a pathfinder for future researchers. In that sense, this select bibliography is not merely a select list of written texts, drawn from various sources, but also a guide for those wishing to pursue enquiries on such a topical theme of left radicalism.

Books

Agarwal, Vineet, *Romance of a Naxalite*, National Paperbacks, Delhi, 2006.
Ahmad, Muzaffar, *Myself and the Communist Party of India, 1920–1929*, Calcutta, 1970.
Ajitha: memoirs of a young revolutionary (translated from Malayalam), Srishti, New Delhi, 2008.
Alam, Javeed, *India: living with modernity*, Oxford University Press, Delhi, 1999.
Alvares, Claude, *Science, Development and Violence: the revolt against modernity*, Oxford University Press, Delhi, 1992.
Arendt, Hannah, *Crisis of the Republic*, Penguin, Harmondsworth, 1973.
Aron, Raymond, *History and the Dialectic of Violence*, Basil Blackwell, Oxford, 1975.
Bakunin, Michael, *Statism and Anarchy*, ed. and tr. M.S. Shastz, Cambridge University Press, Cambridge, 1990.
Balaram, N.E., *Communist Movement in Kerala* (in Malayalam), vol. 1, Prabhat, Trivandrum, 1973.
Banerjee, Sumanta, *India's Simmering Revolution*, Select Book Syndicate, New Delhi, 1984.
Banerjee, Sumanta, *In the Wake of Naxalbari: a history of the Naxalite movement* Subarnarekha, Calcuta, 1980.
Basrur, Rajesh M. (ed.), *Challenges to Democracy in India*, Oxford University Press, New Delhi, 2009.
Basu, Pradip (ed.), *Discourses on Naxalite Movement, 1967–2009: insights into radical left politics*, Setu Prakashani, Kolkata, 2010.
Baviskar, B.S. and George Mathew (eds), *Inclusion and Exclusion in Local Governance: field studies from rural India*, Sage, New Delhi, 2009.
Bergmann, Theodore, *Agrarian Reform in India*, Agricole Publishing Academy, New Delhi, 1984.
Bhaduri, Amit, *Development with Dignity: a case for full employment*, National Book Trust, New Delhi, 2005.
Brinton, Crane, *The Anatomy of Revolution*, Vintage Books, New York, 1952.
Burton, J. and F. Dukes (eds), *Conflict: readings in management and resolution*, Macmillan Press Ltd, 1990.
Calman, Leslie J., *Protest in Democratic India: authority's response to challenge*, Westview Press, Boulder, CO, 1985.
Campbell, D. and M. Dillon (eds), *The Political Subject of Violence*, Manchester University Press, Manchester, 1993.
Chakrabarty, Bidyut, *Forging Power: coalition politics in India*, Oxford University Press, New Delhi, 2006.
Chakrabarty, Bidyut, *Indian Politics and Society since Independence: events, processes and ideology*, Routledge, London and New York, 2008.

Chakrabarty, Bidyut, *Subhas Chandra Bose and Middle Class Racialism: a study of Indian nationalism, 1928–1940*. Oxford University Press, Delhi, 1990.
Chakrabarty, Bidyut, and Rajat Kujur, *Maoism in India: the reincarnation of left-wing extremism in the twenty-first century*, Routledge, London and New York, 2010.
Chatterjee, Partha (ed.), *Wages of Freedom: fifty years of the Indian nation-state*, Oxford University Press, Delhi, 1998.
Chattopadhyay, Suchetana, *An Early Communist: Muzaffar Ahmad in Calcutta, 1913–1929*, Tulika Books, Delhi, 2012.
Corbridge, S., G. Williams, M. Srivastava and R. Vernon, *Seeing the State: governance and governmentality in India*, Cambridge University Press, Cambridge, 2005.
Crossley, Nick, *Making Sense of Social Movements*, Open University Press, Buckingham, 2002.
Dagamar, Vasudha, *Role and Image of Law in India: the tribal experience*, Sage, New Delhi, 2006.
Damas, Marius, *Approaching Naxalbari*, Radical Impression, Calcutta, 1991.
Dasgupta, Biplab, *The Naxalite Movement*, Allied Publishers, Calcutta, 1974.
De Reuck, Anthony (ed.), *Conflict and Society*, Little Brown & Co., Boston, 1966.
Desai, A.R. (ed.), *Agrarian Struggles in India after Independence*, Oxford University Press, Delhi, 1986.
Desai, A.R., *Peasant Struggles in India*, Oxford University Press, Mumbai, 1969.
Desai, Manali, *State Formation and Radical Politics in India*, New York: Routledge. 2007.
Domenach, Jean-Marie et al. (eds), *Violence and Its Causes: methodological and theoretical aspects of recent research on violence*, UNESCO, Paris, 1981.
Downtown, James, *Rebel Leadership: commitment and charisma in the revolutionary process*, Free Press, New York, 1973.
Dube, S.C., *Indian Village*, Oxford University Press, London, 1955.
Duyker, Edward, *Tribal Guerillas: the santals of West Bengal and the Naxalite movement*, Oxford University Press, New Delhi, 1987.
Escobar, A., *Encountering Development: the making and unmaking of the third world*. Princeton University Press, Princeton, NJ, 1995.
Eyerman, R. and A. Jamison, *Social Movements: a cognitive approach*, Polity Press, Cambridge, 1991.
Fanon, Frantz, *The Wretched of the Earth*, tr. C. Farington, Penguin, Harmondsworth, 1980.
Fernandes, Leela, *India's New Middle Class: democratic polity in an era of economic reforms*, Oxford University Press, New Delhi, 2006.
Fic, Victor M., *Kerala, Yenan of India: rise of communist power (1937–1969)*, Nachiketa Publications, Bombay, 1970.
Fox, R. and O. Starn, *Between Resistance and Revolution: cultural policies and social protest*, Rutgers State University, New Brunswick, NJ, 1997.
Franda, Marcus F., *Radical Politics in West Bengal*, MIT Press, Cambridge, MA, 1971.
Franke, Richard W. and Barbara H. Chasin (1989), *Kerala: radical reform as development in an Indian state*, IFDP, San Francisco, 1989.
Fuller, C. and V. Benei (eds), *The Everyday State: anthropological perspective on the state and society in modern India*, C. Hurst, London, 2001.
Ganguly, Sumit, Larry Diamond and Marc F. Plattner (eds), *The State of India's Democracy*, Oxford University Press, New Delhi, 2009.
Gellner, D., *Resistance and the State: Nepalese experience*, Social Science Press, New Delhi, 2003.

230 Select bibliography

Ghosh, Amitav, *Two New Essays: confessions of a xenophile and wild fictions*, Outlook, Delhi, 2008.
Ghosh, Sarkar, *The Naxalite Movement: a Maoist experiment*, Firma K.L. Mukhopadhyay, Culcutta, 1974.
Ghosh, Suniti Kumar (ed.), *The Historic Turning Point: a liberation anthology*, vols 1–2, Pragnana, Calcutta, 1992.
Gibson, Nigel, *Frantz Fanon: the Postcolonial Imagination*, Cambridge University Press, Cambridge and New York, 2003.
Guevara, Che, *Guerrilla Warfare*, tr. J.P. Morray, Vintage Books, New York, 1961.
Guha, Ramchandra, *Patriots and Partisans*, Penguin, New Delhi, 2012.
Gupta, Monobina, *Left Politics in Bengal: time travels among bhadralok Marxists*, Orient Blackswan, New Delhi, 2010.
Gupta, Ranjit Kumar, *The Crimson Agenda: Maoist protest and terror*, Wordsmiths, Delhi, 2004.
Gurr, Ted R., *Why Men Rebel*, Princeton University Press, Princeton, NJ, 1970.
Haralambos, M., *Sociology: themes and perspectives*, Oxford University Press, New Delhi, 1999.
Hasan, Zoya, *Politics of Inclusion: caste, minorities and affirmative action*, Oxford University Press, New Delhi, 2009.
Honderich, Ted, *Violence for Equality: inquiries in political philosophy*, Penguin, Harmondsworth, 1980.
Isaac, T.M. Thomas and Richard Franke (2000), *Local Democracy and Development*, New Delhi: Leftword Books.
Jawaid, Sohail, *The Naxalite Movement in India: origin and failure of Maoist revolutionary strategy in West Bengal*, Associate Publishing House, New Delhi, 1979.
Jeffrey, R., *The Decline of Nayar Dominance*, Holmes & Meier Publications, New York, 1976.
Jeffrey, R., *Politics, Women and Well Being: how Kerala became a 'model'*, London, Macmillan Press, 1992.
Johari, J.C., *Naxalite Politics in India*, Institute of Constitutional & Parliamentary Studies/Research Publications, Delhi, 1972.
Kishwar, Mudhu Purnima, *Deepening of Democracy: challenges of governance and globalization in India*, Oxford University Press, New Delhi, 2005.
Kohli, Atul, *Democracy and Development in India: from socialism to pro-business*, Oxford University Press, New Delhi 2009.
Kohli, Atul, *Democracy and Discontent: India's growing crisis of governability*, Cambridge University Press, Cambridge, 1991.
Kohli, Atul, *Poverty amid Plenty in the New India*, Cambridge University Press, Cambridge, 2012.
Kohli, Atul, *State-Directed Development: global power and industrialization in the global periphery*, Cambridge University Press, Cambridge, 2005.
Kohli, Atul, *The State and Poverty of India*: Cambridge University Press, Cambridge, 1987.
Lieten, G.K., *Continuity and Change in Rural West Bengal*, Sage, New Delhi, 1992.
Lieten, G.K., *Development, Devolution and Democracy: village discourse in West Bengal*, Sage, New Delhi, 1996.
Louis, Prakash, *People Power: the Naxalite movement in central Bihar*, Wordsmiths, Delhi, 2002.
Mallick, Ross, *Development Policy of a Communist Government: West Bengal since 1977*, Cambridge University Press, Cambridge, 1993.

Mallick, Ross, *Indian Communism: opposition, collaboration and institutionalization*, Oxford University Press, Delhi, 1994.
Mao Tse-Tung, *Selected Works of Mao Tse-Tung*, vols 1–4, Foreign Language Press, Peking 1975.
Menon, Dilip, *Caste, Nationalism and Communism in South India*, Cambridge, Cambridge University Press, 1994.
Menon, Nivedita and Aditya Nigam, *Power and Contestation: India since 1989*, Orient Longman, New Delhi, 2007.
Mohanty, Manoranjan, *Revolutionary Violence: a study of Maoist movement in India*, Sterling Publishers, New Delhi, 1977.
Moore, Barrington, *Social Origins of Dictatorship and Democracy: lord and peasant in the making of modern world*, Penguin, Harmodsworth, 1973.
Namboodiripad, E.M.S., *The Communist Party in Kerala: six decades of struggle and advancement*, National Book Centre, New Delhi, 1994.
Navlakha, Gautam, *Days and Nights in the Heartland of Rebellion*, Penguin, New Delhi, 2012.
Nigam, Aditya, *The Insurrection of Little Selves: the crisis of secular-nationalism in India*, Oxford University Press, New Delhi, 2006.
Nilekani, Nandan, *Imagining India: ideas for the new century*, Penguin, New Delhi, 2008.
Nossiter, T.J., *Marxist State Governments in India: politics, economics and society*, New York and London, Pinter Publishers, 1988.
Nossiter, T.J., *Communism in Kerala: a study of political adaptation*, Oxford University Press, Delhi, 1982.
Overstreet, Gene D. and Marshall Windmiller, *Communism in India*, University of California Press, Berkeley and Los Angeles, 1959.
Paul, Santosh, *The Maoist Movement in India: perspectives and counter perspectives*, Routledge, New Delhi, 2013.
Rai, Chowdhuri Satyabrata, *Leftist Movements in India, 1917–1947*, Minerva, Calcutta, 1977.
Rajgopal, P.R., *Social Change and Violence: the Indian experience*, Uppal Publishing House, New Delhi, 1987.
Ram, Mohan, *Indian Communism: split within a split*, Vikash Publications, Delhi, 1969.
Ram, Mohan, *Maoism in India*, Vikas Publications, Delhi, 1971.
Roy, Arundhati, *Walking with the Comrades*, Penguin, New Delhi, 2011.
Roy, Asish Kumar, *The Spring Thunder and After: a survey of Maoist and ultra-leftist movements in India (1962–75)*, Minerva Associates, Calcutta, 1975.
Samaddar, Ranabir, *Passive Revolution in West Bengal, 1977–2011*, Sage, New Delhi, 2013.
Sen, Sunil, *Agrarian Struggle in Bengal*, People's Publishing House, Bombay, 1972.
Shah, Alpa, *In the Shadows of the State: indigenous politics, environmentalism and insurgency in Jharkhand, India*, Duke University Press, Durham, NC, 2010.
Singh, Prakash, *The Naxalite Movement in India*, Rupa & Co, New Delhi, 1995.
Sinha, S., *Maoists in Andhra Pradesh*, Gyan, Delhi, 1989.
Skolnick, Jerome, *The Politics of Protest*, Ballantine Books, New York, 1969.
Sudeep, Chakravarti, *Red Sun: travels in Naxalite country*, Penguin, New Delhi, 2008.
Sundar, Nandini, *Subaltern and Sovereign: an anthropological history of Bastar (1854–2006)*, Oxford University Press, New Delhi, 2008.
Sundaraya, P., *Telangana People's Struggle and Its Lessons*, Communist Party of India (Marxist), Calcutta, 1972.

Thapa, D. and B. Sijapati, *A Kingdom under Siege: Nepal's Maoist insurgency, 1996–2004*, Zed Books, London, 2004.
Tornquist, Olle and P.K. Michael Tharakan, *The Next Left: democratization and attempts to renew the Radical Political Development Project: case of Kerala*, Copenhagen: NIAS Books, 1994.
Webster, Neil, *Panchayati Raj and decentralization of development planning in West Bengal (a case study)*, K.P. Bagchi, Calcutta, 1992.

Articles

A group of citizens, 'Open letters to government and Maoists', *Economic and Political Weekly*, 28 July 2006.
Acharya, Poromesh, '*Panchayats* and left politics in West Bengal', *Economic and Political Weekly*, 29 May 1993.
Alam, Javeed, 'Debates and engagements: a look at communist intervention in India', in V.R. Mehta and Thomas Pantham (eds), *Political Ideas in Modern India: thematic explorations*, Sage, New Delhi, 2006.
Alam, Javeed, 'Nation: discourse and intervention by the communists in India', in T.V. Sathyamurthy (ed.), *State and Nation in the Context of Social Change*, vol. 1, Oxford University Press, Delhi, 1994.
A.M., 'The state of the CPI (M) in West Bengal', *Economic and Political Weekly*, 25 July 2009.
Azad, 'Maoists in India', *Economic and Political Weekly*, 14 October 2006.
Bajpai, Rochana, 'Redefining equality: social justice in the Mandal debate, 1990', in V.R. Mehta and Thomas Pantham (eds), *Political Ideas in Modern India: thematic explorations*, Sage, New Delhi, 2006.
Balagopal, K., 'Maoist movement in Andhra Pradesh', *Economic and Political Weekly*, 22 July 2006.
Balagopal, K., 'Peasant struggle and repression in Pedapally', *Economic and Political Weekly*, 15 May 1982.
Bandyopadhyay, D., 'Land of the overlords: a field trip to Katihar and Purnea', *Mainstream*, 12 March 2007.
Bandyopadhyay, D., 'A visit to two "flaming fields" of Bihar', *Economic and Political Weekly*, 30 December 2006.
Bandyopadhyay, D., 'West Bengal: enduring status quo', *Economic and Political Weekly*, 26 May 2001.
Bandyopadhyay, Sekhar, 'The story of an aborted revolution: communist insurgency in post-independence West Bengal, 1948–50', *Journal of South Asian Development*, vol. 3, no. 1, 2008.
Banerjee, Sumanta, 'Assembly polls: 2006 election: *Jatra* style in West Bengal', *Economic and Political Weekly*, 11 March 2006.
Banerjee, Sumanta, 'Beyond Naxalbari', *Economic and Political Weekly*, 22 July 2006.
Banerjee, Sumanta, 'Naxalbari: between past and present', *Economic and Political Weekly*, 1 June 2002.
Banerjee, Sumanta, 'Naxalites: time for retrospection', *Economic and Political Weekly*, 1 November 2003.
Banerjee, Sumanta, 'Reflections of a one-time Maoist activist', *Dialectical Anthropology*, vol. 33, 2009.

Banerjee, Sumanta, 'West Bengal's next quinquennium, and the future of the Indian left', *Economic and Political Weekly*, 4 June 2011.

Bardhan, Pranab, 'Dominant propertied classes and India's democracy', in Atul Kohli (ed.), *India's Democracy: an analysis of changing state-society relations*, Orient Longman, New Delhi, 1991.

Bardhan, Pranab, Sandip Mitra, Dilip Mookherjee and Abhirup Sarkar, 'Local democracy and clientelism: implications for political stability in West Bengal', *Economic and Political Weekly*, 28 February 2009.

Basu, Dipankar, 'The left and the 15th Lok Sabha election', *Economic and Political Weekly*, 30 May 2009.

Basu, Subho and Auritro Majumdar, 'Dilemmas of parliamentary communism: the rise and fall of the left in West Bengal', *Asian Studies*, vol. 45, no. 2, 2013.

Bhaduri, Amit, 'Development or development of terrorism', *Economic and Political Weekly*, 17 February 2007.

Bhatia, Bela, 'On armed resistance', *Economic and Political Weekly*, 22 July 2006.

Bhatia, Bela, 'Naxalite movement in Central Bihar', *Economic and Political Weekly*, 9 April 2005.

Bhattacharya, Dwaipayan, 'Of control and factions: the changing party-society in rural West Bengal', *Economic and Political Weekly*, 28 February 2009.

Bhattacharya, Dwaipayan, 'Left in the lurch: the demise of the world's longest elected regime?' *Economic and Political Weekly*, 16 January 2010.

Bhattacharyya, Sudipta, 'Operation Barga, "efficiency" and (de)interlinkage in a differentiated structure of tenancy in rural West Bengal', *Journal of South Asian Development*, vol. 2, no. 2, 2007.

Birinder, Pal Singh, 'Violence: a dominant term of discourse', *Studies in Humanities and Social Sciences*, vol. 2, no. 1, 1995.

Biswas, Atharobaki, 'Why Dandyakaranya a failure, why mass exodus, where solution? *The Oppressed Indian*, vol. 4, no. 4, 1982.

Chatterjee, Partha, 'The coming crisis in West Bengal', *Economic and Political Weekly*, 28 February 2009.

Dasgupta, Abhijit, 'On the margins: Muslims in West Bengal', *Economic and Political Weekly*, 18 April 2009.

Dasgupta, Rajarshi, 'The CPI (M) machinery in West Bengal: two village narratives from Kochbehar and Malda', *Economic and Political Weekly*, 28 February 2009.

Dash, Jatindra, 'Mining threatens Orissa's environment', *Indo-Asian News Service*, 5 November 2004.

Dellaporta, Donatella, 'Social movements and democracy at the turn of the millennium', in P. Ibarra (ed.), *Social Movement and Democracy*, Palgrave Macmillan, New York, 2003.

Fernandes, Walter, 'Rehabilitation policy for the displaced', *Economic and Political Weekly*, 20 March 2004.

Fernandes, Walter, 'Singur and the displacement scenario', *Economic and Political Weekly*, 20 Janaury, 2007.

Gallantar, Marc, 'The aborted restoration of indigenous law', in N. Jayaraman and Satish Saberwal (eds), *Social Conflict*, Oxford University Press, New Delhi, 1996.

Ganapathy, 'Open reply to independent citizens' initiative on Dantewada', *Economic and Political Weekly*, 6 January 2007.

Goswami, Sandhya, 'Assam: mandate for peace for development', *Economic and Political Weekly*, 4 June 2010.

Gupta, Tilak, 'Maoism in India: ideology, programme and armed struggle', *Economic and Political Weekly*. 22 July 2006.
Gurukkal, Rajan, 'When a coalition of conflicting interests decentralizes: a theoretical critique of decentralization politics in Kerala', *Social Scientist*. vol. 29, nos 9–10, 2001.
Hardgrave, Robert L., 'The Marxist dilemma in Kerala: administration and/or struggle', *Asian Survey*, vol. 10, no. 11, 1970.
Harish, S. Wankhede, 'The political context of religious conversion in Orissa', *Economic and Political Weekly*, 11 April 2009.
Hebbar, Ritambara, 'Forest bill of 2005 and tribal areas: case of Jharkhand', *Economic and Political Weekly*, 2 December 2006.
Heller, Patrick, 'From class struggle to class compromise: redistribution and growth in South Indian state', *Journal of Development Studies*, vol. 31, no. 5, 1995.
Heller, Patrick, 'Moving the state: the politics of decentralization in Kerala, South Africa and Porto Alegre', *Politics and Society*, vol. 29, no. 1, 2001.
Heller, Patrick and T.M. Thomas Isaac, 'Democracy and development: decentralised planning in Kerala' in Archan Fung and E.O. Wright (eds), *Deepening Democracy: institutional innovations in empowered participatory democracy*, New York, Verso, 2003.
Heller, Patrick, K.N. Harilal and S. Chaudhuri, 'Building local democracy: evaluating the impact of decentralization in Kerala, India', *World Development*, vol. 35, no. 4, 2007.
Isaac, T.M. Thomas, 'Campaign for democratic decentralization in Kerala', *Social Scientist*, vol. 29, nos 9–10, 2001.
Jalais, Annu, 'Dwelling on Marichjhanpi: when tigers became "citizens", refugees "tigerfood"', *Economic and Political Weekly*, 23 April 2005.
Jeffrey, R., 'Peasant movements and the Communist Party in Kerala, 1937–1960', in D.B. Miller (ed.), *Peasants and Politics: grass roots reaction to change in Asia*, New York, Edward Arnold, 1979.
Jena, Manipadma, 'Orissa: draft resettlement and rehabilitation policy, 2006', *Economic and Political Weekly*, 4 February 2006.
Jha, Sanjay Kumar, 'Left wing terror: the MCC in Bihar and Jharkhand', *South Asia Intelligence Review*, vol. 1, no. 40, April 2003.
Jha, Sanjay Kumar, 'Naxalite consolidation in Orissa', *South Asia Intelligence Review*, vol. 2, no. 3, 4 August 2003.
Kannabiran, Kalpana and Volga and Vasanthi Kannabiran, 'Peace and irresponsibility', *Economic and Political Weekly*, 26 March 2005.
Khatua, Sanjay and William Stanley, 'Ecological debt: a case study of Orissa, India: integrated rural development of weaker sections in India', in Athena K. Peralta (ed.), *Ecological Debt: the people of the south are the creditors: cases from Ecuador, Mozambique, Brazil and India*, World Council of Churches, Geneva, 2006.
Kohli, Atul, 'From elite activism to democratic consolidation: the rise of reform communism in West Bengal', in M.S.A. Rao and Francine Frankel (eds), *Dominance and State Power in Modern India: decline of a social order*, vol. 2, Oxford University Press, New Delhi, 1990.
Kujur, Rajat Kumar, 'Naxalism in India', *Human Touch*, vol. 2, no. 6, June 2005.
Kujur, Rajat Kumar, 'Underdevelopment and Naxal mMovement', *Economic and Political Weekly*, vol. 18–24 XLI, no. 7, February 18–24, 2006.
Kunnath, George J., 'Becoming a Naxalite in rural Bihar: class struggle and its contradictions, *Journal of Peasant Studies*, vol. 33, no. 1, January 2006.
Kunnath, George J., 'Smouldering Dalit fires in Bihar, India', *Dialectical Anthropology*, vol. 33, 2009.

Mallick, Ross, 'Refugee resettlement in Forest Reserves: West Bengal policy reversal and the Marichjhapi massacre', *Journal of Asian Studies*, vol. 58, no. 1, 1999.

Mannathukkaren, Nissim, 'The poverty of political society: Partha Chatterjee and the people's plan campaign in Kerala, India', *Third World Quarterly*, vol. 31, no. 2, 2010.

Manor, James, 'Transformation of opposition politics in West Bengal: Congress (I), Trinamul and 1998 Lok Sabha poll', *Economic and Political Weekly*, 15–22 April 1998.

Mehra, Ajay, 'Naxalism and militant peasant movement in India', in K.M. de Silva (ed.), *Conflict and Violence in South Asia*, Sri Lanka International Centre for Ethnic Studies, Kandy, 2000.

Mohanty, Biswaranjan, 'Displacement and rehabilitation of tribals', *Economic and Political Weekly*, 26 March 2005.

Mohanty, Monoranjan, 'Challenges of revolutionary violence: the Naxalite movement in perspective', *Economic and Political Weekly*, 22 July 2006.

Mohanty, Monoranjan, 'Chinese revolution and the Indian communist movement', *China Report*, vol. 27, no. 1, 1991.

Mukherjee, Partha N., 'Naxalbari movement and the peasant revolt', in M.S.A. Rao (ed.), *Social Movements in India*, vol. 1, Manohar, New Delhi, 1979.

Nandy, Ashis, 'The end of arrogance', *Tehleka*, special issue, *Verdict, 2009*, 30 May 2009.

Narayanan, M.K.., 'Naxal movement's cruel spring', *Asian Age*, 28 February 2000.

Nayak, Nihar, 'Managing Naxalism in Tamil Nadu,' *Tamil Nadu Police Journal*, vol. 2, no. 1, January–March 2008.

Nayak, Nihar, 'Maoist movement in Nepal and its tactical digression: a study of strategic revolutionary phases and future implications', *Strategic Analysis*, vol. 31, no. 6, November 2007.

Nayak, Nihar, 'Maoists: contagion in Orissa', *South Asia Intelligence Review*, vol. 3, no. 44, 16 May 2005.

Nayak, Nihar 'Maoists in Nepal and India: tactical alliances and ideological differences,' *Strategic Analysis*, vol. 32, no. 3, May 2008.

Nayak, Nihar, 'Nepal: withering of peace', *Peace and Conflict Monitor* (University of Peace, Costa Rica), 1 February 2006.

Nigam, Aditya, 'Communist politics hegemonized', in Partha Chatterjee (ed.), *Wages of Freedom: fifty years of Indian nation-state*, Oxford University Press, Delhi, 1998.

Nigam, Aditya, 'How the sickle slashed the left', *Tehelka*, 30 May, 2009.

Parthasarathy, G, 'Land reforms and the changing agrarian structure in India', in Anil Kumar Gupta (ed.), *Agrarian Structure and Peasant Revolt in India*, Criterion Publications, New Delhi, 1986.

Punwani, Jyoti, 'Chhattisgarh: traumas of adivasi women in Dantewada', *Economic and Political Weekly*, 27 January 2007.

Rai, Chaudhuri Dipanjan and Satya Sivaraman, 'Nandigram: six months later', *Economic and Political Weekly*, 13 October 2007.

Ram, Mohan, 'The Communist movement in India', in Kathleen Gough and Hari P. Sharma (eds), *Imperialism and Revolution in South Asia*, Monthly Review Press, New York, 1973.

Ramana, P.V., 'Naxalism: trends and government response', *Dialogue*, vol. 8, no. 2, October–December 2006.

Rammohan, K.T. 'Understanding Keralam: the tragedy of radical scholarship', *Monthly Review*, vol. 43, no. 7, 1991.

Rao, D.V., 'Telangana armed struggle and the path of Indian revolution', *Proletarian Path*, Calcutta, 1974.

236 Select bibliography

Rao, K Ranga, 'Peasant movements in Telangana', in M.S.A Rao (ed.), *Social Movements in India*, vol. 1, Manohar, New Delhi, 1979.
Rogaly, Ben, B. Harris-White and S. Bose (eds), *Sonar Bangla? Agricultural agrarian change in West Bengal and Bangladesh*, Sage, New Delhi, 1999.
Rubin, Oliver, 'Analyzing the political dynamics of starvation death in West Bengal', (mimeograph), Institut for Statskundskab, Arbejdspapir, 2008/03.
Rudd, Arild Engelsen, 'Embedded Bengal? The case for politics', *Forum for Development Studies*, no. 2, 1999.
Rudd, Arild Engelsen, 'Land and power: the Marxist conquest of rural Bengal', *Modern Asian Studies*, vol. 28, no. 2, 1994.
Sagar, 'The spring and its thunder', *Economic and Political Weekly*, 22 July 2006.
Sahni, Ajay, 'Bad medicine for a red epidemic', *South Asia Intelligence Review*, vol. 3, no. 12, October 2004.
Sahu, Anadi, 'Naxals in Orissa: then and now', *Shatabdi* (Oriya monthly), 15 September 2001.
Sanyal, Kanu, 'More about Naxalbari', *Proletarian Path*, May–August 1974.
Sarkar, Abhirup, 'Political economy of West Bengal', *Economic and Political Weekly*, 28 January 2006.
Shah, Alpa, 'Markets of protection: the "terrorist" Maoist movement and the state in Jharkhand, India', *Critique of Anthropology*, vol. 36, no. 3, 2006.
Shah, Alpa and Judith Pettigrew, 'Windows into a revolution: ethnographies of Maoism in South Asia', *Dialectical Anthropology*, vol. 33, 2009.
Sharma, Shailendra, 'India in 2010: robust economics amid political stasis', *Asian Survey*, vol. 51, no. 1, 2011.
Shuvaprasanna, 'Ozymandias' certain fall', *Tehelka*, 23 May 2009.
Singh, Prakash, 'Maoism unmasked', *Dialogue*, vol. 6, no. 4, April–June 2005.
Singh, Sekhar, 'Displacement and rehabilitation: a comparison of two policy drafts', *Economic and Political Weekly*, 30 December 2006.
Sinha, Santha, 'Andhra Maoist movement', in G. Ram Reddy and B.A.V. Sharma (eds), *State Government and Politics: Andhra Pradesh*, Sterling Publications, New Delhi, 1979.
Sundar, Nandini, 'Bastar, Maoism and Salwa Judum', *Economic and Political Weekly*, 22 July 2006.
Tharakan, P.K. Michael, 'Communal influence in politics: historical background pertaining to Kerala', *Religion and Society*, vol. 34, no. 1, 1987.
Thirumali, I, '*Dora* and *gadi*: manifestations of landlord domination in Telangana', *Economic and Political Weekly*, 19 February 1972.
Tornquist, Olle 'Movement politics and development: the case of Kerala', *Social Scientist*, vol. 29, nos 11–12, 2001.
Valarian, Rodrigues, 'The Communist Party of India', in Peter Ronald deSouza and E. Sridharan (eds), *India's Political Parties*, Sage, New Delhi, 2006.
Yechuri, Sitaram, 'Learning from experiences and analysis: contrasting approaches of Maoists in Nepal and India', *Economic and Political Weekly*, 22 July 2006.
Zindabad, Inquilab, 'The red sun is rising: revolutionary struggle in India', in Kathleen and Hari P. Sharma (eds), *Imperialism and Revolution in South Asia*, Monthly Review Press, New York, 1973.

Select bibliography 237

Online articles

Armed Conflicts Report, 'India – Maoist insurgency'. www.ploughshares.ca/libraries/ACRText/ACR-IndiaAP.html

Chandran, Suba and Joseph Mallika, 'India: the Naxalite movement, searching for peace in Central and South Asia', Global Partnership for the Prevention of Armed Conflict, 2002. www.conflictprevention.net/page.php?id=40&formid=73&action=show&surveyid=44#2#2

Collier, P., 'Doing well out of war', paper prepared for Conference on Economic Agendas in Civil Wars, London 26–27 April 1999. The World Bank, The Economics of Crime and Violence Project, Washington DC, www.worldbank.org/research/conflict/papers/econagenda.htm

Gupta, Kanchan, 'Naxals, India's enemy within'. http://in.rediff.com/news/2004/nov/25kanch.htm

'History of Naxalism'. Hindustantimes.com

Interview with Muppalla Lakshmana Rao, alias Ganapathy, the then head of the Communist Party of India-Marxist-Leninist People's War. www.rediff.com/news/1998/oct/07gana.htm

Jha, Sanjay Kumar, 'MCC and the Maoists: expanding Naxal violence in Bihar', Article no. 991, Institute of Peace and Conflict Studies, 15 March 2003. www.ipcs.org

Kamboj, Anil, 'Naxalism: India's biggest security challenge', Article no. 1995, Institute of Peace and Conflict Studies, 20 April 2006. www.ipcs.org

Kujur, Rajat Kumar, 'Andhra Pradesh: the Naxal citadel', Article no. 1962, Institute of Peace and Conflict Studies, 14 March 2006. www.ipcs.org

Kujur, Rajat Kumar, 'Andhra Pradesh and Naxal outfits: again on collision course', Article no. 48, Society for the Study of Peace and Conflict, August 25, 2005. ww.sspconline.org

Kujur, Rajat Kumar, 'Dantewada jail break: strategic accomplishment of Naxal designs', Article 2446, Institute of Peace and Conflict Studies, 20 December 2007. www.ipcs.org

Kujur, Rajat Kumar, 'Human rights in the shadow of red terror', Article no. 6712, *Peace Journalism*, issue 12, 10 October 2005. www.peacejournalism.com

Kujur, Rajat Kumar, 'Left extremism in India: Naxal movement in Chhatisgarh and Orissa', IPCS Special Report no. 25, Institute of Peace and Conflict Studies, June 2006. www.ipcs.org

Kujur, Rajat Kumar, 'Naxal war zone in Chhatishgarh', Article no. 50, Society for the Study of Peace and Conflict, 8 September 2005. www.sspconline.org

Kujur, Rajat Kumar, 'Naxal warning in Maharashtra', Article no. 1925, Institute of Peace and Conflict Studies, 14 January 2006. www.ipcs.org

Kujur, Rajat Kumar, 'Red terror over Jharkhand', Article no. 1881, Institute of Peace and Conflict Studies, 3 November 2005. www.ipcs.org

Kujur, Rajat Kumar, 'Resurgent Naxal movement in Bihar', Article no. 1852, Institute of Peace and Conflict Studies, 3 October 2005. www.ipcs.org

Kujur, Rajat Kumar, 'Train hijacking: the new face of red terror', Article no. 1967, Institute of Peace and Conflict Studies, 16 March 2006. www.ipcs.org

'Maoist-Influenced revolutionary organizations in India'. www.massline.info/India/Indian_Groups.htm.

Nayak, K., 'Rourkela: a historical perspective'. www.rourkela.com/history.htm.

Nayak, Nihar, 'Maoist consolidation intensifies in Orissa', Article No: 70, Society for the Study of Peace and Conflict, 16 May 2006. www.sspconline.org

238 Select bibliography

Pant, N.K., 'Naxalite violence and internal security', Article no. 523, Institute of Peace and Conflict Studies, 13 July 2001. www.ipcs.org

Patwardhan, Amrita, 'Dams and tribal people in India'. www.dams.org/

Ramana, P.V., 'Copy cat: PWG and the Al-Qaeda cell model', Article no. 939, Institute of Peace and Conflict Studies, 15 December 2002. www.ipcs.org

Ramana, P.V., 'Left-wing extremism in India', Observer Research Foundation. www.observerindia.com/analysis/A072.htm

Ramana, P.V., 'Unified response can defeat PWG paper tigers', Article no. 819, Institute of Peace and Conflict Studies, 5 August 2002. www.ipcs.org

Rao, Malleshwar, 'Waves of land struggle in South Orissa'. www.cpiml.org/liberation/year_2002/september/activities.htm

Newspapers

The Times of India (English)
The Hindu (English)
The New Indian Express (English)
The Pioneer (English)
The Samaja (Oriya daily)
The Sambada (Oriya daily)
The Prajatantra (Oriya daily)
The Samaya (Oriya daily)
The Dharitri (Oriya daily)

Index

abolition of *bethi* (slavery) in Koraput 189
absence of governance 180
acceptance of neo-liberal economic reforms 178
Adivasi Sanghs 189
agriculture as a bargain sector 34
ahimsa as an instrument for political mobilization 1, 4
AICCCR 190
AITMC 112–13, 119–20; Congress conglomeration 115, 121
alienation from mainstream nationalism 13
All Bengal Teachers' Association (ABTA) 61
All India Committee of Communist Revolutionaries (AICCR) 55
All India Socialist Conference 1934 10
All India Special Conference 1995 71
All India Trinamul Congress (AITMC) 94, 100, 105
Andhra thesis 52
Animal Farm 130
annihilation theory 196
anti-farmer land acquisition policy and Left Front 116–17
anti-Stalinism 64
Anushilan and Jugantor group of revolutionary terrorists 5
Anushilan Samity 62
AOBSZC 195, 199
appreciating parliamentary path of socio-economic changes 219
area-wise seizure 76
articulation of ultra-extremist ideology 177
ascendancy of left radicalism in West Bengal 106–10
Asian Development Bank loans 156
assembly election: in Kerala 2011 154–6; in West Bengal 2011 123

atmosphere of disrespect and arrogance 176
August revolution 1942 222

balance of payment crisis 1991 33
Balimela Dam Project in Chitrakonda 205
battle against intolerable conditions of economic oppression and social humiliation 168
Bengal Criminal Law Amendment Ordinance 62
Bengal Jute Workers' Association strike 6
Bengal-Bihar-Orissa Border Committee 190
bipolar coalitions in Kerala 146–8
birth of CPI (ML) 58–61
BJP 17, 48; poll campaign in West Bengal 2014 105
bourgeois nationalism under the anti-capitalist strategy 81
bureaucratic capital 71

Calcutta Congress 1928 9; of CPI 1948 52
capitalist path of development 31
Central Organization Committee (COC) 181
Centre of Indian Trade Unions (CITU) 115
challenging feudalism and Nizam autocracy 167
challenging one-size-fits-all formula 133
changed environment of globalization 157
changes in health and education in Tripura 96–7
changes in the Maoist strategy in Orissa 202
changing mindset among the voters 129
changing texture of Indian politics 37–9
Chasi Mulia Samiti 194, 208
China as a market socialist society 155

Chinese Communist Party 172
Chitrakinda Conspiracy Case 1969 192
classical Marxism in its reinvented form 102
classical Marxism-Leninism 66, 112–13, 163
collapse of parliamentary left in West Bengal 2011 222
combatting faith in superstitions and black magic 180–1
Comintern and Soviet Union 7
common minimum programme 37
commonsensical idiom of politics 77
communism in two diametrically opposite ways 16
Communist International 50
Communist Party of Great Britain 13, 172
Communist Party of India (Maoist) 73–5
Communist Party of India (Marxist-Leninist) Liberation 67–8
compact revolutionary zone 161, 175
conceptual framework for understanding left radicalism 82
condemning secret assassination by small armed group 171
conflict between CPI (Maoist) and Janashakti 201
Congress: as a multi-class and multi-ethnic political platform 223; electoral debacle in Tripura 90–1
Congress for Democracy 87
Congress Socialist Party 10, 11, 50, 63, 136
Congress-led UPA 44
Congress-minded left radicals 2
consolidation: of civil society activists against Left Front 118; of globalization 32; of left in Tripura 97–8; of Maoism 175–7
constituents of parliamentary left 49–52
constitutional edifice of the country 55
contextual study of Maoism 25
corruption free governance in Tripura 98
critical role of party high command 85
critique of annihilation line 171–3
customary rights of the tribals 203

Dalams 195
Dalit leader Periyar 135
decentralized socialism 11
decline of bhadralok political culture in West Bengal 126
decline of left wingers 10
declining importance of ideology-driven political choice in Kerala 146
deepening of democracy in India 178
deepening of regionalism in India 38

Defence of India Act 190
defending state-centric approach to socio-economic problems 217
defining ideology 23
democratic decentralization 150; in West Bengal 108
democratic participation of the people in political processes 110
democratic politics in Travancore and Cochin 139–40
democratization leading to mass awareness 166
denial mode among the left radicals in West Bengal 128
deterring investments in India's poorest regions 183
developing the tribal language, *Kakabarak* in Tripura 98
development in villages 181
development strategy in Orissa 203
differences among the Left Front constituents 118
Directive Principles of State Policy (Part IV of the Constitution of India) 27
dispossession of little people 33
dissident stand by the West Bengal unit of CPI 54
doctrinal Marxist approach to political mobilization 15
downfall of the left 103
dwindling of the left vote share in West Bengal 120

economic well-being of the people 112
effective social engineering 85
Election Commission of India recognizing CPI (ML) 67
Electoral politics in Travancore-Cochin 1948–57 141–3
emergence of splinter groups in Orissa 194
Emergency 1975–7 58, 130
empowerment of the lower strata of society 166
ethnic cleansing 179
ethnicity in Tripura 89
evolution of Tripura as a constituent state 86–9
expanse of CPI (Maoist) 73
exposing bourgeois nationalist organization 51

Fabian socialism 27
Factional feud among the left radicals in Orissa 193

Index

factional feud among the top leaders 153
factionalism: in CPI (M) 152; in Naxalbari movement 173, 176
faction-ridden Maoists 202
failure to address mal-development 210
fifteen point charter 10
fifth Party Congress 1958 15
first generation nationalist leadership 17
first United Front government in West Bengal 57
food liberation in Koraput 189
Foreign Exchange Regulation 1973 34
formation of guerrilla zone in Orissa 191
formation of Kishan Sabha 6–7
formation of People's Guerrilla Army 72
formation of the Communist Party of India 1920 56
formation of the Planning Commission in 1950 27
Forward Bloc 65–6
fragility of the Left Front 127–8
freedom struggle in Kerala 135–7
future of economic reform in India 32

Gandhi 223; and Congress High Command 10; goal of *Sarvadayo* 97; nonviolence 11
Gandhi–Bose rivalry 8–9
Gandhi-led right wing Congress 3
Gandhism and Soviet Communist Party 63
Gorkhas in Darjeeling 25
government neglect of the downtrodden 207
government rapport with employees 61
gram Panchayat smaitis 110
Gram Sabhas 149, 210
growing consolidation of Maoism in Indian states 165
growing importance of caste in Indian politics 166
guerrilla war as the only tactic of peasants' revolutionary struggle 170
guerrilla zones 76

hardwire of democracy 43
health hazards in Indian villages 179
Hili Station Railway Mail Raid Case 1933 62
Hindustan Socialist Republican Party 62
historic battle against fascism 172
historical electoral victory of Left Front in 1977 123
historical trajectory of left radicalism in West Bengal 104
human emancipation and parliamentary left 44

ideas of Swaraj and direct action in Malabar 137
identical ideological sources for the Naxalites and Maoists 217
ideological: bankruptcy in West Bengal 127; commitment of parliamentary left 49; compatibility among the constituents 77; device for mobilization around relevant socio-economic and political issues 215; fissures in Indian National Congress 139; polarization in CPI (M) 59
ideology as a means for revolution 148
ideology-driven movement 25
imperial war transformed to people's war 13–14
inability of the opposition to sway the masses in West Bengal 107
increasing expansion of Maoism in India 224
India: backward version of capitalism 31; clichéd secular democracy 105; democratic experience since 1947 44; freedom struggle 2; independence 1947 223; interventionist economic strategy 177; not being an enthusiastic reformer 32
India–China war 1962 168
Indian People's Front's victory in Ara (Bihar) 67
industrialization in West Bengal for employment generation 112
institutionalizing benefits for the poor 219
integrated planning 30
integration of the Indian economy into capitalism 31
inter-organizational and intra-organizational conflict among the Naxalites 188
Inter-Provincial Conspiracy case 1933–5 62
involvement of the Maoists in daily struggle for human dignity 218
IPF 193

Janashakti 75, 86, 201
Jungle Surakhya Committee (JSC) 197

Kanpur Bolshevik Conspiracy case 1924 50
Kanpur Communist Conference 1925 56
Karachi Congress 1931 29
Karl Mannheim 23
Kerala Congress (Pillai) 145
Kerala model 156

Kerala Pradesh Congress Committee (KPCC) 140
Kerala Socialist Party (KSP) 140
Khrushchev report on Stalin 53
Kishan Mazdoor Praja Party (KMPP) 141
KMPP 142
Krantikari Kishan Committee (KKC) 197
KSP 142
KSSP 149, 156
Kui Labanga Sangha 194

Labour-Swaraj Party 5
lackadaisical government attitude in Orissa 206
Lahore Congress 1929 10
land reforms and democratic decentralization in West Bengal 114
land-based resources and tribal livelihood 203
later Naxalbari movement 173–6
LDF 144, 146, 148, 151, 156
Left Consolidation Committee 12
left experiments in Kerala, West Bengal and Tripura 19
Left Front 59, 100; a symbol of change and continuity 111; in 2006 election 114–5; in Tripura 88–9
left outperforming the opposition 91
left politics in south Kerala 136
left radicalism: as a powerful ideological construct 216; as vacuous 106; in South America 222; in Tripura 101–3; West Bengal and Telangana 14; of the Maoist variety 162
left-wing faction of the Congress 55, 65
left-wing radicalism in Orissa 187
Leninist principle of democratic centralism 110
liberal democracy of the Westminster variety 17, 43
liberalized-privatized-globalized (LPG) regime 49
Liberation group 69
local participation deficit 149
Lok Sabha poll 2014 103–4, 121
Lok Sabha polls in Tripura 2009 and 2014 92–4
Lok Shakti Manch 195
loosening of organizational control over the leaders in Kerala 152

Madras Congress 1927 8
Mahalanobis Plan 28

Mahatma Gandhi National Rural Employment Guarantee Act 2005 41
Malabar Tenancy Act 1929 139
Maoism: a context-driven ideological response 218, 220; a formidable ideological force 180–1; a politico-ideological force 18; a reinvented Marxism-Leninism in a non-European milieu 175; as lived experiences of the masses 225; in Karnataka 75–6; in Orissa 188–90
Maoist: articulation of socio-economic changes 25; battle for human dignity 225
Maoist Communist Centre (MCC) 70, 72–3, 75, 196–9, 208
Maoists to protect the class interests of the landed gentry 42
market fundamentalism 26, 34
market-driven economic reforms in India 35
market-led development paradigms 163
Marxist class formula 155
Marxist-Leninist method of seizure of power through violence 66, 223
mass struggle for democracy and human dignity 48
meaning of leftism 3
Meerut Conspiracy case 1929 51, 54
Menon ministry in Kerala 145
middle class and parliamentary left 50
mineral resources in Orissa 204
mixed-economy strategy in India 31
MN Roy 12–13
mobile war technology by the Naxalites 201
mobilizational politics and Kishan Sabha 59
mobilizational techniques of the Left Front government in West Bengal 50
mobilizing people based on ascribed identity 134
Monopolies Restrictive Trade Practices Act 1969 35
movements for regional autonomy 39
multinational farms working in Orissa 204
Muslim League reaping the benefit 143
Muslim-dominated Malabar 137

Nair Service Society (NSS) 136
Nandigram and Singur crises 36, 114, 120, 221
National Rural Health Mission 41
Nationalist Congress 1

nature of coalition in India 38–9
nature of left radicalism 216
nature of Maoism 178
Naxal Movement in India 167–70
Naxalites fighting for rights of the poor 209
NDA 37
Nehru's proclivity towards socialism 9
Nehruvian goal of balanced and equitable growth 30
neo-liberal: economic reforms 26–8; route to economic reforms 34; state fulfilling an ideological mission 211
New Democratic Revolution 71
New Economic Policy 1991 33, 165
new leadership in Left Front 121
new phase in the history of parliamentary left 143–4
Ninth Congress 2007 182
Niyamgiri hill and tribals in Orissa 210
North Andhra Guerrilla Mandal 195
North-East Reorganization Act 1971 86
NSS 148

Operation Barga 107, 108, 215
opposing Nizam's dynastic rule 174
opposition to feudalism 14
organizational: election in the Congress 1937 139; questions and left radicals 70
Orissa's tryst with left-wing extremism 187
Orwellian truth 130
OSCC 190–2

Panchayat: election in West Bengal 2008 100; polls in Kerala 2011 154
Panchayats 41, 219, 221; and health care in Tripura 95–6; in Malkangiri 205
parallel campaigns against caste discrimination in Kerala 135
parliamentary communism 53; in West Bengal 101
parliamentary left 109; becoming integral to political processes 81; violence 220
Party Unity 70
party-guided local governance 111
peasant militancy 58
people's army 171
People's Daily 170
People's Liberation Guerrilla Army 183
People's War Group (PWG) 68–9, 173, 187, 194–5, 196, 208; cultural front 195
Peshawar Conspiracy case 1922–3 50
piggybacking on the electoral victory 127
Planning Commission 30–4

planning-driven economic model 161
politicization of social identities in Kerala 134
politico-ideological debates among the Maoists 182
politics in Travancore-Cochin 142
popularity of the left 107
post-independent India's political economy 29
PPC as a vehicle for deepening democracy 149
Praja Socialist Party (PSP) in Kerala 144
pro-active middle class in Kerala 157
processes of democratization 38
programme of *annadan* (offering food) 42
pro-imperialist policies 76
protracted people's war 74; strategy 73
public wrath against private capital 77
pursuing an alternative path of development 225

Quit India Movement 1942 63, 140–1, 172

radical social transformation at the grassroots 150
radical socio-economic transformation 45
Rajiv Gandhi Mahila Vikas Pariyojana 40
Ramgarh Congress 1940 65
Ranadive line 52, 57, 167
red belt 161
red corridor 36, 44, 161, 184, 212, 215, 224
red terror 179, 200
reformism in Kerala politics 16
regionalization of Indian federalism 39
reinvention of Marxism in the non-industrialized world 165
religiously-justified caste discrimination in Kerala 135
reversing the process of de-industrialization 118
review of the Naxalbari movement 169–71
revolution against imperialism, feudalism and comprador bureaucratic capitalism 74
revolutionary: peasants in Darjeeling 169; role of the Congress during the freedom struggle 87; terrorism 4
right wing: Congress leadership 12; faction of CPI 54
rise of mediocrity in the party in West Bengal 127
rising party aristocracy in West Bengal 126
role of coordination committee in Kerala 144

244   Index

role of non-Hindu wealthy families in Kerala 138
role of planning 28–30
role of Tamil Brahmins in Kerala 138
RSP 62–4, 142
rural India as a tinderbox 220
rural peasantry and parliamentary left 50

Sachar Committee 2005 122
Santal Oraon and Munda communities 170
science of social revolution 150
seeking to alter the rural texture 217
self-help groups 40–2
setting up of Rourkela steel plant 205
settlement of *sahukars* and king's men in Koraput 188
Seventy Third Amendment Act 1992 108, 111
SEZ 19, 35–6, 118, 129, 177
sharpening inequity in villages 183
silent revolution in India 40–2
simplicity of local tribals 189
simplistic nationalist approach 155
small-is-beautiful 33
SNDP 136
social prejudices of the Hindu landed gentry 4
social reform movements in Kerala 134–6
socialism as a metaphor 3
Socialist Revolutionary Party (SRP) in Kerala 144
sons of the soil argument 143
South Telangana Guerrilla Mandal 195
Soviet-directed line 52
spreading the disciplined left 101
Spring Thunder 164, 176
Stalinist iron-fist rule 129, 221
Stalinistic mode of authoritarian leadership 122
State assembly elections 1967 39
State Committee Congregation 2012 123
state-guided routes to liberalization 26, 34
state-led development 17, 25, 30
strategy of govern and mobilize 56, 58
struggle against capitalism 2
subaltern struggle 1
Subhas Chandra Bose 12–13, 65
SUCI 64–5

Tebagha movement 174

Telangana Movement 1946–51 167, 174
tenth Five Year Plan 2002–7 208
Territorial Act 1956 86
three caste-communal groups in Kerala 136
three tiers of government – *gram panchayat*, *panchayat samiti* and *zila parishad* 95
transferring land to private investors for industrialization 116
transforming the nature of politics 45
Travancore Congress 137
tribals as pawns 211
Tripura Territorial Council 86
Tripura Tribal Areas Autonomous Development Council (TTAADC) 90, 95, 98
TTNC 142
two contradictory trends in Naxalbari movement 176

UDF 144, 148, 152, 154, 156
understanding Indian Maoism 178
unification of revolutionary groups 74
United Front as an electoral machine 144
universalist-humanistic nature of Marxism, Leninism and Maoism 48
University Grants Commission in India 61
UPA 38
uprisings in Poland and Hungary 53

Vanguard of Indian Independence 50
village folks as reliable customers 41
violence-prone tribal groups 87
violent revolutionary path 15
Vishwa Hindu Parishad 202
VP Singh-led National Front government 16

Washington Consensus 34
West Bengal as a cash-strapped state 57
West European social democratic path 102
withdrawal of Muslim support from Left Front 122
WPP 5–7, 51–2
Writers' Building in Kolkata 115

Zila Parishads 119